THE HOPE FULFILLED

The Rise of Modern Israel

Leslie Stein

Praeger Series on Jewish and Israeli Studies

Westport, Connecticut
London

Library of Congress Cataloging-in-Publication Data

Stein, Leslie.
　The hope fulfilled : the rise of modern Israel / Leslie Stein.
　　p.　cm.—(Praeger series on Jewish and Israeli studies)
　Includes bibliographical references (p.) and index.
　ISBN 0-275-97141-4 (alk. paper) — ISBN 0-275-97815-X (pbk. : alk. paper)
　1. Jews—Palestine—History—19th century.　2. Jews—Palestine—History—
20th century.　3. Zionism—Palestine—History.　4. Palestine—History—
1917–1948.　I. Title.　II. Series.
DS125.S73　2003
956.94'004924—dc21　　　2002070879

British Library Cataloguing in Publication Data is available.

Library of Congress Catalog Card Number: 2002070879
ISBN: 0-275-97141-4
　　　0-275-97815-X (pbk.)

First published in 2003

Praeger Publishers, 88 Post Road West, Westport, CT 06881
An imprint of Greenwood Publishing Group, Inc.
www.praeger.com

Printed in the United States of America

(∞)™

The paper used in this book complies with the
Permanent Paper Standard issued by the National
Information Standards Organization (Z39.48–1984).

10　9　8　7　6　5　4　3　2　1

To my late grandparents, Rachel and Chaim Morchechai Stein,
pious lovers of Zion of a bygone era, who readily ministered to those in need,
regardless of race and creed.

Contents

Illustrations

Palestine in the Mandate Period

Lebanon

Syria

Safed •

Acre •

Haifa •

Nazareth • Lake
            Kinneret

The Mediterranean

Nablus •

Tel Aviv- Jaffa •

Transjordan

Ramalla•

Jerusalem •

Bethlehem •

Dead
Sea

Gaza •

Hebron •

Beersheva •

The Negev

Egypt

Gulf of Aqaba

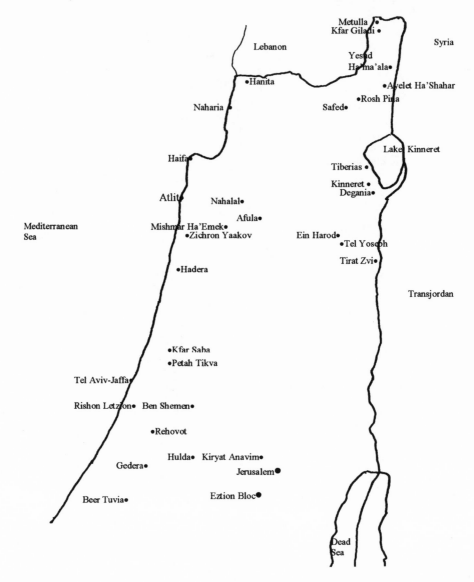

Metulla
Kfar Giladi •

Syria

Lebanon

Yesod
Ha'ma'ala•

•Hanita

•Avelet Ha'Shahar

•Rosh Pina

Naharia •

Safed•

Haifa•

Lake Kinneret

Tiberias •

Kinneret •
Degania•

Atlit•

Nahalal•

Afula•

Mediterranean
Sea

Mishmar Ha'Emek•
•Zichron Yaakov

Ein Harod•
•Tel Yoseph

Tirat Zvi•

•Hadera

Transjordan

•Kfar Saba
•Petah Tikva

Tel Aviv-Jaffa•

Rishon Letzion• Ben Shemen•

•Rehovot

Hulda• Kiryat Anavim•

Gedera•

Jerusalem●

Eztion Bloc●

Beer Tuvia•

Dead
Sea

Preface

In writing this book, I have attempted to provide a concise coverage of the events leading to the formation of Israel. The story commences in 1882, with the beginning of Jewish nationalistic migrations to Palestine, and culminates in May 1948, when the State of Israel was declared.

With publications dealing with Israel being voluminous and apparently endless, some justification for adding yet one more would certainly not be misplaced. In the first instance, I readily concede that there are currently in print some excellent works on Israel's history. However, they are generally rather weighty tomes and deal both with the pre- and post-independence periods. In the process, the first section, which involves a rather different set of problems, is usually treated sketchily. It is my belief that a study of the struggle for the creation of Israel is an important subject in its own right and that it should not be submerged in a volume that gives emphasis to post-1948 developments.

I have tried to capture the essence of pre-state trends within a self-contained work that includes all crucial historic aspects without being too verbose. Apart from accounting for the standard political, diplomatic and military issues, a special effort has been made to describe the social transformation of the Jewish community in Palestine over the course of time. Particular reliance has been placed on Hebrew sources to ferret out information regarding the challenges and lifestyles involving ordinary people.

Although this work is based largely on secondary references, they have been judiciously selected and wherever conflicting accounts appear, mention of this is made in the endnotes. My prime objective has been to provide the reader with a comprehensive, balanced and reasoned narrative. If my endeavors are judged to have been successful, this book ought to appeal to both the general public and to college students pursuing Israeli studies.

Warm words of thanks are due to the staff of Greenwood Press, especially to Heather Ruland Staines, senior editor, Liz Leiba, production editor, and Diana Drew, copyeditor. Reuven Koffler of the Central Zionist Archives, Jerusalem and Tim Slocum and other members of Macquarie University Library's Inter-Lending Department provided useful assistance, as did Debbie Jeffery and Jane Oldroyd.

Valuable comments have been obtained from Ephraim Kleiman and Jerry Tulchinsky, for which I am grateful. Members of my family, that is, my wife, Clara, my son, Mark, and my daughter, Karen, who have either read all or some of the text, have pointed out numerous errors relating to language and style. They have my deep appreciation. In addition, Clara has constantly given me moral and other support and has endured countless hours without my company. In this regard, I do not know how to begin to thank her.

Leslie Stein
Macquarie University
Sydney, Australia

Chapter 1

Introduction: The Early Beginnings

During the Greek and Roman eras, Jewish sovereignty in Judea was in a perilous state. Sometimes it would be totally suppressed and then, on other occasions, such as after the successful Hasmonean revolt, it would temporarily re-emerge. Eventually, when in 135 C.E. Hadrian utterly routed an anti-Roman rebellion, the Jews finally forfeited their independence and for almost another 2,000 years they were rendered homeless. Their land, which Hadrian dubbed Palaestina, subsequently fell under the sway of a series of foreign powers, which, among others, included the Byzantine Empire, the Arabs and the Crusaders. Finally, in 1517, it was incorporated into the Ottoman Empire where, except for a brief Egyptian interlude between 1831 and 1840, it remained until 1917. Throughout all these vicissitudes, despite massive expulsions, not to mention numerous massacres, some Jewish presence in Palestine, albeit at times tenuous in the extreme, was constantly maintained.

By the turn of the nineteenth century, the Jewish population in Palestine numbered roughly 5,000 out of a possible total of 275,000 to 300,000 inhabitants. Nearly forty years later, the British vice-consul estimated that approximately 10,000 Jews lived there. Over half dwelled in Jerusalem, while the rest were concentrated in Safed, Hebron and Tiberias. Within another forty years, that is by 1880, the Jewish population more than doubled, reaching 25,000 out of a total population of 450,000. Two-thirds stayed in Jerusalem, where from 1874 onward, they constituted a residential majority.

The Jews who settled in Palestine were steeped in religion and believed that their presence there fulfilled a divine injunction. Many were drawn to the country to spend their twilight years there in prayer, study and contemplation. The large and sudden upsurge in their numbers that occurred in the first half of the nineteenth century partly reflected developments within Jewish communal life in Eastern Europe. A growing rift between the ultrapious *Hassidim* and

other strictly religious Jews who opposed them, the *Mitnagdim*, induced various Hassidic rabbis to settle, with their adherents, in Palestine. Similarly, a
number of other devout Jews who abhorred the development of Jewish enlightenment (*Haskallah*) and its concomitant secularization, also sought refuge
in Palestine, a country neither contaminated by modernity nor by excessive religious intolerance. Their ability to do so was facilitated by enhanced shipping
connections with Jaffa, Palestine's major port and perhaps more importantly, by
a series of reforms decreed in 1839 by Turkish Sultan Abdul Majid. These reforms paved the way for an improvement in the rule of law and for a general
amelioration of burdens borne by non-Muslims and non-Turkish citizens. Furthermore, by virtue of the capitulations system, foreign citizens were granted
immunity from Turkish courts and were afforded a measure of protection by
their respective consuls. Consequently, Palestine as a destination for would-be
Jewish migrants became somewhat less daunting.

At first, the majority of Palestinian Jews were *Sephardim* (from the Mediterranean Basin and Arab countries). They had been in the country for many
years and were almost all Arabic-speaking Turkish citizens. Most earned their
livelihood by means of commerce or by practicing crafts. A few even undertook
unskilled labor such as porterage. In 1842, the Turkish authorities officially installed the first *Haham Bashi* (chief Sephardi rabbi) in Jerusalem as the recognized head of the Jewish community. A Rabbinical Council was appointed and
directed by him to officiate in matters pertaining to marriage and divorce and
to settle intra-Jewish civil disputes. However, in practice, the Hacham Bashi's
standing was not accepted by the Ashkenazi Jews (those from Central and Eastern Europe) who, by taking advantage of the capitulations system, were able to
set up independent rabbinical courts. By so doing, they effectively fragmented
the community. Unlike the Sephardim, the Ashkenazim were themselves dis-
united and split into numerous subdivisions, each with its own acknowledged
chief rabbi and court. Over time, as more and more Ashkenazim arrived, they
began to outnumber the Sephardim and by 1880, they constituted 60 percent of
the Jewish population.

LIVING OFF CHARITY—THE SHNORRER
(BEGGAR) COMMUNITY

In contrast to the Sephardim, the overwhelming majority of the Ashkenazim
did not engage in any meaningful income-earning activity and largely sub-
sisted on charity, derived in the main from their former compatriots still living
in Europe.[1] Each Ashkenazi community dispatched special emissaries abroad to
solicit funds, playing on the potential donors' sense of obligation to finance
Jews undertaking a life of full-time religious study and devotion. Since practically every Jewish community in Central and Eastern Europe supported local
centers for talmudic study (yeshivot), it was not unduly difficult to persuade

God-fearing Jews to contribute toward the upkeep of similar yeshivot in the Holy Land. While in the European towns and villages (*shtetls*) the full-time seminarists were a small minority supported by a community obtaining its livelihood by dint of hard work, entire communities in Palestine became dependent on handouts.

In some cases, eligible recipients, that is, those recognized as being members of a particular community, were divided into two categories. The first grouping included all residents, regardless of age and status, to whom an equal "living allowance" was issued. The second contained a list of elite mendicants, who were judged to be a cut above the others on the basis of their general public standing and scholastic achievements, as attested by rabbis in their towns of origin. To these fortunate worthies went a supplementary allowance. As for the rank and file, life was anything but a bed of roses. Most were housed in cramped and crowded accommodations devoid of adequate sanitation. Their clothes were ragged and dirty, their diets unsatisfactory and they were constantly plagued by outbreaks of typhoid and typhus. They were kept under the tight control of their communal leaders, who doled out their stipends and were positively discouraged from pursuing profane activities.

The sole purpose of the Ashkenazi community was to further religious observance and to conserve religious dogma. Their male children and young male adults were provided with an education in the Yiddish vernacular that not only excluded run of the mill secular subjects like arithmetic, basic science or foreign languages but also subjects such as Hebrew literature and Jewish history. (Girls and young women were denied formal tuition.) The instruction actually imparted primarily consisted of a study of the Talmud and of rabbinical commentaries. Naturally such a narrowly based curriculum limited the scope of students to secure normal secular employment. Being fully cognizant of just that situation, the Ashkenazi rabbis fought tooth and nail against any initiative that might have liberalized or broadened the schooling available to their charges.

When in 1849, the well-known philanthropist, Sir Moses Montefiore, broached the idea of financing the establishment of a modern school for the benefit of the *Yishuv* (the Jewish population that had settled in Palestine), he was met by a howl of protests from Ashkenazi rabbis. They warned that such a school would lead Jewish children astray and as a result, Montefiore shelved the scheme. Seven years later, Ludwig Fraenkel, an Austrian Jewish writer, proposed founding a school that would go beyond the confines of the curricula then in place. Not surprisingly, he too encountered stiff opposition. Nonetheless, Fraenkel persevered and in 1857, with the blessing of the Hacham Bashi, he accomplished his objective with the opening of the Laemel School. Since all Ashkenazi parents contemplating sending their children there were threatened with a cessation of their allowances, only Sephardi pupils enrolled. Also of note was the experience of the Mikveh Yisrael agricultural school, founded in 1870 by the *Alliance Israelite Universelle.* With unrelenting pressures brought to

bear against prospective participants, the school initially encountered considerable difficulties in recruiting and retaining pupils.

The wrath of the Ashkenazi rabbinate was felt not only by well-meaning
philanthropic outsiders but also by certain eminent religious Ashkenazi Jews
who threw in their lot with the Yishuv. Two glaring instances come to mind.
One relates to Rabbi Yehiel Pines, who arrived in Jerusalem from Russia in
1878 with a brief to recommend to Sir Moses Montefiore various measures that
could be taken to enhance the Yishuv's ability to fend for itself. No sooner had
Rabbi Pines proposed the formation of an agricultural settlement in the environs of Jerusalem, and of various small enterprises within the city, than a group
of clerics assembled at the Western Wall, where to the sound of the shofar
(ram's horn) they duly excommunicated him. Impervious to the shrill voices of
his opponents, Rabbi Pines proceeded to establish a workshop to provide instruction in woodwork. This elicited both a second excommunication and a declaration that Rabbi Pines was a heretic. On that occasion, some of his
unfortunate woodwork apprentices were beaten, thus marking a pattern of violent behavior that has since characterized religious Jewish zealots. The second
case relates to Eliezer Ben Yehuda, the father of modern Hebrew. In 1886 for
the "sin" of advocating that yeshiva students in Jerusalem be taught crafts, he
was excommunicated and, to make matters worse, when his wife died shortly
thereafter, his detractors at first refused to bury her. Only when the Sephardi
rabbis agreed to do so did they finally relent. Some years later, Ben Yehuda was
denounced for publishing an article commemorating the Hasmoneans, who in
166 B.C.E. rebelled against the Seleucid king Antiochus IV and who subsequently purified the defiled temple. This time, the Turkish authorities were informed that Ben Yehuda's writings were essentially subversive and that he was
conspiring against them. As his luck would have it, Ben Yehuda, who had been
born in Lithuania, had opted on his arrival in Palestine for Turkish citizenship.
This had the effect of excluding him from the privileges of the capitulations
system, which afforded foreigners some legal immunity, and as a result of the
rabbis' false evidence (in flagrant violation of the ninth commandment) Ben
Yehuda was sentenced to a year's imprisonment. Fortunately for him, through
the good offices of Baron Edmond de Rothschild, he was soon released.

EARLY ATTEMPTS AT FARMING

It would be grossly unjust to imply that the totality of the early Yishuv fitted into the mold described above. For one, although the Sephardim maintained
a quota of yeshiva students supported by their community, their general rank
and file were not disinclined to pursue normal economic activities. For another,
there were various individual Ashkenazim (apart from Rabbi Pines and Ben
Yehuda) who did not comply with the dictates of their more extreme kinsmen.

In 1878, a small number of families, under the guidance and leadership of Joel Salomon, David Gutman and Jehoshua Stampfer, ventured from Jerusalem to farm a desolate tract of land six miles from Jaffa, which they named *Petah Tikva* (Gate of Hope). They were attracted to the site in question because, among other things, it had fertile soil and was within easy reach of the Yarkon River. On the other hand, the area was infested with malaria and the Yarkon River was polluted. With that in mind, the opinion of Dr. Mezarakis, a local Greek doctor, was sought. From the rooftop of a neighboring house, Dr. Mezarakis observed a total absence of bird life and, on that basis, declared the area to be unfit for human habitation. But having just completed an exhausting and extensive search, and despairing of ever finding a better setting, the leaders threw caution to the wind by deciding not to heed Dr. Mezarakis's advice.

Twelve male settlers, who constituted the group's vanguard, took up residence on their newly acquired land, on an elevated section away from the Yarkon River. Their families either remained in Jerusalem or moved to Jaffa and on every Sabbath the menfolk rejoined them. On the eve of their first Passover, the three founding fathers with their entire families celebrated the Passover seder (feast) on the settlement site. From the reported seder proceedings, it is clear that the settlers not only strove to become farmers but also entertained hopes of engendering a resurrection of Jewish national sovereignty. Numerous speeches were delivered, highlighting their remorse that their ancestral homeland had seemingly become a wasteland. The mood of the hour was captured by Stampfer, who in his peroration declared:

Take comfort Land! Today you have redeemers and if they are currently few in number, in the face of ten will arise one hundred and in the face of a hundred there will be a thousand, then tens of thousands—millions. Neither by day nor by night will we rest until you return to your youthful past and your crowning glory blazes throughout the world at large.[2]

Living in mud shacks, smitten by malaria and toiling on half-empty stomachs, they eventually harvested their first cereal crops. In keeping with ancient biblical practices, the farmers dutifully brought a tenth of their output to Jerusalem. Their entry to the city on a convoy of camels was met by crowds of excited well-wishers who came to witness the first presentation of tithes since the Temple's destruction. The pride and enthusiasm with which the farmers were received demonstrated that they did indeed command the support of at least elements of the Yishuv, some of whom were even inspired to join up with them. Unfortunately, the newcomers settled directly on the banks of the Yarkon, where they soon encountered nothing but distress.

The first year exacted a heavy toll, in that a plague wiped out two-thirds of the settlers' cattle while legal proceedings to register their property drained their financial resources. The following year, the settlement was inundated by flood waters and in the winter of 1880, partly because of internal dissension but largely because of a widespread outbreak of malaria, most of the farmers abandoned the project. By mid-1881, Petach Tikva was completely deserted.

Similarly, a few months before the Petach Tikva venture was launched, seventeen families from Safed attempted to cultivate a plot of land, called Gai Oni (valley of poverty), situated near their city. In that instance, their efforts were barely sustained for a year. The combination of an unfavorable physical environment, a hostile social one and an inability to mobilize help from abroad were more than enough to dampen their farming aspirations. Fund-raising attempts were frustrated by a stream of abuse that the leaders of the Safed community heaped upon them. When their leader, Eliezer Rokach, embarked on an aid-seeking mission, word was put out that he was none other than a nihilist.[3] With the demise of both settlements, the fanatical Ashkenazi rabbinate, it would seem, could rest in peace, for there were no other visible threats to their lifestyle.

NEW ARRIVALS ON THE HORIZON

Suddenly, in 1882, the sense of tranquility of the Yishuv (which we shall now call the "Old Yishuv") was ruffled by the arrival of a different breed of Jewish migrants (representing the "New Yishuv"), many of whom were specifically bent on establishing farming communities. The year 1882 represents a watershed in Jewish history, for it marked the first occasion, in the modern era, when Jews migrated to Palestine in reasonable numbers to restore their presence there not simply as worshipers but also as economically productive agents. They almost all came from Russia and Romania and their unforeseen influx into Palestine is largely explicable in terms of the eruption in 1881, of widespread pogroms in Russia. To understand just why those particular violent events provided a catalyst in inducing the migration of Jews in considerable numbers to Palestine, it is necessary to digress somewhat to examine the general conditions under which Jews in Russia fared.

JEWISH LIFE IN NINETEENTH-CENTURY RUSSIA

Oppression under Czar Nicholas I

Jewish life in Russia in the nineteenth century was more unbearable and more oppressive than in any other major European country. We pick up the threads of this sordid saga from the time when, in 1827, Nicholas I issued his notorious recruitment ukase. Had the benighted Jewish community access to the young czar's diary, they would not have been as dumbfounded as they were when the provisions of the decree were ultimately made known to them. For in 1816, when Nicholas traveled through Russia on a fact-finding tour, he recorded that the ruin of the peasants are the Jews. "They drain the strength of the hapless White Russian people ... They are everything here: merchants, contractors, saloon-keepers, mill-owners, ferry-holders, artisans. ... They are regular leeches."[4] Gradually, an idea crystallized in his mind. The Jews would have to be cleansed of their Judaism and, if possible, Christianized, and an ideal way to accomplish this would be to require of them a lengthy bout of military service.

The term actually decided on was twenty-five years but to compound matters, children as young as twelve years of age could be enlisted and given preparatory training until the age of eighteen, when only then would their term of service officially commence. Every single Jewish community was held responsible for rounding up a given supply of recruits and since volunteers were nonexistent, recruitment agents (known in Yiddish as *chappers*) were allocated the task of forcibly impressing luckless victims.[5] Whenever the chappers were at a loss for sufficient numbers, they showed no compunction in seizing boys as young as eight years old, sometimes even wrenching them from their very mothers' arms. The children's mortified parents invariably lost all hope of ever seeing their loved ones again and mourned them as if they were dead. For many, this was not an unrealistic assumption. Alexander Hertzen, a liberal Russian writer, wrote of his encounter in 1835 with an officer escorting a batch of Jewish cantonists (child recruits). Part of the dialogue was as follows:

"Whom do you carry and to what place?"

"Well, sir, you see, they got together a bunch of these accursed Jewish youngsters between the age of eight and nine ... I have had them on my hands for a hundred versts or thereabouts. The officer that turned them over to me told me they were an awful nuisance. A third of them remained on the road (at this the officer pointed with his finger to the ground). Half of them will not get to their destination," he added.

"Epidemics, I suppose?" I inquired, stirred to the very core.

"No, not exactly epidemics; but they just fall like flies. Well, you know, these Jewish boys are so puny and delicate. They can't stand mixing dirt for ten hours, with dry biscuits to live on. Again everywhere strange folks, no father, no mother, no caresses. Well then, you just hear a cough and the youngster is dead."

Hertzen then appended his own thoughts:

Pale, worn out, with scared looks, this is the way they stood in their uncomfortable, rough soldier uniforms, with their starched, turned-up collars, fixing an inexpressibly helpless and pitiful gaze upon the garrisoned soldiers, who were handling them rudely. White lips, blue lines under the eyes betokened either fever or cold. And these poor children, without care, without a caress, exposed to the wind which blows unhindered from the Arctic Ocean, were marching to their death.[6]

Not all cantonists met with an early death but those that survived were subject to callous physical and psychological abuse, with no effort being spared to convert them to the Russian Orthodox religion. To escape from constant beatings, enforced deprivation of food, water and sleep, most yielded and were permanently lost to the Jewish people. However, against all odds, some held out and refused to succumb. For years a story (quite probably apocryphal but clearly didactic) circulated among the general Jewish population about Jewish cantonists who were assembled for a baptismal ceremony in the city of Kazan. When ordered to jump into the city's river, the boys promptly dove in in unison, drowning themselves en masse.

Potential conscripts adopted all manner of ways to evade military service, with many resorting to self-mutilation of some sort, whether it be lopping off fingers or toes or taking even more drastic measures, such as inflicting damage to their eyesight. With Jewish recruitment levels not meeting expectations, orders were dispatched in 1850 to the effect that whenever a recruit fell short within a given community, three others from the same community were to be forthcoming. Then three years later, an even more macabre decree was issued. Permission was granted to both individuals and communities to substitute any other Jew, from another city or region, caught without a passport. Predictively, this led to the formation of gangs from among the community's baser elements who preyed on innocent travelers, stole their papers and then forcibly dragged them to recruitment stations.

Elsewhere in Europe, the entry of Jews into the armed forces both represented and accompanied their acceptance as legitimate citizens, but not so in Russia. No later than three months after the conscription decree was legally promulgated did the czar take preliminary steps to prohibit Jews from residing in various rural and urban areas. Finally, by 1835, a Pale of Settlement, encompassing Poland and Lithuania, White Russia, Little Russia, the Baltic provinces and the Ukraine (with the exception of Kiev) was designated as the only area in which Jews were allowed to dwell. Temporary entry (limited to six weeks) into other provinces was occasionally granted for urgent judicial and commercial purposes. Even within the Pale of Settlement itself, Jews were forbidden to live in rural areas within fifty kilometers of the western border.

Having imposed the above-mentioned physical liabilities on his Jewish subjects, Nicholas I then mounted a series of assaults on their culture and religion with the clear-cut intention of undermining both. The first onslaught manifested itself in 1836 in the form of the censoring of Hebrew literature. All Hebrew books printed abroad as well as all uncensored locally produced editions (which in practice meant all books then extant) were required to be handed over to local authorities, who, with the assistance of trusted rabbis, were to identify texts "at variance with imperial enactments." Offensive tomes were to be dispatched, under police escort, to St. Petersburg but since the whole process proved to be too unwieldy, the czar ordered that the books in question be burned on the spot.

Next, the government devised a scheme to emasculate Jewish educational institutions. It publicly declared that it intended to form a new category of crown schools to provide Jewish children with both modern and Jewish education. In reality, a secret plan was hatched with the aim of bringing the Jews "nearer to the Christian population and eradicating the prejudices fostered in them by the study of the Talmud."[7] The true nature of the crown schools soon became apparent for only Christians were appointed as principals and only secularly educated Jewish teachers were to be permitted to provide religious instruction. Appreciating the threat to their spiritual life that the proposed system posed, Jews, wherever possible, gave the crown schools a wide berth.[8]

Some Relief under Czar Alexander II

The ascension to the throne of Czar Alexander II following the death in 1855 of his father, Nicholas I, brought swift relief to the Jewish community. One of his first acts of grace involved the abrogation of all child drafting and the placing of Jewish male recruitment on an equal footing with the rest of the population. That is, recruits were to be drawn largely from those not engaged in productive labor and the ability to present alternative persons in one's own or one's community's stead was abolished. The new arrangement's only drawback was that while general child cantonists were to be returned to their parents, forcibly converted Jewish children were to be placed in the permanent care of Christian families.

In response to an imperial order issued in 1856 requiring the revision of all regulations relating to Jews so as to integrate them into Russian society, measures were gradually but persistently taken to lighten their lot. Within official government circles, it was decided that the process of Jewish liberation would commence with individuals of high social standing and whose entry into the social mainstream was eminently desirable. Accordingly, in 1859, top-ranking Jewish merchants, their families and a limited number of their servants, were permitted to live beyond the borders of the Pale. Two years later, Jewish physicians and others with a postgraduate university qualification were admitted into the public service and granted universal residency rights. Finally, in 1879 such rights were bestowed to Jewish graduates at large.

At first, the beneficiaries of Alexander II's reforms represented a very small percentage of the Jewish population, for very few were wealthy merchants and barely any attended tertiary institutes. However, over time, artisans, mechanics and distillers were also allowed to transcend the Pale, provided they continued working within their fields of expertise. More significantly, conditions within the Pale itself, where most Jews remained, were considerably improved. Internal travel restrictions were removed, Jews were permitted to acquire certain types of rural land, they could enter the judiciary and they could participate in rural governing bodies.

Renewed Oppression under Alexander III

Despite Alexander II's general liberal leanings (at least in the Russian context), there were certain reforms that he steadfastly refused to countenance.

These included the provision of a universal franchise and the introduction of a popular representative legislative assembly. Since advocates of democratic reform were ruthlessly suppressed, the regime's obduracy in this regard fostered the growth of a revolutionary movement, which increasingly resorted to violence. On March 1, 1881 (Russian calendar), Alexander II met with an untimely death at the hands of revolutionary terrorists. He was succeeded by his son Alexander III, who was a staunch conservative, an ardent supporter of the Russian Orthodox Church and one with an intense loathing of Jews.

Although some Jews were present within the ranks of revolutionary societies, very few of them were actually involved in sabotage and assassination. Unfortunately, a woman named Hesia Helfman who had played a secondary role in Alexander II's demise, was identified as being Jewish, and from this, the Russian press at large (probably with official backing) inferred that the Jews were generally culpable. Just over a month later, that is, in mid-April and around the time of the Russian Orthodox Easter, when the Passover blood libel was usually raised, a series of pogroms broke out throughout much of South Russia. These disturbances turned out to be the most extensive anti-Jewish activities since the mass slaughter of Polish Jews in the mid-seventeenth century. The first occurred in Yelisavetgrad, where Jewish stores and homes were destroyed and looted. The fact that so many ordinary people—"clerks, saloon and hotel waiters, artisans, drivers, flunkeys, day laborers in the employ of the government, and soldiers on furlough"—all joined in and those that didn't, *displayed complete indifference* "to the havoc wrought before their eyes,"[9] brought home to the Jews their complete vulnerability and isolation.

From Yelisavetgrad, the rioting spread to dozens of surrounding villages and townships. Then a pogrom struck the city of Kiev in which numerous Jews were murdered and many women raped. This was followed by more disturbances in some fifty villages within the same region. Finally, Odessa was subject to three days of anarchy. For a while, calm then prevailed but in early July a new round of anti-Jewish pillage swept through the land. Fortunately, the authorities by then resolved to restore order and by the end of the month everything, except for occasional acts of arson, was under control. The July pogroms brought the total number of Jewish localities affected by that year's disturbances to well over a hundred.

There seemed little doubt that the pogroms were pre-planned and if not government organized then at least government inspired. In most places where riots subsequently ensued, outside agitators first harangued crowds at railroad stations and at other public points of assembly, citing anti-Semitic newspaper articles and suggesting that an imperial ukase had been issued calling on Christians to attack Jews. In addition, the populace were assured that their actions would have the blessing of the civil and military authorities. Considering that in the early stages of almost every pogrom, the military either withdrew or passively looked on as Jews were assaulted, the perpetrators must have taken this as confirmation that their deeds were indeed officially sanctioned.

Even though a limited number of the riffraff were actually brought to trial, the Jews themselves were ultimately held accountable. In Kiev, the public prosecutor, Strelnikov, charged that the real source of the disorders lay in Jewish exploitation. When, in response, Jewish economic disabilities were drawn to Strelnikov's attention, he paraphrased the sentiment of Ignatyev, the minister of the interior, to the effect that "if the eastern frontier is closed to the Jews, the western frontier is open to them; why don't they take advantage of it?" In the words of Dubnow, the famous Jewish Russian historian, "This summons to leave the country, doubly revolting in the mouth of a guardian of the law, addressed to those who under the influence of the pogrom panic had already made up their minds to flee the land of slavery, produced a staggering effect upon the Jewish public. The last ray of hope, the hope for legal justice, vanished."[10]

By May 1882, the unenviable situation in which the Jews were placed resulted not only from threats of physical violence but also from renewed government oppression. Alexander III by virtue of his infamous "temporary rules," effectively prohibited Jews in the Pale from living in rural localities. In practice, this meant that they were to be cooped up in one-tenth of the area previously accessible to them, a factor that limited not only the accommodation available to them but also their general economic opportunities. To impinge on their economic prospects even further, a numeras clausus was introduced, setting strict quotas on the number of Jewish students to be admitted to schools and universities.

The misfortune that befell the Jewish community in 1881–1882 would have been less difficult to bear had the Jews not recently experienced an era of emancipatory progress. After the nightmarish rule of Nicholas I, where the dreaded prospects of being shanghaied for almost a lifetime hung over the heads of young Jewish males, the Jews, under Alexander II, were given notice that they would gradually be accepted into Russian society and that discrimination against them would ultimately end. Having falsely been given cause for hope, the emergence of a violent and officially sponsored campaign of anti-Semitism under Alexander III was an extremely bitter pill to swallow. What made the pill even more bitter was the near total indifference to or even abandonment of the Jews that was evinced by the Russian intellectual community. At the one extreme, revolutionaries belonging to the People's Freedom party openly sided with the pogromists. They rationalized their support on the ground that destitute workers and peasants were confronted by a coalition of Jews, landlords and the Czar. An official party statement issued in August 1881, after analyzing the situation in revolutionary terms, ended with the following exhortation: "Arise, laborers, avenge yourselves on the landlords, plunder the Jews and slay the officials."[11] On the other hand, from the more moderate, tolerant establishment very little solace was forthcoming. The relatively liberal press barely raised its voice in anger and in contrast to Western men of letters, like Victor Hugo, who passionately inveighed against the horror inflicted on the Jews, Russian writers like Ivan Turgenev and Leo Tolstoy remained silent.

JEWISH NATIONAL REVIVAL IN RUSSIA: THE *HOVEVEI ZION* (LOVERS OF ZION) AND THE *BILU*

A significant proportion of Jews reacted to the above-described events by concluding that the future held out nothing for them in Russia. Many were taken by the idea of migrating to more enlightened states in the West and to the United States in particular. Accordingly, they began organizing emigration societies. A small, though not insignificant, minority reasoned that no matter where Jews settled, they would always be regarded as an unwelcome minority and at best be treated on sufferance. Salvation would only be on hand when they returned to their ancestral home and ceased to be strangers in strange lands. They were inspired by a series of articles written by Moses Lilienblum in late 1881, which called for the comprehensive colonization of Palestine and for the preparation of the time when the Jews of Europe would abandon that continent and "settle in the land of our forefathers." A year later, Leon Pinsker came to the fore in the wake of the publication of his classical booklet "Auto-Emancipation." Neither Lilienblum nor Pinsker was among the first to expound Zionist or proto-Zionist views but they were among the first whose clarion calls were met with a warm and moderately wide-ranging response. Of those who preceded them, three readily come to mind, two of whom were orthodox rabbis, Judah Alkalai and Zvi Hirsch Kalischer, while the third, Moses Hess, was a radical secular Jew who at one time had the dubious distinction of being a collaborator of the theoretical founders of communism, Karl Marx and Friedrich Engels.

PROTO-ZIONIST MOVEMENT WRITINGS

In his book *Darhei Noam* (Pleasant Paths), published in 1839, Judah Alkalai first publicly canvassed the need for the formation of Jewish colonies in Palestine as a sine qua non for the coming of the Messiah. Then with the onset of the "Damascus affair" he felt the need to clarify why the renewal of Jewish sovereignty in Palestine had become even more imperative. The affair itself involved an Italian monk in Damascus and his Muslim servant who suddenly disappeared in February 1840. Seven Jews were accused of murdering them for ritual Passover purposes and were subjected to excruciating torture. In addition, sixty-three Jewish children were detained as a means of forcing their parents to reveal where the missing corpses were supposedly hidden. Like the Dreyfus case in France which was to follow later, the Damascus affair became a cause célèbre, invoking the intercession of prominent European Jews, such as Moses Montefiore and Adolphe Cremieux, who by the following September, succeeded in securing the release of all the detainees. For Alkalai, the affair was God's way of issuing a timely reminder that the Jews had to take their fate into their own hands. In 1843 in his booklet "Minchat Yehuda" (The Offering of

Juda), he advocated large-scale land acquisitions in Palestine for the purpose of establishing a Jewish national homeland, in which he envisioned a parliament of Jewish elders, a Jewish army and the revival of Hebrew as a spoken language.

In a similar vein, Zvi Kalischer also saw the need for Jews to assume direct control over their destiny and not to wait passively for the Messiah. His proposals, outlined in his book *Drishat Zion* (Seeking Zion) published in 1862, involved the mobilization of funds under the auspices of Jewish magnates and the deploying of such capital for extensive land purchases, assistance in mass migration and the training of Jewish farmers. On the practical side, in 1870 Kalischer was instrumental in persuading the Alliance Israelite Universelle to establish Mikveh Israel, an agriculture school in Palestine.

Of the writings of the three proto-Zionist thinkers under mention, Moses Hess's *Rome and Jerusalem* ultimately attained the most renown. However, when it was first released in 1862 it barely caused a ripple. Only 160 copies were sold within the initial year of its publication and Hess's exasperated publisher "suggested that Hess ought to buy back the remainder at a reduced price."[12] Even Theodor Herzl, when writing *The Jewish State* in 1895 had not been aware of it. Nevertheless, *Rome and Jerusalem* was eventually acclaimed as an exemplary exposition of modern Zionist thought.

As a literary work, *Rome and Jerusalem* leaves much to be desired. Drafted as a series of letters, it tends to digress into disjointed side issues, such as Spinoza's philosophy and Graetz's exposition of Jesus; despite that, it contains some startling notions, which at the time were highly original. Hess maintained that, above all, the Jews constituted a nation "destined to be resurrected with the rest of civilized nations."[13] Because of endemic anti-Semitism, Jews in countries like Germany, who wished to disassociate themselves from their religion and from the Jewish community in general, would not succeed in doing so. With extraordinary prescience, Hess, in 1862, already discerned the seeds of racial as opposed to religious anti-Semitism. As he noted, "the German hates the Jewish religion less than the race; he objects less to the Jews' peculiar beliefs than to their peculiar noses."[14] That being the case, it is a sham for Jews to proclaim that their religion (which Hess perceived to be "above all, Jewish patriotism,") ought to be considered as being nothing more than a set of moral and ethical beliefs so that Jews could aspire to be accepted as true Germans, Russians or whatever, of the Mosaic persuasion. Ironically, Hess maintained, modern Jews rebuffed by gentiles were more likely to find their life in exile more intolerable than that of their orthodox kinsmen who at least experienced no identity crises. Hess believed that eventually the assimilationists would be driven back into the Jewish fold, as the hard covering encasing their hearts would be shattered "by a blow from without, one that world events are already preparing."[15] Force of circumstances would bring about a revived sense of Jewish nationalism that would ultimately culminate in a renewed sovereign Jewish state in Palestine.

The collective writings of Alkalai, Kalischer and Hess did not appear at a propitious historic moment. With Western Jews harboring assimilationist illusions

and with those in Russia experiencing a period of unexpected benevolent reforms, they made no immediate impact.

PINSKER'S "AUTO-EMANCIPATION"

A few decades later, when Russian Jewry was overwhelmed by the 1881–1882
pogroms, Pinsker found a more receptive readership. Like Hess before him and
Herzl to follow, Pinsker was an emancipated, Westernized Jew, who believed that
he could merge into his country's general social landscape. As a medical doctor,
he volunteered during the Crimean War to work gratuitously in an army hospital, for which he was awarded a citation of honor. However, anti-Semitic rioting
in Odessa in 1871 caused him to question the wisdom of his assimilationist tendencies, and with the advent of the 1881 pogroms, he finally abandoned his previous views. Instead, he adopted a new Jewish nationalistic credo, which found
expression in his essay "Auto-Emancipation," published in September 1882.

In the opening words of his short monograph, Pinsker defined the essence of
the Jewish problem as emanating from "the fact that, in the midst of the nations among whom the Jews reside, they form a distinctive element which cannot be assimilated."[16] Even though many Jews would gladly and shamefacedly
trade their adherence from that of their own people to the nation in which they
happen to dwell, they would inevitably be rebuffed. The world as a whole saw
them as ghostlike members of a bygone nation "no longer alive, and yet moving about the living."[17] Such an eerie apparition paved the way for Judeopho-
bia, which was reinforced by religious prejudice and people's natural aversion
to strangers. Lacking a state of their own, Jews were more exposed than other
foreigners living abroad, for at least the latter could count on some protection
from their homeland or a measure of respect from their host nations.

Since anti-Semitism is basically grounded in a set of irrational beliefs passed
on from generation to generation, there is no point in trying to eradicate it
through discussion and education, "for against superstition even the gods fight
vainly."[18] Conjuring up an imaginary neutral bystander contemplating his people's lot, Pinsker would have him address the Jews thus: "You are truly a silly
and despicable nation. You are silly because being at a loss with regard to your
situation, you demand from human nature something that has always been
lacking—love of one's fellow being. And you are despicable because you have
no self-esteem and no national pride."[19] Pinsker's solution lay in an awakening
of Jewish national consciousness, which would pave the way for the establishment of a sovereign Jewish state.

The Commencement of Emigration from Russia of Nationally Minded Jews to Palestine

Although Pinsker stood at the forefront of Russian Jewish ideologues, the
pogroms of 1881–1882 yielded other national spokesmen, such as Lilienblum
and the Hebrew writer Peretz Smolenskin, who, having despaired of Jewish life

in Russia, became imbued with renewed Jewish settlement in Palestine. To these must be added, the scores of rabbis and students who similarly saw the writing on the wall and who in 1881–1882 spontaneously convened regular *Hovevei Zion* (Lovers of Zion) chapters to champion the cause of migration to Palestine and to raise funds for such purposes. The first Hovevei Zion group saw the light of day in Suvalki near the Polish-Lithuanian border, followed by a number of similar associations in Poland, initiated by Rabbi Shmuel Mohilever of Radom. Essentially, the run-of-the-mill members of the Hovevei Zion movement were orthodox Jews who, like Alkalai and Kalischer before them, adhered to traditional notions relating to the redemption of Israel and the long-awaited future messianic era. Where they differed from other religious Jews who migrated to the Holy Land is that they fused their historical-religious connections to *Eretz Israel* (the land of Israel) with modern nationalism. Of the nationally inspired Jews who left for Palestine in 1882 and in the twenty or so years that followed, most were in this category.

THE BILUIM

Young, more secular-minded Jewish nationalists were attracted to an organization of their own, known as Bilu, a Hebrew acronym for the biblical phrase *Beth Yaakov Lehu Ve-Nelehna*, "O House of Jacob come ye and let us go." In Kharkov, on January 30, 1882, a student by the name of Israel Belkind attended one of the many synagogue services in Russia, convened to commemorate the recent wave of pogroms. At the service's conclusion, Belkind suggested to a group of highly emotionally charged student acquaintances that they meet later in his room to review the general situation. About thirty attended and under Belkind's chairmanship, the Bilu movement was born. It was not all plain sailing, for many of the participants still harbored illusions that general social progress and a more enlightened era would solve the Jewish problem. To counter their arguments, Belkind pointed to Germany, which had already attained constitutional reform and a parliamentary system but where anti-Semitism was nonetheless rife.[20] Even when all were won over to the need to further emigration, agreement that migrants proceed to *Eretz Israel* was not easily come by. In Belkind's words, "Most students who took part in the discussions were far removed from the Bible, from the traditional Hebrew texts and the term *Eretz Israel* sounded strange to them."[21] A short time thereafter, other Bilu-affiliated groups were formed, bringing the number of the movement's membership to approximately 500. The general tone of their innumerable deliberations was often entirely divorced from actual practicalities. For example, the twenty-five students belonging to the Moscow branch devoted hours on end to a debate as to whether the future Jewish state should be based on an absolute monarchy, a constitutional monarchy or on democratic republicanism.

The *Biluim* (that is, Bilu members) were radical militant idealists who saw themselves as national trailblazers willing to face any physical hardship and danger. They were completely won over to the view that the concentration of the majority of Jews in Israel would constitute the sole guarantee of the nation's survival. In a flush of enthusiasm, they spoke of immediately dispatching 500 youngsters to Eretz Israel. There they were to establish a colony that would serve as a model for others to emulate.

Their speech and writings were suffused with flowery, poetic rhetoric. Below, for instance, is an extract from their 1882 manifesto:

> Nearly two thousand years have elapsed since, in an evil hour, after a heroic struggle, the glory of our Temple vanished in fire and our kings and chieftains changed their crowns and diadems for the chains of exile. We lost our country where dwelt our beloved sires. Into exile we took with us, of all our glories, only a spark of the fire by which our Temple, the abode of our Great One, was engirdled, and this little spark kept us alive while the towers of our enemies crumbled into dust, and this spark leapt into celestial flame and shed light on the heroes of our race and inspired them to endure the horrors of the dance of death and the tortures of the autos-da-fé. *And this spark is again kindling and will shine for us, a true pillar of fire going before us on the road to Zion.*[22]

To finance their schemes, the Biluim initially resorted to extortion, threatening wealthy Kharkov Jews with their lives.[23] When such clumsy tactics proved fruitless, they then pinned their hopes on securing funding through the auspices of Lord Laurence Oliphant, who on May 11, 1882, visited Istanbul to advance their cause. That was not the first time that Oliphant made overtures to the Turkish authorities, for in 1880, he had in vain beseeched the sultan to provide what would have amounted to a charter to permit Jewish colonization in a section of Palestine.[24]

Lord Oliphant was one among a growing number of non-Jewish writers and travelers who provided accounts, often accompanied by graphic illustrations, of life in Palestine. In the main, the interest of such writers in the Holy Land sprang from deeply held religious convictions, which, in many cases, included the notion that the return of the Jews to Israel was part of divine providence. In Oliphant's book, *The Land of Gilead*, which was published in 1880 (and eventually translated into Hebrew by Nacham Sokolov with the title *Eretz Hemda* [Desirable Land]), a plan was proposed for the settlement of Jews, under British protection, on the east bank of the Jordan. Although the actual merits of Oliphant's proposal were debatable, it had the effect of persuading Jewish readers that colonization in Palestine was indeed achievable. The growing confidence of Jews in the feasibility of settling in Palestine was also enhanced by a renewed flurry of English, German, French and other Christian philanthropic projects in Palestine that led to improvements in urban living conditions.

As for Oliphant, the Biluim (as well as many general Hovevei Zion adherents) were not only impressed with his book but they regarded him as a key intermediary in facilitating their migration to Palestine. It was expected that he would be able to secure for them free land from the Turkish authorities. When that hope did not materialize, the Biluim nevertheless decided to dispatch an advance guard to Palestine, led by Israel Belkind. The party, which numbered fourteen, set foot in Jaffa in July 1882, with the date of their arrival generally being taken as marking the commencement of the first Zionist immigration wave or *aliyah*[25] (see Glossary). Contemporaneously, hundreds of families emanating from the rank and file of the Hovevei Zion, also uprooted themselves and departed for Palestine. By the year's end, the number of those who made the journey was estimated to be around seven thousand.

NOTES

1. Much but by no means all of the material in this section is derived from Abramov, *Perpetual Dilemma*, 1976, pp. 23–41.

2. As reported by J. Salomon in Eliav, "Early Tribulations," 1978, p. 260.

3. See Eliav, *The First Aliyah*, 1981, vol. 2, p. 173.

4. As quoted by Dubnow, *History of the Jews in Russia*, 1918, vol. 2, p. 14.

5. Certain categories of Jews were granted exemption. These included special classes of merchants and artisans, farmers, rabbis and graduates of a Russian educational institution.

6. As quoted by Dubnow, 1918, vol. 2, pp. 24–25.

7. Excerpts from a secret transcript as quoted by Dubnow, *History of the Jews in Russia*, 1918, vol. 2, p. 58.

8. In their efforts to influence Sir Moses Montefiore, the Jerusalem Ashkenazi rabbis unjustly likened his proposed school to those of the Russian Jewish Crown ones.

9. As quoted by Dubnow, *History of the Jews in Russia*, 1918, vol. 2, p. 250.

10. Ibid., p. 265.

11. Ibid., p. 325.

12. Laqueur, *History of Zionism*, 1989, p. 46.

13. Hess, *Rome and Jerusalem*, 1918, p. 49.

14. Ibid., p. 58.

15. Ibid., p. 177.

16. Pinsker, *Auto-emancipation*, 1936, p. 15.

17. Ibid., p. 18.

18. Ibid., p. 20.

19. Pinsker's *Auto-emancipation* as reproduced in Yevniele, Era of Hibat-Zion, vol. 2, 1961, p. 9.

20. In fact, in September 1882 an anti-Semitic congress was held in Dresden.

21. Belkind, "In the Path," 1983, p. 35.

22. As quoted in Laqueur, *The Israel-Arab Reader*, 1970, p. 19; italics added. As it happened, this italicized sentence left its mark on successive Zionist pioneers, and the concept of a pillar of fire sweeping its way on the road to Zion formed a constant theme in Zionist literature and, more recently, in an award-winning Israeli documentary television program. The notion of a pillar of fire, of course, is derived from the Book of Exodus, where a pillar of fire guided the Israelites in the desert.

23. See Shalmon, "The Bilu Movement," 1981, p. 119.

24. In 1901, Herzl, the founder of modern political Zionism, was to make similar overtures.

25. The supposed exact date marking the commencement of the First Aliyah is an arbitrary one. By the time the Biluim arrived in Palestine, other nationalist visionaries were already there, such as Levontin, the founder of the first Zionist colony, who welcomed them at Jaffa Port.

Chapter 2

The First Aliyah: 1882–1903

Disembarking in Jaffa in the late nineteenth century was commonly regarded as an inherently harrowing experience. With the port not having deepwater berths, ships laid anchor off the coast, so that incoming passengers and
cargo were loaded onto boats rowed by large farouche stevedores. In stormy
weather, the rowing boats would bob up and down and only as the waves momentarily elevated them, would passengers hurriedly be lifted and placed into
the arms of the awaiting rowers. For many, the sight of powerful surly Arab
longshoremen was somewhat intimidating, conjuring up visions of having arrived in a land through which fierce tribesmen stalked. In reality, the immigrants' real moment of reckoning, which occasionally occurred while still on
board ship, was with their encounter with port officials, since the possibility of
being denied access and being deported was by no means insignificant. For most
of the period under review, and certainly during the year 1882, the Turkish authorities forbade the immigration of Eastern European Jews. Accordingly,
would-be immigrants either had to bribe their way in or employ some form of
subterfuge, such as feigning to be temporary pilgrims. Usually, they succeeded
in gaining admission but a favorable outcome was never assured. On occasion,
for want of adequate documentation, entire groups of Jewish passengers were
turned away. In one incident, described by Rabbi Yehiel Pines, all incoming Jews
were refused entry and, as a result, they had to continue on to Beirut. There, on
reaching the shore they were once again deported but this time the ship's captain refused to re-accept them. For the rest of the day "they oscillated between
shore and ship with the sun beating down on their heads and with their souls
in turmoil."[1] Understandably, only once immigrants put Jaffa port behind
them, did they breathe more easily.

Newcomers generally came on their own account either as individuals or as
separate family units, though many also traveled within the framework of orga-

Jaffa in the late nineteenth century (Central Zionist Archives).

nized groups. Most made their way to the main urban centers of Jewish concentration as well as to the cities of Jaffa and Haifa where they attempted to carve
out a niche of some sort for themselves. Some poor families seemed to have arrived with nothing more than unbounded faith. In such cases, they were soon
living on the brink of starvation and were it not for the Alliance Israelite Universelle, which financed their departure, they would have met with a sorry end.

A large number of immigrants arrived with the express purpose of engaging
in farming. As it happened, prospects for realizing their objectives were much
improved by sweeping administrative reforms (*Tanzimat*) that took place between 1839 and 1878. Within the context of these reforms, which affected the
taxation system, land tenure, public administration and other facets of social
organization, land became technically more easily transferable. Added to this,
the fact that a new and, in part, absentee landowning class emerged, conditions
for a land market materialized in which Jewish purchasers could participate.
However, the land market was beset by various encumbrances. Only Turkish
nationals could buy land, and permanent dwellings thereon could not be constructed unless special building permits were secured.

THE FIRST AGRICULTURAL SETTLEMENTS

Between 1882 and 1884, seven agricultural colonies were established. [2] The
total capital and land area (37,000 dunam)[3] of the settlements were meager and

they housed no more than 1,500 people. Yet these colonies, which became an instant source of admiration and pride in the diaspora,[4] were destined to become the backbone of the New Yishuv.

The first settlement was *Rishon Letzion* (First in Zion), established by Jews from Russia and Romania, who on March 19, 1882, formed an eighteen-member founding committee in Jaffa under the leadership of Zalman Levontin. After an eight-week search, the committee, aided by the generosity of Zvi Levontin, Zalman's brother, secured a stretch of uninhabited, uncultivated, sandy land some twelve kilometers southeast of Jaffa. On July 31, 1882, ten members who had a financial stake in the transaction, plus six poor families who joined forces with them, assumed possession of the land.

Next, at the beginning of September 1882, on the very site of the ill-fated Gai Oni settlement near Safed (see chapter 1), a group of thirty financially independent Romanian families picked up where the previous settlers had left off. The new farmers were members of the Association for the Colonization of Eretz Israel (Palestine), which came into being in 1881 in Moinesti in Romania. Their departure from Moinesti generated much fanfare and excitement. From the moment they took leave of their native town until they reached their port of embarkation, they were feted by a multitude of Jewish well-wishers. The sea passage commenced with a hearty send-off by a vast, cheering crowd, but the voyagers' joy was marred by the sudden death of an infant girl. To forestall the possibility of a general and indeterminate quarantine being imposed on the entire party, the girl's mother stoically acted as if the child were still alive.[5] From Beirut, the settlers proceeded over land to Safed, riding on donkeys and mules. That leg of the journey took over three days, during which time one of the women gave birth. Eventually, on reaching the outskirts of Safed, they were welcomed by the city's residents. Renting temporary lodgings in Safed, they commenced working on their farm, which they named *Rosh Pina* (Cornerstone).

The settlement that followed was also formed by Romanians under the aegis of a body commonly known as the Central Committee of the Society for the Colonization of Eretz Israel. This organization saw the light of day in January 1882 at a meeting held in Focsani, Romania, attended by 100 delegates representing thirty-three different Hovevei Zion associations. It was hoped that twenty-two families sponsored by the Central Committee would proceed to Rosh Pina, but when they arrived in Palestine, they decided to stay in Haifa to await the acquisition of land for a settlement of their own. This materialized in October 1882, through the purchase from a Christian effendi, of landholdings on a rocky site at Mount Carmel. Their settlement, which was first named Samarin, was effectively launched on December 16, 1882. Its ultimate name, *Zichron Yaakov* (Memory of Jacob), was bestowed on it in 1884 at the opening of a synagogue financed by Baron Edmond Rothschild in honor of his late father Jacob (James). At first, the settlement depended on support from the Romanian Central Committee, which had hoped to create an average of three new colonies per year. But in practice, it barely managed to muster sufficient funds for Zichron Yaakov and even then for less than a year.

The fourth colony was *Yisud Hamaala* (the Beginning of Immigration), whose settlers originated in Poland and who belonged to a small association affiliated with the Hovevei Zion movement. In August 1883, they purchased 1,500 dunams of land in the Upper Galilee alongside Lake Hula. In the following March, ten families who took up temporary residence in Safed, began commuting to their farmland. Expected reinforcements from Poland and Lithuania did not materialize and this setback compromised the settlement's development from its very inception.

Within much the same time span, *Petah Tikva* (known as the Mother of the Settlements on account of its initial appearance in 1878) was reconstituted. The settlement's then three official owners, Yoel Solomon, David Gutman and Nathan Greengrat, sold off large tracts of land to a Lithuanian group of Hovevei Zion, which also acquired an estate further south. The latter acquisition, which was used exclusively for living quarters, enabled the area alongside the Yarkon River to be cultivated without unduly exposing the farmers to malaria. It was, after all, that disease that took the lives of earlier settlers and that figured in the demise of the original project. On October 8, 1882, with the new arrangement in place, a few of the old-timers who were living in Jerusalem and who had formed a group that they called the Petah Tikva Society returned to Petah Tikva to be joined by the Lithuanians nearly a year later. By the end of 1884, the settlement contained thirty-seven families consisting of wealthy estate owners, poorer estate owners in need of external assistance and landless farm workers.

The sixth settlement came into being following a meeting on September 28, 1882, between Rabbi Shmuel Mohilever (one of the heads of Hovevei Zion in Russia) and Baron Edmond Rothschild. During their discussions, Rabbi Mohilever persuaded the baron to finance a small settlement in Palestine to be run by sturdy young Jews with a prior knowledge of agronomy. Ten Lithuanians, with limited general education but who fitted the bill were chosen to constitute the future settlement's nucleus. The farmers, who were all illiterate, insisted on incorporating an additional person capable of corresponding with their families who were to remain in Lithuania pending the settlement's preparation. After a hazardous journey, in which they were first denied permission to land in Jaffa, they set foot in Palestine in December 1882. Initially they stayed at the Mikveh Israel agricultural school. Eventually, in October 1883, Shmuel Hirsh, the college's principal, secured a fertile stretch of land for them at Akir (a few kilometers south of Rishon Letzion), which was renamed Ekron. Because of delays in obtaining building permits, the settlers first took up residence at a nearby Arab village and only by September 1884 did they begin to construct houses in Ekron itself.

Finally, we turn to the seventh settlement, Gedera, founded in February 1884. Since this was the only settlement sustained by the Biluim, a description of events leading to its establishment will be provided later, in the context of a discussion of the Biluim in Palestine.

Apart for those in Ekron and Gedera, the first wave of pioneers were typically mature, conservative members of the middle to lower-middle classes. Most were petty merchants or minor communal functionaries, such as teachers or ritual slaughterers. Almost all were scrupulously religious.

The settlements themselves and those that followed, both within the First and then the Second Aliyah, were normally sited moderately close to existing Jewish commercial centers, such as Jaffa, Haifa, Safed and Tiberius. Considering that Jerusalem contained the largest concentration of Jews and occupied center stage in religious and ideological terms, it may at first seem baffling that, in the early days, barely any colonies were established within its vicinity. Even the original founders of Petah Tikva ventured to the coastal plain. The answer to this puzzle lies in the fact that the Arabs placed a much higher premium on land in the Judean Hills, particularly terraced, drained land in the mountain valleys, than on land in lower-lying areas. The highlands were exposed to large downfalls of winter rain and even maintained their moisture in the summer months. They were also blessed with an abundance of wells. By contrast, the low-lying land that the Jews acquired was, in the main, sandy, rocky or adjacent to malaria-infested swamps. Such land was relatively easier to acquire, since much of it was either public property or owned by wealthy, absentee landowners amenable to suitable offers. More desirable land in the Judean Hills was normally beyond the reach of Jewish bidders, either because land belonged to entire villages or was held in small segmented parcels.[6]

CHALLENGES TO THE FIRST SETTLERS

The First Aliyah settlers had to contend with a host of daunting problems relating to climatic adaptation and ignorance of local conditions, disease and the near absence of medical treatment, a lack of appropriate agricultural know-how, the opposition of the regime to their entry, land purchase and building restrictions, the untrustworthiness of intermediaries, skyrocketing land prices caused by Jewish speculators, clashes with neighbors and roving Bedouin and the suspicion and hostility from the Old Yishuv. Not only was health care not readily available, but each new settlement had to provide a range of services normally supplied by public authorities, such as sanitation, education and policing. The regime adopted an extreme laissez-faire approach and, apart from raising taxation, it virtually left its rural population, who were largely subsistence farmers, to their own devices. Therefore, it goes without saying that in addition to the deficiency of services already mentioned, transport and communication facilities were few and far between. For example, in a letter from Palestine dated July 29, 1882, Leib Bienstock wrote that "to this day there are no roads, not only between village to village but also between the city of one region to another. The road between Jaffa and Jerusalem is riddled with ridges and potholes even though the coachmen pay excessive taxes. Throughout the entire length of the

road, you will not find a single stone that has been laid properly."[7] The Jaffa to
Jerusalem road was only laid in 1869 to commemorate the official visit of the
Austrian Kaiser Franz Joseph. Up until then, wagons were a sight unseen, with
all transport being undertaken on pack animals.

Little wonder, then, that only a minute proportion of Jews leaving Russia in
the wake of the 1881 pogroms wished to live in Palestine. Even many leading
Biluim and Hovevei Zion activists chose to go to America. Most of those who
actually came were rare individuals whose deep attachment to national religious values fortified them in their day-to-day struggle in an economic, political and cultural backwater in which they were isolated and unwanted. Many did
not stay the course. In Zichron Yaakov, for example, 25 percent of the original
founders left within a matter of months.

As each band of pioneers took possession of their land, they organized their
activities within a cooperative framework in which, for the time being, the land
remained undivided and work activities were centrally coordinated. Land
preparation and, where legally feasible, housing construction were the immediate tasks at hand. These included the laying of an access road, the removal of
rocks and boulders and the burning of weeds. In almost all cases, the provision
of water was highly problematic and to obtain adequate supplies, artesian wells
had to be sunk at great expense and effort.

Settlers who did not readily receive construction permits, which were exclusively authorized by the sultan of Constantinople and whose attainment frequently entailed years of negotiations, slept in tents, thatch huts or even in
neighboring Arab property. In this respect, members of Yisud Hamaala were
particularly hard pressed. Lacking both capital and permission to build their
own houses, they emulated their Bedouin neighbors by erecting huts made of
reeds and matting. They and their children spent three full years in such accommodations, until Baron Rothschild took pity on them and provided them
with solid stone dwellings.

EARLY FINANCIAL TROUBLES AND THE
INTERVENTION OF BARON ROTHSCHILD

Virtually every new settlement faced inordinately high setup charges, primarily in the form of exorbitant legal expenses and bribes relating to the for-
malizing of settlers' rights of access to their duly acquired land and their ability
to construct permanent abodes. Their own funds were totally inadequate and,
within a year, the limited remittances sent by outsiders terminated.

In desperation, the financially stressed settlers appealed to wealthy European
Jews for assistance. Rishon Letzion initiated the process by dispatching Joseph
Feinberg as its emissary. In October 1882, two weeks after Rothschild had met
with Rabbi Mohilever with regard to the settlement Ekron, Feinberg secured an
audience with the baron. On learning of Rishon Letzion's difficulties, the baron

immediately offered to finance its well construction and to provide an agronomist to serve as an adviser. Then in June 1883, the baron expressed a willingness to extend his largesse over a period of years, provided he gained possession of the settlement's title deed and that its affairs be directed by his clerks on his behalf. Having no other alternative, Rishon Letzion acceded to his demands. In October and November 1883, similar arrangements were concluded with Zichron Yaakov and Rosh Pina. This meant that, along with Ekron, Rothschild assumed the patronage of four colonies that were dubbed "the baron's settlements." The remaining three, Petah Tikva, Yisud Hamaala and Gedera were eventually able to derive support of a kind from Hovevei Zion whose branches entered into a general alliance at Kattowitz in November 1884.

THE BARON'S SETTLEMENTS

The timely intervention of the baron in what effectively became his four settlements, set the stage for the solid consolidation and ultimate progress of Jewish agriculture in Palestine. Wishing to remain anonymous, primarily so as not to cross swords with the Turkish authorities who had officially proscribed foreign land ownership, the baron was generally referred to among the Palestinian Jews as the "known benefactor." To those in his settlements, he was an absolute godsend. He honored their debts, fully equipped them with then–state-of-the-art agricultural equipment, provided them with agricultural training and general services and, what is more, built them splendid living quarters. In the realm of education, Rothschild instructed his officials to cover all settlement schooling costs, including expenses relating to the construction of classrooms, the installation and inclusion of suitable equipment as well as salary payments.

On the other hand, the settlers completely forfeited their economic autonomy. All matters relating to farm production and output distribution, as well as those concerned with various services, were placed under the firm management of the baron's clerks. The upshot of it all was that most would-be farmers who had ventured to Palestine in the hopes of carving out their own fate, effectively ended up as the baron's vassals, save that over time, their economic and social conditions improved substantially. (Rabbi Pines defended the new arrangement by declaring that "It is better to be called slaves and live as freemen than to be called freemen and to live as slaves.")[8] The extent to which the settlers' subordinate status was explicitly formalized is indicated in a letter the settlers of Zichron Yaakov were expected to sign in return for the baron's patronage. The letter dated October 14, 1883, read as follows:

We are in your hands. The land of Samarin (Zichron Yaakov's original name) is yours. We deliver ourselves to you. We are obliged, in terms of this letter, to entrust unto you all that you consider that relates to the organization of the settlement. We accept without any question the administration that you choose without any thought of undermining it. We undertake not only to execute any suggestion issued in your name but to comply completely with all manner of instructions.[9]

A negative byproduct of the settlements' affairs being totally entrusted to the baron's staff is that it deprived farmers of any individual initiative. Most felt that they were, in practice, reduced to the status of wage earners and that given that all their basic needs seemed assured, they had little incentive to put in more than a minimally acceptable amount of work. Dr. Hillel Yaffa bewailed the fact that the general administrative system sapped the morale of the farmers. It soon became apparent that, for individuals to progress, they needed to ingratiate themselves with the baron's clerks, who decided which settlers would be sent abroad for training and which would be allocated special jobs and other privileges.

Occasionally, settlers rebelled against the baron's administration. The most notable case occurred in 1887 in Rishon Letzion, where farmers were highly critical of Oesovitsky, the colony's supervisor. Identifying Michal Helpren, who had organized the Yishuv's first workers' association, as a troublemaker, Oesovitsky not only ordered his eviction but called in Turkish soldiers to implement that order. With the entire settlement up in arms and rallying to Helpren's side, Oesovitsky was forced to flee. The baron, who at the time was visiting Palestine, appeared at Rishon Letzion and sternly warned the farmers that anyone disobeying or impugning his clerks would face immediate expulsion. Consequently, the cowed settlers signed a humiliating contract in which they were bound, unless contrary permission was given, not to form any association, not to host any outsider for more than forty-eight hours and not to employ anyone.

No sooner had the baron taken over the reins of control of his settlements than he instituted a thorough revolution in their horticultural structure. Considering that both he and his staff were mainly familiar and comfortable with plantation farming in southern France and in Algeria, it was decided that the Palestinian colonies would shift from varied grain cultivation into monoculture plantations, primarily specializing in grapes but also, to some extent, in almonds and dates. They were encouraged in their resolve to introduce viticulture, in that they observed that some of the Rishon Letzion farmers had already made desultory attempts to plant grape vines. On walking to Jaffa, farmers came across straggly vines emanating from an Arab vineyard. Recalling the bountiful supply of grapes in biblical days, they helped themselves to a handful of green twigs and inserted them in sandy soil on the fringes of their plots. The cuttings flourished and before long they had a vineyard in the making, or at least enough to convince the baron's agronomists that such a potential did indeed exist.

Meanwhile, the Hovevei Zion settlements of Petah Tikva, Yisud Hamaala and Gedera continued to flounder. They were financially weighed down by expenses relating to land registration and building permits and, with the flow of funds from Hovevei Zion being totally inadequate, they had to make do with abysmally low living standards. After repeated pleas to various possible sources of aid, relief was eventually in sight when, in 1887, Rothschild agreed to rescue Petah Tikva and Yisud Hamaala. Within a year, the necessary building permits were secured and the construction of stone houses commenced. Finally, by 1889, the two settlements were fully incorporated into the baron's organization. As for Gedera, some financial dispensation was forthcoming but it remained outside the baron's jurisdiction and continued to be attached to the Hovevei Zion, whose perennial shortage of capital inhibited its development.

THE BILUIM IN ERETZ ISRAEL

As already noted (in chapter 1), on July 6, 1882, fourteen Biluim, purporting to represent the spearhead of their movement, entered Palestine. Having been robbed on board ship and arriving with next to no funds, they borrowed 100 francs from Zalman Levontin, the founder of Rishon Letzion. With that loan, they rented two rooms in a building located near an orange grove outside Jaffa. To support themselves, they secured work at Mikveh Israel. On August 21, 1882, a second contingent consisting of six members joined them. Chaim Chissin of the second group observed that, on their arrival, only nine Bilu members were actively at work at Mikveh Israel. Three were sick (two with malaria and one with sunstroke), Belkind, who acted as the chairman, attended to "movement affairs," while one young girl prepared the meals. Like most newcomers who had never before undertaken manual labor, their initial work experiences seemed backbreaking. In an entry in his diary, dated September 2, 1882, Chissin provides an account of his early encounters with the rigors of physical travail, an account that was matched by countless other pioneers as they successively went through similar paces.

It is now ten days since I last wrote. Up to then, it was not physically possible. My hands are blistered and bloodied. I am unable to straighten my fingers, yet in Russia I dreamt that I would be able to work eight hours in the day and then dedicate the rest of the time to cultural matters. In fact, when one's back seems broken and one is overcome with fatigue, it is quite impossible to become immersed in cultural affairs. On returning from work, one only wishes to grab a quick bite and then lie down and sleep. When I first started work I tended to swing my hoe and to strike sideways, in every direction. But after a short while, my hands would blister. Blood would flow and I would experience horrific pain which would compel me to cast down my hoe. Then I would immediately be stricken by the weakness of my resolve and would admonish myself, saying "Is that how you intend to demonstrate that Jews are capable of physical labor?" An inner voice tauntingly cried out, "You will not withstand this decisive test!" Then with all my resolve and despite the pain, I resumed hoeing. I worked frantically for two full hours and when my strength finally gave in, I collapsed and was immobilized for the rest of the day. My back pain was unbearable, my hands full of wounds, those four morning hours seemed like an eternity.[10]

Shmuel Hirsh, the manager of Mikveh Israel, oversaw their work. In those days, the Biluim believed that he was hostile to them. He had grave reservations regarding their Zionist ideals and stretched them to the limit by restricting their endeavors to hoeing in order to discourage them and prompt them to leave. Meanwhile, they continued to count on securing funds to establish their own settlement. Money was supposed to arrive from their Istanbul branch but when nothing was forthcoming, they turned to Karl Neter of the Alliance Israelite, who promised them help. Unfortunately, he died shortly thereafter and in the wake of his death, social and economic tensions began to undermine their cohesion. Notwithstanding the general lip service paid to the ideals of equality and equal sacrifice, not everyone carried his or her weight. For example, despite a decision to abstain from tea and tobacco consumption to conserve their income, some members bought such goods, ostensibly out of their own pockets. With the principles of equality and solidarity being blatantly flouted, the group fragmented. At the end of September and the beginning of October 1882, a few went to Jerusalem where they were taken under the wing of Rabbi Pines. By the end of October, the thirteen members remaining at Mikveh Israel were at loggerheads with one another, with five constituting their own communa. It seems that the other eight resented the fact that, not only did Belkind not perform agricultural labor, but by describing himself as the Russian-based movement's delegate, he refused to be bound by local decisions. Then in November, under Hirsh's prodding, the two factions at Mikveh Israel reunited and prepared to leave for Rishon Letzion with the baron's blessing.

The transfer of the Biluim to Rishon Letzion raised the ire of those in the movement's Istanbul office, who viewed it as a betrayal and as a shortsighted attempt to resolve their personal problems. Within Rishon Letzion itself, their arrival was not very auspicious. The more elderly farmers, who resented their secular outlook, believed that younger settlers, such as Zalman Levontin and Joseph Fineberg, contrived to incorporate them into the settlement to strengthen their own position. In response, the elderly members sought the support of the settlement's six poor families, claiming that the presence of the Biluim would detract from their allowances. Accordingly, when the Biluim blithely made their entry into Rishon Letzion, they were met with such a hostile reception that they promptly returned to Mikveh Israel. Only when faced with a threat of the total withdrawal of the baron's patronage, did all Rishon Letzion settlers ultimately acquiesce.[11]

During that period, Rabbi Pines gained some authority over the Biluim, by virtue of the fact that some funds supplied by the Hovevei Zion in Russia for Bilu use were entrusted to him. In April 1883, using his newfound leverage, he persuaded seven of the Biluim at Rishon Letzion to return to Mikveh Israel to bide their time there pending the establishment of their own settlement. Those in Mikveh Israel and those still in Jerusalem founded the Bilu Society and severed their ties with those remaining at Rishon Letzion. This rupture caused many to leave the country but the departees were partly offset by new arrivals from the then-disbanded Istanbul office.

The formation of the new Bilu Society gave rise to a new Bilu constitution, calling for the formation of a commune in which everything was to be jointly owned, even clothes. When the baron received a copy of the constitution, his patience snapped. Rejecting requests for aid to found a model settlement, the baron let it be known that he would rather fund the emigration of Biluim from Palestine—an offer that was soon taken up by seven Bilu members (including two leading ones), five of whom went to America and two to France.

Eventually, in December 1884, with the help of Rabbi Pines and based on Hovevei Zion funds, the Biluim finally established their own colony, which they called Gedera. Initially, seven Biluim, accompanied by one independent farmer who planned to buy into the estate, took up possession of the land. A little later, they were joined by two more Biluim.

Conditions in Gedera were pitiful. The pioneers were barely equipped with necessary implements, most of the soil was rocky, there was a shortage of water, they had little agricultural knowledge and limited physical prowess. They suffered from a complete lack of capital, they were isolated and were subject to pillaging by the neighboring Arab peasantry. Because the settlement largely raised field crops, Gedera had to pay taxes according to the estimated value of such crops, which, in practice, often exceeded realized values. Despite all such privations, the settlers managed to persevere.

Monthly allowances remitted by the Hovevei Zion helped to sustain them, and although they were subordinate to an absentee managing director, they ran their own day-to-day affairs. They selected a committee and convened meetings to discuss agricultural problems, work arrangements, the siting of their permanent dwellings and even the social and religious mode of life of the colony.[12]

Gedera soon became embroiled in a dispute with the Hovevei Zion leadership in Russia, which insisted that the settlers pursue a religious lifestyle. The dispute arose as a result of complaints by Old Yishuv rabbis, who were aghast that not only did the Biluim not honor the Sabbath but they also indulged in intersex dancing. Describing the Gedera settlers as "transgressors who pollute the land" the rabbis called on Hovevei Zion to stop providing them with aid.[13] For their part, the Biluim maintained that as Hovevei Zion was essentially a national movement, it ought not concern itself with its members' personal conduct. However, the Hovevei Zion leadership reasoned that since the movement did, in fact, seek national redemption in the religious sense, they were entitled to expect religious compliance from the Biluim at Gedera. Were the Biluim to continue to flaunt their religious disrespect, a shadow would be cast over the movement's general image. Eventually, a compromise was reached whereby Rabbi Pines was appointed as the *mashgiah* (supervisor) of the settlement's religious observances. Part of his responsibility entailed coaxing the settlers to attend synagogue services and to cease work on the eve of the Sabbath. Those refusing to comply were subject to expulsion.

Few of the Bilu organizational objectives were realized. No more than fifty to sixty members actually immigrated to Palestine and by the beginning of 1885, only about twenty remained. Of the fourteen original Biluim who had arrived in Jaffa in 1882, just three lived out their lives in the country.[14] Within the New Yishuv, which soon numbered 5,500, their presence in Palestine was barely perceptible. In the eyes of their contemporaries, the Biluim were seen as idle visionaries; argumentative, apostates, lacking discipline; nihilists; lazy, and in general pathetic.[15] Nevertheless, they were idolized by later youthful idealists who left their mark in subsequent *aliyot* (immigration waves) and by Zionist historians who even incorrectly labeled the First Aliyah, the "Aliyah of the Biluim." Essentially, the Biluim's lasting impression is explicable in terms of their revolutionary zeal and their uncompromising calls to action. Even though a yawning gap emerged between theory and practice, their apparent commitment to Jewish self-labor, their notion of young unmarried members offering at least three years of unpaid service in furtherance of their cause, their declared belief in social equality and their desire to resurrect Hebrew as a living language were all seen as a source of pioneering inspiration.

THE BNEI MOSHE

From its headquarters in Odessa, the Hovevei Zion promoted practical work in Palestine, paying little heed (apart from religious practice) to cultural and spiritual matters. This approach was challenged by Asher Ginsberg, widely known by his pen name, Ahad Ha'Am (one of the people), who believed that a solid infusion of national sentiment, based on Jewish ethical values was of prime importance. In Ahad Ha'Am's view, the Hebrew spirit was exemplified by the ancient prophets whose single-minded pursuit of universal justice and uncompromising vision of righteousness embodied the essence of all that is noble in Judaism. In the diaspora, religious, ghetto-based Jews retained the core of the Jewish tradition but at the expense of an exaggerated adherence to a multitude of regulations executed in all their minutiae. While this preserved the Jewish religion, in practice it reduced it to the mere fulfilment of ritual. Emancipated Jews, on the other hand, ever anxious to absorb the culture of the country in which they resided, could hardly be expected to pay more than lip service to their own national heritage; either way, the Hebrew spirit could not be regenerated in exile. At the very least, to effect a renaissance of authentic Hebrew national life, an autonomous Jewish communal presence in Palestine was required. Such a center, in which the Hebrew language and literature would be revitalized, would serve as a spiritual beacon to the majority of Jews who would continue to live in the diaspora.

With regard to those settlers in Palestine who had an insufficient appreciation of the need for spirituality, Ahad Ha'Am warned that such farmers would
eventually pursue their own personal ends only. That being the case, they
would be ill-prepared to withstand pressures from an unfriendly Turkish authority, a latently hostile Arab population and a life of endless drudgery and
hardship. Even were the settlers able to achieve economic prosperity without
establishing in Palestine a spiritual Jewish center, their efforts would be pointless. For while appreciating the need for Jewish physical autonomy or independence, Ahad Ha'Am was adamant that the homeland also had to safeguard the
Hebrew soul. He believed that Jewish continuity had been attained by heeding
the words of prophets "to respect only the power of the spirit and not to wor-
ship material power."[16] Should a Jewish state merely concern itself with the
day-to-day trappings of nations in general, it would be devoid of Jewish content. In that case, it would fail to inspire world Jewry and would cease to be a
force making for Jewish unity and viability.

In March 1889, in furtherance of his views, Ahad Ha'Am founded a group
known as *Bnei Moshe* (sons of Moses),[17] which was a subset of the Hovevei
Zion movement and which largely consisted of a limited number of free-
thinking intellectuals. Although the group's membership never exceeded 100, it
was, among other things, instrumental in establishing Hebrew schools in Jaffa
and a publishing house in Warsaw. The first Hebrew boys' school was set up in
October 1892 under the joint sponsorship of the Hovevei Zion and the Alliance
Israelite Universelle. Three months later, a comparable girls' school was established. Because the schools were not run along strict religious lines, Rabbi
Pines, who had, up to then, cast his lot with the Bnei Moshe, withdrew his support and joined forces with the Old Yishuv in criticizing Hovevei Zion enterprises. This had a demoralizing effect on Bnei Moshe members, who were
beginning to feel dispirited by a lack of a solid practical program of action and
who were infiltrated by new recruits less concerned with ethical issues.[18] By
1897 the organization ceased to exist.

ECONOMIC DEVELOPMENTS IN PALESTINE UP TO
1903, THE END OF THE FIRST ALIYAH

Within the last decade of the nineteenth century, following a resumption of
oppressive policies on the part of the czar, which involved the forcible expulsion
of Jews from Moscow and the re-emergence of pogroms, the flow of immigrants to Palestine once again gained momentum, with more than 8,000 arriving in 1891 alone. Many of the new immigrants were well-heeled and sought
land for their own use, but most were indigent and were obliged to seek paid
employment. Their absorption was partly facilitated by the prior formation of
new settlements and by an upsurge of urban activity.

Between 1898 and 1904, twenty additional settlements were founded, including Rehovot, Hadera, Mishmar Hayarden, Kfar Tabu and Yavniel. Rehovot and Hadera represented two settlements, apart from Gedera and then later Beer Tuvia, which the Hovevei Zion helped to maintain. Rehovot came into being in 1890 by virtue of support from a society formed in Warsaw, *Menuha V'Nahala* (Rest and Security), which had links with the Bnei Moshe, whereas Hadera arose a year later in response to a Russian-Jewish initiative. As in previous cases, until the baron interceded with the Turkish authorities, both settlements had to make do with makeshift accommodations. In Hadera, surrounding swampland turned out to be larger than anticipated and was not completely drained until 1900 after the extensive planting of eucalyptus trees and the digging of drainage canals.[19] This meant that malaria took a great toll. Many settlers, both young and old and in some cases entire families, were wiped out. As a means of escaping the disease, a large proportion of the settlers evacuated the area each summer. Understandably, Hadera's economic standing proved to be precarious. Its distressed settlers turned to the baron who, in 1893, expressed a willingness to care for them. Rehovot, which was more favorably placed, formally retained its autonomy but nonetheless it depended on the baron as an outlet for its grape harvests.

Having accepted responsibility for the well-being of his settlements, Rothschild continued to widen investments within them. In 1891, a winery (then the world's second largest) began operations at Rishon Letzion to be followed in 1892 by another one at Zichron Yaakov. These two wineries bought all the settlements' grapes "at regular subsidized prices without regard to market conditions in wine."[20] At one stage, grape farmers were paid three times the normal price. Evidently, the wineries, which became a mainstay of the New Yishuv's economy, were not established and run on the basis of commercial considerations alone. They generated a massive agricultural subvention, which in other states and eras would have been publicly funded. Additional projects in which the baron experimented included the opening up of plantations of mulberries, tobacco, spices, sugar cane, tea, raisins and cotton. A silk weaving plant was established at Rosh Pina, as was a perfume factory at Yisud Hamaala and the first citrus orchards were planted at Petah Tikva.

In time, the baron's heavy-handed bureaucratic system mellowed, allowing the direct involvement of settlers in matters relating to both their livelihood and cultural interests. Wine marketing was passed on to a company called Carmel, founded by members of the Menuha V'Nahala, and in so doing, the Hovevei Zion was accorded a key role in the Yishuv's economic affairs. In 1895, the Jewish Colonial Association (JCA) founded in 1891 by Baron Maurice Hirsch and which helped Russian Jews emigrate to Argentina, made its debut in Palestine. There it provided assistance to Mishmar Hayarden, Nes Ziona, Gedera and Rehovot.

In January 1900, the baron dropped a bombshell by announcing his decision to withdraw his patronage and to terminate his settlement administration. In terms of an agreement reached in October 1899, everything was to be transferred to the JCA, along with an endowment of 15 million francs, with the understanding that the baron was to chair the JCA's new Palestine committee. Just why he arrived at that decision remains unclear, but the settlements' poor economic record would almost certainly have been a factor. After eighteen years of effort, in which over £1.5 million had been invested, the settlements were yet to become self-reliant. They were all virtually dependent on one crop, which, in most cases, happened to be grapes. Little consideraton was given to possibilities of delving into other agricultural fields. "Cowsheds were in a shambles. The few cows on hand were of inferior local breeds. There was barely a chicken run to speak of and next to no vegetable cultivation. With the Jewish colonies hardly producing anything of significance to satisfy their own food needs, they had to obtain their requirements from Arabs."[21]

Settlers fearing for their future pleaded with the baron to reconsider his position but not only did their appeals fall on deaf ears but their entreaties angered him. Having an autocratic disposition and not taking kindly to what he considered outside meddling, the baron reprimanded the settlers by declaring: "I colonized Eretz Israel, I alone and no one has the right—be they farmers or societies—to involve themselves in my affairs nor to voice opinions regarding my actions."[22] With their new supervising authority (the JCA) being considerably less generous than its predecessor, the farmers' fears were soon realized.

Unlike the baron, the JCA could not sustain settlements for long years at a stretch that could not pay their own way. The realities of commercial life had to be brought home to the settlers and this was done in a manner that modern economists would recognize as constituting the Yishuv's first structural adjustment process. Funds available to farmers were curtailed and subsidized crop prices were abolished. Because of a wine glut, vine plantings were suspended and older, less productive vineyards, amounting to 50 percent of the total, were uprooted. Instead, the JCA encouraged the growing of alternative crops such as cereals, citrus fruit and almonds, and, for that purpose, each farmer's land acreage was slightly extended. This was accomplished by reducing each settlement's existing population and then either redeploying excess farmers in new settlements or financing their emigration. Within the JCA's own administration, economies were effected in the size of the bureaucracy and in the number of employees providing social and other services. Almost all the baron's clerks were dismissed and the settlement's economic affairs were externally vetted. With the fall in grape prices, wages plummeted. This induced farmers to substitute Arab workers for Jews, with the result that Jewish unemployment rose. Here, too, the needs of the unemployed were partially met by the offer of free passage abroad, which was taken up by a large number, including some of the offspring of the original settlers. By the end of 1900, nearly a quarter of the working-class Jewish families who were present at the year's beginning, departed.[23] The JCA tried to alleviate the plight of those who remained by opening up a training farm at Sejera plus four other settlements, all of which were in the lower Galilee. Despite all its attendant suffering, in purely economic terms, the structural adjustment process could be adjudged a success. For within five years, the settlements had generally become commercially viable.

In terms of the general economic and social development of the New Yishuv, mention should also be made of the fact that Jaffa's Jewish population rose from 400 in 1872 to 3,200 by 1904. In the pre–First Aliyah period, Jaffa only housed a tiny fraction of the Palestinian Jews, most of whom were Sephardim. The city had no organized Jewish community and the charity distribution system existing in Jerusalem was not applied there. As the city's Jewish population was augmented by First Aliyah immigrants, it began to be characterized as being an enlightened one, tolerant of deviations from orthodoxy and open to Western thought and progress. Jaffa began to serve as the New Yishuv's urban center in which were located the headquarters of most organizations on which the New Yishuv depended. It developed good Jewish schools and, among other things, a hospital and an extensive library, both of which opened their doors to the New Yishuv at large.

THE REVIVAL OF HEBREW

The revival of Hebrew as a modern, spoken language ranks as one of Zionism's most remarkable achievements. During the Jewish people's long sojourn in the diaspora, the use of Hebrew was upheld for the purposes of prayer, religious study and writing. Daily speech was conducted in other languages. Central and Eastern European Jews communicated with one another in Yiddish (in which words of German origin account for about 85 percent of the vocabulary).[24] Oriental Jews spoke Arabic and some Sephardi Jews spoke Ladino (based on medieval Castillian). Just as Hebrew was in the process of emerging as a practical spoken language, Theodor Herzl, the founder of modern political Zionism, assumed that the citizens of his envisioned Jewish state would speak German, French or English. It seemed axiomatic to him that Hebrew could not possibly serve as a vehicle for communicating scientific notions, nor for handling modern technological terminology. As he put it, "Who amongst us has a sufficient acquaintance with Hebrew to ask for a railway ticket in that language?"[25]

Even though spoken Hebrew had long fallen into disuse, almost all educated East European Jews were well versed in written Hebrew, since their liturgy was anchored in it. On that basis, with the publication, in the second half of the nineteenth century, of Hebrew newspapers, such as Smolenskin's *Hashahar* (the Dawn) and of modern Hebrew novels, read by enlightened Russian Jews, the possibility of Hebrew being used for nonreligious purposes increasingly began to be canvassed. The need to ensure that Jewry as a whole spoke Hebrew was propagated by Eliezer Ben Yehuda,[26] who reasoned that it would be a cementing factor in binding Jews together. Without the commonality of spoken Hebrew, doubt would invariably be cast as to the intrinsic unity of the Jewish nation and of its ability to forge a unified national consciousness.[27] Subscribing to such views, both the Biluim and many Hovevei Zion adherents aspired to re-constitute Hebrew as the Jewish national language.

Of the two accents used in prayer, Hebraists almost unanimously favored the Sephardi over the Ashkenazi one. The Ashkenazi accent, which developed within the diaspora, was considered to have represented a distorted and per-verse way of pronouncing Hebrew. The Sephardi accent, by contrast, was thought to be more authentic and, in any case, was more widely used by those in Palestine who spoke Hebrew. That is not to say that the decision to adopt the Sephardi accent brooked no opposition. The more extreme religious Jews ar-gued that since, in global terms, the Ashkenazi accent was dominant, jettison-ing it would create even greater problems for Jewish unity. However, their objections were overruled.

The generalized acceptance of spoken Hebrew among Jerusalem's Sephardi, moderate Ashkenazi and enlightened Jewish community was slow in getting off the ground. Hebrew tended to be used only as a means of effecting transcommunal communication. Its use as a lingua franca reflected the fact that nineteenth-century Jerusalem was unrivaled in terms of the ethnic diversity of its Jewish community and, consequently, of the range of languages spoken. Even the extremely religious Ashkenazi Jews at one time resorted to Hebrew when no other commonly understood language would suffice. But as spoken Hebrew eventually began to be associated with the New Yishuv, Old Yishuv stalwarts not only desisted from using it but utterly excoriated those that did. The onus of ushering spoken Hebrew into the Jewish national arena was thus almost entirely borne by the New Yishuv settlements, where the battle for He-brew was joined within the school system.

Without exception, the traditional *heder* (classroom), in which boys were tu-tored in religious scripture through the medium of Yiddish, was at first the only source of formal education within each early settlement. Such an arrange-ment reflected a general willingness on the part of the first settlers to adhere to orthodox norms. Nevertheless, a perceived need to impart some basic secular knowledge, plus a desire to inculcate their children with a Jewish national ethos, soon came to the fore. Subjects like arithmetic were added to the curriculum and Hebrew was introduced and presented as a usable practical language. In time, girls were permitted to study alongside boys and the heders effectively became conventional coeducational schools.

With the transformation of settlement schools into modern nonclerical in-stitutions, the teaching of Hebrew could proceed apace. The first stage involved the explication of Hebrew terms in Yiddish. Then, it was decided that Hebrew would be taught exclusively in Hebrew itself, a step that was made difficult to execute considering the lack of appropriate textbooks and the absence of any precedent on which formal instruction could be based. Ultimately, all subjects were taught in Hebrew. Such a bold move, which was first undertaken in 1888 in Rishon Letzion, was eventually adopted by the other settlements. Progress was, to say the least, rather uneven. Almost everywhere there were innumer-able obstacles that would normally have deterred the fainthearted.

In the first instance, teachers generally lacked appropriate pedagogical training and in their attempts to expound scientific principles or merely to discuss common day-to-day affairs in Hebrew, they groped about for suitable words or phrases. This situation was a natural consequence of the fact that spoken Hebrew had fallen into disuse for nearly 2,000 years. One pupil later recorded that his teacher "did more stuttering than talking."[28] Another observed that "conversations were neither natural nor free flowing and often in the midst of speaking, it was necessary to pause in search of an appropriate word or for one that escaped one's memory. To most, Hebrew speech seemed contrived and sometimes it appeared as if some exercise in mimicry, with hands flailing and with eyes winking, was in progress."[29] For the students, it was quite a revolution. As Yoel Freeman recollected, "Pupils encountered considerable difficulty in shifting from Jargon (the then-common sobriquet for Yiddish) into Hebrew. We kids were used to speaking Jargon in and out of home. Even when we studied the prayer book and the Bible, we translated it into Yiddish, our parental tongue. We neither knew nor dreamt that Hebrew could be a spoken language and then suddenly events took a sharp turn, rendering our lives topsy-turvy."[30]

Aside from Hebrew's then-linguistic shortcomings, a host of external pressures bore down on the teachers. Pupils' parents were not enamored of what seemed to be an artificial and unwarranted imposition of a seemingly sterile language. They themselves would rather have had their children learn a European language and, in this regard, many favored the use of French. In Zichron Yaakov, daughters of leading families were sent to France to complete their education, whereas the youth in general both spoke French and adopted a French attire. Not surprisingly, and to the pride of its inhabitants, Zichron Yaakov soon became known as "Little Paris."[31] When Zeev Yaabetz tried to instill a measure of respect for modern Hebrew in Zichron Yaakov, he was rebuffed and, eventually, in 1890, he was even deprived of his teaching post.

Gradually, attitudes changed. Teachers reached out to parents in their own time, organizing adult Hebrew language classes. Their efforts were endorsed by none other than Baron Rothschild, who, when visiting Zichron Yaakov in 1893, addressed the settlers, saying: "If you do not understand French that is not of any consequence. But speaking Jargon (Yiddish) is unsatisfactory. Jargon is not a real language. It is behoven upon you all to speak the language that our forefathers spoke, that is Hebrew. I hope that next time I call upon you I will find you all speaking Hebrew."[32] Finally, with Hebrew kindergartens being formed, toddlers returned home with Hebrew on their lips and, as a result, parents began to wish to familiarize themselves with that language. Hebrew-speaking groups were soon formed throughout the New Yishuv, and adherents insisted on the language being used at all public functions and gatherings. By the time the First Aliyah ended, Hebrew was becoming a normal and widely accepted spoken language. However, its generalized use was certainly not assured, for within every settlement its strength depended in part on the presence of a sufficient number of enthusiasts. Second Aliyah veterans were wont to declare that spoken Hebrew only became firmly entrenched within their era but, in fact, even at the end of the Second Aliyah in 1914, only a quarter of adult Jews in Palestine spoke Hebrew. The struggle to ensure spoken Hebrew's dominance persisted for many years to come.[33]

Any review of the rejuvenation of spoken Hebrew would be incomplete without highlighting the unique contribution of Eliezer Ben Yehuda and of both his first and second wife. Not only was Ben Yehuda among the vanguard in Jerusalem and elsewhere in initiating various organizations and educational programs for furthering the adoption of spoken Hebrew, but he applied his ideals within the scope of his family life. In 1882, after aborting his medical studies in Paris because he was afflicted with tuberculosis, Ben Yehuda left for Palestine. En route in Vienna, he was joined by his wife-to-be, Deborah, a fellow Lithuanian. As soon as they were on board ship, Ben Yehuda declared that he and Deborah were to spend the rest of their lives conversing in Hebrew only. Up to that point, Deborah could barely utter a single Hebrew expression. Fortunately for Ben Yehuda, she unhesitantly complied.

The couple's determination to create the first Hebrew-speaking household was put to the test when their first child, a son, was born. With absolute ruthlessness they banished all non-Hebrew sounds from their home, lest their son's speech be corrupted by "foreign" terms. For the first three years, their son did not utter a word. Neighbors attributed this to their experiment and even Rabbi Pines, who had previously entered into a pact with Ben Yehuda to speak only Hebrew, tried to persuade Yehuda and Deborah that the inevitable lack of playmates would hinder the child's spiritual growth and cause him to be a social misfit. Notwithstanding such possibilities, Deborah remained resolute. She took upon herself "the obligation of undertaking the first trial—after two thousand years of exile—to resuscitate the dormant Hebrew language within the soul and mouth of her son."[34]

In 1891 Deborah died of tuberculosis, which she contracted from her husband. According to the family physician, Ben Yehuda, who then had two children on his hands, was expected to live no longer than another six months or so. In desperation, he wrote to Deborah's sister, Hemda, who, as a half-assimilated Russian, was studying in Moscow. Like Deborah, Hemda wholeheartedly rallied to Ben Yehuda's call. She married him, learned Hebrew and cared for both her sister's children and her ailing husband. Not only did she provide opportunities for Ben Yehuda to work on the gargantuan task of compiling a modern Hebrew dictionary but, in her own right, she wrote Hebrew prose of some literary merit.

SEPHARDI MIGRANTS

Most people with some inkling of the history of the First Aliyah assume that it was exclusively an Ashkenazi affair. Certainly the overwhelming majority of Jews came from Eastern Europe but 2,500 migrants arrived from Yemen and even smaller contingents made their way from North Africa, Turkey and the Balkan states. They mainly gravitated to Jerusalem and, to a lesser extent, Jaffa, where they made their mark in widening the scope of Jewish urbanization in Palestine. Agricultural pursuits were not entirely bypassed, and Sephardi workers maintained a presence in almost all colonies. In Har Tuv, founded in 1896 by Bulgarian Jews, the Sephardim had a settlement of their own.

Like the Jews throughout most of Eastern Europe, the Jews of Yemen, who numbered 50,000 in the late nineteenth century, were subject to a host of discriminatory practices. There were irritating sumptuary laws that prohibited Jews from wearing attractive clothing. A humiliating prohibition disallowed Jews from riding donkeys and they were unable to construct buildings that may have been deemed large or magnificent. Such restrictions reflected Muslim attitudes toward non-Muslims living in their midst, who were accorded an inferior *Djimi* status. Although irksome, the Yemenite Jews were, by and large, able to cope with such inconveniences. Eventually, when large parts of Yemen were conquered by the Turks, conditions deteriorated and with even more grasping rulers than usual in place, life for most Jews took a distinct turn for the worse. Responding to reports that European Jews were returning to Palestine, and taking advantage of their newly acquired Ottoman citizenship, many set their sights on joining their kinsmen in the Holy Land.[35] They traveled in a series of caravans, which took months to cross a vast expanse of desert and then sailed through the Suez Canal to Jaffa, whence most walked to Jerusalem. Upon their arrival, they showed the effects of their horrendous journey: "Their skin had shrivelled, their faces were wrinkled and naked and barefooted, hungry and thirsty, they were on the verge of death."[36]

Scant assistance, if any, was forthcoming from the Jerusalem Old Yishuv, whose members resented their intrusion. Lacking suitable occupations, many took to begging while taking on whatever casual work came their way. Gradually, a sizable proportion adapted to the local labor market and acquired appropriate skills, particularly in building and stone cutting, areas of activity in which they were the first Jews to break ground.[37] In that sense, they resembled New Yishuv immigrants but considering that they were drawn to Palestine on the wave of deeply held messianic beliefs, they were also akin to the Old Yishuv in terms of their traditionalism, customs and devotion to orthodox religious practices.

TURKISH AUTHORITIES AND JEWISH SETTLERS

In October 1881, the Turks determined that Jews immigrating to the Ottoman Empire were to settle in a dispersed fashion and were not to enter Palestine itself. All Jewish immigrants were obliged to become Ottoman citizens and were to renounce their former ties. A major source of Turkish opposition to large-scale Jewish immigration to Palestine lay in the system of capitulations whereby foreign nationals residing in the Turkish empire were protected by their consuls and were generally placed beyond the jurisdiction of Turkish courts. The capitulations system made life in Palestine somewhat more bearable for Jewish immigrants. It shielded them from excessive arbitrariness on the part of local officials and fortified their resolve not to allow anyone to encroach on their rights. In Ben Yehuda's view, had the capitulations not been in place, not a single settlement would have been established.[38] With few exceptions (such as the founders of Rosh Pina), Russian Jewish immigrants doggedly clung to their formal Russian nationality. This had the effect of strengthening the influence of the Russian consulate in matters that would normally be the province of the local government. In other words, the flow of Russian Jews into Palestine tended to lessen Turkish sovereignty there. For that reason alone, the authorities strove to limit Jewish immigration.[39]

In reality, although many Jews were subsequently deterred from immigrating and some were even refused entry on arrival in Jaffa, Jewish immigration to Palestine continued unabated. Jews requested and received visas as pilgrim visitors and, once in Palestine, they simply stayed on permanently. In 1888, as a result of overtures on the part of the United States, England and France, Turkey finally sanctioned Jewish entry into Palestine, provided the immigrants arrived as individuals and not en masse. By 1891, as the inflow of Jewish immigrants gathered momentum, the Turkish authorities not only revoked the rights of Jewish entry but also prohibited noncitizen Jews from purchasing land.

However, in response to the intervention of the foreign consulates, Jews lawfully resident in Palestine were given permission to purchase land, provided that they did not let nonlawfully resident Jews build on their lots and that they did not extend the number of their settlements. As in the past, the settlers made headway by greasing the palms of venal officials. Luckily for them, the official opposition of the Ottoman government to modern Jewish settlement was experienced mainly in terms of bureaucratic harassment and in terms of the imposition of financial exactions both above and below board. Had the Turkish regime been able to stand up to foreign pressure and had it been run with a modicum of efficiency, clamping down on infringements of all kinds, including graft and corruption, the Jews would not have established even a small toehold in Palestine.

CONFLICT WITH THE OLD YISHUV

The classification of the Yishuv into old and new does not entirely correspond to the sequences of their arrival, for though the Old Yishuv preceded the new one during both the First and Second Aliyahs (or *Aliyot* in correct Hebrew), thousands of immigrants attached themselves to the Old Yishuv. The cleavage between the two has more to do with divergent world views than with their temporal entry onto the Palestinian stage. Even though the two entities were mutually incompatible, each at certain times derived some benefit from the other's existence. For example, the increase of the Old Yishuv prior to 1881, strengthened the Jewish presence in the four holy cities as well as in Jaffa and Haifa and, in so doing, eased the way for the arrival of the first Jewish nationalist settlers.

In general, the Old Yishuv very much resented the appearance of the New Yishuv. Apart from being affronted by the New Yishuv's laxer attitude toward religious practices, the Old Yishuv also feared that the settlements would derive aid at its expense. As early as 1881, Old Yishuv rabbis condemned potential new settlers who were wont to engage in farming, an occupation which in their view was totally uncalled for.[40] Later, in December 1883, Jerusalem rabbis proclaimed that Palestine was incapable of sustaining mass immigration and that the new settlers were "not walking in the road of the Torah and the fear of God and, far from drawing redemption near, they were delaying it, God forbid!"[41]

The Old Yishuv certainly attempted to impose its value system on the new settlers. One lever that it employed related to wine making. For the successful marketing of Palestinian wine, it was absolutely essential that the wine officially be deemed kosher. To obtain the rabbis' imprimatur, their agents were accorded a supervisory status over the wine-making process, which, to conform to religious practice, had to be made exclusively by Jews (a fact that, incidentally, afforded a small measure of protection to Jewish labor). Taking advantage of their ability to disqualify the finished wine product, the religious supervisors usually allowed only seemingly orthodox Jews, that is, those with beards and wearing skullcaps, to serve in the wineries.

The largest bone of contention between the two communities revolved around the question of *shemittah,* the seventh sabbatical year in which, according to the Bible, land was to lie fallow and anything growing on it was to be regarded as ownerless property. Except for a short period in Syria, the practice of shemittah was never applied to Jews living in the diaspora.

The year 1889 was designated as a year of shemittah and, as it drew near, Rothschild's representatives sought a ruling from Rabbi Isaac Spector of Kovno as to whether it would be possible to circumvent the effect of the shemittah injunction without blatantly flouting religious law.[42] Rabbi Spector advised that the matter could be resolved by a temporary "sale" of settlement land to a gentile willing to allow the settlers to sow and harvest it throughout the shemittah year and who would "resell" the land (at the same nominal price) a year later. Rabbi Spector's ruling had the backing of other Russian rabbis and even of the Sephardi Haham Bashi in Jerusalem, Rabbi Eliasher, who was prepared to attach his seal of office to such a transaction. By contrast, the Jerusalem Ashkenazi rabbis were completely unyielding. Salmon, in his seminal study of *Religion and Zionism,* asserted that "There is no doubt that the Ashkenazi leadership exploited the matter of the shemittah to deal a crushing blow to the new settlements and to the Hovevei Zion."[43] They issued a proclamation unambiguously stating that "as the year 5649 [1889] is drawing nigh, we inform our brethren settlers that, in accordance with our religion, they are not permitted to plough, to sow or to reap, or to allow gentiles to perform these agricultural operations."[44] To support the settlers financially throughout the year in question, they called on diaspora Jews to provide donations. The settlers themselves were in a quandary. Many of them, and especially those in Ekron, did not wish to cross swords with the Jerusalem rabbis but the Hovevei Zion as well as numerous Russian rabbis, exhorted them to abide by Rabbi Spector's advice. As a result, the vast majority defied the Jerusalem rabbis and cultivated their land. In ensuing years, the issue was successively raised, giving rise to the view that there existed an apparent "incompatibility of religious tradition with the requirements of a community that sought to be productive and self-supporting."[45]

Religious tensions were present even within the very confines of certain New Yishuv settlements. In Rehovot's case, the founding fathers were middle-aged family men with a very strong sense of religious proprieties. Soon after their arrival, they were joined by free-spirited youngsters, whose zest for life was manifested in their reckless horsemanship, their enthusiastic bouts of dancing and their general disregard for time-honored conventions. Within no time at all, they aroused the enmity of both Rehovot's more elderly members and of the Old Yishuv leadership. Finally, when they attempted to stage Lilien-blum's play, *Zerubbabel*, matters came to a head. Intolerant elements within the orthodox establishment turned to government officials with the suggestion that the play was nothing more than a call to rebellion. In response, a detachment of armed soldiers was dispatched to Rehovot to quell the "uprising." Fortunately, with the timely intervention of Dr. Stein, a respected Jaffa medical practitioner, the powers that be were apprised of the fact that the play's theme was none other than a biblical one. The soldiers were withdrawn and, to the chagrin of the protesters, the performance proceeded.[46]

Notwithstanding the general tension between them, the two Yishuvs were not homogenous entities constantly at loggerheads with one another. When First Aliyah immigrants began arriving, some Old Yishuv Jews (who were clearly not identified with their community's mainstream thinking) aspired to emulate them by establishing farms of their own. However, their ambitions were thwarted for want of both funds and the support of the Hovevei Zion. Nonetheless, a small number did at least obtain wage employment within some of the new settlements.

As for the New Yishuv, most of its original members wished to abide fully by all the religious tenets. The very second clause of Rishon Letzion's founding constitution bound settlement members to conduct themselves within the spirit of the Torah.[47] Accordingly, the Old Yishuv was initially considered to be the primary source for the provision of education for New Yishuv children. What is more, faced with an inappropriate judicial system in which internal disputes could not satisfactorily be arbitrated, settlers and Rothschild's administration alike occasionally deferred to the Old Yishuv's religious courts.

RELATIONS WITH THE ARABS

Arab-Jewish conflicts occurred from the very inception of the First Aliyah. For the most part, they reflected misunderstandings between neighbors stemming from different cultural backgrounds. Commonly, they resulted from attempts on the part of the Jews to enforce capitalist property rights that were neither understood nor accepted by indigenous Arab peasants. Although the initial skirmishes were not directly fueled by interethnic enmity, the general attitudes of both sides toward each other were not conducive to social harmony. The Muslim Arabs regarded the Jews as infidels while many settlers looked down on the "natives" and treated them coarsely. For example, Chissin, the Bilu pioneer, noted with grave misgivings that many of his comrades took pride in the fact that they warded off trespassing Arab shepherds with blows, boasting that in such petty altercations, the spirit of a new fighting Jew emerged.[48] In two visits to Palestine, first in 1891 then in 1903, Ahad Ha'Am expressed his disgust at the settlers' callous treatment of the local inhabitants. During the first visit he recorded that "they behave hostilely and cruelly toward the Arabs encroaching upon them unjustly, beating them disgracefully for no good reason." Later, on his second trip he noted that "the attitude of the colonists toward their land tenants and families is really very much like their attitude toward their animals."[49] In fact, Anita Shapira, an Israeli historian, avows that "the expression 'a people similar to a donkey' was apparently quite commonly used by Jewish farmers with reference to Arab workers."[50] Similarly, the settlers generally stereotyped Arabs as being wild, primitive, dishonest, indifferent and lazy.[51]

On the other hand and without in any way glossing over unprovoked acts of aggression or intimidating behavior on the part of the First Aliyah settlers, it should be borne in mind that most settlements were comparatively isolated and had to fend for themselves within a generally lawless society. Even nineteenth-century Jerusalem closed its gates at night to prevent assaults by marauding Bedouin gangs and the road from Jerusalem to Jaffa was protected by a series of watchtowers. Had the settlers not presented themselves as tough, no-nonsense farmers, they would have been easy pickings for their armed neighbors who were unconstrained by any legal niceties and who had no compunction in plundering vulnerable Jewish settlements.

The first serious Arab-Jewish encounter took place in Petah Tikva in March 1886 as a result of an attempt on the part of the settlers to clear Arab farmers from land that legally belonged to the settlement. For their part, having already commenced cultivation on the land in question, the Arabs invoked a traditional right to continue until the second phase of a two-year crop rotation was completed. Matters soon came to a head when as one of the settlers rode across the disputed field, his horse was taken from him. In an act of reprisal, the Jews seized and impounded nine Arab-owned donkeys. On the following day, a few hundred Arab villagers attacked Petah Tikva, smashing doors and windows, looting houses, retrieving their donkeys and running off with some of the settlement's cattle to boot. Five Jews were injured. Through foreign consular intervention, thirty-one villagers were arrested but in view of a mutually agreed-upon compromise, the matter did not proceed to court. In October 1886, an Arab who was party to the stealing of a horse belonging to a Gedera settler was caught and locked up for the night pending his being handed over to the authorities the following day. Hours later, the prisoner's fellow villagers rushed into Gedera, pelting it with stones while demanding the immediate release of their kinsman. In response, the twenty or so male settlers secured their women in a central building (where, seized by fear, two of them miscarried) and confronted an estimated one hundred assailants in kind, by hurling rocks back at them. Eventually, a settler edged closer to the Arabs and fired his revolver, wounding one intruder and causing the rest to flee. In this case, the termination of hostilities was secured by the arrival on the following day of reinforcements from both Rishon Letzion and Ekron (which gave the melee the characteristic of a national conflict) and by the temporary stationing of government troops in the area. A more serious incident befell Metula. There Druze who felt aggrieved that they had been unjustly evicted from land they considered theirs, stole plow oxen and shot at Jewish farmers, giving rise to one death and a few casualties. That conflict was laid to rest by the baron's clerks who negotiated with the Druze and compensated them for their perceived losses. All told, between 1886 and 1914 (the end of the Second Aliyah), at least thirteen settlements were subject to an onslaught of some kind on the part of Arab bands or neighbors. The settlements were Gedera, Rehovot, Ness Ziona, Ben Shemen, Metula, Rosh Pina, Petah Tikva, Hadera, Mercahavia, Sejera, Yavniel, Beer Tuvia and Kinneret.

Jewish-Arab relations were not entirely negative. There were a number of instances where Jews and Arabs dwelt side by side quite amicably. Shortly before the commencement of the First Aliyah, when Jews from Safed tried to establish a colony at Gai Oni (where Rosh Pina eventually took root), the settlers moved into the Arab village from which they acquired their farmland. Such an arrangement suited the Jewish farmers who feared that had they stayed in their own distinct quarters, they would have been unable to withstand frequently occurring Bedouin raids.[52] As it turned out, when First Aliyah Rosh Pina settlers returned to the abandoned Gai Oni village, they were indeed protected by their Arab neighbors. In David Shov's memoirs, there is an account of an incident in which an Arab youth belonging to a prominent Safed family, was killed by an accidental discharge of a settler's pistol. Seeking to avenge the death of their son, the family with all their manifold kinsmen, converged on Rosh Pina. As Shov described the situation, the local sheik and the peasants who all the while proclaimed that the Jews were innocent "presented themselves as an iron wall in the face of the angry mob and forestalled any bloodshed."[53] Elsewhere in Nes Tziona, neighboring effendis, including Abdul Rahman, a member of the Supreme Muslim Council, chose to build their homes within the Jewish settlement. For the entire period until the Israeli War of Independence (1947–1949), Jews and Arabs in Nes Tziona continued to cohabit peacefully.

Arabs living adjacent to Jewish settlements were able to obtain regular wage employment and, as a result, their living standards appreciated. With such improvements, the Arab population in the vicinity of Jewish settlements rose faster than the Arab population as a whole. For example, a settler teacher named Grazovsky recorded that whereas in Rishon Letzion the early pioneers numbered 40 Jewish families, some 400 Arab families soon took up residence in the surrounding semi-arid villages.[54] Developments of that kind, add credence to reported views of Arab peasants who described the Jewish farmers as "good men who paid well."[55] In the course of time, some Arab villages were subject to a certain modernizing influence on the part of their Jewish neighbors.[56]

From the point of view of the Jewish settlements that specialized in plantation crops, Arab farmers were a welcome source of supply of vegetables, poultry, eggs and wheat. In terms of services, many settlers depended on Arabs for labor and for the transportation of their grapes to the wineries. When they were in no position to take on hired help, they often leased out land to neighboring Arabs to circumvent the prospect of uncultivated soil being forfeited to the state. However, leaseholdings were a mixed blessing, for they tended to constitute the basis of future strife when Jews eventually wished to resume cultivating their land.

Political opposition on the part of the Palestinian Arab community to the Zionist enterprise first appeared on June 24, 1891, when Muslim notables in Jerusalem telegraphed the sultan in Constantinople appealing for the immediate prohibition of Jewish immigration. They based their case on an assumed oversupply of labor and argued that if more Jews arrived, "the Muslims themselves would be greatly the sufferers, as, the European Jews being skilled in all different kinds of trades, the Muslims could not compete against them."[57] Their petition was swiftly granted. In July 1891, all Jewish immigration was banned but, as mentioned above, their victory turned out to be only a temporary one, for after a short while, the ban was no longer enforced. Another overt sign of political opposition to Jewish migration appeared in 1899, when in the Jerusalem Administrative Council, the mufti of Jerusalem, Muhammad Tahir al-Husseini, formally proposed that Jewish newcomers be physically assaulted and then expelled.[58] Unlike the first petition, al-Husseini's proposal met with a firm rejection.

It has often been alleged that the early Zionists were totally unaware of the existence of a large Arab population in Palestine and believed that the Jews, "a people without a land, could settle in a land without a people." (Ironically, such a phrase was first coined in May 1854, by a non-Jew, Lord Shaftesbury.)[59] If ever indeed such an illusion was maintained, it surely could not have been long-lasting. The first settlers found themselves as tiny enclaves in a land that was predominantly Arab and it is inconceivable that they would have not passed on such information to both the budding Hovevei Zion societies and the Russian Jewish press. Even on the eve of the First Aliyah, when the Russian pogroms were in full swing, in a call put out by a group of Jerusalem Jews to their brethren abroad to join them, the Arab presence was taken into account. To assuage concerns that potential immigrants might feel threatened by the large indigenous Arab majority, it was asserted that "the Arabs do not have any repressed hatred towards Jews and if we approach them with peaceful intent they will respond in kind."[60] Before departing to Palestine, Bilu members acknowledged the country's Arab presence by letting it be known that they intended to learn Arabic in order to relate to and establish good neighborly relations with their Semitic cousins.[61] Their ability to do so was facilitated by the publication in 1882 of an Arab language manual, written in Yiddish by a Hovevei Zion member. In his preface, the author, Itzak Neistein, wrote, "It is necessary to know the language of the country's population."[62] In 1886, in a polemic against the Zionist movement, Ilia Rubanovich (a Jewish revolutionary) directly confronted Palestinophiles (who saw a return to Palestine as a panacea for their woes) with the Arab issue. He pointedly asked whether "the Jews expect to be strangers among the Arabs or would they want to make the Arabs strangers among themselves?" Then, with some prophetic foresight, Rubanovich went on to adumbrate the potential essence of the Palestinian problem by stating that "the Arabs have exactly the same historical right and it will be unfortunate for you if—taking your stand under the protection of international plunderers, using the underhand dealings and intrigue of a corrupt diplomacy—you make the peaceful Arabs defend *their* right. They will answer tears with blood and bury your diplomatic documents in the ashes of your own homes."[63] Rubanovich's critique may have had a limited readership and even if no Palestinophile actually came across it directly, the enlightened youth among them would very likely have confronted similar notions articulated by Jewish left-wing opponents, who wished to disabuse them of their faith in the possibility of a Jewish national reawakening in Palestine. If any would-be or actual settlers may have preferred to cast the Arab presence out of their minds, it must surely have been lurking somewhere in the background. They certainly could not claim that their own leaders had kept them in the dark. Ahad Ha'Am stated the facts quite clearly. In 1891 in a report titled "Truth From Eretz Israel," he wrote, "We tend to believe abroad that Palestine is nowadays almost completely deserted, a noncultivated wilderness, and anyone can come there and buy as much land as his heart desires. But in reality this is not the case. It is difficult to find anywhere in the country Arab land which lies fallow; the only areas which are not cultivated are sand dunes or stony mountains, which can only be planted with trees, and even so only after investing much labor and capital for land clearance and preparation."[64] At the Second Zionist Congress in

1898, Leo Motzkin reported that "in whole stretches throughout the land one constantly comes across large Arab villages, and it is an established fact that the most fertile areas of our country are occupied by Arabs."[65] Notwithstanding Motzkin's observations, the issue was not effectively debated until the Seventh Congress in 1905.

Until then, the settlers were preoccupied with day-to-day economic challenges and with warding off obstacles and difficulties placed before them by the Turkish regime. With Palestine being an integral part of the Ottoman Empire and with the settlers being generally contemptuous of the Arabs, who, like them, lacked political sovereignty, attention was focused on relations with the powers that be.

THE ACHIEVEMENTS OF THE FIRST ALIYAH

Within the First Aliyah period, approximately 60,000 Jews arrived in Palestine but at least half subsequently emigrated. Those who remained accounted for a very small proportion (about 3 percent) of the million or so Jews who, by the end of the century, had turned their backs on Europe. Most reinforced the population of the Old Yishuv.

By 1904, a year after the First Aliyah ended, twenty-eight Jewish agricultural settlements had been established in Palestine. Their members numbered approximately 5,500, that is, 10 percent of the 55,000 Jews then in the country. Second Aliyah immigrants may have ungenerously viewed them as being largely staid gentleman farmers relying on hired labor and wanting in the idealism of their youth but they could not gainsay the fact that without them, their ventures in Palestine would have been infinitely more risky and uncertain. Not only did the First Aliyah settlers bequeath future immigrants a budding Jewish economic base, but they also made a significant contribution to the renaissance of Hebrew culture. They represented the first modern Jewish generation in which the use of spoken Hebrew was revitalized, and although they did not produce any outstanding men or women of letters, they prepared the groundwork for those who followed.

BARON ROTHSCHILD: AN EVALUATION

In 1881 (the year the Russian pogroms erupted) Baron Edmond de Rothschild, then thirty-six years of age, set out on family business to the Baku oil fields. As his train passed through southern Russian stations, he was besieged by hordes of Jewish well-wishers whose poverty and distress impelled him to become actively involved in relief work. Up to that point in time, despite having had a very good grounding in Jewish education, most of his spare time was absorbed by his art collection and in studying natural science, with barely any attention given to philanthropy or similar matters. Once having become fully cognizant of the wretched state of Jewish life, his thoughts increasingly turned to palliatives and by the time he was approached by Rabbi Mohilever, he had independently reached the conclusion that Jews ought to be encouraged to become farmers. As to where Jews should farm, Rothschild reasoned that "in order for a person to become a farmer it is necessary for him to be devoted to the land. There is a need to have an attachment to it based on historic memory and tradition. In this respect, Palestine is the land in which Jews are linked."[66]

Rothschild's first commitments to Palestinian settlements were rather tentative, but he soon became financially entangled in almost the entire enterprise, giving generously in furtherance of both economic activities and of social needs. His involvement was not simply a fiscal one; as a devout Jew, he soon identified more closely with the New Yishuv, realizing that it would play a major role in his people's future. Unlike the typical wealthy benefactor, Rothschild was not primarily motivated by an egotistical desire to achieve fame and universal recognition. On the contrary, he adopted a very low profile, always placing the well-being of the colonization process above all other considerations. First Aliyah immigrants were graced with visits from him on three separate occasions. Their efforts in setting up a framework for a Jewish national identity were fully appreciated by him, even though at times he was vexed by perceived ingratitude and insubordination. As he himself made clear, he had rallied to their aid not because they were needy, for there were other Jews just as badly off, but because he wished to further the "glorified ideal" of establishing Jewish settlements in Eretz Israel.[67]

Admittedly, he was impervious to unsolicited advice. He made many mistakes in the choice of the crops that he selected for cultivation, in the inappropriate use of expensive machinery and in pampering his wards with living conditions that did not reflect their productivity. Needless to say, such miscalculations were met at his own cost and while other magnates looked on him with incredulity as he seemingly squandered his family fortune, he alone stood among his wealthy peers in support of the Yishuv. Had he not stepped into the breach and stretched out a helping hand, early pioneering endeavors would probably have come to naught and Zionist aspirations may never have materialized.

NOTES

1. Written in an article published in Hamalitz 1883 and reproduced in Eliav, *The First Aliyah*, 1981, vol. 2, pp. 59–61.

2. Much, although by no means all, of the information in this section is derived from Arenson, "Stages," 1981.

3. A dunam is equal to a quarter of an acre.

4. In 1885, a large menorah (candelabrum) symbolizing the seven settlements was kindled in Odessa.

5. David Shov in Yaari, *Memoirs*, 1947, p. 502.

6. On the geographic aspects of the First Aliyah settlements, see Ben Arye, "Geographic Aspects," 1981, from which most of this paragraph is drawn.

7. Reproduced in Eliav, *First Aliyah*, 1981, vol. 2, p. 245.

8. Ibid., p. 266.

9. From A. Samsonov, *The Book of Zichron Yaakov*, as cited by Giladi 1981, p. 186.

10. As quoted by Shalmon, "The Bilu Movement," 1981, p. 127.

11. This account, which is based on Belkind, "In the Path," 1983, p. 82, differs somewhat from that of Meirowitz, "In the Days," 1942, p. 28, where it is alleged that the Biluim first stayed at Rishon Letzion for a short time before returning to Mikveh Israel.

12. Arenson, "Stages," 1981, p. 36, and Shalmon, "The Bilu Movement," 1981, p. 135.

13. Abramov, *Perpetual Dilemma*, 1976, p. 46.

14. Be'eri, *Beginning*, 1985, p. 49.

15. Shalmon, "The Bilu Movement," 1981, p. 140.

16. Ahad Ha'am's article on "The Jewish State and the Jewish Problem" as reproduced by Hertzberg 1959, p. 268.

17. Ahad Ha'am, like others, considered Moses to be the greatest of all Hebrew prophets.

18. Laskov, "Chovevei Zion," 1981, p. 161.

19. Three hundred Egyptians were employed to undertake the bulk of the drainage work.

20. Arenson, "Stages," 1981, p. 58.

21. Even-Shoshan, *History*, vol. 1, 1955, p. 17.

22. As cited by Giladi 1981, p. 203.

23. Laskov, "Chovevei Zion," 1981, p. 168.

24. Wigoder, *Encyclopedia*, 1977, p. 1994.

25. Herzl, *The Jewish State*, 1988, p. 145.

26. Born in 1858 in Lushki, near Vilna. His father's and his original surname was Perlman.

27. Vlack, "Development," 1981, p. 409.

28. As quoted in Harmeti, "Revival," 1981, p. 432.

29. Ibid.

30. As quoted by Vlack, "Development," 1981, p. 419.

31. Vlack, "Development," 1981, p. 420.

32. As quoted by Vlack, "Development," 1981, p. 419.

33. Harmeti, "Revival," 1981, p. 446.

34. Quoted by David Yudelivitz in Yaari, *Memoirs*, 1947, p. 479.

35. Within Yemen a false rumor had also gained currency that Baron Rothschild was about to buy land that would be distributed to all migrants free of charge.

36. From Yaakov Goldman, as cited by Druyen, "Immigration," 1981, p. 212.

37. Druyen, "Immigration," 1981, p. 217.

38. Yaari, *Memoirs*, 1947, p. 16.

39. Carmel, "Jewish Settlement," 1981, p. 103.

40. As quoted by Abramov, *Perpetual Dilemma*, 1976, p. 46.

41. As quoted in Shalmon, "The Bilu Movement," 1981, p. 136.

42. Orthodox rabbis can be rather adept at finding ways to circumvent troublesome religious edicts. For example, although Jewish law prohibits people from carrying articles in public places on the Sabbath, it allows them to do so within their own home. However, if a village or town is surrounded by some sort of continuous border, represented even by a length of cord, no distinction is made between private and public places, for they are all fictionally within the same enclosure.

43. Salmon, *Religion and Zionism*, 1990, p. 132.

44. As quoted by Abramov, *Perpetual Dilemma*, 1976, p. 49.

45. Ibid., p. 50.

46. Stein-Ashkenazi, *The Balfour Declaration*, 1980, p. 157.

47. Similar clauses were adopted by other settlements.

48. As cited by Shalmon, "The Bilu Movement," 1981, p. 130.

49. As cited by Shapira, *Land and Power*, 1992, p. 58.

50. Ibid.

51. Roi, "The Zionist Attitude," 1981, p. 246.

52. Avneri, *Claim of Dispossession*, 1984, pp. 85–86.

53. David Shov in Yaari, *Memoirs*, 1947, p. 511.

54. As mentioned in Kollet, "Workers," 1981, p. 347.

55. Hirst 1984, p. 24.

56. Roi, "The Zionist Attitude," 1981, p. 249.

57. As cited in Gilbert, *Exile and Return*, 1978, p. 43.

58. Vital, *Zionism*, 1982, pp. 378–379. As it happens the mufti was the father of an even more notorious one, namely Haj Amin al-Husseini.

59. Be'eri, *Beginning*, 1985, p. 36.

60. The Association for the Establishment of Settlement, Chavazelet July 27, 1881. Reproduced in Yavnieli, *Era of Hibat-Zion*, 1961, vol. 1, p. 114.

61. Shalmon, "The Bilu Movement," 1981, p. 124.

62. Be'eri, *Beginning*, 1985, p. 41.

63. As quoted by Frankel, *Prophecy and Politics*, 1981, p. 129. Italics in the original.

64. Ahad Ha'am, as quoted by Avineri, *Making of Modern Zionism*, 1981, p. 122.

65. As quoted by Pawell, *Labyrinth of Exile*, 1989, p. 358.

66. From the memoirs of Henry Frank as reported in Eliav, *First Aliyah*, 1981, vol. 2, p. 42.

67. Yavnieli, *Era of Hibat-Zion*, 1961, vol. 2, p. 23 (Introduction).

Chapter 3

Modern Political Zionism

Toward the end of the nineteenth century, the Hovevei Zion continued to lend support to the few settlements in Palestine to which they were committed. However, their financial remittances, which had always been small, became even more sparing. Their increasingly dismal pecuniary position reflected a deepening malaise. After nearly two decades of existence, their societies, which were attenuated in terms of both branch numbers and overall membership, were essentially reduced to small-scale charitable institutions. They neither formed a coherent and unified body, nor did they bequeath to world Jewry a national organization capable of speaking and negotiating on its behalf. In 1897, with the appearance onto the world stage of a modern, well-organized political Zionist movement, the situation altered radically.

Amazingly, the formation of that movement essentially resulted from the Herculean efforts of one charismatic person, Theodor Herzl. Born on May 2, 1860, in Budapest, of wealthy parents who adhered to reform Judaism, he was given the Hebrew name Zeev, along with the Hungarian Tivadar and the German Wolf Theodor. From 1866 to 1869, he attended a Jewish parochial school where he was exposed to some biblical Hebrew and religious studies and, in 1870, he enrolled in a technical high school. As he began to acquire literary tastes, his interests in science-based learning waned and eventually he transferred to a conventional high school where a more classical education was provided. In 1878, shortly after the death of his only sister, Pauline, the family moved to Vienna. There Herzl attended the University of Vienna, where he studied for a law degree.

As a student he totally associated himself with the gentile world. He took to gambling with gusto, joined a dueling fraternity called Albia, participated in its drinking binges and fought the obligatory duel to obtain full fraternity membership. Suddenly, in March 1883, his blissful association with his carousing comrades ended. During a memorial service for Richard Wagner, an Albia dele-gate delivered a blatantly anti-Semitic speech. A shocked Herzl tendered his resignation. He protested against the fraternity's failure to condemn its spokesman and drew the conclusion that their very silence implied complicity.[1]

The Albia incident was not the first occasion that Herzl came across anti-Semitism. Almost a year earlier he encountered it in one of its literary guises when reading Karl Duhring's book, *The Jewish Question As a Question of Race, Morality and Culture*. The book, which set out to deny that the Jews ever made a useful contribution to civilization, concluded with a demand for their exclusion from public life.[2] However, Herzl still held to the illusion, so common among Austria's assimilated Jews, that anti-Semitism was simply a passing phenomenon that would be eradicated by economic progress and social enlightenment. That does not mean to say that he was never mortified by anti-Semitic jibes directed at him personally. He carried vivid memories of two inci-dents in particular. The first, which occurred in 1888 at Mainz, involved a lout shouting "hep hep" at him as he was leaving a tavern to the accompaniment of boisterous laughter. The second took place later near Vienna when someone called out "dirty Jew" as he rode past in a carriage. As he recalled, "that shout went deeper because it resounded on my 'home' soil."[3]

On completing his university studies and serving out his probationary year in court, he turned his back on the legal profession to devote himself to literary pursuits. This entailed a combination of freelance journalism and numerous at-tempts at becoming a successful playwright. Most of his thirty-odd plays were lighthearted romps that, while poking fun at upper-class marriage and moral-ity, were largely devoid of either serious social criticism or of characters with even a semblance of credibility. Almost all were promptly rejected. While that caused Herzl acute disappointment, he never wavered in his belief that he had the makings of a fine dramaturge. He persevered, churning out one manuscript after another. Where he did succeed was by becoming a highly respected feuil-letonist.

In 1891, on the basis of well-received casual contributions submitted to the prestigious *Neue Freie Presse*, Herzl was appointed as its regular Paris corre-spondent. That assignment represented a watershed in his professional career. Not only was he working for one of Europe's leading newspapers but his Paris brief required of him the reportage of a very broad sweep of French life. In ad-dition to covering financial and political matters, he was to comment on the French cultural scene and on anything else that he deemed to be of interest. Above all, Herzl began to acquire a thorough knowledge of the workings of the French parliamentary system and of power politics at play, factors that stood him in good stead when he himself entered the political arena.

As a key journalist for the *Neue Freie Presse*, Herzl established innumerable contacts with the pillars of French society. His set of acquaintances included leading figures in literature, the arts and politics. Usually he related to them on a fairly superficial basis but included among them was Max Nordau, with whom he established a warm and intimate friendship. Also born in Budapest (in 1849), Nordau, a son of an orthodox rabbi, qualified as a medical doctor and settled in Paris where he specialized in psychiatry. Like Herzl, he was drawn to the world of letters and also at one time wrote feuilletons to supplement his income. Unlike Herzl, Nordau's books, *The Conventional Lies of Our Civilization*, *Paradoxes*, and *Degeneration*, made a big impact on discerning European and American readers.

Of more significance, Herzl was able to observe French anti-Semitism at close range. When he arrived in Paris, approximately 40,000 Jews lived in France, constituting about 0.2 percent of the total population. Only about 1,000 French Jews were strictly observant, with the rest seeking to assimilate, in various degrees, into French society. Neither their small number, their willingness to discard their Jewishness nor the so-called French enlightenment spared French Jews the ogre of anti-Semitism. In 1882, nine years before Herzl took up his Paris assignment, the collapse of a Catholic bank, the Union Générale, was blamed on the House of Rothschild. With thousands of small investors ruined, many priests distributed anti-Jewish pamphlets that were couched in the most venomous of terms. This tide of hate-mongering culminated in 1886 with the publication of Edouard Drumont's *La France Juive*. Drumont's monstrous work, which deftly raked up a wide array of anti-Semitic charges based on religion, racism and general xenophobia, was a runaway bestseller, appearing in over two hundred editions.[4] Buoyed by the favorable response to his book, Drumont launched a weekly paper, *La Libre Parole*, in 1892 which was dedicated "to the defence of Catholic France against atheists, republicans, Free Masons and Jews." Shortly after the paper's inauguration, Drumont was charged with libeling Auguste Burdeau, vice president of the Chamber of Deputies, as a hireling of the Rothschilds. During the trial, in which he was sentenced to three months' imprisonment, his supporters bombarded the court with cries of "down with the Jews." Around the same time, Drumont sustained an injury as a result of dueling with a Jewish cavalry captain. His second, the Marquis de Mores, then challenged Captain Armand Mayer, a supporter of Drumont's opponent. Mayer, whose right arm was severely crippled and who was barely capable of lifting a sword, nevertheless accepted the challenge lest he be accused of "Jewish cowardice." He was killed within the duel's opening moments. His funeral, held on June 26, 1892, drew a crowd of mourners, estimated between 20,000 and 100,000, marking the largest public demonstration against anti-Semitism that Paris had yet seen. Herzl, who attended the funeral, reported on both the Drumont trial and the Mayer tragedy.

A couple of months after Mayer's death, Herzl mordantly surveyed French anti-Semitism. Among other things, he noted that "Jewish money is resented only if they have any.... And if a Jew carries native cunning to the point of sacrificing his life in a noble and knightly manner, he will earn widespread murmurs of approval. This is more or less what happened to Captain Mayer: even his opponent, the Marquis de Mores, declared that he 'regretted the death of this honourable man.' A Jew can certainly not ask for more without appearing greedy."[5]

Two years later, in October 1894, while posing for a bust statue being sculpted by Beer, a fellow Jew from Budapest, Herzl engaged the artist in a conversation on the Jewish question, a question that was increasingly haunting him. They agreed that it did the Jews no good to become artists and to liberate themselves from the money taint. The curse stuck to them regardless. As the conversation progressed, Herzl observed, "We cannot break out of the ghetto," and with that thought in mind, he left the studio in a state of excitement, set on writing a play on the Jewish condition. Applying himself wholeheartedly to that task, he completed *The New Ghetto* within three weeks. The play represents an expression of Herzl's emotional anguish. Fueled by the realization that social anti-Jewish barriers were just as potent as legal ones, it climaxes in a duel fought by a Jew to redeem both his and his people's honor. Like Captain Mayer, the hero promptly receives a mortal wound. In his final moments and just prior to the curtain fall, he murmurs, "Jews, my brothers they won't let you live until you learn to die. ... I want out—out of the Ghetto."

According to conventional wisdom, Herzl showed no interest in Jewish affairs until the Dreyfus trial. The trial itself and its sequel, which Herzl personally observed, supposedly beckoned him to his people. In fact, anti-Semitism and the plight of the Jews had been concerning him for a number of years prior to Dreyfus's arrest in October 1894. When news of the affair first came to light, Herzl was already working on *The New Ghetto*. Earlier, he had toyed with a number of fanciful schemes, which he hoped might lay the Jewish problem to rest. These ranged from a mass conversion of all Jewry to Christianity, the challenging by Herzl of key anti-Semites to duels and a comprehensive scientific study of the major centers of Jewish life so that the situation of world Jewry might be better and more sympathetically understood. The Dreyfus affair, coming as it did in France, where the notions of liberty, equality and fraternity were first expounded, certainly made a strong impact on Herzl. It reinforced his growing belief that Jews would forever be excluded from the mainstream of European social and economic life, and it was a strong catalyst edging him on to the adoption of full-scale Zionism.

The affair itself divided French society into those who thought Dreyfus guilty and those who thought him innocent. It began in October 1894, when Captain Alfred Dreyfus, a Jewish officer born in Alsace, was arrested on a charge of spying for the Germans. His trial, which opened on December 19, was held behind closed doors. It concluded on December 22, when all seven judges agreed on a verdict of guilt and sentenced Dreyfus to permanent deportation to Devil's Island in French Guiana. There, for over four years, he suffered intolerable hardships. He lived in complete isolation and was forbidden to utter a solitary word. The shack in which he was confined was surrounded by a high fence, which blocked his view to the outside world and at night his feet were shackled. As he lay in pain on his cot, insects and spiders crawled over him and on more than one occasion, he was threatened by poisonous snakes. In time, he was stricken by malaria and a host of other tropical and intestinal ailments. All the while, not only was he completely innocent but his prosecutors were well aware of that.

Evidence of espionage had indeed come to light but in the absence of an obvious suspect, Dreyfus, on account of his Jewishness and Alsacian background, was targeted. His accusers pinned their hopes on matching Dreyfus's handwriting with an incriminating document, but when that failed, they relied on perjured testimony given by a high-ranking officer who claimed, without naming his source, that "an absolutely honourable person" had informed him that Dreyfus was an enemy agent. The judges found such flimsy "evidence" to be more than sufficient to convict him.

Dreyfus's brother Mathieu, worked tirelessly to vindicate him. Assisted by competent and faithful legal counselors and by writers such as Bernard Lazare and Emile Zola, Mathieu eventually attracted a very broad range of supporters from among prominent socialists and liberals who constituted the camp of Dreyfusards, as opposed to a coalition of anti-Semitic clerics and royalists who endorsed his conviction. Stage by stage, the case unraveled. The actual spy, Commandant Marie Walsin-Esterhazy, was exposed. Commandant Hubert Joseph Henry, on whose "evidence" Dreyfus was prosecuted, confessed to having inserted forged documents in Dreyfus's file and then committed suicide. Eventually, in 1899, Dreyfus was brought back to France for a retrial. Despite all evidence to the contrary, he was once again convicted but was soon pardoned. Only in 1904, at a trial of the High Court of Appeal, was Dreyfus cleared of all previous charges and reinstated as an officer in the French Army. Even at that trial, when every shred of evidence favored Dreyfus, eighteen of the forty-nine judges voted to confirm the decision of the 1899 trial. The French Army and right-wing establishment had become so compromised, that for them the issue was no longer Dreyfus but their "honor."

Herzl's immediate reactions to the initial trial were rather muted but, prompted by Nordau, who sensed that a miscarriage of justice was being perpetrated, he soon took a keener interest in its proceedings. He reported the court's unanimous verdict without comment but his dispatch of December 27, 1894, allowed for the possibility that Dreyfus was persecuted because he was a Jew.[6] On January 5, 1895, Herzl was present at the inner courtyard of the Ecole Militaire where Dreyfus was publicly disgraced. Wearing the uniform of an artillery army captain, Dreyfus was brought before a mounted general who sternly proclaimed, "Alfred Dreyfus, you are not worthy of bearing arms. In the name of the French people, we degrade you."[7] In response, Dreyfus raised both his hands and shouted, "Soldiers, they are degrading an innocent man." Then to the accompaniment of rolling drums, a military bailiff stripped Dreyfus of his buttons and straps and snapped his sword in two. Finally, as Dreyfus filed past the troops, a group of officers yelling "Jew, Traitor," he turned toward them and in an admonishing tone said, "You have no right to insult me." His general demeanor made a deep impression on many of those present. As for Herzl himself, the mob cries of "Death to the Jews," which permeated the streets of Paris, must have made no less of an impression. As if to provide him with even more food for thought, Drumont then wrote in his anti-Semitic tabloid that in point of fact Dreyfus "committed no crime against his country. To betray one's country, one must first have one."[8]

In March 1895, Herzl visited his parents in Vienna where Lueger's Anti-Semitic Christian Social party had just come within striking distance of securing the majority of Vienna's City Council. When, a month later he returned to Paris, he was emotionally and intellectually in turmoil. The writing of *The New Ghetto* had failed to provide a catharsis for his tormented soul, and he was seized by the notion that he had to do something more concrete for the Jewish people. In the weeks that followed, he thought of nothing else and then suddenly the solution emerged. The Jews had to have a state of their own! Whether they liked it or not, the gathering forces of anti-Semitism dictated that no other realistic alternative would do. From the moment that Herzl grasped this, he was completely metamorphosed. For the rest of his short life, he devoted all his energies not only propagating that idea but also ensuring its practical implementation. As he saw things, the only real problems related to the accumulation of the necessary finances. With sufficient capital, all else would fall into place, for once the scheme was made known, both its feasibility and desirability would be obvious to all people of good will, be they Jews or gentiles.

Herzl hoped that Baron Maurice de Hirsch, as a leading financial magnate, would be won over to his newfound cause. Hirsch, who was one of the richest men in the world, was also an extremely generous Jewish benefactor. Among other things, he had, in 1891, founded the Jewish Colonization Society (JCA) for the purpose of establishing farming settlements for Russian Jews in Argentina and elsewhere. Taking the bull by the horns, Herzl, who had never met Hirsch, wrote to him. He requested a lengthy interview, stressing that weighty matters were at stake that could only be discussed face-to-face. Hirsch, who was regularly beseeched by all manner of supplicants, replied that Herzl ought to state his business in writing. This induced Herzl to respond provocatively: "What you have undertaken now has been as magnanimous as it has been misapplied, as costly as it was pointless. You have hitherto been only a philanthropist, a Peabody; I want to show you the way to become something more."[9] This second letter produced the desired results, in that two days later, Herzl received an invitation to meet with Hirsch (on June 2, 1895) at his Paris residence.

Herzl prepared himself well for the encounter. He made copious notes summarizing his proposal and gave careful thought to his sartorial appearance: "The day before I had purposely broken in a new pair of gloves so that they might still look new but not fresh from the shop. One must not show rich people too much deference."[10] Hirsch received him cordially but when Herzl attempted to unravel his plan, the conversation took an unfortunate turn. It bogged down in an exchange of views over Hirsch's own approach to the Jewish question. After a series of pointless discussions, the conversation ran its course without Herzl being able to complete his submission. With some annoyance and with what must have seemed to Hirsch as arrogant youthful bravado, Herzl, as he recorded in his diary, let be known that he was left with no other recourse than to approach the German kaiser. "To the kaiser I shall say: Let our people go! We are strangers here; we are not permitted to assimilate with the people, nor are we able to do so. Let us go! I will tell you the ways and the means which I want to use for our exodus, so that no economic crisis or vacuum may follow our departure. Hirsch asked, 'Where will you get the money? Rothschild will subscribe five hundred francs.' The money? I said with a defiant laugh. I shall raise a Jewish National Loan Fund of ten million marks. 'A fantasy!' smiled the Baron. 'The rich Jews will give nothing.'"[11] On that note, the interview ended.

Far from being discouraged by the debacle with Hirsch, Herzl resolved to present his case to the Rothschilds. He consoled himself with the thought that it was Hirsch, not he, who had failed to seize an historic opportunity to shape Jewish destiny. In approaching the Rothschilds, Herzl planned to submit a comprehensive memorandum outlining the full extent of the reasons why the creation of a Jewish state was imperative and, more to the point, the manifold organizational arrangements required to secure suitable territory, initiate mass Jewish migration and absorb the immigrants in their new homeland. He wished to formulate his proposals in a rational and coherent manner to forestall all possible doubts and objections. During the next few weeks he worked in a trance-like state, neglected his physical needs and drifted about in uncharacteristic dishevelment. Every now and then, he wondered whether he was taking leave of his senses. He summarized his experience as follows: "For some time past I have been occupied with a work of infinite grandeur. At the moment I do not know whether I shall carry it through. It looks like a mighty dream. But for days and weeks it has possessed me beyond the limits of consciousness; it accompanies me wherever I go, hovers behind my ordinary talk, looks over my shoulder at my comically trivial journalistic work, disturbs me and intoxicates me."[12] Eventually, he hammered out a document which in effect became the prototype of his book, *The Jewish State*.

It was at that time that Herzl concluded that he could serve the Jewish cause more effectively if he operated from his homeground in Austria. He successfully applied to the *Neue Freie Presse* for a transfer to Vienna and took leave of Paris toward the end of July 1895. In Vienna he discussed his prospective submission to the Rothschilds with several confidants, including Chief Rabbi Moritz Gudemann. The general consensus was that an approach to the Rothschild family would prove to be fruitless. In the opinion of his father, a more appropriate course of action would entail bypassing the wealthy Jews, by appealing directly to the Jewish masses. This could be accomplished through the publication of an inspiring pamphlet. Herzl had independently considered the same course of action and had hoped that his own newspaper would support him. Bacher and Benedikt, the paper's joint editors, both of whom were Jewish, would have none of it. They did, however, imply that if he could secure a group of influential people in France and England, who might constitute some sort of study commission, they would consider reporting its findings. To pursue the matter, Herzl was given a short leave of absence and in November 1895 he returned to Paris. There he had an interview with Rabbi Zadok Kahn and with other leading French Jews, none of whom responded with undue enthusiasm. However, when Herzl visited his old friend Max Nordau, he met not only with Nordau's instant understanding but with a commitment to follow him through thick and thin. Nordau arranged for the English writer Israel Zangwill, whose novels depicted Jewish life in the East End of London, to receive Herzl on his arrival in England. Much to Herzl's satisfaction, not only did Zangwill accept his ideas with open arms but so did a string of other influential Jews. Among them was Asher Myers, the editor of the *Jewish Chronicle*, who requested a condensed version of the booklet that Herzl mentioned he was thinking of writing.

Back in Austria, a publishing contract was secured with Max Breitenstein, a Viennese bookstore owner. On January 17, 1896, the *Jewish Chronicle* devoted two full pages to Herzl's summary and on February 14, 1896, the booklet, which Herzl titled *The Jewish State—An Attempt at a Modern Solution of the Jewish Question*, first saw the light of day.

The appearance of *The Jewish State* represents a landmark in Zionist history. It issued the first modern call for the Jewish problem to be addressed by the international community at large. For, as Herzl maintained, the Jewish question "is a national question, which can only be solved by making it a political world-question to be discussed and settled by the civilized nations of the world in council."[13]

The booklet opens with a short discourse on the Jewish Question. In Herzl's view, all nations in which the Jews dwelled were "either covertly or openly anti-Semitic."[14] Where Jews attained formal legal rights, they were "debarred from filling even moderately high positions, either in the army, or in any public or private capacity."[15] Migrating to relatively moderate states was self-defeating, for as the proportion of Jews in the total population rises, so does the degree of anti-Semitism. Placing one's trust in human progress is equally pointless for "he who would found his hope for improved conditions on the ultimate perfection of humanity would indeed be relying upon a Utopia!"[16] By virtue of historical factors and because of a shared experience of suffering, the Jews "are a people—one people."[17] That being the case, they were entitled to national sovereignty. Like Pinsker before him, Herzl did not, at first, specify the actual territory in which the Jewish state was to have been located. Nevertheless, he was soon persuaded that only Palestine would evoke the necessary effort and sacrifices required of the Jews in establishing their homeland.

The remainder of the booklet was devoted to practical considerations. Anticipating that the notion of a Jewish state would be seen by many as a chimera beyond the realm of attainability, Herzl carefully drafted a workable blueprint

for the realization of his ideal. In his scheme of things, he envisioned the formation of two agencies, one of which, the Society of Jews, would effectively
serve as the political organ of the Jewish people. It would promote and represent the national interest. In the process, it would secure sovereign rights "over
a portion of the globe sufficiently large to satisfy our just requirements."[18]
After that had been achieved, the Society of Jews would constitute the nucleus
of the future state's public institutions. The other agency, the Jewish Company,
would handle all the economic problems associated with the mass migration of
Jews to their new state and the construction of appropriate economic infra-
structures. Everything would be managed in a planned and orderly fashion,
with the entire procedure spanning many years. In this regard, Herzl gave detailed thought to a host of possible eventualities, including the liquidation of
Jewish property in Europe, the selection of migrants required by each phase of
the state's development, the distribution of land, town planning, labor laws,
welfare relief, industrial investment and so on. Finally, the booklet concludes,
"The Jews who wish for a State will have it. We shall live at last as free men on
our own soil and die peacefully in our own homes."[19]

Before considering the general reaction to the publication of *The Jewish
State*, we might at this stage first dwell on some of Herzl's personal views regarding the character and nature of the homeland that he envisioned. These are
contained both in *The Jewish State* and in his utopian novel *Altneuland* (Old
New Land), which appeared in 1902. Through the medium of his novel, which
is prefaced by the motto "if you would wish it, it is no legend," Herzl depicted
how he expected the state to unfold. *Altneuland*'s plot involves a brief visit to
Palestine at the turn of the century by two disillusioned men intent on leading
lives of reclusion on a Polynesian island. The overall neglect and decay that
they encountered in Palestine appalled them. Twenty years later, they return to
civilization and en route to Europe via the Suez Canal, they decide to make a
detour to revisit Palestine. There, to their absolute amazement, they discover a
newly founded Jewish state, way ahead of other countries in terms of its application of modern technology and progressive social reforms.

Herzl hoped that the Jewish state would not only put to use all that applied
science had to offer but that European social graces and refinements would be
second nature to its upper classes. In *Altneuland*, the elite attend opera wearing
white gloves. Liveried Africans serve the wealthy in their palatial homes and
chauffeur them in their motorized vehicles. Within the country at large, no
luxury or amenity generally available abroad is found wanting. Modeled on an
ideal European paradigm, Herzl's state would readily accommodate people of
all beliefs and religious persuasions. Ahad Ha'Am and others complained that
Herzl seemed to be promoting a state devoid of Jewish content rather than a
Jewish state permeated with spoken Hebrew, Jewish customs and traditions.
There was a ring of truth to their charges but they tended to judge Herzl too
harshly, for he was handicapped by a rather superficial Jewish upbringing and
by years of total estrangement from Jewish life. Early in his marriage, he was

so remote from his Jewish roots that he never even had his son, Hans, circumcized, nor did he bestow on him a Jewish name. At Christmas, he would decorate a tree.

Taking Herzl's personal circumstances into account, it could be argued that when writing *Altneuland*, some effort was indeed made to highlight specifically Jewish features. For instance, Passover is celebrated by families in the traditional manner, the Sabbath is generally upheld, especially in Jerusalem, where after noon on Friday "very few motor cars were to be seen; all the shops were closed. Slowly and peacefully the Sabbath fell upon the bustling city."[20] The Temple is rebuilt, the biblical jubilee year is enforced and the currency is the shekel. In the eyes of purists, these points may not amount to much, but their paucity may simply reflect Herzl's limited Jewish cultural horizons rather than any deliberate act of omission on his part.

If Herzl's thoughts were not unduly concerned with distinctly Jewish aspects of his desired state, his aspirations regarding its general social structure were creatively imaginative, innovative and downright prophetic. Essentially, he favored an enlightened capitalist society that would encourage independent entrepreneurship and competition but that would also restrain antisocial forces and behavior. Workers would be granted a seven-hour working day, the unemployed would be provided with work-relief schemes and numerous producer and consumer cooperatives would be formed. The country would be highly electrified, there would be a large chemical complex at the Dead Sea and a canal cut through from the Mediterranean to the Dead Sea would constitute an important source of hydroelectric power. Most importantly, the country would be thoroughly democratic and tolerant. Arabs living within it would be accorded full-citizen status and would be so well treated that they would be genuinely pleased that the Jews had returned home. In keeping with his liberal philosophy, Herzl paid due attention to potential conflicts with the religious establishment. In *The Jewish State* he devoted a section to the problem under the heading "Theocracy." It is worth citing the first paragraph in full:

Shall we end up having a theocracy? No, indeed. Faith unites us, knowledge gives us freedom. We shall therefore prevent any theocratic tendencies from coming to the fore on the part of our priesthood. We shall keep our priests within the confines of their temples in the same way as we shall keep our professional army within the confines of their barracks. Army and priesthood shall receive honors high as their valuable functions deserve. But they must not interfere in the administration of the State which confers distinction upon them, *else they will conjure up difficulties without and within.*[21]

So suspicious was Herzl of the integrity of certain elements within the rabbinate that in *Altneuland*, the sole threat to the state's democracy emanated from a rabbi. In addressing a small assembly of the electorate, a Mr. Steineck denounces an extremist movement headed by a Rabbi Geyer. Steineck reminds his listeners that in the prestate period, Geyer and his ilk objected to a return to Zion on the grounds that the Jews had a God-given mission to remain in the diaspora to enlighten the gentiles. Now Geyer "is more Palestinian than any of us. Now he is the Patriot, the nationalist Jew. And we—we are the friends of the alien."[22] Geyer, who believed that "a non-Jew must not be accepted by the New Society,"[23] was remarkably akin to Rabbi Meir Kahane, who in the 1970s organized a religious fascist movement in Israel, and also similar to a host of other right-wing clerics who now strut about the West Bank. Although Herzl's forebodings have materialized, the response that he counseled still provides food for thought. Again, through the enlightened Mr. Steineck, we are told that we "must hold fast to the things that have made us great; to liberality, tolerance, love of mankind. Only then is Zion truly Zion!"[24] The notion that the Jewish state had to be founded on ethically sound principles is one that Herzl kept emphasizing. In his view, were the Jews simply to establish a new society lacking in social justice, it would not have been worthwhile taking even a single step in that direction.[25]

Turning now to the reaction to the publication of *The Jewish State*, two contrasting variants emerged. On the one hand, negative and even abusive criticism was leveled by elements representing establishment Jewry; that is, by wealthy and privileged Jews and by various rabbis who either identified with them or who had their own ideological reasons for opposing Zionism. Among such critics were those who were scandalized that Herzl had the temerity to suggest that the Jews constituted a distinct nation. Fearful that such a declaration would jeopardize their civil rights, they unrelentingly inveighed against his pronouncements. Typical of the criticism leveled against him were the arguments of Vienna's chief rabbi, Rabbi Gudemann. Although Gudemann had previously likened Herzl to Moses and had endorsed his ideas, he succumbed to pressures from within his affluent congregation. In a strident attack on Herzl, he maintained that Jewish commonality resided only in their belief in God and that Zionism was incompatible with Judaic teachings.[26] Others simply labeled Herzl a mad visionary, the "Jules Verne of the Jews." He was the butt of jokes circulated by what Herzl himself termed "stock-exchange Jews" and their empty-headed retinue. Herzl had both anticipated and steeled himself against such ridicule. He either completely ignored wags who made snide comments at his expense or answered them in kind. For example, on February 23, 1895, Herzl's diary records:

At the Concordia Club yesterday Government Councillor Hahn from the Correspondence Bureau tried to make fun of me: "What do you want to be in your Jewish State? Prime Minister or President of the Chamber of Deputies?" I answered "Anyone who undertakes the sort of thing I am undertaking must naturally be prepared that at first the street urchins will be on his heels."[27]

Although critical reactions to *The Jewish State* were widespread, they were no match for the effusively warm responses from Jewish intellectuals and from rank-and-file East European Jews who were captivated by Herzl's ideas. When David Wolffsohn, a prosperous Cologne timber merchant and a Hovevei Zion adherent, read the book, he noted, "I felt that I had become another man. ... The broad perspectives, and the faith, strong as a vision, which speaks from every line of the Judenstaat [Jewish State], has opened before me a new world, whose existence I had indeed long suspected, but which I had never beheld."[28] Typical of the reaction of the "common man" was a communication from Semlin, where Herzl's pious grandfather and Rabbi Judah Alkali once lived. It stated that the entire community stood ready to emigrate.[29] Day after day, Herzl received encouraging and grateful letters and, in time, he was overwhelmed by numerous callers volunteering their personal services. Among such well-wishers, was David Wolffsohn himself, who was destined to become one of Herzl's most stalwart and reliable supporters. Out of nowhere, as it were, a new Zionist movement was in the process of spontaneous formation. It did not of course develop in a vacuum. Many of its earliest cadres were drawn from extant Hovevei Zion chapters and from Zionist-oriented student fellowships, such as the Vienna Kadimah Society.

Of all Herzl's visitors, the Reverend William H. Hechler, chaplain to the British embassy in Vienna, was perhaps the most eccentric. As it turned out, he was also among the most helpful. In March 1896, Hechler bounded into Herzl's office declaring that in accordance with his own calculations based on biblical prophecy, Palestine would be restored to the Jews between 1897 and 1898. It seems that on reading Herzl's book, Hechler felt that "the fore-ordained movement" had arrived.[30] Wishing to be an active participant in the divine enterprise, he offered to place Herzl's tract in the hands of German princes. His ability to do so stemmed from the fact that he had once been a tutor in the household of the grand duke of Baden. Intrigued by Hechler's "naive enthusiasm," Herzl implored him to secure an audience for him, preferably with the German kaiser, or, at the very least, with a German prince. Armed with a portrait photograph of Herzl, to impress upon prospective potentates that Herzl was no "shabby Jew," Hechler promised to do whatever he could.

Toward the end of April 1896, Hechler secured a meeting with the kaiser's uncle, the grand duke of Baden. The meeting itself, which took place at Karlsruhe, went off well, with Herzl and the grand duke striking a warm accord. As Hechler and Herzl were about to take their leave, the grand duke firmly shook Herzl's hand, and with sincere words of encouragement and an expressed willingness to receive letters from Herzl, he bade his Jewish guest farewell.

Although nothing concrete emerged, Herzl wrote, "I was slightly intoxicated with the success of our conference."[31] And well he might have been. On this, his first encounter with a royal personage, Herzl handled himself with due decorum. He spoke deferentially, but at the same time he spoke as a self-respecting representative of the Jewish people. The favorable impression made on the grand duke reflected Herzl's own aristocratic bearing. His command of German was impeccable, as was his command of French and Hungarian. He was a natural diplomat and an excellent conversationalist. Moreover, he had a most appealing physical appearance. He was moderately tall, stately, stunningly handsome and exceedingly well-groomed. His beautiful face, graced with large doe-like brown eyes and bedecked with a large, flowing black beard, bespoke both wisdom and kindness. In short, he was magnetic. Up to then, he had felt some disquiet in dealing with people in power. One significant outcome of his encounter with the grand duke was that such misgivings were finally overcome.

Herzl returned from Karlsruhe brimming with self-confidence and ready to launch a general diplomatic offensive in furtherance of his cause. Aiming his sights at no less than the Turkish sultan, he, through the auspices of an early Zionist stalwart, made contact with Baron Philip de Nevlinsky. Like Hechler, Nevlinsky was a colorful character. Having participated in an abortive Polish uprising against Russian rule, Nevlinsky forfeited all his estates.[32] He then conned his way into becoming a freelance diplomatic agent for a number of countries simultaneously. While serving as a press attaché to the Austrian embassy in Constantinople from 1874 to 1878, he cultivated intimate ties with key Turkish officials as well as with the sultan himself. He was therefore well-placed to assist Herzl in gaining entrée to Yildiz Kiosk (the sultan's palace).

When, in May 1896, Herzl first met Nevlinsky, he discovered that not only had he read his booklet but that on his latest trip to Constantinople he had actually discussed it with the sultan. The sultan informed Nevlinsky that he could never part with Jerusalem since the Mosque of Omar had to remain in Muslim hands. On hearing this, Herzl asserted, "We shall extra-territorialise Jerusalem, which will then belong to nobody and yet to everybody—the holy places will be the joint possession of all believers."[33] Thereupon, he deployed all his charm in obtaining a commitment on Nevlinsky's part to represent him, a commitment that Herzl financed at his own expense.

After some prevarication, Nevlinsky finally agreed to accompany Herzl to Constantinople. They set out on June 15, 1896, on the Orient Express. On arrival, they checked in at the Hotel Royal from which Nevlinsky proceeded to try to make contact with the sultan. Herzl's plan of action entailed an offer of £20 million, on the part of the Jewish people, to Turkey, to rid itself of its international debt. In return, Palestine was to be ceded to the Jews. Although Herzl commanded neither an organization nor financial backing of any kind, he felt sure that if only the sultan would accept his proposals, grateful Jewish millionaires would readily fall into line.

Nevlinsky did, in fact, succeed in talking with the sultan but he was unable to persuade him to grant Herzl an audience. During the eleven days that they spent in Constantinople, Herzl met with various high-ranking officials, including the grand vizier, (whose position was that of a prime minister); Izzet Bey, the first secretary of the sultan; Nuri Bey, the general secretary of the Foreign Ministry; and Daoud Effendi, chief dragoman. Most demonstrated a positive interest in his designs but it was patently clear that the sultan alone had the final say and, alas, that say was unambiguously negative. According to Nevlinsky, when he sounded out the possibility of granting the Jews national rights in Palestine, the sultan emphatically asserted:

If Mr Herzl is as much your friend as you are mine, then advise him not to take another step in this matter. I cannot sell even a foot of land, for it does not belong to me, but to my people. My people have won this empire by fighting for it with their blood and have fertilised it with their blood. We will again cover it with our blood before we allow it to be wrested away from us.... Let the Jews save their billions. When my Empire is partitioned, they may get Palestine for nothing. But only our corpse will be divided. I will not agree to vivisection.[34]

On receiving Nevlinsky's report, Herzl put on a brave face. He continued to lobby every Turkish official with whom he came into contact and sustained the hope that ultimately he would be able to put his case in person to the sultan. There was indeed some basis for such optimism. While still in Constantinople, Herzl learned that although the sultan was adamant that he would not receive him as a journalist, he would receive him as a friend, but only after Herzl influenced the European press "to handle the Armenian question in a spirit more friendly to the Turks."[35] During the return journey to Vienna, Nevlinsky elaborated on his final sessions with the sultan. He recalled that though the sultan could not accede to Herzl's request as it was then presented, the sultan did suggest that "the Jews are intelligent; they will find some acceptable formula."[36] Nevlinsky then informed Herzl that in addition to providing help on the Armenian question, the sultan expected him to secure for Turkey an immediate loan of £2 million, with light-house revenue as security. As the conversation progressed, the two interlocutors became more upbeat. Nevlinsky hit on the idea of enlisting Bismarck, through a trusted friend, to write to the sultan, appealing to him to offer the Jews Palestine under Turkish suzerainty. Then, in a burst of extravagant wishful thinking, Nevlinsky declaimed, "If you succeed in pacifying the Armenians, if you make a loan of two million pounds on the light-house and if we have Bismarck's letter—we will carry the thing off in a week."[37] So receptive was Herzl to the prospect of success that he took Nevlinsky's pronouncement as a fact. He was convinced that a charter for a Jewish state was available for the asking. All that he had to do was to attend to the Armenian issue and to raise the loan capital.

In July 1896, with great expectations, Herzl hastened to London. There, to his disappointment, the one person on whom he thought he could completely rely, Sir Samuel Montagu, expressed reservations about raising the necessary capital. Herzl had talked expansively about a sum of £20 million with which he thought Palestine could be secured. Montagu did at least promise that, provided both the executors of the Hirsch estate, who had some discretionary power, and Baron Edmond de Rothschild were willing to cooperate, he too would play a part.

Before leaving for Paris to negotiate with Rothschild, Herzl addressed a mass meeting at the Jewish Workingmen's Club in Whitechapel. Montagu, not wishing to involve lower-class Jews, advised Herzl to cancel the engagement, but Herzl, who was beginning to be leery of the Jewish elite, refused. The hall was packed to capacity and in the words of Jacob De Haas, Herzl's honorary English secretary, Herzl's "personality, his glowing eyes, his fine simple gestures, his open deprecating of himself and the natural touch of mystery with which he spoke of diplomatic affairs, won an audience keyed up by its youthful, resourceful, exuberant leaders to the point where they, not he, challenged all Jewry to follow."[38] The upshot of it all was that Herzl was able to discern a grassroots Zionist movement taking shape, one that appealed to ordinary Jews and which, as a last resort, he could utilize should the wealthy fail him.

The meeting with Edmond de Rothschild took place on July 18, 1896, at the Baron's Paris banking house. It was a complete flop. After being lectured by Herzl on the nature of his Zionist plans, the baron let it be known that apart from his having no faith in Turkish promises, he dreaded the possibility of a sudden influx of 150,000 *shnorrers* (beggars) turning up on the shores of Palestine expecting to be fed. He was not up to such a task for "there might be mishaps." To this Herzl interjected, "Are there none now? Isn't anti-Semitism a permanent mishap with loss of honour, life and property?" Getting nowhere, Herzl eventually reached for his umbrella and rose. Before leaving he told the baron, "You were the keystone of the entire combination. If you refuse, everything will fall to pieces. I shall then be obliged to do it in a different way. I shall start a mass agitation, and that will be even harder to keep the masses under control. ... This is precisely what I wanted to avoid."[39]

In Vienna, Herzl assembled a core of followers to assist in fashioning an international Zionist movement with tangible organizational structures. Drawing on his own financial resources, he opened a Zionist office, recruited a small staff and published a series of pamphlets. In addition, he orchestrated, by correspondence, Zionist agitation in other European countries and even in America.

By the beginning of 1897, Herzl decided to convene a Zionist Congress composed of delegates of all general and local Zionist organizations and from as many different countries as possible.[40] Originally, the Congress was slated for Munich where Russian delegates were less likely to be subject to Russian secret police surveillance and where a wide range of kosher restaurants were available. But because of strong opposition on the part of the Munich Jewish community, who feared that an overt demonstration of Jewish national aspirations would open a hornet's nest of anti-Semitism, the venue was changed to Basel. The Congress was scheduled to open on August 29, 1897. Some three months beforehand, Herzl inaugurated a Zionist weekly, named *Die Welt* (The World).[41] Its masthead consisted of a star of David enclosing a globe centered on Palestine, wedged between the words *Die* and *Welt*. This project was also largely financed by Herzl, or, if truth be told, through his wife's dowry. Herzl not only edited *Die Welt* but anonymously wrote most of its articles. What is more, while remaining on the full-time staff of the *Neue Freie Presse*, he continued to handle endless general Zionist organizational matters.

Naturally, the forthcoming Congress demanded most of his attention. Soon after it was announced and invitations to delegates went out, a wall of opposition to it emerged. Assimilationist Jews considered the prospect of an assembly of coreligionists proclaiming its desire for a Jewish homeland distinctly embarrassing. Their views were echoed by the German Rabbinical Council that accused the Zionists of contravening the messianic promise and the obligation to serve one's fatherland.[42] In response, many prospective West European delegates began to plead all manner of excuses as to why they might not be able to attend. In desperation, Herzl wooed the cream of Russian Jewry, a source of support that he had hitherto neglected. From that source, he obtained the blessing of Rabbi Mohilever, one of the founding fathers of Hovevei Zion, and firm commitments from Zionist luminaries such as Lilienblum, Ussishkin, Sokolow and Ahad Ha'Am.[43] With such dignitaries under his belt, most of the waverers fell into line and the Congress became a foregone conclusion.

It opened as planned on Sunday morning, August 29, 1897. The delegates, all dressed in tails and white tie, assembled in the concert hall of Basel's Municipal Casino. The atmosphere was one of complete decorum. The delegates' formal attire set a sedate and solemn tone to the proceedings. A large blue and white flag hung over the hall's entrance, while within, on a dais draped in green, stood a long green table, with an elevated seat for the president. Separate tables were set aside for stenographers and the press. When the opportunity arose, Herzl surveyed the entire scene from the back of the hall. He noted that "the Congress was magnificent" and that the visual impression it created overawed him.[44] The actual number in attendance is not known precisely. According to Pawel, it was somewhere between 199 and 246, with sixty-nine delegates representing communities or organizations. All in all, they came from twenty different countries, including the United States.[45] Every Jewish male had a vote. Women participants were only enfranchised at the second Congress.[46]

The proceedings were opened by Dr. Karpel Lippe, a stalwart Hovevei Zion adherent, who commenced with a traditional Hebrew blessing thanking God "for giving us life, preserving us and bringing us to this point in time." Dr. Lippe, who was to speak for no more than ten minutes, hugged the limelight and incoherently rambled on. With his patience beginning to wear thin, Herzl signaled on four separate occasions for Dr. Lippe to bring his maladroit speech (which included a note of thanks to the Turkish sultan) to a close. Only when Herzl issued him a direct order to do so did Dr. Lippe finally yield. Then as Herzl mounted the rostrum, he was greeted with a wild emotional outburst that lasted for some fifteen minutes. Wave after wave of applause were punctured by cries of "long live the king." Herzl himself maintained a calm composure and refrained from making any gesture that could be interpreted as putting on airs.[47] His opening speech, which outlined the essence of his Zionist credo, was "listened to with spell-bound, tense, ear-straining attention."[48] The second keynote address was given by Max Nordau, an inspiring orator, who adroitly surveyed the contemporary Jewish condition. In his overview, Nordau stressed that even where, in countries such as France, Jewish emancipation was bestowed, it was done not because of any fraternal feelings toward Jews as a downtrodden people but only for the sake of logical consistency. So moved was

Herzl by Nordau's address, that, as he returned to the main table, Herzl approached him, praising his delivery as *"Monumentum aere perennis*—a monument more lasting than bronze."[49]

With the introductory speeches behind them, the delegates turned to the main business of the hour, which was to define their objectives and the means to achieve them. After a lengthy debate, they arrived at a consensus, defining Zionism as a movement that "seeks to secure the creation of a home for the Jewish people in Palestine secured by public law," henceforth known as the Basel Program. Recommended practical steps included the encouragement of the migration of productive farmers and laborers to Palestine; the mobilization of world Jewry into organized Zionist groupings; the promotion of Jewish national consciousness; and finally, the adoption of appropriate measures to secure international support and endorsement for their enterprise. The Zionist Congress was transformed into the supreme organ of the movement. A central action committee consisting of twenty-three members was to oversee its activities between Congresses, while five of its members were to constitute a working executive, resident in Vienna, to attend to day-to-day matters. Future Congress delegates were to be elected on the basis of 1 per 100 members. To become a member, one needed to be over eighteen years old, to abide by the Basel Program and to pay a yearly membership fee of one *shekel* (then, 1 shilling or 25 cents).

At the end of the third day, when all issues and possibilities for the future were fully aired, Max Mandelstam, a lecturer in ophthalmology at Kiev and a Hovevei Zion veteran, lavishly thanked Herzl for all his efforts. Mandelstam's sentiments were echoed by all those present, who expressed their gratitude through a round of enthusiastic cheering and clapping. Thus ended "the first authoritative assembly of the Jewish people since their dispersion under the Roman Empire."[50] Unlike the 1884 Hovevei Zion Kattowitz conference, which largely went unnoticed, the Zionist Congress was extensively reported in both the Jewish and the non-Jewish press.

In his own summation of the Congress, Herzl wrote in his diary, "Were I to sum up the Basel Congress in a word—which I shall guard against pronouncing publicly—it would be this. At Basel I founded the Jewish State. If I said this out loud today, I would be answered by universal laughter. Perhaps in five years, and certainly in fifty, everyone will know it."[51] In fact, fifty years and eight and a half months later, the State of Israel was proclaimed by David Ben Gurion while standing in front of a large photograph of Herzl.

By the time the Second Zionist Congress was convened in Basel in August 1898, the movement had made large strides. The number of Zionist branches had risen from 117 to 913, from which 349 Congress delegates were elected. The Congress itself began to take on the character of a regular house of parliament in which divisions based on principle emerged. Through skillful leadership and an ability to compromise, Herzl's personal authority remained intact. He had clashed with Hovevei Zion old guards who wished to reinforce First

Herzl with a British Zionist delegation. Herzl is seated on front bench, fourth from the right, between his mother and Israel Zangwill (Central Zionist Archives).

Aliyah settlements, for he opposed what he regarded as premature attempts at colonization. In his view, in the absence of securing an official Zionist charter giving the Jews legal authority to settle in Palestine, gradualism or slow infiltration would rouse the opposition of both the native population and local authorities, who would then contrive to stifle further Jewish immigration. Therefore, interim settlements ought to be suspended until internationally recognized national rights were obtained. On the other hand, bowing to strong opposition, Herzl lent his support to settlements already in place. Also, against his better judgment, the Congress adopted a policy sponsored by cultural Zionists, of fostering by means of education, a sense of Jewish national identity. This move was seen by the Orthodox as a secular encroachment on rabbinical affairs and to this very day, the issue has not been resolved. Perhaps the most practical achievement of the Second Congress was the endorsement of Herzl's efforts to form a national bank, which was to be called the Jewish Colonial Bank for Palestine and Syria.

Almost immediately after the second Congress, Herzl, along with Hechler, held a second meeting with the grand duke of Baden at his summer residence at Castle Maine. The grand duke informed Herzl that he had briefed the kaiser on the Zionist movement and that the kaiser, in turn, had instructed Count Eulenberg, his closest friend and adviser, to present him with a detailed study of the subject. Following this up, Herzl wrote to Count Eulenberg, who was then serving as Germany's ambassador at Vienna, offering to provide him with supplementary information. His offer was readily accepted, and on September 16, 1898, Herzl met with him at the Embassy Palace. Eulenberg reacted positively and sympathetically to Herzl's standard Zionist discourse and promised to try to secure an audience for him with the kaiser. On October 1, a much-astonished Herzl received a letter from Count Eulenberg, informing him of the kaiser's sympathy for the Zionist movement.[52] To crown it all, Eulenberg went on to declare that the kaiser would receive a Zionist deputation headed by Herzl during his forthcoming visit to Jerusalem. A few days later, at a subsequent meeting with Eulenberg, this time at his manor house at Liebenberg, Herzl was advised that prior to proceeding to Jerusalem, he ought also to make himself available at Constantinople (where the kaiser would be making his first call), should the kaiser also wish to see him there. But most wonderful of all, as Herzl described it, Eulenberg let it be known that the kaiser was keen on Herzl's suggestion that Germany, with the sultan's blessing, ought to take it upon itself to provide a protectorate for the nascent Jewish state. In Eulenberg's opinion, "the kaiser did not doubt that the sultan would receive his advice favourably." The very next evening, in consulting with the grand duke of Baden, Herzl received confirmation regarding the kaiser's pro-Zionist position. The kaiser, as the grand duke told Herzl, had "been thoroughly informed about the matter and is full of enthusiasm. That word is not too strong; he has taken to your ideas quite warmly."[53] For Herzl, all this was a dream come true. He gathered four leading Zionist colleagues, Wolffsohn, Bodenheimer, Schnirer and Seidener, who, with him, were to constitute an official delegation and hurried off to Constantinople, arriving there on October 16, 1898.

Two days later, he was indeed summoned to appear before the kaiser. The audience exceeded his expectations. Dazzled as he was by the kaiser's regal presence, he retained his self-control and was given free rein to enunciate his case. In turn, the kaiser explained why the Zionist movement appealed to him and indicated full accord with all that Herzl had to say. As the interview ended, the kaiser asked Herzl to state in a word what he was to seek from the sultan. "A Chartered Company—under German protection," replied Herzl. To which the kaiser affirmed, "Good! A Chartered Company," and then he shook Herzl's hand.

With time being of the essence, Herzl and his party scrambled aboard a Russian freighter headed to Alexandria; from there they transferred to another Russian ship that took them to Jaffa. They reached Palestine on October 26. Within hours of their arrival, they visited Mikveh Yisrael and then spent the night at Rishon Letzion. The following day they were welcomed to Rehovot by a cavalcade of some twenty young Jewish farmers. The sight of "those fleet, daring horsemen into whom our young trouser-salesmen can be transformed," brought tears to Herzl's eyes.[54]

On October 28, Herzl reappeared at Mikveh Yisrael. The kaiser was due to ride past on the adjoining highway to Jerusalem, and Herzl wished to salute him as a prelude to the Jerusalem meeting. Taking up a position alongside a plow and removing his pith helmet, he awaited the royal party. Herzl described the scene as follows:

The Kaiser recognised me even at a distance. It gave him a bit of a start; he guided his horse in my direction—and pulled up in front of me. I took two steps forward; and when he leaned down over the neck of the horse and held his hand down to me, I stepped up quite close to his horse, stretched up my own hand, and stood before him with my head bared.

He laughed and flashed his imperious eyes at me.

"How are you?"

"Thanks, Your Majesty! I am having a look at the country. And how has the journey agreed with Your Majesty so far?"

He blinked grandly with his eyes: "Very hot! But the country has a future."

"At the moment it is still sick," I said.

"Water is what it needs, a lot of water!" he said from above me.

"Yes, Your Majesty! Irrigation on a large scale!"

He repeated: "It is a land of the future!"

Perhaps he said some other things which have escaped me, for he stopped with me for several minutes. Then he held down his hand to me again and trotted off.[55]

The trite exchange that took place did nothing to impair Herzl's confidence that in Jerusalem, the kaiser would formally issue a proclamation heralding Jewish statehood. Later that day, in sweltering heat, Herzl and his party took the train to Jerusalem, where they awaited the kaiser's bidding in a state of great excitement. To their mortification, one day followed another with no call emanating from the kaiser's camp. Just as they were beginning to despair, they were instructed to appear at the imperial tent on Wednesday, November 2, five days after first setting foot in the Holy City. On entering the imperial tent, Herzl formally introduced the members of his delegation and then proceeded to read a speech, which had been vetted and modified by the minister of state, Count Bulow. Thanks to Bulow's hostile intervention, Zionist and Jewish national aspirations were expunged from the original draft, leaving Herzl with the task of delivering a speech rich only in innocuous platitudes. Although Herzl reluctantly cooperated with Bulow, he remained convinced that Bulow's and the kaiser's views diverged and that his encounter with the kaiser that day would yield incalculable benefits to the Jewish people. Herzl was quickly disabused of his illusions. As he concluded his speech, the kaiser thanked him for his communication and then hastened to add, "The matter, in any case, still requires thorough study and further discussion."[56] Herzl was completely crestfallen. He tried to console himself with the thought that the kaiser "said neither yes nor no."

Cut off from all communication with the outside world, Herzl's party had absolutely no notion as to how their audience was reported. Even though nothing tangible resulted from their encounter with the kaiser, they took it for granted that the mere fact that such a meeting had occurred would be acknowledged as a Zionist triumph. Over a week later, on disembarking at Naples, they came across a dispatch issued by the German news agency. It simply recounted that the kaiser had received a Jewish delegation that presented him with an album of pictures of the Jewish colonies in Palestine and that the kaiser reaffirmed his interest in the welfare of the Turkish empire and his respect for the sovereignty of the sultan. Instantly, Herzl's companions fell into a state of deep depression but an undaunted Herzl reasoned that perhaps they would, after all, be better off without German involvement.

There was no apparent reason why the kaiser held out grounds for hope to Herzl in Constantinople only to dash them in Jerusalem. However, Herzl more or less guessed what had happened. The kaiser did indeed raise the protectorate issue with the sultan who told him that though he personally was not well disposed toward requests for an autonomous Jewish entity in Palestine, he would instruct his foreign minister to look into the matter.[57] Interpreting the sultan's response as a polite rejection, the kaiser determined to distance himself from Zionism. As a royal sovereign, he obviously could not explicitly explain the situation to Herzl.

Faced with a total anticlimax, which provided fuel to internal critics who were beginning to question both Herzl's leadership style and competence, Herzl desperately tried to obtain direct access to both the Russian czar and the Turkish sultan. Through the help of well-placed intermediaries, the czar was approached but no positive response ensued. Attempts to reach out to the sultan were even more problematic, for in the meantime, Nevlinsky, Herzl's go-between, passed away. Nuri Bey of the Turkish foreign ministry offered to plead Herzl's case but all that Herzl saw for Nuri Bey's "efforts" were exorbitant exactions.

Eventually, it dawned on Herzl that, in addition to Nuri Bey, help might be forthcoming from an Hungarian Jew, Arminius Vambery. Like Hechler and Nevlinsky, Vambery was a flamboyant character. He had mastered twelve languages, at one time or another professed five religions, served as a priest in two of them and then ultimately became an atheist. More to the point, in Turkey he had worked his way up from being a coffee house singer to the grand vizier's confidant, meeting on intimate terms with the sultan. On June 16, 1900, Herzl paid him a call. Harping on their common Hungarian Jewish background and addressing Vambery as "uncle," Herzl pulled out all the stops in trying to induce Vambery to arrange an audience with the sultan. Vambery, for his part, appeared evasive and when Herzl took leave of him, he was uncertain of his intentions. Finally, after numerous entreaties, Vambery agreed to visit the sultan to intercede personally on Herzl's behalf. His mission proved to be successful and in early May 1901, Herzl's wishes were granted. He was to proceed to

Turkey where the sultan would receive him, "not as a Zionist but as Chief of the Jews and an influential journalist."[58] Under no circumstances was the issue of Zionism explicitly to be raised.

Accompanied by Wolffsohn and Marmorek, Herzl arrived in Constantinople on May 13, 1901. The audience took place four days later. After being ushered into the reception room Herzl was welcomed by the sultan, who appeared to be small and shabby. His beard was badly dyed, he had a hooked nose, "long yellow teeth with a big gap on the upper right," a bleating voice and "feeble hands in white, oversize gloves."[59] After an exchange of salutations and small talk, Herzl made it known that he was devoted to the sultan on account of his benevolence toward the Jews. Then by means of a well-chosen parable, Herzl offered to assist Turkey in exchange for as-yet-unspecified favors. He likened the situation to Androcles and the lion. The sultan was the lion with a thorn in his side (the Turkish debt), which Herzl, acting as Androcles, was ready to remove. However, in exchange for the redemption of the debt, the sultan would have to undertake a measure that was highly favorable to the Jews and that needed to be proclaimed in an appropriate manner. The wily sultan, whom Herzl had grossly underestimated, replied that he could say something favorable about the Jews to either his Jewish court jeweler or to the chief rabbi. Herzl countered that that was not what he had in mind and that, with the sultan's permission, he would later suggest an appropriate declaration. As for the Turkish debt, the sultan informed Herzl that plans were afoot to consolidate it, in order to yield a saving of at least £1 million. Affecting astonishment, Herzl exclaimed, "What? So little?"[60] To which the sultan shrugged his shoulders with a sad smile. Herzl then requested that he be issued with all the details of Turkey's financial situation and the debt consolidation project so that he could determine how he could be of assistance. At that point, their conversation, which lasted two full hours, came to a conclusion. Although not a word was said about Zionism or Palestine, Herzl deluded himself into believing that he had successfully entered into the first stage of negotiations over a colonial charter. As he left the palace, he was convinced that victory was within his grasp.[61]

During the following seven days, through senior government officials, indirect contact with the sultan was maintained. By such means, Herzl was requested to provide an immediate loan of £4 million in return for which, the exploitation of five state monopolies was offered. As for the Jews, the sultan informed Herzl that they were welcome to immigrate, provided they became Turkish citizens, served in the army and that they settled in a dispersed fashion with "five families here and five there—scattered without connection."[62] Indicating that, in principle, Herzl had no objection to such a proposal, he stressed that technical and economic considerations favored concentrated settlement and then, chancing his luck, he ventured to add: "Surely there is land enough in Palestine which could be used for such a purpose."[63] Izzet Bey immediately relayed Herzl's reply to the sultan. When he returned bearing a cordial farewell greeting, Herzl took that as an omen that the negotiations over the charter were moving onto a higher plane.

Fortified by his "success" in Constantinople, Herzl headed for Paris and London to drum up financial backing for his dealings with the sultan. Practically everyone he approached turned him down and, to make matters worse, despite the dispatch of endless letters to Turkey reassuring the sultan that he was in the process of creating a financial consortium on his behalf, his epistles went unanswered. By December 1901, Herzl begged the sultan to send him a good-will telegram on the occasion of the Fifth Zionist Congress scheduled at the end of the month in Basel. He desperately needed some tangible token that his Constantinople visit had borne a positive outcome and feared that the sultan might yet deny that they had struck up a relationship. When the coveted telegram materialized, he noted with relief that, "with this wire, my situation is certified and regularised."[64]

The Fifth Zionist Congress marked the entry of a "Democratic Zionist Faction," which contained some of the Zionist movement's most illustrious young intellectuals, such as Chaim Weizmann, Martin Buber and Leo Motzkin.[65] Their insistence on emphasizing cultural matters, including the need to establish a Hebrew University in Jerusalem and a Jewish publishing house irritated Herzl, who wished to confine attention to grand political strategies. When he tried to curb a debate on their proposals, thirty-seven delegates walked out of the hall in protest. This represented the first serious challenge to Herzl's hegemony, which Herzl tried to placate by adopting a more conciliatory tone. Unfortunately, he inwardly harbored a grudge against the Democratic Faction, for what he regarded as a personal insult, "a clear case of lèse-majesté," and in order to neutralize their influence, he secretly called on religious Zionists to form their own party. In March 1902, at a convention in Vilna, which was personally subsidized by Herzl, the Orthodox Zionist Mizrahi Party was founded.[66] Pawel, Herzl's biographer, observes that this act of double dealing on Herzl's part, fed the myth of his having become religious.[67] In fact, although criticized by Weizmann for having "excessive respect for the Jewish clergy,"[68] Herzl never abandoned his philosophy of liberal tolerance, in which all streams in the Jewish religion were to be given their equal due. Finally, on a more positive note, the Fifth Congress ushered in the foundation of the Jewish National Fund, charged with undertaking collective land purchases in Palestine.

On February 5, 1902, after months without hearing anything concrete from Turkey, Herzl received a telegram requesting him to proceed immediately to Constantinople in order to clarify the nature of the assistance he supposedly could provide. He arrived there on February 15, to learn that the sultan wished him to form a syndicate for the consolidation of the public debt and to assume responsibility for the exploitation of the empire's oil and minerals. In exchange, Jews would be welcome to settle in any part of the empire, bar Palestine. Herzl promptly, albeit courteously, rejected what he termed "a Charter without Palestine" and then returned to Vienna. In July 1902, Herzl once again visited Constantinople but as on all the previous occasions no progress was made. The Turks were merely using Herzl's known presence in Turkey as a foil to extract improved financial terms from European bankers who would certainly not trouble them with demands for a colonial charter or the like. It was then that Herzl concluded that the chances of reaching an agreement with Turkey within a reasonable time frame, were minute.

Troubled by the growing misery of East European Jews, for whom the need for a refuge was becoming more urgent, Herzl decided to seek a temporary alternative to Palestine. That was not the first time that the idea of finding a "half-way station" entered Herzl's mind. Four years earlier (in July 1898), he recorded, "I am thinking of giving the movement a closer territorial goal, preserving Zion as the final goal. The masses need immediate help, and Turkey is not yet so desperate as to accede to our wishes.... Perhaps we can demand Cyprus from England, and even keep an eye on South Africa or America—until Turkey is dissolved."[69] However, on this occasion, he took active steps to implement his decision. Through an English Zionist, Leopold Greenberg, Herzl secured an introduction to Joseph Chamberlain, the British colonial secretary. They met in London on October 22, 1902.

After providing Chamberlain with an explanation of Zionism and the problems he had experienced in negotiating with the Turks, Herzl quickly came to the point and requested that England accord the Jews settlement rights in Cyprus, El Arish and the Sinai Peninsula. He had hoped that once the Jews established a strong foothold there, their bargaining position vis-à-vis Turkey would be strengthened and if worst came to worst, they could use those territories as bases from which they might wrest Palestine by force. Obviously, he could not divulge such thoughts to Chamberlain, who, as it happened, was very well disposed to Herzl's request. Unfortunately, as Chamberlain explained, since Cyprus was already inhabited by Greeks and Muslims, he could not displace them for the sake of the Jews. As for the other two areas, they were under the jurisdiction of the Foreign Office. For Herzl to pursue the matter, he needed to speak to Lord Lansdowne. No serious objections were raised by Lansdowne who informed Herzl that to reach a decision, it was first necessary to ascertain the views of Lord Cromer, Britain's consul general in Cairo. To facilitate matters, Lansdowne agreed to introduce Herzl's representative, Leopold Greenberg, to Cromer.

Greenberg dutifully sailed to Cairo, where he was well received not only by Cromer but also by Boutros Gali Pasha, the nominal Egyptian prime minister. Then on December 21, Herzl received a letter from the British Foreign Office informing him that the prospective Sinai Peninsula project would probably meet with their approval subject to an expeditionary commission's positive findings. In consultation with the Foreign Office, Herzl nominated a team consisting of a South African mining engineer, an architect, an agronomist, a physician, a nominee of Cromer and Colonel Albert Goldsmid. Except for Cromer's nominee, all of the above were Jewish Zionists. Mounted on camels, the team soon set off from Cairo leaving Greenberg to liaise with Cromer.

As far as Herzl was concerned everything seemed cut and dried. So certain was he of obtaining a British charter, that he foreshadowed his resignation from the *Neue Freie Presse* and failed to take up an option to purchase a crypt alongside that of his late father. In cooperation with Lord Rothschild of England, he mobilized Jewish financial backers and impatiently waited for the expected nod from the British Foreign Office. By late February 1903, dispatches from Greenberg, which up to then indicated nothing untoward, began to augur badly. In early March, Herzl realized that the Egyptian prime minister was creating some difficulties and despairing of Greenberg's negotiating position, he decided to intercede personally. On March 24, he arrived in Cairo and the following day he was in Cromer's office. Cromer seemed to resent Herzl's intrusion.[70] Herzl for his part, described Cromer as "the most disagreeable Englishman I have ever faced."[71] Even so, Cromer did not at that point give Herzl to understand that the project was stillborn. At that stage, both he and Boutros Gali Pasha were prepared to await the verdict of their water expert, William Garstin. In the meantime, to boost support for the project, Herzl went to London to see both Chamberlain and Lansdowne. Despite their conviviality, the proposed scheme soon received the kiss of death when in May 1903, Garstin reported that Herzl's study commission's estimate of water requirements was five times less than his and that a proposal to drain off surplus Nile water was impractical.

During Herzl's conversation with Chamberlain on April 24, 1903, in which they both noted that the Sinai Peninsula was not exactly a land of milk and honey, Chamberlain made an aside, which prefaced an issue that was soon to shake the Zionist movement to its very core. Having recently returned from a tour in Africa, Chamberlain mentioned, "I have just seen a land for you on my travels and that's Uganda. [In reality, present-day Kenya.] It's hot on the coast, but farther inland the climate becomes excellent, even for Europeans. You can raise sugar and cotton there. And I thought to myself, that would be a land for Dr. Herzl. But of course he wants to go only to Palestine or its vicinity."[72] In reply, Herzl conceded that he did in fact prefer land either in or near Palestine.

A month later, Chamberlain repeated his offer of Uganda to Greenberg who relayed it to Herzl. This time, Herzl decided that the matter warranted serious consideration and instructed Greenberg to ascertain just what Chamberlain had in mind. Reasons for Herzl's change of heart are not difficult to fathom. Apart from his stalemate with the Turks and the El Arish fiasco, a terrible pogrom erupted in Kishinev, a city in Russian Bessarabia. There, on April 6, 1903, a frenzied mob, actively supported by, among others, Plehve, the minister of the interior, and Pobyedonostsev, the procurator of the Holy Synod, ran amok. Forty-seven Jews were killed, hundreds were wounded and some 1,500 stores were looted and destroyed. The Kishinev pogrom was a particularly gruesome outrage. "Nails were driven into victims' skulls, eyes gouged out, and babies thrown from the higher stories of buildings to the pavement. Men were castrated, women were raped." All the while, "the local bishop drove in his carriage through the crowd, blessing it as he passed."[73] By the time order was re-stored, 20 percent of the Jewish population were left homeless.

Although by twentieth-century standards the Kishinev pogrom was a rela-tively minor affair, at the time it was responsible for more deaths and injuries than the hundreds of pogroms that shook Russia in 1881.[74] The Kishinev pogrom itself and its aftershock, which reverberated throughout the civilized world, highlighted the physical vulnerability of Eastern European Jews. It em-phasized, if ever the point needed emphasizing, the absolute urgency of secur-ing a Jewish homeland. Uganda was obviously not what the Zionists had in mind but Herzl reasoned that it would have to make do as a temporary expedi-ent until Palestine was obtained. On August 14, 1903, in response to negotia-tions undertaken by Greenberg, the British government officially confirmed that, in principle, it was willing to grant the Jewish Colonial Trust (the Zionist movement's newly formed bank), territorial concessions in Uganda. What was envisioned was some form of internal Jewish autonomy subject to overall British control.

An early indication of the vigorous opposition that the Ugandan option was to encounter arose when, in early July, Herzl briefed Nordau. Much to Herzl's surprise, Nordau responded negatively, asserting that the probable exploitation of black labor would impede the moral regeneration of the Jews. He correctly foresaw that the proposal would threaten the cohesion of the Zionist move-ment and advised Herzl to drop the idea forthwith.[75] But Herzl remained adamant. He conceded that the Ugandan option was highly flawed but argued that an Ugandan charter could be brandished in front of the sultan in order to elicit a similar one for Palestine. To make the proposal even more palatable, Herzl developed a theory of an inverted colonial process. Unlike other nations, which created their colonies as an offshoot of their homelands, the Jews would create their homeland as an offshoot of their colonies. Nordau remained un-convinced but agreed not to oppose the plan openly.

During much the same period, Herzl received news that Plehve, the czar's minister for internal affairs, was planning to outlaw the Russian Zionist move-ment. Herzl promptly wrote to him requesting an interview. Receiving no reply, he then turned to Madam von Korvin-Piatrovska, who was personally friendly with Plehve, begging her to intercede on his behalf. This bore fruit, for on July 23, he received a letter from her telling him that not only had Plehve agreed to see him but he was "looking forward to making the acquaintance of so interesting a personality as Dr Herzl."[76] On August 10, 1903, Herzl entered Plehve's office. The conversation began with Plehve bemoaning the difficulties of assimilating Russian Jewry. In that context, he turned to the Russian Zion-ists, complaining that they were more concerned with fostering a localized Jew-ish nationalism than with migrating to Palestine. Such a tendency, Plehve affirmed, impeded Jewish assimilation. Plehve went on to reveal that he was aware of the fact that certain Russian Zionists were beginning to question Herzl's leadership. Impressed by Plehve's knowledge, Herzl cleverly turned matters to his own advantage by making a comparison with Christopher Columbus's disgruntled crew who had begun to lose hope of ever encountering land. Facing Plehve, Herzl stated, "Help me to reach land sooner, and the revolt will end."[77] When Plehve asked what sort of help he could provide, Herzl stipulated the following three points: (1) the Russian government was to recommend to the Turkish sultan that he grant the Jews a colonial charter in Palestine, (2) the Russian government was to subsidize emigration to Palestine out of taxes from Jewish sources, (3) Russian Zionist Societies based on the Basel program were to be legalized. Much to Herzl's satisfaction, Plehve readily agreed to recommend all three measures to the czar on the understanding that the Sixth Zionist Congress, scheduled for August 23, 1903, would refrain from criticizing the Russian regime. Three days later, Plehve announced that the czar had approved Herzl's three-point request. (In practice, no official overture on the part of the czar to the sultan was subsequently made.)

With everything more or less straightened out with Plehve, Herzl called upon Witte, the minister responsible for finance, to ensure that restrictions placed on selling Jewish Colonial Trust shares be rescinded. Here, too, he was successful but not until he was subjected to Witte's views on the Jewish question. After declaring that there were legitimate reasons for becoming an anti-Semite, for the Jews were arrogant, dirty and involved in nasty pursuits such as pimping and usury, Witte disclosed that he personally was their friend. Then the "Jewish friend" went on to relate that he used to say to the czar, "Your Majesty, if it is possible to drown the six or seven million Jews in the Black Sea, I have absolutely no objection to it. But if it isn't possible, we must let them live."[78]

From Russia, Herzl made a beeline for Basel, arriving there on August 21, 1903, two days before the opening of the Sixth Zionist Congress. A pre-Congress meeting of the Greater Actions Committee was convened at which Herzl reported on his Russian tour and on England's Uganda offer. Instead of applauding his efforts, which was what Herzl had anticipated, many committee members were horrified that he had made personal contact with Plehve, the "butcher of Kishinev." They begged Herzl not to publicize an official letter from Plehve agreeing to Herzl's three-point request, but Herzl emphatically refused to do so. Finally, little was said of the Ugandan offer since with the Sabbath drawing near, the meeting had to be adjourned

On Sunday morning, August 23, 592 delegates, the largest contingent within the movement's first half-century, assembled for the Sixth Congress's opening session. As was customary, Herzl was the first to speak and from the very beginning, the question of Uganda came to the fore. Herzl emphasized the context in which the proposal had arisen, that is, the sultan's unyielding obduracy, the unsuccessful bid to obtain El Arish and the Kishinev pogrom, which Herzl described as a portent of even worse to come. Given all these factors, Herzl asserted that he would surely have been irresponsible had he not at least submitted the Uganda proposal for the Congress's consideration. The next day, in a

strongly worded speech, Nordau backed Herzl. While acknowledging the absolute and unchanging primacy of Palestine as a Zionist objective, Nordau
stressed that a *nachtasyl* (night shelter) had to be provided for the multitude of
Jews whose lives and property were currently imperiled.

The issue was then open for general discussion and though it was formulated
in terms of whether approval should be given to the establishment of a commission of inquiry to report on the feasibility of the Uganda option, everyone
realized that fundamental Zionist principles were at stake. The nub of the matter was whether the movement should or should not concentrate exclusively
on securing Palestine. The ensuing debate was extremely acrimonious. Those
that opposed quests for alternative, interim solutions feared that the movement
would become permanently sidetracked and that Palestine, its ultimate objective, would be forsaken. Russian delegates mostly argued against the motion,
with the most strident among them, the "Zion Zionists," being secularists. By
contrast, the bulk of the orthodox sided with Herzl. The explanation for this lies
in the fact, that at that stage, the orthodox partly approached the Zionist endeavor essentially as a means of providing physical relief to the Jewish people,
whose ultimate redemption in Zion would occur in God's given time. As Rabbi
Isaac Reines explained, "We support the African proposal because we have paid
more heed to the needs of our dear people than the matter of land."[79] By contrast, the secularly inclined Jews saw Zionism as a process of national redemption in its own right. Since they believed that an authentic Jewish national
renewal could only occur within Palestine, they were not prepared to consider
alternatives.[80] Finally, late on Wednesday afternoon (August 26) the resolution
was put to the vote: 295 were in favor, 177 against, with 120 abstaining. Although technically a victory for the Ugandan option supporters, less than half
of all delegates present positively endorsed the proposal.[81] Of the few Russians
who sided with Herzl, almost all did so out of personal loyalty and not out of
conviction.[82] When the tally was announced, most of the dissidents promptly
stormed out.[83]

The rejectionists regrouped in an adjoining hall where many wept openly.
Some sat on the floor in keeping with traditional mourning rites. Virtually all
believed that they were witnessing the demise of the Zionist movement. Their
noisy protestations continued well into the night and when word of this
reached Herzl, who apart from normal fatigue, was heavily burdened by a deteriorating heart, he summoned all his remaining strength and returned from
his hotel to the Congress center. There he found that the door to the hall in
which the dissidents were assembled, was locked. Only after a debate of some
kind was he finally admitted. Tired and haggard as well as emotionally exhausted, Herzl reasoned with them while they listened in silence. Without offering any concessions, he did his utmost to reassure them of his love for Zion.
As a result, the following morning they all resumed their seats at the main conference hall. On their behalf, Shemarya Levin, read a declaration indicating that
their withdrawal was not to be taken as a demonstration but rather as a "spon-

taneous expression of a profound spiritual shock."[84] For his part, Herzl went out of his way to placate his opponents by accepting that the Uganda investigating committee would not be financed by shekels or other official Zionist funds. Finally, in his closing Congress speech, Herzl raised his right hand and, in Hebrew, solemnly declared, "If I forget thee, O Jerusalem, let my right hand forget her cunning."[85] He uttered the words solemnly, "as if he had himself fashioned the ancient oath on the spot. The Congress was swept by a storm of applause."[86] While a complete and formal rift in the movement was averted, divisions in the ranks endured, with the Uganda issue continuing to fester over the following two years.

In mid-November 1903, under Menahem Ussishkin's leadership, a pocket of open rebellion flared up in Russia. Nine Russian members of the Greater Action Committee, who assembled at Kharkov, issued Herzl an ultimatum. If he continued to pursue the Uganda project, they would proceed to organize a new Zionist Organization that would exclude him. In response, Herzl treated their demands with disdain. He published their ultimatum in *Die Welt* and rallied the rank-and-file Zionist members to his side. Even those who took issue with him, were appalled at the brazen attempt of a minority faction to impose its will on the majority. By the end of December, Ussishkin's prospective coup totally disintegrated.

Meanwhile, on December 19, 1903, at a Hanukkah ball in Paris, a deranged Russian Jewish student by the name of Chaim Loubon, fired two pistol shots at Nordau, shouting "Death to the East African." Fortunately, Nordau escaped unscathed. The wild passions that the Uganda project unleashed, were not confined to its opponents. Strong support soon emerged from a seemingly unlikely source; that is, from within the heartland of Palestine's New Yishuv. Eliezer Ben Yehuda, for one, cast his lot with the Ugandists and used his newspaper to advance their cause. In Rishon Letzion, veteran farmers vigorously attempted to silence the Uganda project's critics. As a case in point, a new migrant, Shlomo Tzemach, was beaten by administrators at Rishon Letzion's winery because he objected to the fact that workers were being coerced to support the project.[87]

The surprising endorsement of Herzl's stand from among large sections of the New Yishuv reflected a degree of demoralization wrought by years of relative isolation and insubstantial consolidation. The 5,000–6,000 Jewish farmers present in Palestine felt that they were but a drop in an ocean of hordes of Muslim subjects and, as Ben Yehuda told Herzl, it would merely need some vague hint by the authorities for the indigenous population to set their hatchet-men on them, as had been done to the Armenians.[88] For that reason, they felt that a British charter would provide a securer basis for Jewish settlement.

Within a short while, the Uganda project soon began to lose some of its gloss. The moment British settlers in East Africa realized that plans were afoot to grant Jews a measure of autonomy, they mounted a spirited campaign to nip the scheme in the bud. Their newspaper, the *East African Standard*, railed against what was termed "Jewganda" into which masses of unproductive Jewish hawkers were expected to arrive.[89] Bowing to such pressures, the British Foreign Office, on January 25, 1904, offered the Zionists a much more limited area of land near Lake Victoria.[90] Rather than turning it down completely, the Zionists grudgingly accepted the new British proposal but decided not to act on it, pending further internal deliberations.

As promised, Herzl did not lose sight of the goal of securing Palestine. In late January 1904, to whip up support for such ends, he went to Italy. Pausing for a short stop in Venice before journeying to Rome, Herzl popped into a pub. There he was recognized and approached by Berthold Lippay, a papal count and painter. Lippay, who also originated in Budapest, promised to arrange an audience for Herzl with the Pope. At first, Herzl thought that he was dealing with a mere braggart, but Lippay was true to his word and by January 25, Herzl was in the Vatican face-to-face with Pope Pius X. Despite Lippay's advice, Herzl refrained from kneeling and kissing the Pontiff's hand, an omission that in retrospect, Herzl thought may have affronted the Pope. When Herzl requested that the Catholic Church lend its moral support to the Zionist movement, the Pope was totally unyielding. He said, "We cannot prevent the Jews from going to Jerusalem—but we could never sanction it. ... The Jews have not recognized our Lord, therefore we cannot recognize the Jewish people. ... The Jews who ought to have been the first to acknowledge Jesus Christ have not done so to this day."[91] As Herzl noted, "It was on the tip of my tongue to say, 'That's what happens in every family. No one believes his own relatives.' "[92] Instead, he went on to suggest that the Church's use of terror and persecution was not an appropriate way of enlightening the Jews, but it all fell on deaf ears. A little earlier, a much more constructive encounter had taken place with the king of Italy, who was remarkably well disposed toward Zionism but who had little international clout.

For the next few months of 1904, Herzl spent an inordinately large amount of time writing to various dignitaries, seeking to initiate another dramatic diplomatic demarche. His poor health, which had recently given rise to fainting fits and to heart palpitations, steadily worsened. Doctors diagnosed serious cardiac disorders and counseled long bouts of rest, but Herzl soldiered on, maintaining a daily work schedule that would have exhausted even the most physically robust of people. Delegates to the Sixth Congress noticed a distinctive transformation in his appearance. His face was gaunt, his hair and beard had premature streaks of gray and his eyes were encircled by black rings. By June 1904, he was exceeding ill and was attended to by various medical specialists. Finally, he succumbed to pneumonia and on July 2 he died, a young man of forty-four. His funeral was held on July 7 at the Doebling Cemetery in Vienna. Many eulogized him but perhaps Stafan Zweig's memories of Herzl's funeral best captured the total impact of the man. After noting the uninhibited mass hysteria and grief displayed by mourners who streamed in from all parts of Europe, he conceded that he had finally realized just how much hope and inspiration Herzl had given to the Jewish people. The Jews were not simply burying some second-rate writer but one whose prophetic vision had immensely up-lifted them.[93]

Not only did Herzl give Jews grounds for hope, but he propelled them on to the world stage, not simply as passive observers but as active participants determined to mold their own fate. He bequeathed to his people a Zionist movement with a resilient institutional framework, which was no longer dependent on the will and energy of a single person and which successfully served as the nation's vanguard in trailblazing its path to statehood.

In August 1949, in accordance with his wishes, Herzl's remains, as were those of his parents and sister, were reburied on Mount Herzl in Jerusalem. His wife, who died in 1907, was cremated. Her ashes were misplaced by her son, Hans. Pauline, Herzl's eldest daughter, died in 1930 in Bordeaux as a result of a mor-phine addiction. Hans, who felt some responsibility for her lot, shot himself in Bordeaux, hours before Pauline's funeral. Herzl's remaining daughter, Trude, died of hunger in March 1943 in the Theresienstadt ghetto. She had a son, Stephen, but he committed suicide in November 1946, a day or two after he fi-nally received confirmation that his parents had met their deaths while in Nazi captivity.

After Herzl's demise, the overall stewardship of the movement was en-trusted to his loyal supporter, David Wolffsohn. The main Zionist offices were moved to Cologne, where Wolffsohn lived. Instead of Cologne becoming the nerve center of the movement, it tended to adopt a rather low-key position. Si-multaneously, in Russia, where the world Jewish population was largely con-centrated, local Zionists adopted a more autonomous stance. In the absence of additional serious diplomatic moves, at least until the tail end of World War I, and with more sober expectations of the likelihood of them being successful, the movement turned to more prosaic tasks. Attention was placed on the provi-sion of assistance to budding settlements in Palestine. However, support was somewhat limited and certainly no plans were afoot to embark on anything even vaguely approaching mass migration. With the onset of the 1905 Russian Revolution, the movement encouraged its members to engage in the struggle for general political reform, in the belief that by so doing, the situation of Rus-sian Jewry in both individual and communal terms would improve.

In July 1905, at a special session of the Seventh Congress, the Uganda scheme was finally laid to rest. After a noisy two-day debate, it was decided (by acclamation) that in thanking the British government for its good will, the movement's exclusive devotion to Eretz Israel would simultaneously be reaf-firmed. Consequently, under the leadership of Israel Zangwill, thirty-one diehard territorialists (that is, those who favored a Jewish state wherever feasi-ble) withdrew from both the Congress and Zionist Movement to form the Jew-ish Territorial Organization. Their new movement (which dissolved in 1925) never posed any significant threat to Zionism and never even came within any-thing like striking distance of achieving its objectives. While the territorialists did not outflank the Zionists, the Zionist movement had to compete vigorously for Jewish allegiance against other forces. At the political level, its main rivals were the Bund and the anti-Zionist religious establishment.

The Bund, which was also established in 1897 (in Vilna) was a Marxist organization. It came into being bearing its full Yiddish title as *Der Allgemeiner Yiddisher Arbeter Bund in Lite, Poilen un Russland* (the General Jewish Workers' Organization in Lithuania, Poland and Russia). Its founding members, who subscribed to classical Marxist revolutionary tenets, rejected Zionism as a reactionary nationalist movement which, in offering an illusory panacea, diverted Jewish workers from the class struggle. Although they themselves cast their lot with the international proletariat, the Bund's leaders realized that, in view of current conditions in Russia and Poland, Jewish workers could only be won over to their cause by appealing to them in Yiddish and by seducing them with some token form of linguistic autonomy. As an active trade union body, it attracted large numbers of Jewish laborers and was particularly successful in pre–Second World War Poland. In time, the Communist regimes smothered it and by 1947 it had virtually disappeared.

At the other end of the political spectrum, a serious challenge was posed by the anti-Zionist religious establishment. On an ideological plane, it opposed Zionism as a heretical movement, arrogating to itself a mission that could only be executed by divine fiat. Hassidic and other extremely devout rabbis were appalled by the dominant role that secular Jews played in the movement. They were convinced that militant secular Zionists were essentially Jews who realized that because of anti-Semitism, they could not comfortably be absorbed in the countries in which they resided. Accordingly (as many rabbis argued), they effectively sought a form of collective assimilation, through the medium of a modern secular Jewish state, that to all intents and purposes would be devoid of Jewishness. Such a prospect was seen as far more threatening to the continuity of Judaism than, say, a process of a relaxation of religious observances on the part of individual Jews. In the latter case, wayward Jews could still be coaxed back into the fold but the Zionists, by contrast, who were effectively sponsoring a new form of Jewish existence, represented an organized direct frontal attack on orthodoxy and its way of life. This was manifested by Zionist efforts to capture control of communal bodies and by the promotion of cultural activities in which extremely devout rabbis had no input. As for attempts to settle in Palestine, since the extremely religious Jews rejected all modern Jewish nationalist notions and since in their eyes Palestine was a holy land, they felt that the country ought not to be fouled by the presence of disbelievers whose profanity would incur the wrath of God.

The "cultural question" did, in fact, constitute a threatening challenge to religious Jews, for its advocates were motivated by a loathing of traditional diaspora lifestyles. They bore negative feelings toward orthodoxy and hoped to bring about a renaissance of Jewish culture on the basis of a selective use of historical Jewish traditions.[94] Matters came to a head in 1911, when at the Tenth Zionist Congress, the dissemination of culture was firmly entrenched as a crucial ingredient in the Zionist platform. This development precipitated the withdrawal of the remnant of extremely religious Jews from the Zionist Movement,[95] who a year later made common cause with like-minded individuals in forming an organization named *Agudat Israel* (the Association of Israel), which was dedicated to the negation of everything for which Zionism stood. It gathered a fairly widespread following, claiming by 1939, around half a million members.

Formidable as the challenges of both the Bund and Agudat Israel may have been, the biggest bugbear of the Zionist Movement, especially in the West, lay in other channels. To some extent, it had to cope with the hostility that emanated from assimilationist Jews, who feared that Zionism would compromise their civil rights. However, its biggest drawback was its inability to enthuse a large multitude of the Jewish population, who either discounted its practical possibilities or, like ordinary people generally, were not prepared to sacrifice themselves for seemingly nebulous ideals in Palestine, while opportunities for a better life were available to them in America or elsewhere. For all these reasons, the Zionist Movement, though claiming to represent world Jewry as a whole, never attained majority support until after the end of the Second World War.

NOTES

1. Pawel, *Labyrinth of Exile,* 1989, p. 70.
2. Pawel, *Labyrinth of Exile,* 1989, p. 76.
3. Herzl, *Diaries,* 1960, p. 6.
4. Pawel, *Labyrinth of Exile,* 1989, p. 163.
5. Bein, *Theodore Herzl,* 1940, p. 143.
6. Pawel, *Labyrinth of Exile,* 1989, p. 206.
7. Burns, *Dreyfus,* 1993, p. 151.
8. As quoted by O'Brien, *Siege,* 1986, p. 64.
9. Herzl, *Diaries,* 1960, p. 16.
10. Ibid., p. 18.
11. Ibid., p. 23.
12. Ibid., p. 3.
13. Ibid., p. 76.
14. Ibid., p. 86.
15. Ibid., p. 85.
16. Ibid., p. 91.
17. Ibid., p. 76.
18. Ibid., p. 141.
19. Ibid., p. 157.
20. Ibid., p. 248.
21. Ibid., p. 146. Italics added.

22. Ibid., p. 138.

23. Ibid., p. 139.

24. Ibid., p. 139.

25. Bein, *History,* 1970, p. 15.

26. Laqueur, *History of Zionism,* 1989, p. 96.

27. Herzl, *Diaries,* 1960, p. 305.

28. As quoted by Bein, *Theodore Herzl,* 1940, p. 183.

29. Ibid., p. 308.

30. Ibid., p. 210.

31. Ibid., p. 341.

32. Pawel, *Labyrinth of Exile,* 1989, p. 284.

33. Herzl, *Diaries,* 1960, p. 346.

34. Ibid., p. 378.

35. Ibid., p. 387.

36. Ibid., p. 400.

37. Ibid., p. 404.

38. De Haas, *Theodore Herzl,* 1927, p. 120.

39. Herzl, *Diaries,* 1960, p. 428.

40. Pawel, *Labyrinth of Exile,* 1989, p. 320.

41. Herzl proudly referred to *Die Welt* as a *Judenblatt,* a Jew's sheet, a term used by anti-Semites in describing liberal papers under Jewish ownership. (See Hertzberg, 1959, p. 203.)

42. Pawel, *Labyrinth of Exile,* 1989, p. 327.

43. It should be noted that Ahad Ha'am arrived at the first congress with grave misgivings about political Zionism, describing himself as "a mourner at a wedding." He was highly critical of Herzl's approach to the Jewish question and never attended subsequent congresses.

44. Herzl, *Diaries,* 1960, p. 586.

45. Pawel, *Labyrinth of Exile,* 1989, p. 333.

46. At that time women were commonly denied the right to vote. In Britain, for example, women only won a complete franchise in 1928.

47. Ibid., p. 584.

48. De Haas, *Theodore Herzl,* 1927, p. 173.

49. Herzl, *Diaries,* 1960, p. 584.

50. Elon, *Herzl,* 1975, p. 244.

51. Ibid., p. 581.

52. Pawel, *Labyrinth of Exile,* 1989, p. 367.

53. Herzl, *Diaries,* 1960, p. 696.

54. Ibid., p. 742.

55. Ibid., p. 743.

56. Ibid., p. 755.

57. Pawel, *Labyrinth of Exile,* 1989, p. 378.

58. Herzl, *Diaries,* 1960, p. 1093.

59. Ibid., p. 1128.

60. Ibid., p. 1116.

61. Pawel, *Labyrinth of Exile*, 1989, p. 446.

62. Herzl, *Diaries*, 1960, p. 1135.

63. Ibid., p. 1135.

64. Ibid., p. 1190.

65. As an organized opposition grouping, the Democratic Zionist Faction was short-lived. It merged into the general opposition to Herzl that arose in the following (Sixth) Congress.

66. Pawel, *Labyrinth of Exile*, 1989, p. 453. The term *mizrahi* means eastern, but in this context it is an acronym for *merkaz ruach*, spiritual center.

67. Ibid., p. 453.

68. Weizmann, *Trial and Error*, 1949, p. 63.

69. Herzl, *Diaries*, 1960, p. 644.

70. Pawel, *Labyrinth of Exile*, 1989, p. 483.

71. Herzl, *Diaries*, 1960, p. 1446.

72. Ibid., p. 1473.

73. Elon, *Herzl*, 1975, p. 373.

74. Lindemann, *Jew Accused*, 1991, p. 154.

75. Pawel, *Labyrinth of Exile*, 1989, p. 495.

76. Herzl, *Diaries*, 1960, p. 1514.

77. Ibid., p. 1526.

78. Ibid., p. 1530.

79. As quoted by Almog, *Zionism*, 1982, p. 203.

80. Ironically, many years later, when a strong Jewish state would debate whether to cede territory to the Palestinians, the orthodox would proclaim that Palestine is, by divine decree, indivisible, whereas secular descendants of the "Zion Zionists" would be more accommodating. However, the matter is not black and white, for a large number of socialist Zionists also supported the Uganda proposal. See Frankel, *Prophecy and Politics*, 1981, p. 322.

81. The actual number of those voting and their preferences are subject to dispute. For example, Vital asserts that, in reality, there were 611 (not 592) delegates in all, with 292 voting for the resolution, 176 voting against and 143 abstaining. See Vital, *Zionism*, 1982, p. 302.

82. Ibid., p. 1552.

83. Pawel, *Labyrinth of Exile*, 1989, p. 509.

84. Bein, *Theodore Herzl*, 1940, p. 463.

85. Ibid., p. 464.

86. Ibid., p. 464.

87. See S. Tzemach, *First Year*, 1965.

88. Herzl, *Diaries*, 1960, p. 804.

89. Elon, *Herzl*, 1975, p. 390.

90. Pawel, *Labyrinth of Exile*, 1989, p. 514.

91. Herzl, *Diaries,* 1960, p. 1603.

92. Ibid., p. 1603.

93. Pawel, *Labyrinth of Exile,* 1989, p. 531.

94. Almog, *Zionism,* 1982, p. 129.

95. The mainstream orthodox, adhering to the Mizrachi party, remained in the Zionist fold.

Chapter 4

The Second Aliyah: 1904–1914

PIONEER WORKERS

At the onset of the twentieth century, life for Russian Jews took a distinct turn
for the worse. Almost one in five became severely impoverished as incomes
drastically declined.[1] This resulted from a marked increase in the Jewish population at a time when Jews were confined to areas with limited job prospects and
from the displacement, through industrialization, of traditional Jewish crafts,
such as tailoring and shoemaking. The fall in living standards coincided with an
upsurge in general social turmoil, which culminated in the October 1905 Revolution.

Both in the years immediately prior to the revolution and in the period
shortly thereafter, when reactionary forces regrouped to undermine the democratic reforms, a series of pogroms swept through the country. The first one
took place in April 1903 in Kishinev. Later, in September of the same year, violence broke out in Homel. Then in October 1905, at the height of the revolutionary fervor, approximately 690 separate pogroms, mainly in the Ukraine,
were recorded. All told, an estimated 876 Jews were slaughtered. Faced with
such tribulations, many Jews decided to put Russia behind them. Between 1904
and 1914, approximately a quarter of the Jewish population, numbering 1.2
million, migrated, mostly to the United States.

The Zionist Movement in Russia did not encourage Jews to migrate en masse
to Palestine, for it was then generally believed that such a course of action was
not feasible. Nonetheless, between 1904 and 1914, a large body of Jews actually
did settle there. Estimates of the number of migrants vary. Some sources report
a floor of 20,000[2] while others suggest that there may have been as many as
40,000.[3] Whatever the true figure, there is no doubt that in the period in question, a significant increase in the Jewish presence in Palestine occurred, for at
the 1904 base year, the Jewish population stood at only 55,000.

The Jewish migratory influx into Palestine between 1904 and 1914 became known as the Second Aliyah, as opposed to the First Aliyah of 1882–1903. As with the First Aliyah, most Second Aliyah migrants were non-Zionist orthodox Jews who reinforced the presence of the old religious Yishuv. Perhaps a quarter, or at most a third of all the newcomers were young Zionists. Yet when the term "Second Aliyah" is used, it refers specifically to the latter category because it was essentially the actions of the young idealistic settlers that drastically altered the course of the New Yishuv's development.

In contrast to many First Aliyah migrants, who journeyed to Palestine within the confines of organized groups supported by Hovevei Zion societies, those of the Second Aliyah almost all arrived as individuals. Some came during the Russian-Japanese War to avoid military service and were known in Palestine as "the Japanese." Others sought refuge from pogroms, escape from police persecution for involvement in seditious activity or relief from endemic poverty. However, a large majority set foot in Eretz Israel fired with unbounded enthusiasm for the national cause. Although most were overwhelmingly secular in outlook, many originated from very religious families imbued with a love of Israel and a longing for Zion. A third of the men had studied in a *yeshiva* (rabbinical seminary) and over half had acquired an excellent knowledge of Hebrew even before leaving home.[4] For instance, David Ben Gurion (Israel's first prime minister), who migrated to Palestine in 1906, gave a rousing speech in Hebrew a few days after his arrival.[5] About 13 percent were sons of rabbis, cantors, ritual slaughterers or teachers of religion.[6] On the other hand, some hailed from assimilated families and spoke only Russian. Joseph Trumpeldor, who became a legendary Zionist hero, was one of them. In general, the Zionist pioneers were young (many were less than twenty years old), unmarried and from the lower middle class.

Typically, they decided to migrate to Palestine after some involvement in political activity and/or after extensive readings and discussions regarding Zionism and Jewish affairs. There does not seem to have been any single common factor that galvanized them; instead, various separate influences were operative. Among these was a feeling of shame regarding the Jewish humiliation experienced in the pogroms. Many also recoiled from the seemingly parasitic economic lifestyle of diaspora Jewry. Being under the sway of revolutionary dogma, they upheld that only manual labor was free of the taint of exploitation. To restore Jewish honor and self-respect, they considered it essential that a strong Jewish working class be established. This could not materialize in the diaspora and certainly not in Russia, where even Jewish employers preferred hiring gentiles.

The malaise permeating Zionism, and the blow to the organization's morale following the Uganda episode, were also instrumental in persuading young people that it was incumbent on them not to bide their time in exile any longer. A loathing of a perceived abandonment of traditional Zionism—which they took to include the centrality of Palestine, the revival of Hebrew and agricultural colonization—induced a reaction in Jewish youth that aroused them to rebel against the Zionist establishment. Many were convinced that the movement stood on the brink of collapse. Far from this leading to apathy, the more stout-hearted among them echoed Chaim Brenner's sentiments, that "if we are the last generation and that if history has decreed that we have no national future, at least we shall not abandon the final battle and we shall man the wall to the last."[7] Such views were bolstered by a 1905 proclamation issued by Joseph Vitkin, calling on diaspora youth to migrate to Palestine without further ado to work in the Jewish settlements and urban areas. A similar appeal was made by Ussishkin, except that he thought in terms of youth volunteering to serve in Palestine for only a limited period of time. These, plus a steady flow of literature from two newly founded Zionist workers' parties in Palestine, which described, in grandiose terms, the efforts of the young Jewish laborers already there, all left their imprint. Vitkin's *cri de coeur* was particularly telling in that it appealed to youth to rally behind practical Zionism, not on the basis of Jewish distress in exile but in order to rescue work efforts in Palestine, as the following extract indicates:

Awaken, awaken, youth of Israel. Arise to the aid of the nation. Our nation is dying. In just a while, its land will be lost to us forever. Hurry, hasten to its rescue! Prepare yourselves.... Forget all that has been dear to you until now. Put aside everything forever and without any hesitation come forward to perform the national task. You are not as superfluous as you are accustomed to think. You are vital to the nation and land just as air is for breathing. Equip yourselves with unbridled love for the nation and land, with the love of freedom and labor and with infinite patience and come. Renew the days of the Biluim with greater vigour lest we perish.[8]

In many ways, Vitkin's proclamation appealed to revolutionary Zionist youth who believed that to effect a rejuvenation of the Jewish nation, a new breed of Zionists had to supplant existing ones who were long on loquaciousness but short on action. The needs of the hour demanded youth yearning to attain self-realization in pioneering. As Even-Shoshan so eloquently put it, "The revolutionary fervor of the Second Aliyah pioneers was cast in the mode of self-realization. They were revolutionaries but in an original sense. They first of all sought to alter themselves and by means of personal example, to influence others. And in the final analysis to bring about a change in the reality of the Yishuv."[9]

Among the first to go to Palestine, was a small band from Homel, numbering fourteen, which had participated in defending Jewish lives and property during the September 1903 pogrom. Some had even been wounded. Had members of that group not fled Russia, they would undoubtedly have been arraigned with thirty-six fellow Homel Jews who were charged by the Kiev Department of Justice with assuming an aggressive attitude, necessitating an armed military response.[10] They arrived in Jaffa on December 5, 1903.

With the exception of the Homel group and a few others, such as a band of thirty from Rostov, not only did Second Aliyah migrants journey to Eretz Israel as isolated individuals, but in most instances, they encountered discouragement from one source or another. Sometimes this arose even from within the ranks of fellow Zionists. After all, did not Ber Borochov, the Zionist socialist theoretician, postulate that a migratory process would inevitably eventuate when irresistible political and sociological forces would drive the Jewish people into Palestine? Why then trouble oneself prematurely with "artificial" migration?[11] As difficult as it was in coping with disparaging comments from intimate local associates, be they family members, friends or general communal functionaries, such reproaches were nothing compared with the cutting rebukes directed against them, first by newly disillusioned migrants in the process of leaving Palestine and then, by established First Aliyah settlers. Berl Katznelson on reaching Jaffa, received a distinctly unfriendly reception. He bitterly recalled, "With every oncoming boat, people left their work and ran to the port to greet the immigrants. And what greeted us is beyond description. The first question was 'Why did you come?' After that they emitted a series of derogatory comments concerning Eretz Israel, as well as witticisms and mockery about us dimwits. Such was our initial welcome."[12] Similarly, Natan Hofshi remembered his first day in Jaffa, when he entered the dining room of Haim Baruch's hotel. "The noise was deafening and grew louder still as youngsters rose to greet us newcomers and to make space for us to sit down. From every side questions rained down on us, mostly in Yiddish. They left a nasty impression both on account of their tone and the language in which they were conveyed. Sitting next to me was a tall lad with an upright bearing. Hershl Schleifer was his name. He was a guard at the vineyard at Rechovot. He wore a black shirt with red embroidery. He turned to me and asked 'Why have you come? Have you any money left over? A boat is sailing today from Jaffa to Russia. You had better return home before you are stranded here penniless.'... I cannot recall anything about the contents of my first meal in Eretz Israel, for I was very upset by that encounter. As I was told, everyone in that room was set on leaving the country."[13]

On arrival at Jaffa, the young newcomers would most likely spend a night or two at a small, Jewish-owned and -managed hotel and then walk to one of the Jewish settlements, such as Rishon Letzion, Rehovot or Petah Tikva. There, bearing their satchels containing their entire worldly belongings, they confronted a situation that both dismayed and disgusted them. Contrary to their expectations, instead of being greeted by welcoming Zionist stalwarts, delighted at the arrival of young and eager reinforcements, they were usually met with undisguised hostility. Years of being pampered and corrupted by Rothschild's patronage had the effect of transforming most First Aliyah settlers from a group of starry-eyed national visionaries into a coterie of gentleman farmers entirely devoid of any vestiges of their earlier idealism. Very few worked their farms directly, relying instead on foremen to supervise a labor force made up almost entirely of Arab peasants, some of whom even resided in the settlement itself. As the Hebrew writer, Tzemach recorded, the Rishon Letzion farmer in whose house he managed to secure lodgings, spent the entire day at home in his dressing gown playing cards with his neighbors.[14] The womenfolk, bedecked in the latest Paris fashions, delegated the housekeeping chores to their Arab maids. Most of their grown-up sons were studying in Paris, where they hoped to remain, while their daughters who were still at home, spoke French. As Dr. Arthur Ruppin noted, the near total absence of farmers' sons conveyed the impression that the settlements were "homes for the aged."[15]

Almost all the farmers were ardent Ugandan Territorialists, who had given up on Hebrew and who had reverted to Yiddish. They were totally out of sympathy with the aspirations of the newcomers, neither understanding them nor concerning themselves with their plight. Differences between the migrants of the two Aliyot were quite fundamental. Those of the First Aliyah went to Palestine at a fairly advanced age. They were religious, and, apart from their prior Zionist beliefs, they were essentially of a conservative frame of mind. By contrast, the Second Aliyah arrivals were rather young, secularists and enthused with socialist visions. The clear-cut differentiation and separation of old and new settler worked to forge close ties among the newcomers, which in time fortified them in their resolve to endure all the hardships that they encountered.

Those who appeared in the very early stages of the Second Aliyah probably bore the main brunt of it. They had no acquaintances, contacts or other forerunners who could assist them and had to turn alone to one farmer after another, begging to be hired. Securing employment was no easy feat. The young job seeker, who often seemed as if he had just stepped out of a yeshiva, would present himself at a farmer's doorstep, or, alternatively, he would rise early in the morning to join a band of Arab workers assembled at some point, awaiting work selection. Either way, the process was invariably a degrading one.

At home, the farmer berated the job applicant, making fun of him in front of his entire family. When Eliyahu Even-Tov first went in search of work in Petah Tikva, he stood on the threshold of a farmer's abode while the farmer and his family carried on with their evening meal. Between sips of drink and bites of food, the farmer cast his eyes on him, examining him from head to toe, as if Even-Tov were of some rare species. Eventually, speaking in Yiddish, the farmer grunted, "You idiots. This is the land of the Ishmaelites (Arabs) and not the land of Israel. If fellows like you would only go to America where you would make a fortune, then even here things would not be so bad." As Even-Tov later wrote, "Twenty-five years have passed since then and still within my heart, there lingers the painful image of my standing alongside that door."[16]

At the labor pick-up point, the young Jewish worker was generally ignored. If he was lucky, a farmer might deign to take him on for the day, pending a report from Arab workers toiling alongside him. Little concern was shown for the youngster's general welfare. This is clearly illustrated by Neta Herpaz's experience on his first workday. "When everything was finished, the Arab workers invited me to sit in the wagon and return with them to the settlement. They loaded a plough with its sharp blade facing upward, which they covered with a sack. Then, with devious courtesy, they suggested that I sit on the sack. I was so tired and in need of a rest that I hurriedly clambered onto the wagon and sat where they indicated. The moment the wagon budged, I experienced a terrible pain. The plough's blade sliced into my flesh and blood trickled down my trousers. However, I saw no point in censoring the Arabs and in any case, I could not speak Arabic.... When we arrived at the winegrower's courtyard, I rushed over to a faucet to wash my wounded foot. Opposite me stood the farmer and his wife, while the workers were relating how they had tricked me. The conversation was punctuated by bursts of laughter on the part of both farmer and wife. It was obvious that they enjoyed the 'joke' and did nothing to reprimand the culprits, nor did they provide me with even a word of comfort. ... The insult seared into my inner soul. Never in my wildest imagination did I expect such a first encounter with a Hebrew winegrower."[17]

As in most cases, there were exceptions to the rule, for a small minority of farmers were decent and kind to the Jewish workers. They were soon identified and recommended to the newcomers. They did whatever they could to help them, but their numbers were small, as was their communal influence.

Work hours were seemingly endless and, sometimes, next to no time was left for newcomers to stock up on food provisions. Their general accommodations were to say the least, stark. They either slept on rooftops, under thatch coverings or in shared crowded rooms. No matter where, they were plagued by mites, fleas, flies, mosquitoes, mice, lice, scorpions, snakes and simply dirt. Furniture was improvised through the use of old packing cases and tins. Only one hot meal a day was secured, and that consisted of very basic ingredients. Some broth, tea, tinned fish, olives and pita bread were the staples. Their state of health was frequently undermined by bouts of dysentery, typhus and, of course, malaria. Practically everyone succumbed to malarial attacks, leaving them in a feverish and enervated state. Usually, no doctor was readily available and, in extremely critical cases, the sick were loaded onto pack animals to be transported to a hospital. Many died en route.

THE CONQUEST OF LABOR

The key challenge that the Second Aliyah migrants faced was the "Conquest of Labor." This was a two-pronged challenge. One part related to the personal adaptation of the newcomer to a life of physical toil. Almost instantly, the young migrant had to demonstrate that he was capable of maintaining a sustained and vigorous work effort. Workers' memoirs frequently recall instances of Jewish overseers surrounding Jewish tyros with hardened fellahs (peasants). They would then goad the Arabs to till at breakneck speed, by challenging them to show the "Muscovites" (as the young migrants were derisively called) the fellahs' true work mettle. Rising to the bait, the fellahs would start hoeing frenziedly, leaving the hapless Jewish workers trailing behind. Both as a point of pride and fearing for their jobs, the Jewish workers somehow or other had to mobilize all their remaining strength to stay abreast. Discovering that they had hit on a ready means of raising the work tempo, the overseers made a habit of engineering such "competitions." Fortunately for the newcomers, the Arab workers grew tired of the foremen's machinations, which, of course, also rebounded against their interests. Unofficial pacts were soon concluded between them and the Jewish youngsters to abide by more reasonable work paces.

The second aspect of the Conquest of Labor had deep sociological ramifications. At issue was the general nature of the development of the New Yishuv. The First Aliyah settlers had come to terms with an economic structure in which farm plantations were based on the exploitation of cheap, casual labor. Although socially undesirable, such a practice did not in itself threaten the Zionist enterprise. What did undermine it was the fact that while the farm owners were Jewish, virtually all their employees were Arabs. On average, each farmer employed the services of three Arab families, which meant that literally thousands of Arabs worked in the settlements.[18] A situation was evolving, which to all intents and purposes, was a replica of the colonial settler societies that existed in Algeria, Kenya and in other European colonies. Had such a state of affairs persisted, the Arab natives would sooner or later have overthrown their alien taskmasters and a Jewish state in Palestine would have been no more than a pipe dream. To their credit, the Second Aliyah migrants fully grasped all the implications of the paucity of Jewish labor, not only in existing settlements but within the country at large. It was obvious to them that unless the New Yishuv were a self-contained unit—in the sense that all the major factors of production, that is, land, labor and capital, were firmly in Jewish hands—Jewish national autonomy would never be realized. Even if their political prognosis was erroneous, they and the Zionist movement generally, would certainly not have wanted a Jewish state based on the South African Apartheid mode. That would have stymied all efforts to "normalize" the Jewish people and to eliminate Borochov's inverted Jewish social pyramid.[19] It not only would have deprived the Zionists of a moral claim to Jewish sovereignty in Palestine, but would also have limited the capacity of the state to absorb the Jewish masses.

Most of the Second Aliyah migrants came to Palestine precisely to address the problem of Jewish labor. They were unrelenting in their demands that Arab labor be avoided at all costs. Arab labor was referred to as "foreign work." In Hebrew, the term *foreign work (avodah zarah)* literally means "idolatry," a crime that in biblical days was subject to capital punishment. In pursuit of their objectives, they were prepared to resort to physical violence; on occasion, they did. Force was sometimes even employed within their own ranks, when, for instance, a worker's home was vandalized because Arab workers paved its flooring.[20] The poor worker in question, who certainly could not afford to have engaged more expensive Jewish labor, was totally beside himself. Such an incident revealed a blind and insensitive fanaticism that characterized some Second Aliyah migrants.

Grape harvesting at Rishon Letzion, at the beginning of the twentieth century (Central Zionist Archives).

In time, an ideology of sorts, which elevated the status of manual labor, evolved. A prime mover in this regard was Aharon David Gordon, who in 1904 at the age of forty-eight, left an administrative post in Russia to work as an agricultural laborer in Palestine. Gordon propounded a general philosophy that was somewhat shrouded in mysticism. He maintained that an attachment to agricultural labor, involving direct contact with nature, is spiritually uplifting. In communing with nature, suggested Gordon, one gains an appreciation of the glory of creation and, in a sense, one participates in its ongoing process.

As for general social issues, Gordon believed that to realize a just society, what mattered most was not a country's economic or social system but the nature of its individuals. Without individual rectification of behavior, mankind as a whole would be beyond redemption. Such an emphasis on personal responsibility had a marked appeal to Second Aliyah migrants who arrived in Palestine as isolated individuals. It was also of great comfort to them that someone of his age could so radically alter the course of his own life to toil alongside them.

Partly taking their cue from Gordon, Second Aliyah migrants made a fetish of manual labor. Their problem was that their views were not shared by the existing settlement farmers. After abandoning their original Zionist objectives, First Aliyah settlers had embraced personal gain as their sole concern. In that regard, it was clearly in their interests to hire Arabs as opposed to Jews. The former were willing and able to work for a pittance. (In fact, they had access to their own farm land, run by their families, so their wage earnings were merely supplementary.) Jewish workers, who were totally inexperienced, talked in terms of earnings consistent with minimum cultural standards. What is more, they were neither exceptionally compliant nor respectful. Their excessive show of Jewish nationalistic zeal, combined with their secularism, irritated their employers. Farmers certainly disliked the Second Aliyah migrants' tendency to spend their evenings in political discussions followed by endless rounds of singing and dancing until the early hours of the morning. "How could such people be relied on to put in a day's work?" they would frequently ask.

The antagonism between the Jewish farmers and the young Second Aliyah workers reached a flashpoint in Petah Tikva. Most newcomers made Petah Tikva, their first port of call, and the number of young Jewish workers there gradually rose. The farmers were particularly concerned about the free-thinking ideas that the workers introduced, and were worried lest their own children be influenced by them. In December 1905, when news of the October pogroms in Russia reached Palestine, the newly arrived migrants decided to forsake a planned Hanukkah party for a meeting of solidarity with pogrom victims. Displeased by the secular workers' behavior at assemblies and festive evenings, in which even girls participated, the orthodox members of Petah Tikva's council opposed the holding of the planned assembly.[21] Nonetheless, the function was held, even though Arab guards were posted to prevent a crowd from gathering. The council was affronted by such a blatant violation of its authority. When, a few days later, one of the workers desecrated the Sabbath by smoking, it was decided that the young workers finally had to be brought into line. They were provided with an ultimatum. Either they signed an agreement promising to abide by all the precepts of the Jewish religion, to refrain from participating in public assemblies and to uphold all settlement regulations, or else they would no longer be permitted to live and work there. The workers, who felt that their rights to free expression and democracy were being undermined, refused to comply and, as a result, a work ban was imposed on them. For the next few months, a sort of shadow war ensued. An attenuated number of workers remained in the settlement, assisted by a few of Petah Tikva's more tolerant and independent-minded members. Eventually, although never canceled, the ban became a dead issue.

Usually, when work was obtained in one settlement or another, it was of short duration. With the fulfillment of their assignments, workers either sought alternative employment in the same settlement, or, more realistically, they would try their luck elsewhere. This meant that most Second Aliyah migrants led a rather nomadic form of existence, wandering about as itinerant workers from one settlement to the next. Many accepted their peripatetic lifestyle with good grace, regarding it as a golden opportunity not only to travel throughout the length and breadth of the New Yishuv but also to promote the cause of Jewish labor in as many settlements as possible. A few, like Yona

Horvitz, even discerned that they were overcome by a wanderlust that "impelled many of the Second Aliyah workers to always set out somewhere else to start afresh. That hidden force made me suddenly abandon my dear friends and without any thought for the morrow, I would once more enter into a new life with unknown gray areas."[22] The young workers would sometimes team up with a few newfound friends to pool their resources into a *communa* (collective) as a means of providing themselves with a rough-and-ready form of social security. When the groups inevitably disbanded, the individuals would go their separate ways, perhaps linking with yet others in their never-ending quest for greener pastures.

Hadera was considered a rather important way station. The farmers there were particularly prone to malaria and, in consequence, there was a widespread loss of life. With their attitude to the young workers being somewhat more positive than those of most other settlers, many Second Aliyah migrants regarded it as a point of honor to put in some time there. The harsh conditions that prevailed in Hadera were to some extent alleviated by the establishment of a workers' kitchen, which supplied laborers with a hot evening meal. Workers' kitchens were commonplace in many settlements. In addition to their catering function, they also served as a cultural and political venue. However, they were often of a limited life span either because of mismanagement or because of seasonal membership losses, which adversely affected their revenue. A classic description of a workers' kitchen in Hadera is contained in Zvi Lieberman's memoirs.

> The room was spacious with many windows, as in a synagogue. All the windowpanes were smashed and the rickety window frames swayed in the wind, opening and shutting with a noisy clamor. It was evening. The workers were seated at long tables. Only a few managed to change from their workclothes.... With much impatience, stimulated by pangs of hunger following a day's work, they glanced at a small hatch linked to the kitchen. Before the server appeared, David Bader handed out quinine tablets. Those aware of the implications of contracting malaria swallowed two or even three pills.... The main course was groat or lentil soup, which either lacked salt or was far too salty. The soup contained foul, yellowish-blue liquid in which floated a few groats.... After the soup, there was porridge, made from the same water and groats and with oil and salt.... Someone remarked that it was once again burnt. Everyone then shouted "railway train," while placing their plates adjacent to one another as if they were miniature coaches. The hall was astir with noise, clanging and humming.[23]

On that occasion, humiliated by the fun made of her cooking, the young woman who daily put in twelve hours of work to ensure that her comrades were given a warm meal, rushed out of the kitchen to fall on her bed, where she wept uncontrollably. Meanwhile, the workers satiated their hunger with bread and then had tea speckled with oil globules, which was poured into cracked and rusty iron mugs. Finally, the "last course" commenced. It was the hora. "It was danced with enthusiasm, with warmth, with fire, inspired by a superior spirit. The dance seemed to liberate one from all suffering, from all blows. The dance with hand on shoulder, draws hearts together and purifies the soul. One is freed from all encumbrances, at one with one's lofty dream."[24] It seems that dancing the hora was generally felt to be cathartic. A similar appraisal was given by a member of Degania. "It was not simply a dance but a kind of wordless shouting, a relief from all that amassed in the heart. There was something about the dance that gave rise to conciliation after bursts of anger or after blunt exchanges between comrades. The hora seemed like an open book from which I could discern people's hardships of life."[25]

Without underrating Hadera, the locality that by far exerted the most magnetic attraction was the Galilee, which contained some training farms, as well as small rural homesteads, operated by former workers who provided the traveler with a warm welcome. With cereal cultivation in the Galilee being the norm, farming there corresponded with Second Aliyah migrants' preconceived views as to what constituted the essence of horticulture. The remoteness and exposure to Arab attacks of the frontier-type Jewish settlements, added to the Galilee's allure, as did its appealing terrain and enchanting views of Lake Kinneret (the Sea of Galilee). The romanticism of the Galilee resembled the idealizations, in North America, of the Wild West. Practically every young worker wished to make a pilgrimage to the Galilee, where, in time, the Second Aliyah's leading settlements were founded.

POLITICAL PARTIES AND OTHER ASSOCIATIONS

Faced with both feelings of isolation and alienation from the First Aliyah establishment, the Second Aliyah workers formed organizations of their own, which reflected their aspirations and which sought to ameliorate their distressing material conditions. In short succession, two separate political parties came into being. The first, *Hapoel Hatzair* (the Young Worker), was founded in October 1905 by nine inaugural members, who included Eliezer Shohat, Aharon David Gordon, Shlomo Tzemach and Sara Malkin. Although Hapoel Hatzair believed that the growth of a strong Jewish working class was a Zionist prerequisite, it neither propagated socialism nor did it advance the notion of a class struggle. Instead, it concentrated its efforts on practical ways to assist workers, such as the creation of cooperative workers' kitchens and stores, sick funds, labor exchanges and workers' libraries.

A month later, in November 1905, *Poalei Zion* (Workers of Zion) was established, which prided itself on having full bona fide Marxist credentials. Initially, it contained two factions. One headed by Yitzhak Ben-Zvi, insisted on the primacy of socialism, while the other led by Ben Gurion, placed more weight on nationalism. The party adhered to the international labor movement and celebrated May Days with a flurry of red flags.

At its inception, Hapoel Hatzair recruited ninety members, Poalei Zion sixty. By 1910, their combined membership hovered around the five hundred mark.

Mention should also be made of a third group of workers who were unattached to any party but who were nonetheless actively involved in Jewish labor affairs. The nonparty workers seemed to share a common approach and some saw them as belonging to a "nonparty party."

Each of the two official parties fielded its own journal and propagandists, vying for membership by stressing the relevance of their seemingly distinct platforms. (When in Jaffa, members lodged at separate hostels, that of Spector for Poalei Zion and Haim Baruch's inn for Hapoel Hatzair.) Yet in practice, there was little to distinguish them. Poalei Zion's supposedly anti–free enterprise bias, did not prevent it from echoing Hapoel Hatzair's views, that the Jewish state in the making had to depend on a strong and dynamic capitalist base.[26]

On the trade union front, in 1906, an association of farm workers in the Galilee, known as *Hahoresh* (the Ploughman), was formed. It represented farm worker interests but its total membership was very limited, with over half concentrated in the Jewish Colonial Association farm at Sejera. A similar association was formed for workers on the coastal plain.

DEVELOPMENT OF ZIONIST INSTITUTIONS

A number of Zionist institutions, which provided important props for the overall development of the New Yishuv, were either consolidated or formed within the Second Aliyah period. In 1903, the Anglo-Palestine Bank, which was first named the Anglo-Palestine Company (APAC), opened its doors in Jaffa. Headed by Zalmon Levontin (one of the founders of Rishon Letzion), it functioned as a subsidiary of the Zionist movement's Jewish Colonial Trust, which Herzl had so assiduously promoted. Also in 1903, the Sixth Zionist Congress authorized the commencement of operations of the Jewish National Fund (JNF). Although the fund had been founded a couple of years earlier, it had remained dormant for want of its minimum capital target of £200,000. Congress approval for the activation of the JNF enabled the Zionists to purchase more land for Jewish settlement. At the Eighth Zionist Congress in 1907, a Palestine Department (of the Small Actions Committee), chaired by Otto Warburg and situated in Berlin, was established. With a quarter of the entire Zionist budget at its disposal, it decided to set up a branch office in Jaffa, under the directorship of Dr. Arthur Ruppin and with Dr. Yaakov Thon as its first secretary. The opening of the Palestine office, in early 1908, constituted a turning point in general Zionist strategy. In Herzl's day, practically the entire thrust of its operations was on diplomatic overtures. Now the emphasis switched to fairly modest, yet more productive activities, involving the gradual acquisition of more Palestinian land and the establishment of new settlements.

Both Drs. Ruppin and Thon were ardent Zionists in the true sense of the term and lent their total support to the New Yishuv. Dr. Ruppin in particular, who had only recently joined the movement, immediately grasped the importance of ensuring the effective integration of Jewish workers within the settlement community. Consequently, he did everything possible to facilitate their absorption and their transition to self-sustaining farmers. In 1907, before taking up full-time residence in Palestine, Dr. Ruppin was sent to the country on a fact-finding mission. Having published a book in 1904, titled *The Jews of Today*, described by Alex Bein, as "the point of departure for all sociological literature on Jewish life that has been written since,"[27] and having served in the Berlin-based Bureau of Jewish Statistics (where Dr. Thon was his secretary), Dr. Ruppin was eminently qualified for the task at hand. After a six-month investigation, he presented his report to the Small Actions Committee. His main recommendations focused on the urgent need to obtain more land in both Judea and in the Galilee. For that purpose, he proposed the formation of a body to be charged with parceling out the newly acquired land to Jews, on easy financial terms. For those with no agricultural knowledge, Dr. Ruppin wished to establish a training farm. He thought in terms of affording suitable trainees who had obtained a few years of practical exposure to farming, with the opportunity of becoming tenant farmers. In 1908, accepting Dr. Ruppin's submissions, the Actions Committee formed the Palestine Land Development Company (PLDC) with a commission to prepare JNF land for farming and to provide novices with schooling in agricultural techniques. Finally, in 1907 an Olive Tree Fund was inaugurated. It was responsible for planting a forest of olive trees as a memorial to Herzl and was placed under the control of the Palestine Department. Up until then, olives had been rarely cultivated by Jewish farmers, since they take eight to ten years to produce their first yields, as opposed to grapes, oranges and almonds, which take half as long. At the outset of its operations, the Olive Tree project was shrouded in controversy. The agronomist Moshe Berman, who was put in charge, began by employing Arabs. This sparked an immediate reaction on the part of Jewish workers, who were particularly affronted by the fact that of all employers, a Zionist body was flouting the principle of the Conquest of Labor. From Petah Tikva, a group of workers, known as the Romni group,[28] hurried to the Beit Arif nursery (where the forest's saplings were being cultivated) and demanded that Berman hire them. Berman, who explained that Arabs were employed only because Jewish labor was seemingly not forthcoming, complied.

THE EXPANSION OF JEWISH SETTLEMENTS, THE FIRST FARMING COLLECTIVES AND THE FIRST KVUTZA (COLLECTIVE FARM)

On assuming his Palestine appointment, Dr. Ruppin decided to establish a Palestine Land Development Company farm on land alongside Lake Kinneret. He was particularly interested in fostering settlements in that general area, since it was rather sparsely populated and therefore offered a chance for Jews to maintain a relatively large presence there. More to the point, he had great hopes of eventually increasing the Jewish population on the coastal plain to 200,000 and the numbers around Tiberias to 15,000. He envisioned that the two areas would be linked by a narrow band of Jewish-owned land. On that basis, he reasoned, a convincing case could ultimately be presented to the sultan for some form of Jewish autonomy.[29] The farmland alongside Lake Kinneret was originally known as Daleike-Umm Juni, but Dr. Ruppin, at the suggestion of his Hebrew teacher, Shmuel Agnon,[30] renamed the estate "Kinneret."[31] The agronomist Moshe Berman was selected to manage the enterprise. He, in turn, enlisted a party of eight workers (the Romni group), who had previously served under him at the Beit Arif tree nursery. On June 8, 1908, they took possession of the site, settling in a one-room, ruined khan (see Glossary) situated on a hill-top.[32] After cleaning it out, they organized within it a kitchen, a dining room and a first aid station. Their sleeping quarters were on the khan's flat roof. Initially, meals were prepared by each member on a roster basis but given their poor cooking abilities, they decided to overrule their previous decision not to involve female participation because of the generally harsh conditions and lack of security that prevailed. They appealed to Sara Malkin to join them and after some hesitation, she agreed. Upon her arrival, a semblance of normality returned to their lives. Although one could not say the same for that of Sara Malkin. She slept in the khan itself, which lacked windows, a floor and a ceiling. As she later recalled, "at night, mice often tried to gnaw at my fingers and the hissing of snakes interrupted my sleep."[33]

The workers were provided both with full board plus a monthly cash allowance. In addition, they were offered an end-of-year bonus equal to the value of the wheat yield on five dunams of land. At first, an atmosphere of full cooperation between worker and management prevailed. Berman lived with his employees on an equal basis, eating and sleeping with them. Despite the usual hazards of widespread malaria and of constant pilfering and attacks on the part of surrounding Arabs, farm work proceeded steadily. The soil was prepared, fields were sown and a stable was erected. All this effort called for more labor, and by the beginning of 1909, forty-three workers were engaged. Some of the newcomers worked in teams of independent contractors, undertaking to complete specific tasks, which partially met their aspirations for a degree of worker autonomy.

Contrary to Berman's expectations, the first year did not end well. A large deficit was recorded and relations between Berman and his workers soured. The latter occurred partly as a result of the increased work force, which reduced intimate ties between Berman and the workers and which induced Berman to assert his role as chief executive. In the process, Berman was seen as becoming more autocratic and less inclined to accept any vestige of joint decision making. Matters came to a head when Arab laborers were taken on to help complete the threshing. (A number of Jewish workers were stricken with malaria and it was feared that large piles of cereal were likely to be soaked by impending rain.)

Faced with what was perceived as a blatant violation of the principle of hiring only Jewish labor, the original eight Romni workers, plus three more who joined them, withdrew to Hadera. Those who remained at Kinneret questioned Berman's general competence and suitability. Not knowing how to handle the situation, Berman appealed to Dr. Ruppin to come to his aid. Dr. Ruppin convened a meeting at Tiberias, where Berman and the workers could state their grievances on more neutral territory. The workers, through their association, Hahoresh, demanded Berman's immediate resignation and that the farm be worker controlled. As Ruppin recalled, they argued their case for self-management on the grounds that "the manager (Berman) with his salary and personal expenses on journeys etc., was an intolerable burden for the farm."[34] (A two-story house was eventually built for Berman and his family.)While Dr. Ruppin rejected the workers' general requests, he did provide an opportunity for at least some of them to farm on an independent basis, even if only for a limited period. In concrete terms, he expressed a willingness to place 1,500 dunam of Kinneret land, east of the Jordan (formerly Umm Juni, as-yet unconnected by any bridge), plus sufficient draft animals, tools and other essentials, at the disposal of a small group. This group, in turn, would be expected to work the land for a year. Besides monthly wage payments of forty-five francs per worker, the group would be entitled to half of the net profits. After giving the matter some consideration, Dr. Ruppin's offer was accepted and on December 1, 1909, six men and one woman formally entered into a contract with him. (One of the men was Y. Bloch who was summoned from the Romni group then in Hadera, to join the party.) Taking possession of some shacks put at their disposal by neighboring Arabs, the group set to work. Their efforts bore fruit in that at the end of the agricultural cycle, a net profit of 4,000 francs (£160) was realized.

On discharging all its obligations, the group disbanded, with most heading for Merhavia, which had recently been purchased. As for Dr. Ruppin, having observed, with no small amount of gratification, that given sufficient incentives, the young workers could confidently be left to farm on their own, he decided to replicate the arrangement. This time, at Bloch's suggestion, he turned to the Romni group. They not only responded positively but expressed a desire to move to the Umm Juni site on a permanent basis. On October 28, 1910, ten men and two women arrived to take over the inventory and accommodations vacated by the first group. From the start, they lived together in a communal framework, with every member receiving the same monthly wage, paid by the Palestine Office. The concept of meeting everyone's needs in kind, in lieu of wages, had not yet been developed. In fact, the mother of the first baby was paid less than a full wage to offset time spent with her infant.[35] Specializing at first in grain, they renamed the site Degania (Cornflower).

Degania stands out in the history of the Zionist movement as its founding kibbutz. Although it has a legitimate claim to that position, in its formative years it really ought to be viewed as a small-scale kibbutz prototype. While exhibiting many of the qualitative characteristics of the kibbutzim that followed and while it was able to claim credit for some of the groundwork in kibbutz evolution, its small and intimate membership really endowed it with the features of an extended family. (The first true full-size kibbutz saw the light of day in 1922 at Ein Harod.) Degania's overall membership, which in time included Aharon David Gordon, grew slowly. By 1911 it contained fifteen comrades. When the first child was born, everyone related to it as if they had familial rights, picking it up without prior parental approval and bringing it to the dining room for all to behold and enjoy.[36] Within the first three years of its existence, the settlement had no formal organizational structure. All members would sit around a table to thrash out problems of the day. Only in 1913 did they elect a management committee composed of officials responsible for work allocation and other pressing matters. From the very beginning, the Romni veterans deposited their wages into a common pool but others, after meeting communal obligations, such as kitchen expenses, remained free to use their earnings as they saw fit. Complete consumer collectivization evolved gradually. It was fully realized in 1922 when personal wages were abolished and everyone received their basic requirements in kind.[37]

Constantly harassed by hostile neighbors, Degania experienced its first fatality in November 1913, with the murder of eighteen-year-old Moshe Barsky. On receiving news of Moshe's death, his father sent a letter from Russia to members of Degania. In it he wrote:

Dear Brothers! The unexpected occurred. We have suffered a terrible calamity. But I believe that your spirit will not flag and that you will not retreat, God Forbid! On the contrary, I hope that the memory of my late son will bestow upon you strength and courage to withstand all the difficulties in this Holy endeavor, until we realize our great ideal for which my son sacrificed his life and soul.[38]

Shortly thereafter, the father sent his other remaining son to Degania to take Moshe's place.[39] Members of Degania did indeed cherish Moshe's memory, for in 1915, Shmuel Dayan, one of the settlement's founders, named his first son after him. (Moshe Dayan was later to become Israel's chief of staff and defense minister.)

Conventional wisdom notwithstanding, Degania, the first *kvutza*, was certainly not the product of preconceived ideological beliefs. When at Kinneret and then at Hadera, the Romni group began to consider itself as a distinct and permanent collective, its members were not all of one mind as to the exact nature of its desired future. In fact, some were reluctant to accept Dr. Ruppin's offer to occupy Umm Juni in the first place, and only through Joseph Busel's persuasive powers did they all agree to do so.[40] (Busel was the group's most charismatic member. In 1918, he drowned in Lake Kinneret.) Not long after Degania's formation, dreams began to be floated of moving to a more distant area in what is now Syria. The group was intoxicated with the experience of opening up new tracts of land in outlying areas, thereafter to be handed over to more staid farmer settlers. To counter this tendency, Busel had to emphasize that unless

Early days at Degania (Central Zionist Archives).

the dreamers purged themselves of the impulse to uproot themselves, no pioneering assignment would ever be fully consummated.[41] If Yoseph Bratz's testimony is taken at face value, "The most important motivation for taking up work at Umm Juni (Degania) was the aspiration for self-labor, with independent responsibility—without there being any mastery and supervision from an external source."[42]

As Degania began to take shape, it came to occupy center stage as far as the young Second Aliyah workers were concerned. It attracted numerous visitors and delegations and played host to political party conferences and conventions. Over time, with the development of a kvutza ideology, Degania was perceived not simply as a means to reach a desired goal (self-worker management), but as an end in itself.

In Kinneret, on the other hand, general economic and social difficulties persisted. Having relinquished the best of its land to Degania, Kinneret went from one yearly deficit to another. Relations between Berman and the workers remained tense. In February 1911 matters came to a head. This was precipitated by the workers wishing to use one set of wagons more than Berman allowed so they could attend the funeral in Tiberias of one of their comrades struck down by yellow fever. Angered by what they perceived as Berman's insensitivity, the mourners set out on foot in pelting rain. On their return, they declared a strike, calling for Berman's removal. (Berl Katznelson was one of the strike leaders.) Dr. Ruppin was once again summoned, but on this occasion all the disputants

lost out. Both Berman and the striking workers were given their marching orders. They were replaced by the agronomist Yoel Golde and a new set of workers, but some of the newly dismissed laborers were also allowed to return. Then
in October 1912, the farm was entrusted to a handful of Americans, who belonged to an organization called *Haikar Hatzair* (the Young Farmer). Since
only four of its members arrived in Palestine, another eight hands who had formerly worked in Kinneret were recruited. A host of new farming techniques
and equipment was introduced. In effect, the first experiment in comprehensive
mixed farming was conducted. Unfortunately, crop damage caused by trespassing bedouin and the poor quality of Kinneret's soil took their toll. Within a
year, the Americans were forced to throw in the towel. Finally, a group of old-
timers, consisting of thirteen men and three women, were coaxed back to assume responsibility for the farm. Also on site was an experimental women's
agricultural training school under Hanna Meisal's direction. Together, the two
units began to show positive results but by then the First World War had begun
and Kinneret, along with all other Jewish settlements was soon bedeviled by
widespread depredations perpetrated by the Turkish army.

WOMEN IN THE SECOND ALIYAH

Hanna Meisal's attempts to teach women farming techniques helped to up-
grade the role and status of women workers. Women pioneers were a distinct
minority. For instance, at one stage in Hadera, there were 150 male workers and
only 6 female ones.[43] Estimates place the proportion of Second Aliyah female
workers out of the total work force at 6–7 percent.[44] Taking the early-twentieth-
century social milieu into account, it is not surprising that women pioneers
were so few in number. Parental opposition to girls wanting to go to Palestine
was much stiffer than was the case with boys.

As difficult as it was for young male workers to secure employment, it was
far harder for women. Few believed that they were physically and psychologically capable of arduous field work. Religious farmers of Petah Tikva and elsewhere had qualms about letting them toil alongside men, but there were also
grounds for worrying about their personal security lest they be left on their
own in isolated areas. Apart from Hanna Meisal, who was a trained agronomist,
the women workers had no knowledge of farming and it never occurred to anyone else to remedy that situation. The general consensus was that women
should concentrate on household chores. Their potential productivity elsewhere was regarded with skepticism. In Degania's early days, there was considerable reluctance to admit more than a handful of women, on the grounds that
too many of them would constitute an economic burden.[45]

Even in the sphere of cooking, the Second Aliyah women were found wanting. Most lacked familiarity with the most basic of culinary skills. When they
were put to work in the kitchen, "They received absolutely no expert training.

The little knowledge that they gleaned was passed on from woman to woman with all its faults and defects. This was especially the case with regard to the baking of bread, which was either half burnt or completely soggy."[46] Sometimes accumulated uneaten bread was simply used as cattle fodder. Meanwhile, the female cooks would work endlessly, securing their ingredients, fetching water, washing dishes, igniting wood-burning stoves and ovens and preparing meals, almost single-handedly, for scores of workers. At one workers' kitchen in Rehovot, two girls, cooking for thirty-five others, slaved away from five in the morning until ten at night.[47] There were occasions when a few forlorn young women who felt that they could not rise to the challenge of kitchen work committed suicide. Seemingly, they could not live with themselves for "failing" what seemed to be a crucial pioneering test. Not surprisingly, at the first reasonable opportunity, many fled the kitchen.

Only gradually was it appreciated that unless women were involved in milking, poultry management, vegetable gardening and other facets of farm activity, the Jewish farming community would be relatively disadvantaged. By asserting themselves in organized women's work gangs and by means of exclusively female political action groups, the women's demands to be recognized as equal pioneering participants were ultimately taken seriously.

HASHOMER (THE GUARD)

At the beginning of the First Aliyah, farmers confronted by threats to their property, personally guarded their settlements. But in the same way that they eventually ceased relying on their own farm labor, so too did they relinquish security concerns to others. The hired strongmen were usually local Arabs or, sometimes, Circassians. As far as the Second Aliyah immigrants were concerned, such an arrangement was fraught with danger. Not only were the settlements based on non-Jewish labor but adding insult to injury, their general protection was entrusted to the very people most likely to plunder them.

It soon became obvious that the struggle for the Conquest of Labor had to include guard duty. Consequently, in 1908 seven young men, under Israel Shochet and Israel Giladi's leadership, gathered in Ben-Zvi's house to form a society named Bar Giora, after one of the heroes in a Jewish revolt against the Romans. The society, which was a secret one, adopted the slogan: "In blood and fire Judea fell, in blood and fire Judea shall rise."[48] Considering themselves the crème de la crème of a new breed of Zionist pioneers, the Bar Giora association aimed to fulfill a range of tasks, from the protecting of existing settlements to the securing and occupation of vulnerable and isolated tracts of land acquired by the JNF. In keeping with their socialist principles, they also wished to establish new collective forms of Jewish agricultural settlements. In that regard, they assembled at Sejera, a training farm in the Galilee, where they hoped to base themselves as a prelude to the widening of their activities.

At Sejera, they were allocated some equipment and a patch of land, which they contracted to cultivate on an independent basis in return for daily workers' wages and prospects of receiving 20 percent of the land's net return. Ten members were in place at the start, with their numbers soon rising to eighteen. Under Manya Shochet's inspiration, they worked for a year as a completely autonomous unit without any external control and supervision. Known simply as the "Collective," they preceded the experiment at Umm Juni (Degania) by a year.

Naturally, members of Bar Giora also turned their hands to what they regarded as their major objective, that is, the mounting of guards. After some equivocation, the manager of the Sejera training farm agreed to let them assume watch on a trial basis, as did the adjoining farming settlement (also named Sejera). In both cases, it was realized that the Circassians who had been previously hired were derelict in their duty. This was drawn to the manager's attention one night by the Jewish workers "stealing" a prize horse and then reporting the loss. In seeking out the watchman, the manager, to his chagrin, found him in a drunken state in a nearby village. Soon thereafter, a small settlement in the lower Galilee, Mesha, was also placed under Bar Giora protection.

By 1909, in the wake of the 1908 Young Turk revolution, the general security situation in the Galilee became even more precarious. Arabs in the vicinity of Jewish settlements acted more brazenly, with instances of violence and theft becoming more commonplace. As each settlement turned to the Bar Giora group for assistance, it became obvious that the society's limited membership could not meet the growing demands put on it. To widen its ranks, it was decided to create a successor organization that would not only function openly (at least within the Jewish community) but would attract a larger general membership. This organization, named *Hashomer* (the Guard), was officially launched during the 1909 Passover, at a founding conference at Mesha. It was administered by a committee of three, elected at a general meeting. To assist members in acquiring arms and horses, a loan fund was established. Like Bar Giora before it, almost all of Hashomer's founding members belonged to Poalei Zion. Adherents of Hapoel Hatzair, who were largely pacifists, refused to take part, fearing that the movement had a touch of militarism about it.[49] Hashomer soon had its work cut out for it, with one settlement after another enlisting its services. Among the larger establishments, Hadera was first in line, followed by Rehovot and Rishon Letzion. Only in Petah Tikva and Zichron Yaakov was Hashomer not welcomed. In order to patrol all the settlements that sought its aid, the young guardsmen abandoned their collective farm work at Sejera.

Members of Hashomer had a romantic and heroic aura about them. They tended to dress in Arabic garments, complete with keffiyas (headscarfs) held in place by thick woolen bands. With their dazzling moustaches, their bandoliers and large riding boots, they cut dashing figures as they mounted their caparisoned horses. All were armed, some sporting rifles and revolvers and some even brandishing swords. Priding themselves on their horsemanship, they

Members of Hashomer (Central Zionist Archives).

sometimes competed in racing against neighboring Arab riders and on occasions when they outpaced them, their defeated rivals retreated in ignominy. Unquestionably, they were very courageous. Single-handedly, they thought nothing of challenging entire groups of intruders.

Toward the eve of World War I, Hashomer's stocks within the New Yishuv began to fall. A combination of factors contributed to this. Prime among them was the higher cost of employing Jewish guards as opposed to Arabs. It could of course be argued that since Hashomer was infinitely more vigilant, the farmers were in fact more than compensated for Hashomer's more expensive fees. Nonetheless, such a line of reasoning did not go down well. Farmers began to feel that the provocative behavior and posturing of some of the Jewish guards created unnecessary friction with Arab neighbors and simply invited avoidable clashes. In 1913 Hadera canceled its contract with Hashomer and then Rehovot followed suit. The latter withdrawal occurred immediately after the settlement was besieged by hysterical Arabs demanding blood in revenge for the loss of one of their kinsman shot when caught stealing. In the same incident, two Hashomer members were killed. Even so, the farmers felt that trouble enough was brought upon them "just for a bunch of grapes" and that the Jewish guards had to go.[50]

Not only the farmers but many Second Aliyah migrants had various misgivings regarding Hashomer. Some resented their higher rates of pay and their seemingly large amount of leisure time. Others were alienated by their perceived arrogance and their frequent use of Yiddish. As one contemporary writer bemoaned, "the moral state of Hashomer is totally unsatisfactory."[51] What troubled many was its organizational nature, for it was a disciplined, self-contained body that answered to no other, not even to Poalei Zion, from whom its founding members sprang.

For its part, Hashomer felt that its sacrifices were not sufficiently valued. On occasions when they were burying their dead, streams of Arab laborers would flood past them to work in the very settlements their comrades had died defending. They were convinced that among such laborers were the perpetrators of previous outrages. In any event, the charge that Hashomer stimulated Arab violence was not entirely valid. Much effort had been expended in trying to foster good relations with neighboring Arabs. To this end, a number of Hashomer members learned some Arabic. Arab dignitaries were welcomed with all due solemnity in a specially constructed visitors' reception room. Social calls were frequently made to surrounding villages where the *Shomrim* (members of Hashomer) were sometimes hosted for two or three days at a stretch and every effort was made to refrain from any unwarranted use of firearms.

Hashomer's attitude to the Arabs was at times ambivalent. They objected to their employment in Jewish settlements and kept a leery eye on them as potential thieves and assailants. Nevertheless, they emulated their dress, respected their customs and admired their fighting spirit. They were none too proud to learn from them. On one occasion, two of their members spent a full year living among Bedouin as apprentice shepherds.[52]

Full Hashomer members over the period from 1908 to 1920 rarely totaled more than 100. The highest number at any given moment was only forty. However, between 1909 and 1913, eleven members lost their lives in its service. Despite its small following, Hashomer made a very significant contribution to Jewish self-defense, the Conquest of Labor and the spread of settlement holdings. Young diaspora Jews followed its activities with interest and admiration. In time, it provided the inspiration for the founding of new pioneering movements. One of the major ones, Hashomer Hatzair (the Young Watchman), derived its name from it.

ARAB NATIONALISM AND THE JEWISH RESPONSE

In the twenty-six year period from 1882 to 1908—that is, from the beginning of the First Aliyah to the Young Turk Revolution—violent clashes between Arabs and Jews were rather limited in scope. A total of thirteen Jews were killed, but only four could be said to have died within the context of intercommunal strife. The other nine were victims of purely random criminal acts.[53]

In 1908 an Arab-Jewish clash occurred in Jaffa. In March of that year, while strolling in the city's streets, two Jews were seriously assaulted by Arab youths. On hearing of this, incensed Second Aliyah workers began to organize vigilante patrols. An altercation soon broke out between them and some Arabs, who were forced to seek refuge in a nearby store. The Jews followed them and in the heat of a scuffle, an Arab was stabbed. The Jews then fled to two inns. Instead of protecting them, as he was entitled to do under the capitulations system, the Russian vice-consul, who was an inveterate anti-Semite, incited the Turkish authorities to pursue the Jewish fugitives. Five were arrested and beaten; in addition, both soldiers and Arab citizens ransacked the Specter Hotel, injuring thirteen of its residents in the process. Compared with previous Arab-Jewish clashes, this incident represented a qualitative change. It was the first to occur within an urban area and the first in which government officials sided against the Jews. The Zionists promptly mobilized all their forces abroad in protest against Asaf Bey, the kaymakan (subgovernor) in Jaffa. Their efforts were rewarded, in that he was hastily transferred to Istanbul and the five detained Jews were released without charges.[54] In reporting the above-described event to David Wolffsohn, president of the World Zionist Organization, the director of the Anglo-Palestine Bank, Zalman Levontin, wrote, "In this particular incident, only the kaymakan was the guilty party, but the youngsters associated with Poalei Zion had been very provocative. They tended to parade around the streets of Jaffa openly bearing weapons and displaying undisguised arrogance and contempt toward local Arab residents."[55]

To a certain extent, the clash in Jaffa encapsulates some of the early ingredients of Arab-Jewish friction. Highlighted among these was a growing awareness among Arabs of an increasing and potentially threatening Jewish presence, coupled with the development of a determined if not aggressive assertion of actual and perceived rights on the part of some Jews. Because Jaffa was the gateway to Palestine, it always seemed to be brimming with Jews who were both entering and leaving the country, thus creating an exaggerated impression of their actual numbers.[56] New Jewish immigrants retained their foreign citizenship, which yielded them special privileges, such as exemption from certain taxes and military service and which generally placed them beyond the reach of the judicial authorities. This very much rankled the indigenous population. In the cities they were resented by established traders and artisans, who feared that they would lose ground to them. Their legitimate concerns were also tinged with a tincture of anti-Semitism, for the introduction of which into Palestinian society, certain Christian missionaries and ecclesiastical societies could claim much credit.

Violent clashes between Arabs and Jews began to occur with increasing levels of intensity and frequency in the northern regions of Palestine. In April 1909, an incident that seemed to herald the start of a new era of conflict, took place at Sejera. It began with a group of four Arab peasants robbing a Jewish worker. In attempting to defend himself, the worker shot one of his assailants, who died two days later. This gave rise to stormy attacks on Sejera by fifty or so Arab villagers, in which two Jews were murdered and two badly hurt. Two years later, within the same region, four more Jews were slain. There were no subsequent convictions. In the summer of 1913, two Jews were killed in the Mutasaariflik of Jerusalem and in the winter of 1913–1914, the northern settlements experienced a renewed spate of bloodshed.

Within Palestine, Arab nationalism began to be canvassed with a degree of vigor only after the successful 1908 Young Turk Revolution, which promised constitutional rule and a measure of free speech. Yet even before then, there were clear signs that an Arab national consciousness was developing and that Jews were beginning to be perceived as potentially serious obstacles to Arab aspirations. For example, in 1905, Neguib Azoury, a one-time assistant to the Turkish pasha of Jerusalem, published a book, *The Awakening of the Arab Nation in Turkish Asia.* Among other things, he wrote:

Two important phenomena, with the same characteristics but which are diametrically opposed to each other, and which have so far not attracted notice, are appearing in Turkish Asia. They are the Arab national awakening and the latent efforts of Jews to re-establish, on a grand scale, their ancient kingdom of Israel. These two phenomena are destined to be locked in perpetual battle until one prevails over the other.[57]

At the time of its release, Azoury's book, written in French and published in Paris, attracted little attention and caused few, if any ripples. It simply served as a marker, showing the way in which future Arab nationalists would view the issue. What is of interest is that Azoury was a rabid anti-Semite, who foreshadowed writing a book, exposing the "Jewish menace" to the world at large. In this respect, he was not typical of other early anti-Zionist Arabs, who were prepared to make a distinction between Zionism and Judaism. Some opponents of Zionism even acknowledged the justice of its cause but rejected it on practical grounds, citing concerns of the Palestinian Arabs. For example, in 1899 in a letter to Rabbi Zadoc Kahn, the chief rabbi of Paris, Yusuf al-Khalidi, a prominent Jerusalem Arab wrote, "Who can challenge the rights of the Jews to Palestine? Good lord, historically it is really your country." However, he then went on to indicate that the native population would not countenance Zionism. Instead, the Jews should settle in an uninhabited part of the world. "That would be the best, the most rational solution to the Jewish question. But in the name of God, let Palestine be left in peace."[58]

On the Zionist side, the "Arab issue" was first seriously aired in 1905 during the Seventh Zionist Congress at Basel. In a separately convened meeting, sponsored by the Ivriyah Society (for the promotion of Hebrew), Yitzhak Epstein, a teacher from Palestine, described the Arab question as the most pressing problem with which the Zionists had to contend. (The lecture was later published under the title, "The Hidden Question.") Without mincing his words, Epstein informed Congress delegates "that in our beloved land there lives an entire people that has been dwelling there for many centuries and has never considered leaving it."[59] Not only that, "while we harbor fierce sentiments toward the land of our fathers, we forget that the nation now living there is also endowed with a sensitive heart and loving soul. The Arab, like all other men, is strongly attached to his homeland."[60] In drawing attention to occasional displacements of fellahin arising from Jewish land purchases, Epstein considered not only the moral issues at stake but also the practical implications of arousing Arab enmity. He cautioned against awakening a sleeping lion. Alternatively, he likened the situation to a heap of smoldering cinder covered by sand but with a possi-

bility that a single spark could be released to set off an inextinguishable inferno. Jewish security could only be guaranteed through "the righteousness of
our ways and the integrity of our aims."[61] Among other things, his suggested
panaceas involved a generous allocation of resources to promote Arab health
and education. Epstein's proposals were rejected both because of insufficient
Zionist funds and because the majority of delegates considered it futile to try to
buy the friendship of anyone exhibiting anti-Jewish hostility.[62]

Like so many other well-meaning Zionists both of his and of later generations,
Epstein failed to comprehend that the nub of the matter was not the compensation of any hardships that Jewish migration may inadvertently have caused but
rather the coming to terms with a rival nationalist movement aspiring to full sovereignty in the very land in which the Zionists were staking their own claim.
Zionists generally found it difficult, if not impossible to accept that a genuine
Arab nationalist movement, seeking objectives that were incompatible with
theirs, was in the making. In time, by way of coping with the Arab issue, various
schools of thought emerged. One, in which "Rabbi Benyamin" (an alias of Joshua
Radler-Feldmann) was a leading exponent, either believed in fully incorporating
the Arabs into a future Jewish majority population, or at least ministering to
their social, economic and cultural needs to the fullest extent possible. Others
thought it totally inappropriate for Jews to concern themselves with Arab aspirations, on the grounds that they had a moral duty to care exclusively for themselves. In challenging the first group, Haim Brenner wrote, "Why does Rabbi
Benyamin talk about neighborly love with our indigenous neighbors since we are
soul enemies? ... There has to be hatred between us and it will continue to be
so.... We have to accustom ourselves to this hatred and use all the means in our
weak hands to persevere.... The soft lovers are a cursed lot."[63] A third party took
the middle ground. They saw the issue merely in terms of a lack of mutual understanding between Jews and Arabs. Dr. Ruppin, a member of this group, favored
approaching influential Arabs to persuade them that they had nothing to fear
from Zionism.[64] Finally, many Second Aliyah workers, especially Poalei Zion adherents, faced an agonizing quandary in reconciling their demands to displace
Arabs in the work force, with their supposed beliefs in international worker solidarity. One way in which they resolved their dilemma, and certainly not an intellectually honest way, was that they concluded that, because the fellahin were
not members of the proletariat, in purely Marxist terms class-conscious Jewish
workers were entitled to advance their case at the Arabs' expense.[65]

Returning to the consequences of the Young Turk Revolution, it seemed as if
the proverbial genie had been let out of its bottle. The young Turkish officers
and their supporters wished to restructure Turkey as a modern industrial state.
In the process, they were more concerned with consolidating the Turkish mainland than with the Empire as a whole. The shift toward Turkish national su-
premacy weakened the general feelings of cohesion, based on a common
adherence to Islam, previously felt by Ottoman subjects. Arab citizens began to
sense that, in the new scheme of things, they were becoming increasingly mar-

ginalized. In response, they began to demand greater degrees of regional autonomy. This in turn set wheels in motion that eventually led to a full-blown Arab nationalist movement striving toward complete Arab sovereignty.

The new liberal political atmosphere allowed for a more outspoken Arab press, of which the Haifa newspaper, *Al Karmel,* founded in 1909, became a leading anti-Zionist organ. It not only called on Arabs not to sell land to Jews but demanded an immediate and total halt to Jewish immigration. The paper's views were fairly widely disseminated and, by word of mouth, its message penetrated into the outlying homes of illiterate peasants. Within a few years, additional Arab nationalistic newspapers came into being, such as *Falestin,* founded in 1911 in Jaffa and Jerusalem's *Al Muntada,* which appeared in 1912.

The issue of land sales to Jews was the main focus of attention of the early Palestinian nationalists. A transfer that aroused much controversy was the one concerning Pola, the site of the Jewish settlement Merhavia, which *Al Karmel* denounced in forthright terms. For a while, with the kaymakan in Nazareth, Shukrei Al-Asali, joining forces with the Arabs, it seemed as if *Al Karmel's* negative campaign would succeed. Al-Asali resorted to every conceivable legal device to nullify the Pola land transaction. His efforts included an open letter, published both in Istanbul and Haifa, addressed to the Ottoman army commander in Syria. In it he asserted that the Jews were gathering arms and were engaging in military training. They had, he claimed, already assumed control over entire Galilee regions. Finally he warned, "If the Government does not set a limit to this torrential stream, no time will pass before you see that Palestine has become a property of the Zionist Organization."[66] Significantly, Al-Asali used the nom de plume *Salach Ad-Din* (Saladin), the name of the Arab warrior who defeated the Crusaders. As Be'eri presciently noted, "So began the analogy of the Crusaders, which in the course of time became one of the foundation stones in Arab national historiography and anti-Zionist propaganda—the likening of the Zionist enterprise to the invasion of foreign Christians in the Middle Ages and the suggestion that it would be but a passing episode."[67]

Some attribute the struggle for the Conquest of Labor as an added ingredient in fueling Arab-Jewish animosity. Had the Conquest of Labor been fully realized, thousands of Arab workers doubtlessly would have been dismissed. But in practice, just as Jewish workers were sparsely employed at the beginning of the Second Aliyah, so were they at its end. In 1914, for example, only 21 and 30 Jewish workers, respectively were employed in Hadera and Zichron Yaakov, compared with 240 and 300 *regular* Arab workers.[68] Taking into account all Jewish farms and villages, the number of Jewish agricultural laborers, which amounted to approximately 2,000, did not represent more than 10 percent of the total hired work force.[69] What did seem to raise the ire of educated Arabs were articles in the Jewish press calling for the total displacement of Arab labor, an approach that, in retrospect, can be seen as lacking in tact.

In the political arena, the first of a series of three elections to the Turkish parliament took place in October 1908. Although they faced prospects of securing democratically elected representatives, the Arabs felt cheated. Throughout the entire empire, they outnumbered the Turks by a ratio of three to two, yet they were only assigned 60 seats to the 142 earmarked for Turkish delegates. In Palestine, 5 seats were allocated, 3 in the Jerusalem region and 1 each in the regions of Nablus and Acre. Naturally, only Ottoman citizens were entitled to vote and of the 50,000 Jews who dwelled in Jerusalem, only 6,277 were enfranchised.[70] This meant that the Jews had no hope of electing a representative of their own. As it happened, the 5 elected Palestinian delegates were all Muslim Arabs, which betokened an eclipse of early Christian-Arab leadership within the Palestinian movement. The Palestinian parliamentarians soon distinguished themselves in the National Assembly by expressing their fears of and objections to Zionism. In the process, they made common cause with fellow Arab nationalists from the rest of the empire. With each successive parliamentary session, anti-Zionist sentiment was articulated with increased ferocity. Palestinian Arabs began to perceive Zionism not as merely one of a number of obstacles blocking their path to independence, but as the prime hurdle. In May 1910, anti-Zionist lobbying in the Ottoman capital was reinforced by the publication in major Istanbul newspapers of a telegram sent by Arab notables in Nazareth. After drawing attention to the increasing Jewish presence in Palestine, the telegram warned that "the Zionists intend to deprive us of our estates and their intentions pose for us a question of life and death."[71] This was followed in March 1911 by another telegram, signed by more than 150 prominent Arabs, voicing similar concerns.

By 1913, it appeared that some thaw in Arab-Zionist antagonism was in the offing. The Arabs, striving for tangible measures of regional autonomy, began to seek Jewish support, hoping to mobilize what they considered to be the influential Jewish press. More specifically, Salim Naguir, who was active in the Arab Decentralist Party, approached Sami Hochberg, the Jewish editor of *Jeune Turc*. Hochberg was told that in exchange for favorable reportage about Arab demands, the Arabs in turn would advocate an extension of Jewish rights in the field of immigration and property ownership. As a good-will gesture, the Arabs, in an important national conference that took place in Paris, did indeed tone down their anti-Zionist rhetoric. Following up on this breakthrough, Zionist leaders met with their Arab counterparts and it was agreed that a conference be called consisting of ten Jewish and ten Arab delegates, to thrash out Jewish-Arab differences. Just before the conference was scheduled to commence, World War I erupted.

Not only were all efforts at effecting an Arab-Jewish concord permanently suspended, but so too was the New Yishuv's contacts with the Arabs. In any case, the Arabs with whom the Jews were trying to relate were mostly non-Palestinian residents and just one among a number of existing factions and associations. Some of the non-Palestinian Arabs took a pan-Arabic national view in which some accommodation with Zionists was feasible. As opposed to them, the Palestinian Arabs directly confronted a growing Jewish presence. Their nationalism was based more on parochial requirements, in which it was next to impossible for them to accept further Jewish immigration. Some genuinely feared that not only would they be overwhelmed by Jewish migrants but that they might even be totally dispossessed in the future. This was poignantly stated in a pre–World War I letter printed in *Falestin* in which Zionism was described as an "omen of our future exile from our homeland."[72] Reviewing the Arab nationalist movement up to the outbreak of World War I, Roi concluded that "the more extremist among them made it abundantly clear that their plans left no room for both an Arab and a Jewish nationalist revival in one and the same place."[73] Reluctantly, the Zionists had to accept the fact that the chances of a rapprochement between them and the Arabs were all but nonexistent.

MIGRANTS FROM YEMEN

Midway through the Second Aliyah period, around the years 1908–1911, when it became evident that Jewish workers had made little headway in penetrating the established settlements, the notion of the Conquest of Labor began to be reassessed. At that time, the influx of migrants tapered off to a very small trickle, just when disaffected workers increasingly emigrated. The economy was buoyant and jobs were plentiful but young Jewish workers were suddenly insufficiently available. Instead, they began to strive for the Conquest of Land, and by means of the creation of new farming communities, they hoped to work on their own account.

Apart from the sudden scarcity of Jewish workers, two factors seemed to operate against their hired presence in established settlements. First, there was the old chestnut about them not being able to compete with Arabs in terms of wages. Second, very few Jewish workers stayed put in a particular job for an appreciable length of time. Even the more idealistic among them began to concede that it was, after all, unrealistic to expect educated young people to transform themselves into simple farm laborers for life. Inevitably, they would rebel against the endless monotony and physical travail of unskilled work and leave in search of white-collar posts. If the Yishuv was to employ Jewish workers, there seemed no alternative but to recruit so-called "natural workers," who by coming to Palestine as experienced laborers would not encounter any deterioration in lifestyle. Within Eastern Europe, pockets of such "natural workers" seemed to exist. But they were not "natural workers" in the full sense of the term. They did not arise from the ranks of a proletariat who for ages had been members of the working class. On the contrary, many were only first- or second-generation workers, who had fallen down the rungs of the social ladder and who were anxious once more to ascend it. If they were to migrate from Eastern Europe, they would only do so to better themselves and not merely to relocate elsewhere. In short, few, if any, "natural workers" of Ashkenazi stock, were likely to come to Palestine. Eventually, the answer to the problem of sourcing "natural workers" appeared to lie in the hands of the Jews from Yemen.

Between 1904 and 1906, Yemenites entered Palestine in modest numbers, mainly settling in Jaffa. By 1907, twenty or so Yemenite families spontaneously arrived in Palestine, largely concentrating in Rehovot and Rishon Letzion. Within a year, they were joined by another forty families. To members of the Hapoel Hatzair, who took an interest in their welfare, they seemed to constitute the elusive natural Jewish workers. In their view, there appeared to be three advantages in the Yemenites' favor. First, it was thought that because they had come from a comparatively backward country, they were accustomed to few needs and would be satisfied with low wages. In any case, they could still accumulate some savings by allowing their wives to work as domestic servants and letting their children help out in busy harvesting and fruit-picking seasons. Second, they were religious, compliant and spoke both Hebrew and Arabic. Hapoel Hatzair activists were convinced that these two considerations ought to have mollified the reluctance of First Aliyah farmers in employing them and, accordingly, progress in the Conquest of Labor ought to be made. The third factor that enhanced the attractiveness of immigration from Yemen was the belief that, in contrast to European migrants, Yemenites were more likely to remain in Palestine permanently. It was assumed that their social and religious background, as well as their meager secular educational qualifications, lessened the chances of them being able to try their luck elsewhere. This assumption was borne out by the fact that no more than 10 percent of migrants from Yemen ultimately left the country.

The belief that the Yemenites represented a reliable reservoir of Jewish workers was shared by Dr. Ruppin. In 1910 he commissioned Shmuel Yavnieli as his recruiting agent. Responding with enthusiasm, Yavnieli grew a beard and sidelocks, adopted the alias "Eliezer Ben Yoseph" and in December of that year, posing as a rabbinical emissary, he left for Yemen. Over a four-month period, he toured various towns and villages in which Jews resided. At each encounter, Yavnieli spread the word about the budding New Yishuv in Eretz Israel, exhorting his listeners to join hands with the pioneers who were already there. Yavnieli's message was well received. By 1912, nearly 1,500 Yemenites had migrated to Palestine.[74]

Unlike the young Ashkenazi workers, the Yemenite workers, who ranged in age from twenty to forty, arrived with their families. However, the process of their adaptation was anything but smooth. With adequate housing difficult to come by, families slept in barns, stables or cellars. The few who did secure accommodation in buildings, found that the roofs leaked, they were cold in winter, hot in summer and were very crowded. On their arrival, many farmers showed a measure of concern for them. But as time went by, the farmers seemed incapable of sustaining an ongoing interest. Gradually, they detached themselves from them entirely. As one Yemenite recalled, "The farmers neither rejoiced in our happiness nor shared in our sorrows. We were like strangers in a strange land."[75] Another wrote that they were reviled and humiliated being called "dogs and Goyim (gentiles)."[76]

Employment was not readily attainable and for those who were both advanced in years and not used to physical labor, life in Palestine, was at first very taxing.

In any case, very few Yemenites were truly "natural workers." The huge majority were artisans of one kind or another. Furthermore, they were weak and exhausted from their trying journey and were generally in a poor state of health. There were times, stretching from days to weeks, during which no work of any kind was obtained. In those dreadful periods, the Yemenites, driven by hunger, sent their children to beg for food. When work was forthcoming, Yemenites were paid less, for the same effort, than their Ashkenazi coworkers.[77] In Hadera, at one point, they were even paid less than Arabs and were expected to put in longer hours, on the spurious grounds that their living quarters were closer to the settlement.[78] Jewish foremen often handled them coarsely "and there were even incidences of Yemenite workers being struck with whips."[79]

Some effort was indeed made to alleviate their plight. In this regard, the settlements of Rehovot, Petah Tikva and Hadera allocated landholdings on which impoverished Yemenite families could establish homes and cultivate small plots. Thus the auxiliary farms of Shaarayim, Mahaneh Yehuda and Nahaliel were founded. However, the homes that ultimately were built for them, and that were financed from general Zionist revenue, were smaller than the few homes built for Ashkenazi workers. In most instances, the Yemenites were located at some distance from the center of the settlements, often entailing a half-hour walk. Their physical separation, which added to their generally inferior social status, compounded their feelings of alienation. They did not have ready access to the settlements' public services. In particular, they lacked an adequate water supply, even for drinking purposes. Their diets were deficient in nutrients, and diseases were rampant. They suffered from malaria, pneumonia, tuberculosis, various stomach disorders and from trachoma, all of which were exacerbated by overcrowded living conditions. Not surprisingly, mortality rates, especially among infants, were excessively high. In Petah Tikva and Hadera, nearly sixty migrants died within the first year of their arrival.[80]

Through no fault of their own, the Yemenites did not fulfill expectations that they would ensure the Conquest of Labor. By 1913, thousands of Arabs were employed in the major settlements. Even so, of the 800 Jewish workers engaged, 310 (that is 39 percent) were Yemenites.[81] In other words, the Yemenites certainly represented a very significant component of the small Jewish agricultural work force. In Rehovot and Hadera, their numbers actually exceeded those of the farmer members.

THE ESTABLISHMENT OF TEL AVIV

At the beginning of the twentieth century, the Jewish population in Jaffa numbered around 5,000 out of a total of 40,000. With its narrow lanes and passages, general lack of sanitation and with filth and foul odors being all-pervasive, the city was anything but salubrious. Running water was unavailable and the wells from which it was drawn were frequently contaminated, giving rise to repetitive outbreaks of typhoid. There were no shops selling fresh food, which could only be secured in an Oriental-style bazaar or in open-air markets. For good measure, a shortage of accommodation led to high rental costs.

In 1907, to alleviate their living conditions, some sixty Jewish Jaffa residents formed an association named *Ahuzat Habayit* (Housing Estate). It consisted mainly of middle-class merchants but also included were a few teachers and members of the professions. They fixed their sights on establishing a new urban neighborhood on the outskirts of Jaffa. Their aim was to build "sixty houses in an orderly manner, with wide and attractive streets, to include, inasmuch as possible, sanitary installations, such as sewage drains, water pipes and so on, and to set an exemplary standard for the general development of urban Jewish settlement."[82] Unable to finance the project entirely out of their own resources, they banked on securing a long-term loan, possibly from the Jewish National Fund. In July 1907, their spokesman, Akiba Weiss, approached Dr. Arthur Ruppin, who was on a study mission to Palestine, and asked for his assistance. Dr. Ruppin eagerly embraced the scheme and at the Seventh Zionist Congress, held a few weeks later, the Jewish National Fund was authorized to issue the appropriate funding.

At a closed meeting, Ahuzat Habayit decided to acquire land north of Jaffa. The decision was intended to be kept under wraps to forestall land speculation, but somehow word got out and, as a result, the price of the land in question tripled. Once the land was purchased, the association had to grease bureaucratic palms to secure construction permits. Then, as soon as the association was about to commence its operations, the authorities suddenly chose to start building a barracks right in the middle of what was projected as the estate's main thoroughfare. With Turkish law precluding the establishment of private property within the vicinity of a barracks, it seemed as if Ahuzat Habayit's plans were in complete disarray. Not only were their objections totally disregarded, but the building tempo of the barracks was stepped up to a pace that was without precedent, either in Turkey in general or in Palestine in particular.[83] As "luck" would have it, for an exorbitant sum, Ahuzat Habayit eventually succeeded in buying the barracks. It was then promptly demolished and so it seemed was the association's remaining obstacle. But there was one more surprise in store for them. Overnight, an armed band of Arabs pitched their tents on the hill designated for the Hebrew Gymnasium (high school) and laid claim to the land. The Turkish authorities made only token efforts to dislodge them. Out of desperation, Ahuzat Habayit "compensated" the supposed landowners to the tune of 35,000 gold francs and then all hindrances were at last finally cast aside.

By 1910, most of Ahuzat Habayit's members were able to take up residence in their new quarters. By and large, each house, which was surrounded by garden space, accommodated only one family. As planned, the estate was set out on a wide and straight road (Herzl Street), at the end of which stood the Herzlia Gymnasium. In the same year (1910) the new estate was called Tel Aviv (Hill of Spring), the name adopted by Sokolov for his Hebrew translation of Herzl's

Founding meeting of Tel Aviv (Central Zionist Archives).

novel, *Altneuland*. Soon another housing association was formed, called *Nahalat Benyamin* (Benjamin's Estate, after Baron Rothschild). Composed of tradesmen and clerical workers, it too secured financial assistance from the Jewish National Fund and proceeded to develop its housing alongside that of Ahuzat Habayit. They, in turn, were followed by another group who were fully privately funded.

In 1914, Tel Aviv (which was still formally part of Jaffa) had 139 private dwellings, housing 1,419 people.[84] The Palestine Office moved into the area, as did a few workshops. Under the mayoralty of Meier Dizengoff, Tel Aviv assumed the role of the center of the New Yishuv. As Dr. Ruppin declared: "You will find in the Jewish neighborhood (Tel Aviv) an effervescent Jewish life that possibly has no counterpart anywhere else in the world."[85]

A POSTSCRIPT ON HEBREW

Most of the Second Aliyah migrants were Yiddish speakers and even at party meetings, Yiddish was spoken. Often this would elicit strong protests from supporters of Hebrew. Sohovolski recalls that at the third general meeting of Hapoel Hatzair, where the proceedings were conducted in Yiddish, a strident vocal majority sponsored a resolution prohibiting the use of "the jargon" (Yiddish) at any party proceeding, whether it be in the form of a play, a soiree or any other function.[86] The problem was that very few of the newcomers were sufficiently conversant in Hebrew and frequently, from a practical point of view, Yiddish simply had to be used. There were also those in the workers' ranks who believed in utilizing Yiddish as a link with the rest of East European Jews. Some were under the sway of a new sense of pride in that language, caused by a growth of "Yiddishism" from which the Bund's influence was not far removed. For such reasons, Poalei Zion's first Palestine newspaper was published in Yiddish, not Hebrew. Gradually, the mood in the party changed and the Yiddish paper was supplanted by a Hebrew one called *Achdut* (Unity). Both political parties invested considerable efforts in inculcating Hebrew. Classes were arranged for those lacking knowledge of the language and just as earlier streams of Second Aliyah workers were totally uncompromising in the call for the Conquest of Labor, so did zealous Hebraists insist that, at all times, only Hebrew be used. Their vigilance in this regard ensured that Hebrew was spoken at both work and play and throughout the New Yishuv at large.

The final battle for the ascendancy of Hebrew occurred just before the First World War. In October 1913, a few months prior to the proposed opening of the Technion at Haifa, the board of the *Hilfsverein der Deutschen Juden*, which financed the project, decided that German would be the language of the college's instruction. This produced a swift reaction on the part of Jewish teachers throughout Palestine, who organized a series of protest strikes. They demanded that all subjects be taught in Hebrew and regarded the issue as a test case that would determine whether or not Hebrew would finally reign supreme in all key Jewish institutions. Fortified by support from abroad, the teachers prevailed. It was agreed that within four years, Hebrew would be used exclusively, with some courses even resorting to that language forthwith. As it happened, classes did not actually commence until after World War I.

CONCLUSION

By 1914, the Jewish population in Palestine had reached approximately 85,000 out of an overall figure of 700,000. Membership in the New Yishuv numbered approximately 35,000, of whom 11,990 were in rural villages and areas.[87] Ben Gurion was convinced that no more than 10 percent of the workers who ventured to Palestine in the entire Second Aliyah period remained.[88] Assuming Ben Gurion to be correct, this means that the dropout rate, amounting to 90 percent, was enormous. Bearing in mind the daunting problems that the young workers encountered, one might, of course, marvel at the fact that as many as 10 percent persevered. For in opting out, one could immediately forsake a life of seemingly endless drudgery, poverty and insecurity in exchange for a comparatively easy life in America, Europe and Australia, where most ultimately went. In Ben Gurion's view, it was less the trying conditions in which Second Aliyah workers operated that impelled so many to fall by the wayside but rather their feeling that they were but a small drop in the ocean. With the passing of every year, their numbers seemed to remain stationary. They saw little return for their prodigious efforts and began to wonder if they would ever make a significant contribution to the New Yishuv.

In fact, their actual impact on society was far greater than they realized at the time. The diehards were an extraordinarily tough breed of individuals, who, having been forged in Eretz Israel's fiery crucible, were strongly steeled. Their timely arrival in Palestine transformed the New Yishuv from a tendency to degenerate into a typical colonial settler society into a dynamic, self-assured body, conscious of its destiny and the sacrifices required to achieve it. They not only provided a core of formidable leaders, who ultimately stewarded the New Yishuv into statehood, but they set the stage for the formation of Israel's unique labor institutions, such as the kibbutz, the *Histadrut* (Labor Federation), the *Kupat Holim* (Health Fund, which was first mooted in 1912) and other associated cooperative societies. In the realm of defense, Hashomer was the forerunner of the Hagana, which in turn became the Israel Defense Force. Virtually all the key organs on which the budding State of Israel relied were at least inspired, if not established, by Second Aliyah pioneers.

NOTES

1. Lowe, *Tsars and the Jew,* 1978, p. 93.
2. Frankel, *Prophecy and Politics,* 1981, p. 366.
3. Wigoder, *Encyclopedia,* 1977, p. 73.
4. Frankel, *Prophecy and Politics,* 1981, p. 368.
5. Laqueur, *History,* 1989, p. 280.
6. Frankel, *Prophecy and Politics,* 1981, p. 368.
7. Katznelson, "The Miracle of the Second Aliyah," in Habbas, *Second Aliyah,* 1947, p. 12.
8. From Joseph Vitkin's proclamation as reproduced in Eliav, *First Aliyah,* 1981, vol. 2, p. 401.
9. Even-Shoshan, *History,* 1955, vol. 1, p. 9.
10. Dubnow, *History of the Jews in Russia,* 1920, vol. 3, p. 102.
11. Mandel Zinger, "From Brodi to Eretz Israel," in Habbas, *Second Aliyah,* 1947, p. 118.
12. Katznelson, "My Road to Eretz Israel," in Habbas, *Second Aliyah,* 1947, p. 85.
13. Natan Hofshi, "Pioneers of Zion," in Habbas, *Second Aliyah,* 1947, p. 138.
14. Tzemach, *First Year,* 1965.
15. Ruppin, *Three Decades,* 1936, p. 36.
16. Eliyahu Even-Tov, "In Petach Tikva at the Time of the Ban," in Habbas, *Second Aliyah,* 1947, p. 183.
17. Neta Herpaz, "Tribulations of Conquest," in Habbas, *Second Aliyah,* 1947, p. 221.
18. Gvati, *Hundred Years,* 1985, p. 34.
19. According to Borochov, unlike other nations that were based on a large stratum of farmers and workers supporting smaller numbers of tertiary workers and capitalists,

the Jews were in a different situation. At the base of their society was a small stratum of laborers and as one moved higher up the social scale, the layers of tertiary workers and traders became larger; hence, the Jews maintained an "inverted social pyramid."

20. Y. Horvitz, "From Conquest of Labor to Settlement," in Habbas, *Second Aliyah*, 1947, p. 208.

21. Gvati, *Hundred Years*, 1985, p. 35.

22. Y. Horvitz, op. cit., p. 215.

23. Zvi Lieberman, "The Workers' Kitchen at Hadera," in Habbas, *Second Aliyah*, 1947, pp. 272–274.

24. Ibid., p. 273.

25. E. Shidlovski, "Tribulations of Absorption," in Habbas, *Second Aliyah*, 1947, p. 557.

26. Frankel, *Prophecy and Politics*, 1981, p. 371.

27. Alex Bein, "Introduction," in Ruppin, *Memoirs*, 1971, p. xiii.

28. Most had originated in the Ukrainian town called Romni.

29. Bein, *History*, 1970, p. 36.

30. In 1966, at age 78, Shmuel Agnon was awarded a Nobel Prize in recognition of his contribution to Hebrew literature.

31. Others, such as Radler-Feldman, also laid claim to suggesting the name "Kinneret." Since the farm lay alongside the lake, the farm's appropriate name may have been obvious to most observers.

32. Months later, the khan was extended to six rooms and was surrounded by a wall.

33. S. Malkin, "My Journeys through the Land," in Habbas, *Second Aliyah*, 1947, p. 498.

34. Ruppin, *Memoirs*, 1971, p. 102.

35. Miriam Bratz, "The First Family in the First Kvutza," in Habbas, *Second Aliyah*, 1947, p. 529.

36. Ibid.

37. Viteles, *History*, 1967, p. 46.

38. As quoted by Yosef Bratz, in Gidon, *Pathways*, 1955, p. 82.

39. Ruppin, *Memoirs*, 1971, p. 105.

40. Gvati, *Hundred Years*, 1985, p. 43.

41. Ibid.

42. As quoted in Gidon, "Aspiration," 1980, p. 43.

43. Zvi Lieberman, in Habbas, *Second Aliyah*, 1947, p. 273.

44. Even-Shoshan, *History*, 1995, p. 208.

45. Ibid., p. 213.

46. Zvi Lieberman, in Habbas, *Second Aliyah*, 1947, p. 273.

47. Hana Laskov, "Wanderings of a Young Woman Worker," in Habbas, *Second Aliyah*, 1947, p. 563.

48. This slogan, which originated in a poem by Jacob Cohen, was also used by defense groups in Russia organized by the Poalei Zion.

49. Laqueur, *History*, 1989, p. 285.

50. A. Kolar, "Road of Tribulations of One Settlement," in Habbas, *Second Aliyah*, 1947, p. 462.

51. As quoted by Frankel, *Prophecy and Politics,* 1981, p. 421.

52. Alexander Zeid, "In Early Days," in Habbas, *Second Aliyah,* 1947, p. 177.

53. Be'eri, *Beginning,* 1985, p. 65.

54. Ibid., pp. 115–16.

55. Ellsberg, "Arab Question," 1965, p. 163.

56. Mandel, *Arabs and Zionism,* 1976, p. 39.

57. As quoted by Be'eri, *Beginning,* 1985, p. 119.

58. As quoted by Mandel, *Arabs and Zionism,* 1976, pp. 47–48.

59. As quoted by Shapira, *Land and Power,* 1992, p. 45.

60. As quoted by Gorny, *Zionism and the Arabs,* 1987, p. 43.

61. As quoted by Be'eri, *Beginning,* 1985, p. 124.

62. Laqueur, *History,* 1989, p. 215.

63. As quoted by Be'eri, *Beginning,* 1985, p. 128. Brenner was killed by Arabs in the 1921 riots. His attitude to Arabs had changed shortly before his death. He began to see them as fellow human beings, rather than as enemies, and had resolved to study Arabic.

64. Ruppin, *Three Decades,* 1936, p. 64.

65. Be'eri, *Beginning,* 1985, p. 110.

66. As quoted by Mandel, *Arabs and Zionism,* 1976, p. 89.

67. Be'eri, *Beginning,* 1985, p. 158.

68. Ibid., p. 180.

69. Roi, "Zionist Attitude," 1968, p. 202.

70. Ellsberg, "Arab Question," 1965, p. 164.

71. Ibid., p. 167.

72. Mandel, *Arabs and Zionism,* 1976, p. 122.

73. Roi, "Zionist Attitude," 1968, p. 236.

74. Druyen, "Immigration," 1981, p. 98.

75. As quoted by Y. Sprinzik, "With the Yemenites," in Habbas, *Second Aliyah,* 1947, p. 336.

76. As quoted by Druyen, "Immigration," 1981, p. 99.

77. Shafir, *Land, Labor,* 1989, p. 103.

78. D. Bader, "Detail," in Habbas, *Second Aliyah,* 1947, p. 219.

79. Druyen, "Immigration," 1981, p. 100.

80. Ibid., p. 104.

81. Meir, *Zionist Movement,* 1983, p. 95.

82. As quoted by Bein, *History,* 1970, p. 103.

83. David Smilensky in Avraham Yaari, *Memoirs,* 1947, vol. 2, p. 913.

84. Bein, *History,* 1970, p. 105.

85. As quoted by Bein, *History,* 1970, p. 105.

86. T. Sohovolski, "The Beginnings of Hapoel Hatzair," in Habbas, *Second Aliyah,* 1947, p. 617.

87. Gross, 1997, p. 29.

88. D. Ben-Gurion, "In Celebrating a Quarter of a Century," in Habbas, *Second Aliyah,* 1947, p. 17.

Chapter 5

The First World War and the Balfour Declaration

PALESTINE IN THE WAR YEARS

On November 5, 1914, Turkey entered World War I on behalf of the Central Powers, that is, Austria-Hungary and Germany. In the process, the capitulations system fell by the wayside and Palestinian Jews of Russian citizenship suddenly became enemy aliens. They did at least have the option of normalizing their status by becoming Ottoman citizens. But that entailed being subject to military conscription with the attendant risk that if Turkey were defeated or if conscripts were captured by Russian forces, they would be tried for treason. To provide some room for maneuver, leaders of the New Yishuv negotiated an agreement with the Turkish authorities that allowed for the immediate drafting of new citizens into local labor brigades but which deferred, for at least a two-year period, conscription into the regular armed forces. Given this understanding, approximately 12,000 Jews responded to calls by leading Zionists to opt for Ottoman citizenship. However, Ottomanization was both costly and tardy. A large application fee was imposed and the authorities deliberately stalled the citizenship process to limit the number of Jews eligible for permanent residence.

In December 1914, 7,000 non-Ottoman Jews fled or were expelled to Egypt, to be joined by another 4,000 during 1915. Expulsion procedures were sometimes swift and brutal. The first batch of exiled Russian Jews were simply given a few hours to gather their belongings. Then 750 of them were forced onto a series of rowboats that were anchored in pitch darkness alongside the vessel that was to transport them. Not all succeeded in boarding the ship and, in the ensuing confusion, a number of children became separated from their parents and either went off without them or were left stranded in Jaffa.[1]

Although the majority of Palestinian Jews were essentially loyal to Turkey, that did not ensure their well-being. It was their misfortune that in 1914 Jemal

Pasha became commander-in-chief of Syria (which included Palestine). Jemal Pasha was an unmitigated and cruel tyrant who implacably suppressed both Arab and Jewish nationalism. On taking up his post, he lost no time in introducing a series of stringent measures designed to harass the Zionist movement. The public display of Hebrew signs was prohibited, as was the possession of JNF stamps. Jewish self-defense groups were outlawed, letters were not to be written in Hebrew and the newspapers of the two labor parties, *Hapoel Hatzair* and *Ahdut*, were banned.

Even without Jemal Pasha's heavy hand, matters would have been bad enough. The war brought about a marked decline in both internationally traded goods and monetary transfers from abroad. Exports of wine, citrus fruits and almonds all but ceased. Imported foodstuffs and fuel oil were in very short supply, and with the inability to access funds from donors in England, Russia and Poland, the Old Yishuv was deprived of its major source of subsistence.

Some measure of relief materialized through the timely actions of Henry Morgenthau. Serving at the time as the American ambassador in Constantinople, Morgenthau, a non-Zionist Jew, visited Palestine in 1914 at Dr. Ruppin's behest. Realizing that the situation called for a large philanthropic endeavor, he alerted American Jewish organizations to provide the necessary assistance. Accordingly, both money and food provisions were dispatched, with the first consignment arriving in September.

An emergency committee, under the chairmanship of Meier Dizengoff, assumed responsibility for securing and distributing food aid, for stimulating employment and for sustaining those without any income. To augment job prospects, the emergency committee lent aid money to settlements on condition that Jewish labor be hired. Those that obtained employment were paid at reduced rates and in the form of "chits," which were barely exchangeable for anything other than meals. Workers themselves took their collective fate in hand. They organized public kitchens, their Sick Fund ministered to their ill and they tended to pool their earnings to sustain active and non-active workers alike. A workers' collective, known as *Ahava* (Brotherhood), established in 1914 in Petah Tikva, was a model of cooperative enterprise. It contracted for assignments that assumed responsibility for the cultivation of orchards and vineyards. Out of its proceeds it acquired basic commodities that were distributed to its members on the basis of individual and family needs.

Foreign aid only temporarily and partly helped to sustain the Yishuv. In the spring of 1915, a locust plague devastated the countryside, devouring most of the standing crops. Then, in 1916, Turkish war needs were met by the widespread and indiscriminate sequestration of livestock and food. To obtain material for railroad construction, numerous fruit trees were felled. By winter, because of intensified submarine warfare, neutral American ships stopped calling on Palestine. This led to an abrupt and serious decline in the availability of imported wheat flour.

Shortfalls in food supplies were partially made good by Jewish settlements in the Galilee, which produced grain over and above their own requirements. To ensure that the Galilee grain was accessible to as wide a market as was possible, a cooperative known as *Hamashbir* (Food Provider), was established. It operated from Kinneret, where Meier Rothberg managed its warehouse and from which wheat was dispatched to workers in the coastal plain, at below market prices.

By April 1917, the lot of the Yishuv, both old and new, reached its nadir. In anticipation of a British invasion, Jews were evacuated from Jaffa, Tel Aviv and the surrounding area. Most found refuge of a sort in the settlements of the Galilee. But adequate accommodation was not really available, and many displaced Jews had to sleep in crudely constructed huts, tents and, as in Hadera, shelters made of eucalyptus branches.

The evacuation of settlers in the Tel Aviv region was not in fact absolute. Mindful of general food shortages, the Turks exempted those who were directly engaged in agriculture. The settlements themselves had to make a determination of just who fitted into that category, for a number of their members were employed as teachers, clerks and in other white-collar occupations. As far as possible, all such people were fictitiously classified as "farm workers," but the settlements were still left with the invidious task of supplying a reasonable quota of evacuees. This was tackled by singling out the Yemenite workers. "The Yemenites were the first and sometimes the only victims who were sacrificed to ransom settlements from the expulsion decree. They were the scapegoats that filled the train stations of Rosh El Ayin and Afula and died en masse on the banks of the Kinneret."[2]

The war years wrought the greatest havoc on members of the Old Yishuv who lived in the cities of Jerusalem, Hebron, Safed and Tiberias. Cut off from their overseas charitable lifelines, they were subject to the ravages of famine. During the early part of 1917, it is thought that in Jerusalem alone, some 300 Jews starved to death each month.[3] By the time hostilities ultimately ended, the Jewish population in Palestine had receded to around 56,000. This number was close to what it was at the beginning of the Second Aliyah in 1904 and represented only about 10 percent of the total postwar Palestinian population.

THE ZIONIST MOVEMENT IN THE WAR YEARS

David Wolffsohn's presidency of the Zionist Executive came to an end in 1911. Instead of a successor immediately being elected, Otto Warburg was appointed as the Executive's chairman. Eventually, he was elevated to the post of president, which he retained until 1920.

The outbreak of war placed the Zionist Movement in a terrible dilemma. With its members residing in opposite warring camps, the Zionists had an urgent need to stress their neutrality. A natural corollary would have been the transfer of Zionist headquarters from Berlin, where it was situated when Warburg took over the movement's reins, to a nonbelligerent state. However, the situation was complicated by an overriding need not to antagonize the Germans, whose good will was needed to restrain their impetuous Turkish allies from harming the Palestinian Jews. An uneasy compromise was reached. The Central Zionist Office remained in Berlin at the same time as a bureau was opened in Copenhagen, which liaised with the German office, while, in the United States, an American Provisional Committee coordinated Zionists' interests there. The American committee, whose full title was "The Provisional Executive Committee for General Zionist Affairs," assumed interim responsibility for activities and decisions that had previously been the prerogative of the Zionist General Council. It was headed by Louis Brandeis, who in 1916 became a U.S. Supreme Court justice and who enjoyed personal ties with President Woodrow Wilson.

THE ZION MULE CORPS

As already mentioned, most of the Russian Jews expelled from Palestine found refuge in Egypt. Among those who headed for Alexandria was Joseph Trumpeldor, the legendary soldier renowned for his exploits in the Russian-Japanese War. In August 1904, in the battle of Port Arthur, Trumpeldor's left arm was injured by shell fragments and had to be amputated. After his convalescence, Trumpeldor resumed active combat duty until he was captured by the Japanese. In recognition of his outstanding valor, he was decorated by the czar. In 1912, he settled in Palestine. Coincidentally, Ze'ev Jabotinsky, a leading Zionist and newspaper correspondent, was also in Alexandria. The two met and agreed that the Jews ought to contribute to an anticipated British invasion of Palestine. What they had in mind was the formation of a Jewish battalion attached to the British Army and recruited from among Palestinian exiles.

In March 1915, they sought an interview with General Maxwell, the British military governor in Cairo. After prolonged negotiations, Maxwell rejected their submission but proposed as an alternative the establishment of a battalion of muleteers, to be known as the "Zion Mule Corps." Maxwell's offer was not initially well received. Trumpeldor, Jabotinsky and their followers, were hoping that by means of a distinct fighting force, the Jews would be given the opportunity to help liberate Palestine and thereby share in the sacrifices. Maxwell's suggestion that they serve in the capacity of a nonfighting auxiliary unit, in this case as food and ammunition transporters, seemed demeaning.

When it became known that instead of being assigned to the Palestinian front, the Jewish volunteers would be sent to the Gallipoli Peninsula, Jabotinsky decided not to participate. Trumpeldor, by contrast, was more accommodating. He reasoned that since the Turks were the designated enemy, it mattered not where one engaged them. Even though he would have preferred to have been enlisted as a regular soldier, he realized that by helping to deliver vital supplies, he could still make a valuable contribution to the British war effort. Accordingly, he accepted Maxwell's offer. To some extent, Maxwell made it easier for him to do so by claiming to speak on behalf of the British to the Jewish people, promising them a friendship "which will certainly continue in the future in Jewish Palestine."[4] Captivated by Maxwell's use of the term "Jewish Palestine," Trumpeldor recorded, "We were won over, and replied that we agreed to everything—unconditionally."[5]

Official Jewish involvement with the Allies was not favored by the Zionists as a whole. Realizing that the fate of the Yishuv in Palestine hinged on the good will of the Turks, to many it seemed axiomatic that any activity that was patently anti-Turkish invited wholesale reprisals. Trumpeldor, by contrast, banked on a swift Allied victory, which, if assisted by the Zionists, would, he believed, have promoted Jewish Statehood.

The Zion Mule Corps officially came into existence at the end of March 1915. It was commanded by Colonel Patterson and contained five British and eight Jewish officers. Trumpeldor, commissioned as a captain, was the most senior Jewish recruit. All told, some 500 Jews were formally inducted. Wearing caps bearing the Star of David, they took the oath of allegiance in the presence of Alexandria's chief rabbi, Rabbi Raphael de la Pergola, who blessed them and exhorted them to serve honorably.

Supplied with twenty riding horses, 750 pack mules and rifles captured from the Turks, the Corps underwent brief training. Although Hebrew was the language generally used, drilling, which lasted a mere three weeks, took place in English. Then, on April 17, 1915, they left for Gallipoli. Half the Corps were placed on H.M. Transport *Hymettas* and the other half on H.M. Transport *Anglo-Egyptian*. Both ships first made for the Greek port of Lemnos, where a number of other transports assembled. To Colonel Patterson's dismay, orders were given for the Zion Mule Corps to be divided. Those sailing on the *Anglo-Egyptian* went with the Australians and New Zealanders, while those on *Hymettas*, which included Patterson, Trumpeldor and most of the other officers, joined the 29th British Division. As Patterson foresaw, because the two companies that linked up with the Anzacs (Australian and New Zealand Army Corps) were without sufficient leadership and were inadequately prepared, they were incapable of functioning properly. After an interval of a few weeks, they were returned to Alexandria where they were demobilized.

Things turned out differently with regard to the other half of the Corps. They landed in Southern Gallipoli after a beachhead had been secured and promptly set to work. Their tasks were grueling ones. Loaded mules had to be directed in the darkness of night toward the front trenches. In the process, they would come under enemy fire. As Patterson wrote, "It must not be supposed that we only came under fire on specific occasions. It broke upon us at all times, night and day, without warning."[6] Nerves of steel were needed to ensure that the mules did not bolt and that they pressed on in the face of such dangers. To their credit, the Corps acquitted themselves well, drawing praise from Sir Ian Hamilton, the overall commander of the Gallipoli campaign. In a letter to a New York Jewish newspaper that inquired if the Zion Mule Corps really existed, Hamilton stated:

It may interest you to know that I have here, fighting under my orders, a purely Jewish unit. As far as I know, this is the first time in the Christian era that such a thing has happened. The men who compose it were cruelly driven out of Jerusalem by the Turks, and arrived in Egypt, with families, absolutely destitute and starving. A complete transport Corps was there raised from them, for voluntary service with me against the Turks, whom they naturally detest. These troops were officially described as the "Zion Mule Corps," and the officers and rank and file have shown great courage in taking water, supplies and ammunition up to the fighting line under heavy fire. One of the private soldiers has been specially recommended by me for gallantry and has duly received from the King the Distinguished Conduct Medal.[7]

As the days and weeks went by, with the Corps working around the clock, fatigue caught up with them. Many either became ill or were wounded. Some, like their doctor who constantly tended to the injured under a hail of gunfire, became shell shocked and had to be discharged. It was then that incessant grumbling set in. Many complained that they were paid less than the regular British troops and, as a result, their families in Alexandria could not cope. With their ranks being depleted on account of sicknesses and injuries, the workload of those remaining on duty increased. A small minority, still smarting from the fact that they were denied the right to fight in Palestine, became increasingly restless.

At the end of July 1915, Patterson and Trumpeldor went to Alexandria to round up an additional batch of volunteers. They returned to Gallipoli with two hundred enthusiastic men, most of whom were Sephardi Jews. On their arrival, the general tone of things vastly improved and the Corps once more functioned smoothly.

On December 28, 1915, it was suddenly announced that the Corps was to be disbanded. At first Trumpeldor was at a loss as to the reason why, for General Hamilton had again recently praised them. In a letter to Jabotinsky, Hamilton wrote that the soldiers of the Corps "calmly carried on under fire of bullets and shells and even at times displayed greater heroism than frontline soldiers, for the latter were at least assisted by the intoxication of battle which diverted their minds from all dangers."[8] It soon became clear that the termination of the Zion Mule Corps emanated from the general evacuation of Gallipoli, which commenced at the beginning of January 1916.

Within its short tour of duty, the Zion Mule Corps lost eight under fire and suffered fifty-five casualties. Among the wounded was Trumpeldor himself. He was shot in the left shoulder, with the bullet projecting out on the other side. Once it was removed, he continued as if nothing untoward had occurred. Considering the brevity of the men's training, the Zion Mule Corps performed admirably. Colonel Patterson, in a communication to the Russian consul in Cairo, singled out nine Jews of Russian citizenship for special mention.

THE BALFOUR DECLARATION

On November 2, 1917, Arthur Balfour, the British Foreign Secretary in Lloyd George's cabinet, addressed a letter to Lord Rothschild. The letter, which became known as the Balfour Declaration, read as follows:

I have much pleasure in conveying to you, on behalf of His Majesty's Government, the following declaration of sympathy with Jewish Zionist aspirations which has been submitted to, and approved by, the Cabinet.

"His Majesty's Government view with favour the establishment in Palestine of a national home for the Jewish people, and will use their best endeavours to facilitate the achievement of this object, it being clearly understood that nothing shall be done which may prejudice the civil and religious rights of existing non-Jewish communities in Palestine, or the rights and political status enjoyed by Jews in any other country."

I should be grateful if you would bring this declaration to the knowledge of the Zionist Federation.

The Balfour Declaration represented the elusive political charter for which Herzl so desperately strove. It not only consisted of official backing of Zionist objectives by a great European power but one that was soon destined to assume total control of Palestine. With subsequent endorsements by the United States and France and, ultimately, by the League of Nations, the Balfour Declaration became, in effect, the Jews' title deed to, at the very least, a portion of Palestine.

The issuing of the Balfour Declaration followed tortuous shifts of British foreign policy. At the outbreak of the First World War, Britain had not put in a bid for an eventual stake in Palestine and by implication had left the field open to the French. The latter, in turn, had their hearts set on being the pre-eminent force in Syria, which was generally taken to include Palestine. Early in 1915, British officials began to review the consequences of ceding territory immediately to the east of the Suez Canal to a European rival, with whom permanent amicable relations could never be guaranteed. To ward off potential threats to its holdings in Egypt, the British began to float proposals for alternative postwar agreements. Such reconsiderations were preceded by the ruminations of Herbert Samuel, a Jew, who served in Asquith's Cabinet as president of the Local Government Board. In November 1914, in separate conversations with Lloyd George and Sir Edward Grey, the foreign secretary, Samuel suggested that the security of Britain's eastern Suez Canal flank might best be assured by the formation, under British auspices, of a Jewish state in Palestine. While he

did not actively pursue Samuel's suggestion, Grey indicated that he was senti-
mentally attracted to such a viewpoint. Apparently, so did Lloyd George. Then
in January 1915, Samuel refined his thoughts and summarized them in a memorandum that he circulated to some of his cabinet colleagues. He recognized
that because the Palestinian Jews were still a small minority of the total population, it was unrealistic to assume that initially they could be entrusted with
the country without British patronage. Samuel's ideas, while not obtaining the
imprint of British policy, were tabled and provided food for thought. They did
at least prepare some of the groundwork for later policy changes, along the
lines he advocated.

With growing British concern to ward off an unfettered French postwar
foothold in Palestine, Sir Mark Sykes, a parliamentarian with an extensive
knowledge of Middle Eastern affairs, was authorized to secure a suitable understanding with the French. His negotiating partner was François Georges-
Picot, an experienced diplomat. Their discussions, which took place toward the
end of December 1915, culminated in what became known as the Sykes-Picot
Agreement, formally ratified in May 1916. The agreement, which was shrouded
in secrecy, made provision for a mutually acceptable division of British and
French spheres of influence in what was to be a dismembered Turkish Empire.
With specific regard to Palestine, it was resolved that the French were to control
an area west of the Jordan River north of a line running slightly north of Acre
to a point near the head of Lake Kinneret. Britain would possess Haifa and Acre
and the area south of the French sphere down to a line running from just north
of Gaza through Hebron, and the northern reaches of the Dead Sea were to be
under some form of international authority.

Prior to the negotiations with France, a pledge was given to Husain, the
sharif of Mecca, that, subject to certain explicit exclusions with regard to various areas west of Damascus, Britain was "prepared to recognize and uphold the
independence of the Arabs in all the regions that the Sharif had previously proposed."[9] This commitment was forwarded, in a note dated October 24, 1915, by
Henry McMahon. Subsequently, the question of whether Britain effectively
indicated that Palestine was to be included as part of an independent Arab state
was subject to controversy. In Antonius's view, since Palestine was not explicitly excluded, "It must be held to have formed part of the territory accepted by
Great Britain as the area of Arab independence."[10] A contrary opinion was
maintained by Kedourie, who argued that "between the Sykes-Picot Agreement and the promises of McMahon, there could be and there was no incompatibility."[11]

Meanwhile, Dr. Chaim Weizmann, who had been lecturing in chemistry at
Manchester University since 1904, was drawn to the attention of Lloyd George,
who at the time headed the Ministry of Munitions. Weizmann's friend, C.P.
Scott, the influential editor of the *Manchester Guardian*, acted as an intermediary. Weizmann had made pioneering progress in a fermentation process that
could facilitate the production of acetone, needed for explosives. In addition, he

held the position of co–vice president of the British Zionist Federation and was also a member of the World Zionist General Council.

In September 1915, Weizmann was appointed as a chemical adviser both to the Ministry of Munitions and the Admiralty. His research on behalf of the government certainly placed him in close contact with Lloyd George, whose respect and admiration he soon earned. Years later, a myth evolved that the Balfour Declaration was Weizmann's reward for his contribution to the war effort. Yet, as Leonard Stein noted, it is "nonsensical to imagine that the Declaration was handed to him as a kind of good conduct prize."[12]

In December 1916, the Asquith government was replaced by one headed by Lloyd George, with Balfour becoming the Foreign Secretary. All major policy decisions were made by a small War Cabinet. Instead of resting content with a neutralization of French pretensions in much of Palestine, as allowed for by the Sykes-Picot Agreement, the Lloyd George government veered toward an option whereby the French would be totally excluded. In practice, this could have been achieved simply by means of a purely British military victory and presence in Palestine, but expected French protestations would almost certainly have been problematic. Giving some consideration to this matter, Sykes began to toy with the notion of persuading the French that the Jews were not only totally aghast at any prospect of Palestine falling under an international condominium, but were anxious for Britain to provide them with a trusteeship. Putting it that way, it would appear as if Britain herself did not wish to occupy Palestine but was prepared to do so for the sake of a downtrodden third party. With such views gaining ground in Sykes's and other British politicians' minds, the British began to be more receptive to Zionist overtures. Their openness in this regard was by no means based exclusively on considerations of self-interest. Many of the leading actors had a warm regard for Jewry and supported the re-establishment of a Jewish state on the basis of deeply held religious or idealistic beliefs.

On January 28, 1917, Sykes conferred with Weizmann to arrange a meeting with top-ranking Zionists. On Sykes's suggestion, a short statement summarizing Zionist goals was to be submitted prior to the meeting. The statement in question concluded as follows:

Palestine to be recognised as the Jewish National Home, with liberty of immigration to Jews of all countries, who are to enjoy full national political and civic rights; a Charter to be granted to a Jewish Company; local government to be accorded to the Jewish population; and the Hebrew language to be officially recognised.[13]

The meeting, held at the beginning of February, was attended by Sykes, Rabbi Moses Gaster, Herbert Samuel, Chaim Weizmann, Nahum Sokolow (a member of the World Zionist Executive), Lord Rothschild, James de Rothschild, Joseph Cowen, Harry Sacher and Herbert Bentwich. Contrary to the secret Sykes-Picot Agreement, the Zionists were assured that the question of Palestine's future remained an open one.

To provide some momentum toward a shift in British policy more favorable to the Zionists, Weizmann entered into conversations with both Balfour and Lloyd George. Both men gave Weizmann the impression that they were entirely amenable to a postwar arrangement which would be in keeping with Zionist aspirations in Palestine. A short while later, Sokolow went to Paris and Rome to rally French and Italian support. After a number of interviews with French government functionaries, Sokolow succeeded in extracting from Jules Cambon, the secretary-general of the Ministry of Foreign Affairs, a letter, dated June 4, 1917, which effectively amounted to a miniature Balfour-type Declaration. In it, Cambon wrote:

You were good enough to present the project to which you are devoting your efforts, which has for its object the development of Jewish colonization in Palestine. You consider that, circumstances permitting, and the independence of the Holy Places being safeguarded on the other hand, it would be a deed of justice and of reparation to assist, by the protection of the Allied Powers, in the renaissance of the Jewish nationality in that land from which the people of Israel were exiled so many centuries ago.

The French Government, which entered this present war to defend a people wrongly attacked and which continues the struggle to assure the victory of right over might, can but feel sympathy for your cause, the triumph of which is bound up with that of the allies.

I am happy to give you herewith such assurances.[14]

On returning to England, Sokolow deposited a copy of Cambon's letter with the Foreign Office. The letter was not published, possibly because the Zionists were reluctant to give France any credit for siding with them before they had secured an official British statement to similar effect. In any case, they were at one with the British in that a multinational Allied force was to be excluded from Palestine. The importance of Cambon's written statement is that not only did it create a precedent for the British to follow, but it placed on record France's endorsement of Zionist objectives. Such an endorsement could later be flaunted to quell any French resistance to the scuttling of the Sykes-Picot Agreement and the placing of Palestine under a British mandate.

In the course of 1917, the Zionists were certainly edging toward some accord with the British, reflected in Sykes's overtures to them and Weizmann's friendly talks with Balfour and Lloyd George. The leaders of the old establishment English Jewry, who were bitterly anti-Zionist, soon sensed which way the wind was blowing. In desperation, they mounted a vigorous campaign to counter Zionist influences. They made it clear that they did not deny that Palestine had some significance for Jews in the same way that it was venerated by both Christians and Muslims. Nor did they object to the natural development of a Jewish community there, which may in time manifest national characteristics. What really raised their ire was the view, advanced by the Zionists, that Jews were not simply coreligionists but also conationals. They dreaded the possibility that the British government might officially concur with the Zionists that a national home of the Jewish people ought to be constituted in Palestine. To their way of thinking, that would belittle their claims to full British citizenship. Although unable to turn the tide against the Zionists, their detractors, as shown further below, were at least able to ruffle their feathers and deprive them of their most preferred outcome.

By mid-June 1917, with the securing of the Cambon letter and with rumors circulating that the Germans were on the verge of issuing a statement in support of Zionism, Weizmann appealed to British government officials to publicly announce what they had privately assured him; namely, that they were in complete sympathy with Zionist aspirations. In response, Balfour personally told Weizmann and Lord Rothschild that he was ready to move in that direction, pending the submission of a proposed declaration by the Zionists, which he could reasonably be expected to present to the War Cabinet. For their part, the Zionists, wishing to appear neutral in relation to the warring countries, decided that it would be preferable that the draft be sent not by their organization but in a personal letter by Lord Rothschild. Sokolow assumed responsibility for drawing up the document and dispatched it (in Rothschild's name) on July 18. Although the document was ostensibly a representation of purely Zionist objectives, it was drafted in full consultation with Mark Sykes and high-ranking members of the British Foreign Office. It therefore reflected a measure of negotiation between the British government and the Zionists and a compromise by both sides. It allowed for the recognition of a Jewish chartered company with sweeping powers to settle Jews in Palestine. However, the draft declaration that was actually considered by the government was somewhat more terse, worded as follows:

His Majesty's Government accepts the principle that Palestine should be reconstituted as the National Home of the Jewish People.

His Majesty's Government will use its best endeavours to secure the achievement of this object and will discuss the necessary methods and means with the Zionist Organisation.[15]

It was presented to the War Cabinet at the beginning of September. At that time the War Cabinet consisted of Lloyd George, Bonar Law, George Curzon, Alfred Milner, George Barnes, Sir Edward Carson and General Jan Smuts. Balfour himself was not an official member of the inner War Cabinet but he periodically appeared before it. Apart from Balfour and Lloyd George, Smuts, Barnes and Milner were all considered by Weizmann to be well disposed to his cause. The same could not be said of Edwin Montagu, who, as secretary of state for India, was elevated to the General Cabinet, though not the War Cabinet. A first cousin of Herbert Samuel, Montagu was an assimilated Jew who absolutely abhorred Zionism. His intense opposition to Zionism was based on his personal experiences. He is reputed to have once remarked that he had been striving throughout his life to escape from the ghetto and greatly feared that the forces of Zionism might ineluctably drive him back.[16] In June 1917, the *Morning Post* in criticizing his selection as chairman of a committee on labor unrest, questioned whether British workers would regard him as a true Englishman. Then a month later, the same paper depicted him as "a politico-financial Jew," who ought to be disqualified for public office on account of having a dual allegiance.[17] As Montagu saw things, nothing could be more personally disastrous than a British Declaration, which, he assumed, would delineate him as a Jew whose real focus of loyalty was in Palestine.[18]

Although not a member of the War Cabinet, Montagu's views regarding Lord Rothschild's memorandum, were sought at its session held on September 3. As might be expected, Montagu pulled no punches in arguing against it. His diatribe was not without effect and, partly as a result, the War Cabinet decided to ascertain President Wilson's position. On September 11, a telegram arrived from the United States indicating that Wilson thought that "the time was not opportune for any definite statement."[19] Such a response was the last thing the Zionists needed, for it had the potential of shelving the entire matter indefinitely. A deeply distraught Weizmann made urgent contact with Louis Brandeis who, in turn, replied to him by wire sent through the British War Office (so that the British Government would be party to the communication). Brandeis informed Weizmann that on the basis of talks he had with the president and his advisers, he could safely assure him that Wilson was in fact "in entire sympathy" with the proposed declaration.[20] Without further ado, Weizmann met with Balfour and then later with Lloyd George. The meeting with the latter was of only a few minutes' duration. It was contrived by Scott of the *Manchester Guardian*, who had arranged to have breakfast with the prime minister and to have Weizmann waiting in the wings, to speak with him should the opportunity arise. On the basis of a brief exchange between Weizmann and Lloyd George, the Balfour Declaration was saved from oblivion, for it was determined that it would once again be placed on the War Cabinet agenda.

At the following War Cabinet meeting, held on October 3, the issue was reaired. Once again, Montagu was in attendance. This time, his anti-Zionist rhetoric was even more barbed than before. Referring to his portfolio as secretary of state for India, he demanded to know how he would be able to represent Britain "if the world had just been told that His Majesty's government regarded his national home as being in Turkish territory?"[21] Balfour for his part tried to reassure the cabinet that the proposed declaration would be well received in the international arena. Putting the Cambon letter to good use, he read it out to reassure his colleagues that French feathers would not be ruffled.[22] As to President Woodrow Wilson, with Brandeis's telegram to Weizmann in mind, Balfour indicated that he had reason to assume that Wilson was in fact well disposed toward Zionism. However, since Wilson had already indicated that he had reservations about the timing of the Balfour Declaration, it was decided that he would once again be approached to ascertain whether he still stood firm on that matter. In addition, as a concession to Montagu, it was agreed that the government would consider arguments presented both by the Zionists and their opponents.

The unrelenting hostility evinced by Montagu and his associates, plus reservations expressed by others, began to take their toll. Milner in conjunction with Leopold Amery drafted an alternative declaration to the one proposed by Rothschild. Their goal was to placate both the Jewish anti-Zionists and those who were expressing concerns about Arab interests. Their suggested declaration read:

His Majesty's Government views with favour the establishment in Palestine of a national home for the Jewish race and will use its best endeavours to facilitate the achievements of this object, it being clearly understood that nothing shall be done which may prejudice the civil and religious rights of existing non-Jewish communities in Palestine, or the rights and political status enjoyed in any other country by such Jews who are fully contented with their existing nationality.[23]

The Milner-Amery draft was transmitted to President Wilson, who, in mid-October, let it be known that he approved the text and no longer saw any need to delay the declaration. Wilson's endorsement heartened the Zionists, but their satisfaction in this regard was tempered by a significant difference between the Rothschild proposal and the one now bearing the government's imprimatur. Whereas the Rothschild document proclaimed "that Palestine should be reconstituted as the national home of the Jewish People," the document superseding it referred to the "establishment *in* Palestine of *a* national home."[24] In the course of the years to follow, these amendments were to prove to be a source of immense distress to the Jewish people.

Finally, on October 31, the matter of the declaration was brought before the War Cabinet for the third and last time. Cognizant of the potential propaganda dividends that were expected to be accrued from a grateful world Jewish public, the issue was favorably resolved with little serious dissension, Montagu's well-known staunch opposition notwithstanding. The Milner-Amery draft was officially approved with minor amendments. The term "Jewish race" was replaced by "Jewish people," and the ending was abridged. The phrase "the rights and political status enjoyed in any other country by such Jews who are fully contented with their existing nationality," was replaced by a more succinct one: "the rights and political status enjoyed by Jews in any other country." On November 2, the Balfour Declaration was officially conveyed to Lord Rothschild.

Jewish reaction to the announcement of the Balfour Declaration was one of unbounded jubilation. As the news filtered through to the shtetls (villages) of Russia and the rest of Eastern Europe, there was a general feeling that all the hardships and misfortunes that they had suffered as Jews were about to be compensated by the recognition of Britain and other great powers that they were entitled to a national home in Palestine. Naturally, the Jews living in Palestine were particularly gratified. Those falling in areas liberated by General

Allenby, at the year's end, received the news promptly. As for the others, who were cut off from all communication with the outside world, it took a while before they learned what had transpired. In late 1918, hundreds of exiles from Jaffa and Tel Aviv were cooped up in Kfar Saba, which had then become a frontline village. Most were living in tents, which they had to share with German troops. Among the Germans was a Jewish lieutenant. After he felt comfortable with his tentmate Menachem Kleivner, he lent him a copy of a German Zionist newspaper written in Yiddish. As Kleivner and his friends began reading the paper in a generally depressed state of mind, they were astonished to find a report of the Balfour Declaration. They could not help but compare their current circumstances with what the Balfour Declaration heralded for their future. As Kleivner put it, "Here we are ground into the dust and there they are raising us to the heavens."[25]

THE JEWISH LEGION

After the disbandment of the Zion Mule Corps, Jabotinsky, aided by Trumpeldor, continued to lobby for the formation of a Jewish Legion to fight for the liberation of Palestine under the wing of one of the Allied Powers, preferably Britain. Their efforts were eventually rewarded when, in August 1917, the British Cabinet decided to create a Jewish Regiment consisting of three battalions. A factor predisposing the Cabinet to respond favorably to Jabotinsky and Trumpeldor's request was the presence in Britain of 20,000 Russian Jews of military age who, because of their alien status, were escaping conscription.[26]

As in the Zion Mule Corps, the first battalion was commanded by Colonel Patterson. The government had indicated that the regiment's name and insignia, a menorah (an ancient Jewish candelabra), would clearly highlight its Jewish character. But thanks to the intercession of the anti-Zionist Jewish establishment, whose leaders hurriedly met with Lord Derby, the secretary of state for war, the Jewish battalions were simply to be known as "the Royal Fusiliers." The prospect of specific British army units being identified as being distinctly Jewish was as distasteful to the anti-Zionist Jews as was the prospect of the government announcing, through the Balfour Declaration, that it recognized the Jews as having their own valid national aspirations. To attempt to neutralize the influence of the anti-Zionists, a delegation representing the mainstream of English Jewry appealed to Lord Derby to abide by the government's original decision. Being reluctant to become embroiled in intra-Jewish politics and not wishing to appear indecisive, Lord Derby tried to placate them by promising that if the soldiers acquitted themselves well in battle, they would then receive a Jewish title and badge. On the other hand, they would immediately be supplied with kosher food, the Jewish Sabbath would be honored and all Jewish festivals would, wherever possible, be upheld. The Jewish units were in practice universally known as the "Jewish Battalions" or "Jewish Legion."[27]

Recruits for the first Jewish unit, the 38th Battalion of the Royal Fusiliers, were enrolled in London and then sent to Plymouth for training.[28] Of the battalion's thirty officers, twenty were Jews who were transferred from other regiments.[29] The nucleus of the Jewish Legion consisted of Zion Mule Corps veterans who, at Patterson's request, were transferred from the 20th Battalion of the London Regiment. When the Zion Mule Corps was disbanded, 120 of the muleteers volunteered for service in France. The ship transporting them was torpedoed but they all survived by clinging to floating debris and, after drifting to Crete, they were brought to England. (Trumpeldor also wished to be included in the Jewish Legion but, even though he had served as a captain in the Zion Mule Corps, he was rejected because foreigners were not allowed to become officers in the British Army.)[30] Gradually, more and more men, of whom most were new immigrants from Russia, arrived at the Plymouth training base. They possessed a variety of callings and included among them was Jacob Epstein, the eminent sculptor. Of all trades, that of tailoring was the most prominent and for that reason, the battalion was lightheartedly referred to as "the Tailors." Their military instruction proceeded smoothly and the men's general behavior was beyond reproach. Patterson mentioned with pride that not a single case of civil offense was leveled against them, a fact that he regarded as being quite remarkable. With perhaps an even greater degree of astonishment, he also went on to note that "yet another record was created by this unique Battalion. The Wet Canteen, where beer only was sold, had to be closed, for not a single pint was drunk all the time it was open."[31]

While still in Plymouth, Patterson received instructions to form two more Jewish battalions, in addition to the 38th, as soon as numbers warranted it. Accordingly, the 39th Battalion was soon commissioned. It was originally commanded by Major Knowles, then Colonel Samuel and ultimately by Major Eliezer Margolin. Margolin, who was Russian born, lived in Palestine during the First Aliyah period. After a while, he left for Australia, where he settled permanently. At the outbreak of the war, he volunteered for the Australian army, was commissioned as an officer and was transported to Europe. The 39th Battalion largely consisted of volunteers from the United States, organized by Pinhas Rutenberg, David Ben Gurion and Yitzhak Ben-Zvi. The latter two had arrived in the United States in 1915 after their expulsion from Palestine.

The 38th Battalion was set to sail from Southampton to Egypt on February 5, 1918. Two days beforehand, half the troops were ordered to London to parade through the City and the East End. On February 4, after spending a night at the Tower, they marched through the streets of London in full battle dress and with fixed bayonets. They were led by the band of the Coldstream Guards and by two flagbearers (one of whom was Jabotinsky), who bore the Union Jack and the Zionist blue and white emblem containing the Star of David. At the Mansion House, the Lord Mayor, dressed in his mayoral robes, took the salute, while Jewish onlookers cheered and waved ecstatically. The following day, the entire battalion set off for Alexandria via Italy, arriving at their destination on February 28.

A few days later, Patterson received the first of what were to be a series of shocks and rebuffs from the hierarchy of the [British] Egyptian Expeditionary Force (EEF). In a letter to General Allenby, the commander-in-chief, Patterson raised the matter of the 38th and 39th Battalions being augmented by a 40th Battalion, composed of Jewish volunteers from Palestine. Patterson hoped that a full-scale Jewish brigade would be formed, a prospect, he was given to understand, that had War Office support. In response, Patterson was summoned to General Headquarters, where both Allenby and his chief of staff, Major General Bols, made it patently clear that neither of them took kindly to the presence of the 38th Battalion. Bols, in particular, indicated "that he was not favorably disposed toward Jewish aspirations."[32] In fact, almost the entire British officer Corps of the EEF adopted a hostile stance toward Zionism and Jews in general. Some, including well-placed senior officers, were anti-Semites of the highest order. That their government had issued a Declaration in favor of Zionism and espoused a policy of fraternal friendship toward the Jewish people meant nothing to them. In this sphere, they felt neither duty nor honor bound to fulfill Cabinet decisions.

Nonetheless, the Jewish military presence within the EEF began to be consolidated. At the end of April, the 39th Battalion, under the command of Margolin, landed in Alexandria. On June 5, the 38th Battalion traveled by train to Palestine. There they were stationed at Umm Suffah, near Shechem (Nablus) in the Judean Hills, where they occupied a series of elevations facing the Turks. Between them and the enemy was a valley into which they made forays at night, taking up positions behind hastily constructed stone barriers. Very little serious action took place and most of the time spent in that area was filled with routine patrols. In August, the Battalion was relocated to a site in the Jordan Valley, 1,200 feet below sea level and for over seven weeks, they languished in sweltering heat. No other British unit was subjected to such climatic extremes for such a length of time. As Patterson remarked, even the Bedouin "flee from the accursed place in these two dreaded months."[33] Their camp was on the extreme eastern and northern section of the British Army. Surrounded by vastly superior Turkish forces on three sides, they had "the most exposed piece of front to guard which it is possible to conceive."[34] On September 15, Margolin's 39th Battalion took up a position in support of the 38th Battalion. (By then the Jewish Legion's forces in Palestine numbered 5,000.)[35] Finally, on September 20, after a few days of repeatedly raiding the enemy, the 38th Battalion, with some backing from the 39th Battalion, attacked and overran the Umm esh Shert Ford over the Jordan River. The conquered ground was well protected by a series of trenches, by barbed wire entanglements and by the fortified Jordan cliffs. Its capture threw Turkish communications out of kilter and enabled the First Australian Light Horse Brigade to cross the river and gallop to Es Salt, where a large enemy concentration was routed.

By the beginning of October, the 39th Battalion was posted at Ludd, and after Turkey's surrender on October 31, they were directed to Rafa. From there they were responsible for protecting installations over a large stretch of land. Fortunately for them, they were reinforced by the arrival of a company of soldiers from the 40th Battalion. The 40th Battalion consisted of Palestinian Jews who volunteered their services when the southern part of the country was liberated by British forces and after the Balfour Declaration was announced. The initiative came from a group of students at Tel Aviv's Herzlia Gymnasium, headed by Eliyahu Golomb. Shortly, they were joined by numerous members of Poalei Zion and eventually even by members of Hapoel Hatzair, once they overcame their passivistic leanings.

Immediately after the war, the 39th and 40th Battalions were merged into the 38th Battalion and for a short time, the Judeans were responsible for the public safety of much of the country. But this was not to last, for most of them were discharged toward the end of 1919 and the rest in 1921. In its short history, in which the Judeans lost thirty-three men, twenty-one were honored with medals and laudatory mentions in dispatches.

THE NILI SPIES

In the unfolding drama of the Nili spy ring, there were a number of key players, of whom the most senior was Aaron Aaronson, the eldest of six siblings.[36] He was reared in Zichron Yaakov, where he settled at the age of six when he and his parents arrived from Romania. On turning eighteen, he studied agriculture in France, courtesy of Baron Rothschild. Two years later, after receiving his diploma, he was appointed as an agronomist at Metulla in northern Palestine. He did not stay long at that post and soon found himself working as an overseer in a large estate in Turkey, acquiring a fluent knowledge of Turkish. Aaronson's work in Turkey ended after a couple of years, bringing him back to Palestine, where he drifted about without securing a fixed position. He spent a good deal of his time exploring the country's flora, fauna and geological structure, accumulating an immense stock of knowledge in such matters. Perhaps his greatest achievement was his discovery of wild wheat, which he found growing in parts of the Upper Galilee and along the slopes of Mount Hermon. When scientists in the United States learned that he was cultivating the newly found wild wheat at his father's farm, they invited him to America. Impressing his hosts with his botanical ingenuity, he secured funding for an agricultural experimental station, which, in 1910 he established at Atlit, approximately eight kilometers northwest of Zichron Yaakov. A little later, Aaronson set up a branch of the experimental station at Hadera, placing it under the management of Absalom Feinberg, a native-born Jew who spoke fluent Arabic.

At the outbreak of war, detachments of Turkish soldiers arrived in Zichron Yaakov and Hadera as well as in other Jewish settlements along the coastal plain. They confiscated the settlers' weapons and then handed over some of them to neighboring Arabs. Finding themselves suddenly placed in such a precarious situation, many settlers prayed for a swift British invasion. To further that end, Aaronson and Feinberg decided to provide the British with strategic information, using the station at Atlit as an espionage base.

Because of his agricultural research, Aaronson was able to strike up an accord of a kind with Jemal Pasha, the Turkish commander, who had an interest in such matters. When the locust plague broke out, Aaronson was given the rare privilege of being able to travel freely throughout Palestine. This enabled him to survey the totality of Turkish and German forces stationed there. Although a vast amount of intelligence was accumulated, no contact was secured with British ships expected to appear in the vicinity. It seems that agreed signaling procedures, conveyed to Feinberg on a furtive visit to Egypt, had been altered without them being apprised of the change. To clarify the situation, Feinberg made another attempt to reach Egypt. He penetrated the Turkish ground forces by riding a horse dressed in the uniform of Aaronson's locust brigade and as he ventured further southward, he disguised himself as a Bedouin. Just as he was nearing the Suez Canal, he was intercepted by a Turkish patrol and taken to a prison in Beersheba to be hanged as a spy. He was saved at the eleventh hour by Aaronson, who insisted that his locust assistant had been mistakenly arrested.

The task of recontacting the British still had to be accomplished. This time Aaronson took it upon himself. He obtained permission from Jemal Pasha to travel to Germany, where he ostensibly wished to consult with fellow scientists. From Germany he went to Copenhagen and then boarded a ship bound for America, having made a prior arrangement for the British to intercept it and "arrest" him. After being debriefed in London, Aaronson was sent to Egypt to work with British officers.

While Aaronson was in Egypt, Sara, his eldest sister, left Constantinople where she had been living and returned to Zichron Yaakov to join Feinberg. Since nothing had been heard from Aaronson, Feinberg embarked on yet another dash to the British front, this time accompanied by Yoseph Lishansky. On January 25, 1917, Aaronson was summoned to Port Said to find Lishansky recovering from gunshot wounds. He recounted that when he and Feinberg had approached the canal zone, they were surrounded by hostile Bedouin. A gunfight ensued, which led to Feinberg's death and Lishansky's wounds. The Bedouin assumed that Lishansky was dead and, miraculously, he was rescued by British scouts.

At about that juncture, Major Deedes suggested to Aaronson that he seek out a stouthearted man capable of swimming at least four hundred meters in choppy seas and who was familiar with the Atlit vicinity. The plan was to lower him from a boat anchored off Atlit so that he might make his way ashore and then to Atlit to inform Sara of the new signaling arrangements. Leibel Bornstein, an ex–Zion Mule Corps soldier who once worked as a coach driver on the road from Hadera to Haifa, turned out to be the man in question. Bornstein was taken aboard a ship bound for the Palestinian coast. As planned, he swam ashore and dutifully restored the lost contact between the British and the spy ring, which by then termed itself Nili (an acronym of the Hebrew phrase "the eternity of Israel shall not be falsified" [*netzah Yisrael lo yishaker*]). From then on Nili began operating in earnest, sending messages on a regular basis. Through a system of flashing light signals at night, passing ships would send out a small boat to the shore to hand over money and instructions and to receive in turn Nili's dispatches. On one of such ships, Lishansky returned to help Sara Aaronson.

In time, Nili was provided with a set of homing pigeons, which were occasionally used to bear urgent messages to the British, who were then preparing to march on Beersheba. On September 3, 1917, one of the birds released by Sara Aaronson landed at Caesarea at the very spot where the moudir, the head of the police, was feeding his own pigeons. He readily identified it as not being his and noticed a little cylinder, containing a coded message, attached to its leg. Although the message was not deciphered, it was obvious that an active spy ring was at large. The Turks did not have long to wait for further confirmation. Naaman Belkind, one of Nili's members, was caught while attempting to reach Egypt by camel. By plying him with wine, doping him with hashish and then torturing him, the Turks were able to extract enough information for them to zero in on Zichron Yaakov. They seized Sara Aaronson, her brother Zvi and her father Ephraim. Lishansky escaped at the last moment. For three whole days Sara was subjected to cruel and hideous forms of torture. Not giving anything away other than a declaration that she had acted entirely on her own, Sara was to be transferred to Nazareth, where the Turks hoped that they would break her spirit. Before the journey, she was given permission to change her clothes and while alone in her bathroom, she reached for a pistol placed behind a panel and shot herself through the mouth. She died three days later.

Thereafter, a bounty of gold was placed on Lishansky's head, fourteen elders of Zichron Yaakov were taken as hostages and the rest of the settlers were threatened with all manner of horrors should they not surrender Lishansky. Running and hiding from place to place, Lishansky was eventually picked up by three members of Hashomer, who were making their way in a wagon to Tel Adas, in the northern part of the Galilee. When they arrived at their destination, the appearance of Lishansky created quite a furor. Everyone knew that he was a fugitive and that his presence there placed them all at substantial risk. In addition, there was a longstanding enmity between Hashomer and Lishansky, who in the past had been ejected from its ranks for recklessly killing an Arab. One member of Hashomer tried to shoot Lishansky and as he fled, he was wounded by gunfire. Somehow or other, Lishansky, disguised as a Bedouin, managed to reach an Arab village not far from Rishon Letzion, where he was recognized and handed over to the Turks. An embittered Lishansky freely provided his capturers with the names, including nicknames, of every Hashomer member he could recall, directly implicating them in the Nili spy ring. Both he and Naaman Belkind were hanged in Damascus.

THE OPPRESSIVE SEQUEL TO NILI'S DEMISE

Almost immediately after Lishansky's detention, wholesale arrests were conducted throughout the length and breadth of the country, with the Turks rounding up anyone thought to be linked to Hashomer. Not only did the Turks suspect that Hashomer was involved in espionage but they also believed that it was preparing an armed uprising and that it had stockpiled a large amount of ammunition. Assushkin recalled that he and his comrades were chained to one another and marched off over a three-day period from Kfar Giladi to Nazareth, where 130 prisoners were being held. In his memoirs Assushkin expressed a reluctance "to recount in full detail the investigation and torture in Nazareth and on the sadistic procedures adopted by Hasan Beck (a doctor by profession)."[37] Suffice it to say, they were severely manhandled and then transported to Damascus. According to Bela Rozenfeld, 150 prisoners were marched to Afula. They walked "barefooted with injured feet. Most were debilitated and ill, hungry and thirsty. They were herded like a pack of dogs. They were not allowed to break their thirst from wells that they passed, nor were they granted any respite whatsoever. The rifle butt did its job and under a shower of blows and wild threats they arrived sick and tormented at Afula station. There they were squeezed into cattle cars whose doors were never once opened to allow them to attend to the call of nature."[38] On another occasion, Y. Segal had the misfortune to be transported by train from Jerusalem to Damascus. He reported that "for eight days we were imprisoned in those terrible coaches. For eight days we did not manage to sleep. Eight continuous days with eighty to a coach! Locked up and deprived of the ability to move and of fresh air, with refuse, mire and filth, with lice and pests, with people having to excrete as they stood. Thus we traveled to Damascus."[39] Many German soldiers bore witness to the way the Jews were treated and transported and it is more than probable that they conveyed the benefit of their findings to the Nazi regime established in their country a decade and a half later.

Were it not for the intervention of Chaim Kalvarisky from Rosh Pina, who risked his life in pleading before Jemal Pasha and in arguing that Hashomer was innocent of the charges brought against it, all the prisoners would have been executed. Those that landed in a Damascus jail were greatly assisted by Avraham Herzfeld and Yitzak Ben-Yaakov from Degania, who managed to supply them with food (prepared by two women pioneers from the Galilee) and other necessities. Before assistance reached them, the Jewish inmates were fed unclean, partly cooked soup and porridge. They slept on cold floors in filthy cells and within a matter of months at least thirty-eight of them perished.[40] Herzfeld and Ben-Yaakov even managed to meet with and bribe the chief warden to permit selected prisoners "temporary" leave of absence and then to smuggle them back into Palestine.

THE CONQUEST OF PALESTINE

Having entered the war in late 1914, the Turks, in 1915, twice attempted to wrest control of the Suez Canal. In both instances, superior British forces repelled them. The following year, the British seized the initiative by opening up, within northern Sinai, an offensive that ended on the Palestine border. Then in March and April 1917, the British attacked Gaza but were repulsed. Soon after the appointment of General Allenby as overall British commander, a break-through was achieved toward the end of October with the Turks losing Beer-sheba. A few weeks later, Jaffa fell. By December, Allenby was able to turn to and conquer Jerusalem. With British forces being deficient in numbers, a mili-tary stalemate resulted, leaving sections of Palestine under opposing forces. It was not until September 1918 that fighting resumed. The British mounted a major operation on the coastal plain, which culminated in horse-mounted Anzac troops sweeping through Megiddo (Armageddon) and then pushing on to Damascus. Palestine was liberated, the prisoners in Damascus were set free and an oppressive yoke was lifted off the shoulders of the Yishuv.

It is highly probable that, had Turkey prevailed, the New Yishuv would have been totally eradicated. Turkish leaders like Jemal Pasha were uncompromising nationalists who, given a free hand, would have snuffed out all movements and tendencies toward the establishment of autonomous Arab or Jewish regions, just as they cruelly dispatched hundreds of thousands of Armenians. That such a fate did not befall the New Yishuv in the war years is attributable to the re-straining influence of Germany and the show of support to the Jews of Pales-tine both by their kinsmen in America and by the American government. In 1917, a Turkish officer candidly explained the situation to one of the Jews ban-ished from Jaffa in the following terms: "As soon as some misfortune is im-posed on you (the Jews), you raise such a hue and cry that it reverberates around the world. Were it not for that, no one among you would have been left to survive."[41]

NOTES

1. Yoseph Shalosh, "Ottomanization and the Expulsion of Foreign Nationals," in Yaari, *Memoirs*, 1947, p. 1000.

2. Yoseph Sprinzak, as quoted by Meir, *Zionist Movement*, 1983, p. 138.

3. Halevi et al., *Banker*, 1977, p. 41.

4. As quoted by Lipovetzky, *Joseph Trumpeldor*, 1953, p. 49.

5. Ibid.

6. Patterson, *With the Zionists*, 1916, p. 106.

7. As quoted by Patterson, *With the Zionists*, 1916, pp. 213–14.

8. As quoted by Laskov, *Trumpeldor*, 1972, p. 128.

9. Antonius, *Arab Awakening*, 1969, p. 170.

10. Ibid., p. 177.

11. Kedourie, *England*, 1956, p. 57.

12. Stein, *Balfour Declaration*, 1961, p. 120.

13. As quoted by Stein, *Balfour Declaration*, 1961, p. 369.

14. As quoted by Stein, *Balfour Declaration*, 1961, p. 417.

15. As quoted by Stein, *Balfour Declaration*, 1961, p. 470.

16. Ibid., p. 498.

17. The *Morning Post*, June 5, and July 10, 1917.

18. Stein, *Balfour Declaration*, 1961, p. 499.

19. Ibid., p. 505.

20. Ibid., p. 507.

21. Ibid., p. 515.

22. Ibid., p. 419.

23. As quoted by Stein, *Balfour Declaration*, 1961, p. 521.

24. Italics added.

25. M. Kleivner, "Kfar Saba Centre for Jaffa and Tel Aviv Refugees," in Yaari, *Memoirs*, 1947, p. 1068.

26. Stein, *Balfour Declaration*, 1961, p. 488.

27. Patterson, *With the Judeans*, 1922, p. 24.

28. Ibid., p. 34.

29. Jabotinsky, *Jewish Legion*, 1945, p. 105.

30. Instead, Trumpeldor went to Russia where he organized the *Hechalutz* movement. See chapter 6.

31. Patterson, *With the Judeans*, 1922, p. 34.

32. Ibid., p. 57.

33. Ibid., p. 110.

34. Ibid., p. 105.

35. The composition of the 5,000 was roughly 40 percent from North America, 28 percent from England, 30 percent from Palestine and the remaining 2 percent from elsewhere, including Argentina. See Jabotinsky, *Jewish Legion*, 1945, p. 164.

36. Most of the information in this section is derived from Engle, *Nili Spies*, 1959.

37. Assushkin, "The Founding of Kfar Giladi," in Habbas, *Second Aliyah*, 1947, p. 459.

38. Bela Rozenfeld, "In the Years of War and Distress," in Habbas, *Second Aliyah*, 1947, p. 653.

39. Y. Segal, "Oppression Because of Suspicion of Espionage," in Yaari, *Memoirs*, 1947, p. 1104.

40. A. Herzfeld, "In the Years of War and Distress," in Habbas, *Memoirs*, 1947, p. 646.

41. As quoted in Bein, *History*, 1970, p. 131.

Chapter 6

The Early Years of British Rule in Palestine:
1917–1930

With postwar Palestine firmly in British hands and with the Balfour Declaration still ringing in their ears, the Zionists seemingly had good cause for believing that they were on the brink of national redemption. But, in reality, the situation was not quite that auspicious. The country was placed under a military regime that subscribed to the proposition that as an occupying force, it was bound by international law to preserve the status quo. This meant that until the country's final status was determined at an International Peace Conference, no special privileges were to be granted to the Zionists. Jewish immigration, except for postwar returnees, was not permitted. Few Jews were appointed to public posts and Hebrew was not recognized as having any official standing. Above all, copies of the Balfour Declaration were not locally released.

Nevertheless, as a measure of good faith, the British government authorized the formation of a Zionist Commission, which was meant to coordinate with and assist the Palestine administration in facilitating the establishment of a Jewish National Home. The Commission arrived in Palestine in April 1918 under Weizmann's chairmanship.[1] As might have been expected, the military did not take kindly to its presence and it had, in effect, little, if any, influence on policy. Weizmann was however advised by high-ranking British officers to seek a modus vivendi with the Arabs.

Acting on such advice, on June 4, 1918, Weizmann visited Emir Faisal,[2] at his headquarters near Aqaba. The visit represented an earnest attempt to reassure the Arabs that Zionism had no sinister intentions. In that light, Weizmann informed Faisal that the Jews wished to develop Palestine with full regard to legitimate Arab concerns. For his part, Faisal reassured his interlocutor that he believed that such aspirations were feasible.[3]

Just over six months later, in January 1919, on the eve of the Peace Conference, Weizmann and Faisal met again, this time in London. Their meeting culminated in the issuing of a jointly signed statement providing for harmonious relations between Arabs and Jews. Faisal accepted the Balfour Declaration with all that it entailed, while Weizmann committed Zionist assistance for an Arab state that Faisal was expecting to establish.

Then the following February, when the Zionists were appearing before the Paris Peace Conference, the Emir Faisal gave an interview to the French newspaper *le Matin* in which he expressed hostility to Zionism. In view of the cordiality that he and Weizmann seemed to have struck, Felix Frankfurter, an American Zionist, approached the Emir to clarify his position. The atmosphere at the meeting was convivial and a few days later the Emir sent Frankfurter a letter in which, *inter alia*, he stated, "We feel that Arabs and Jews are cousins in race, suffering similar oppressions at the hand of powers stronger than themselves, and by a happy coincidence have been able to take the first step toward the attainment of their national ideals together. We Arabs, especially the educated among us, look with the deepest sympathy on the Zionist movement. Our deputation here in Paris is fully acquainted with the proposals submitted by the Zionist Organisation to the Peace Conference, and we regard them as moderate and proper. We will do our best, inasfar as we are concerned to help them through; we will wish the Jews a most hearty welcome home."[4]

The Emir's letter to Frankfurter, coupled with the joint Faisal-Weizmann January agreement, was widely touted by the Zionists as evidence of Arab acceptance of their position. What they played down was Faisal's own publicly stated reservations and the attitudes of the rest of the Arab nationalist leadership. When cosigning the declaration with Weizmann, Faisal appended, in Arabic, the following proviso:

Provided the Arabs obtain their independence as demanded in my Memorandum dated the 4th of January, 1919 to the Foreign Office of the Government of Great Britain, I shall concur in the above Articles. But if the slightest modification or departure were to be made (in relation to the demands in the Memorandum) I shall not then be bound by a single word of the present Agreement, which shall be deemed void and of no account or validity, and I shall not be answerable in any way whatsoever.[5]

In a rather short passage of time, Faisal's hopes for an independent Arab state in Syria were dashed. In 1920, the French occupied Syria, declared it their protectorate and displaced Faisal. To compensate him, the British made him king of Iraq. Even if Faisal's ambitions were not undermined, he was never in any position to guarantee the Zionists that his early expressions of sympathy would be shared by the Arabs as a whole. A short time before Faisal's Syrian aspirations were foiled, the Syrian (Arab) Congress, which assembled in July 1919, totally rejected Zionist plans for the establishment of a Jewish homeland in Palestine and opposed further Jewish immigration. By September 1919, Faisal himself explicitly stated that the Arabs could never yield Palestine to the Jews.[6]

Within Palestine, Arab opposition to Zionism was rapidly gaining momentum. As early as January 1919, more or less at the same time that Weizmann was conferring with Faisal in London, an all-Arab Palestine Conference called for the repudiation of the Balfour Declaration. A month later, the Arab mayor of Jerusalem, Mussa Kassem, marched at the head of a procession denouncing Zionism. Prior to the procession, a proclamation was issued that likened the Jews to poisonous vipers who bring about misfortune to the world at large. The proclamation ended with the assertion that Palestine belongs exclusively to the Arabs and that they will defend it to the end just as they had done at the beginning.[7]

The military authorities, ever eager to scuttle Zionist objectives, picked up as their cue the growing and overt Arab resistance to official pro-Jewish policy. On May 2, 1919, General Clayton (the chief political officer) in endorsing General Money's (the chief administrator) advice that Britain jettison the Balfour Declaration, telegraphed London that Arab "fear and distrust of Zionist aims grow daily and no amount of persuasion or propaganda will dispel it."[8] In response, the government firmly rejected Clayton and Money's overtures and informed the military authorities that they intended to abide by their former commitments.

A month later, a two-man commission consisting of Dr. Henry King and Charles Crane, both from the United States, arrived in Palestine. The Commission, known as the King-Crane Commission, was charged by the Paris Peace Conference with the task of determining the wishes of the local population regarding their political future. Little time was lost by Arab dignitaries in voicing to the Commission their total opposition to Zionism. In Jerusalem, their chief spokesman, Aref Pasha Dajani, explained that wherever in the world Jews are present "they always arrive to suck the blood of everybody," and that "if the League of Nations will not listen to the appeal of the Arabs this country will become a river of blood."[9] Influenced by Arab anti-Zionist protestations, the King-Crane Commission recommended that Palestine be combined with Syria in a mandate to be administered by either the United States or Britain. Fortunately for the Zionists, its report was shelved and soon fell into oblivion.

By the beginning of 1920, a newly formed Muslim-Christian League, in no small way fostered by British officers and administrators, became the major source of anti-Zionist activity. Agitation against the budding Jewish community had advanced to such a point, that Arab-Jewish clashes were only a matter of time. The first serious bout of violence was occasioned by a temporary power vacuum in the northern region of the country.

THE BATTLE OF TEL HAI

In the aftermath of the First World War, when Britain occupied Palestine and the French, in terms of the Sykes-Picot Agreement, assumed control of Lebanon, the northeastern district of Palestine, where the four Jewish settlements of Metulla, Hamra, Kfar Giladi and Tel Hai were located, momentarily became a virtual no man's land.[10] In September 1919, the British, in deference to the French, withdrew from the northern Galilee to a point slightly north of Ayelet Hashahar. However, the French did not firmly assert their presence in the vacated territory. As a result, the region fell prey to roving Bedouin, armed with stockpiles of ammunition abandoned by the Turkish army. The Bedouin constantly harassed the French forces that occasionally made a perfunctory appearance and attacked and looted local Christian Arab villages.

For the most part, the settlers at Metulla and Hamra, realizing that they were almost certain to be subject to an armed assault that they would be incapable of repelling, chose to leave the area until some semblance of law and order was restored. Not so the handful of young workers at Kfar Giladi and Tel Hai, who all stayed put. Their resolve was reflected in an article written by Aaron Sher, which appeared two months before the battle of Tel Hai. On behalf of his coworkers, Sher appealed to the leaders of the Jewish community in Palestine to rally to their aid by providing them with material provisions and physical reinforcements. Emphasizing the need for urgent action, his article asserted that "a place once settled is not to be abandoned,"[11] a phrase that subsequently became a slogan of the Labor Zionist movement. The Provisional Council of Jews in Palestine was divided as to how they ought to have responded. Jabotinsky believed that the workers stood no chance of resisting an attack and advised them to let discretion be the better part of valor by withdrawing. Labor delegates were, in theory, inclined to mobilize support for their beleaguered comrades; in practice, however, they were tardy in organizing the delivery of needed men and supplies. Apart from isolated individual volunteers (of whom Aaron Sher was one), no organized reinforcements arrived in the time of need.

In December 1919, Joseph Trumpeldor, who had returned to Palestine to prepare the groundwork for the immigration of Russian Jewish pioneers, was asked by Israel Shochet, one of the heads of Hashomer, to pay a visit to the four northern settlements and to report on their situation. On his arrival there, Trumpeldor assumed command of Tel Hai and began drilling the settlers in preparation for an imminent attack. Even with the handful of volunteers who had rallied to their aid, the combined fighting force of Tel Hai and Kfar Giladi did not exceed fifty-nine. At first, little serious harm befell them, but on December 12, 1919, Shnior Shefoshnik was murdered as he stepped outside Tel Hai's precincts. Then on February 6, 1920, Sher was fatally shot during a brief melee with Arab robbers in the settlement's fields.

The fragile position of the settlers was noted in a diary entry of Trumpeldor dated January 4, 1920. After French forces in the area were routed, Trumpeldor wrote: "The question was raised, if a battalion of French troops equipped with [cannons] and machine guns was unable to withstand an Arab assault, how could we, a small handful of people armed only with rifles, do so?...At a hastily arranged meeting it was decided that we would remain in place, come what may ...and that when the decisive moment comes we shall hold firm and shall raise the cost of our lives to the utmost."[12]

Matters came to a head when on March 1, 1920, Tel Hai was surrounded by hundreds of Bedouin. From their ranks, five armed men stepped forward. One of them, a resident of a neighboring village was known to the settlers. They expressed a wish to enter Tel Hai's compound to satisfy themselves that French soldiers were not present. Since this had become a fairly routine request, the settlers did not demur.

To appreciate the sequence of events, one needs to picture Tel Hai's layout. The settlement was built as a rectangular stockade. One end was bounded by the living quarters, in which sand bags were placed in the outward-facing windows. The remainder of the complex, which included a yard and stables, was enclosed by a fortified wall. Entry into the house could only be gained via the yard, which in turn could only be accessed through a large gate in the middle of the bordering wall opposite the house. The house was single-story, but there was a small attic room, in the center of the building. The latter was approached through an open set of stairs that led up to a small landing, both of which faced and were exposed to the yard.

As Trumpeldor accompanied the five Arabs into the yard, they set their sights on inspecting the attic room. Meanwhile, another Arab with a machine gun, slipped in unobserved and secreted himself somewhere in the living quarters. In the attic room at the time, were Tel Hai's two women members and three men. Just as Trumpeldor was ascending the attic stairs, he was informed by a comrade who understood Arabic that the Arabs were in fact conspiring to seize all their weapons. Trumpeldor instantly rushed downstairs, sped into the yard and discharged his pistol both as a signal and order for everyone to open fire. The Arab with the machine gun was quickly discovered and killed. But before Trumpeldor could take another step, he was shot in the hand and then in the stomach. The five Arabs on the attic landing tossed a grenade into the attic room, instantly killing the two women and two of the three men there. From their high vantage point overlooking the yard, the intruders shot Jaboc Tocker, a volunteer from the American segment of the Jewish Legion. A bullet pierced his head, completely shattering his brain.

Events were taking an entirely unexpected turn. Never had the settlers allowed for the possibility of engaging in a battle in which some of the enemy would be internally ensconced. By the same token, the surrounding Bedouin were separated from their leaders and lacked initiative. They were beaten back by a constant volley of shots fired from the settlement's fortified windows. Two pioneers, under protective cover, lifted a prostrate Trumpeldor from the yard and carried him into the living quarters, where they rested him on the floor. As he lay there, he bid the medical orderly to reinsert his exposed entrails into his abdomen. Not knowing how to execute such a request, Trumpeldor himself guided him. With the first aid equipment being in the attic room and hence out of reach, the orderly dressed Trumpeldor's stomach with a towel. When that was completed, Trumpeldor declared, "These are my last moments, tell everyone that they must stand firm till the very end for the sake of the people of Israel's honour."[13] Thereafter he lay quietly so as not to be a burden to anyone.

At some point, the five Arabs were able to extricate themselves both from the attic landing and from the yard. The general exchange of fire then intensified and continued for three solid hours. Eventually, a short cease-fire was arranged that enabled the attackers to gather fourteen of their dead and many more of their wounded. When the cease-fire ended, the defenders, armed with the intruder's machine gun and with extra ammunition that had previously been inaccessible to them, held the attackers at bay. By nightfall, three men slipped away to seek medical assistance for Trumpeldor and four others. When the doctor arrived, he asked Trumpeldor how he was feeling. With a wry smile, Trumpeldor replied, "It is no matter, it is good to die for our country."[14] The doctor ordered all the injured to be taken to Kfar Giladi. In the absence of stretchers, they were borne on blankets; en route, Trumpeldor died. Apprised of the fact that masses of Arab reinforcements were gathering for a renewed assault and bearing in mind that they then had merely 150 bullets per person and enough food for only one more day, the settlers reluctantly decided to abandon both Tel Hai and Kfar Giladi.

Numerous heroic stands, like that at Tel Hai, have occurred in Israel's short history. But the battle of Tel Hai stands out as a turning point in the annals of the heroic efforts made to secure and sustain the Jewish state. As already mentioned, French troops with mechanized weaponry beat a hasty retreat when confronted with a lesser force than that which surrounded Tel Hai and when the settlers ultimately left the area, the Arabs were amazed to see just how scanty their numbers were. Judging by their stubborn resistance, they estimated that they would have to have been no less than a few hundred.[15]

The exploits of Trumpeldor and his comrades instantly became a source of inspiration for thousands of young Jews in Russia and Eastern Europe, who hastily left for Palestine. In time, Tel Hai became a focal point where youth in Palestine paid homage to the fallen eight (six during the actual battle and the two killed shortly beforehand) and where they pledged to follow in their footsteps. Of no less significance, in December 1920, at the San Remo Conference, because of (among other factors) the blood shed by the young Zionist pioneers, the entire Upper Galilee was transferred to the British as part of Mandated Palestine.

Today, in an era in which personal sacrifice for the commonweal seems like an anachronism, there are some Israelis who heap scorn on the idea that Trumpeldor willingly gave of himself for the national cause. Some even go as far as to suggest that not only was Trumpeldor incapable of expressing his final words in Hebrew but more probably he cursed in Russian. However, the only two eyewitnesses at the time, Dr. Gary and Shneerson, independently corroborated the story.[16] It certainly was not true that Trumpeldor knew no Hebrew, for there are various documents extant written by him partly in that language. Moreover, many have testified that Trumpeldor commonly spoke of his willingness to pay the ultimate price and that the phrase *ein davar* (it does not matter), was frequently on his tongue. Whether Trumpeldor actually explicitly stated that "It is no matter; it is good to die for our country" is of no consequence; all his living actions clearly indicated that that was, in fact, his credo.

Having drawn Jewish blood in the battle of Tel Hai but having incurred large losses themselves, Arab nationalists sought a much softer target for their next encounter. Weeks later, they turned on the vulnerable Old Yishuv Jews of Jerusalem.

THE 1920 JERUSALEM POGROM

On April 4, 1920, a crowd from Hebron and Nablus, associated with the annual Muslim Nebi Musa pilgrimage that had taken place two days earlier, assembled near the Jaffa Gate of the Old City of Jerusalem. (The Nebi Musa pilgrimage commemorated the supposed carrying of Moses' body, by a Bedouin, to a grave across the Jordan known as Nebi Musa, Moses' shrine.) At the Jerusalem gathering, the pilgrims' emotions were skillfully aroused by the public display of a picture of King Faisal, the declaration of his "reign in Palestine" and by an appeal to set upon the Jews. After some preliminary shop looting and the assaulting of Jews who happened to be in the area, the crowd surged through the Jaffa Gate into the heart of the Old City. Until then, the British forces remained passive. Only once the rampaging mob was well within the walls of the Old City did they spring into action. They surrounded the Old City and with fixed bayonets prevented anyone from entering it. As a consequence, while the rioters were having a field day, Jewish defense groups were largely unable to reach their imperiled brethren. Members of the Jewish Legion (who then numbered about 400) were confined to their barracks and the few who made their way to Jerusalem were detained by military police.[17] The mayhem that claimed the lives of 8 Jews and ended up wounding 211 others continued for three days.

Although there were prior rumors afloat of an impending attack on Jews, inhabitants of the Jewish Quarter seem to have been caught unawares and offered virtually no resistance.[18] A small group, under the active leadership of Jabotinsky, that did fight back, was promptly arrested. Jabotinsky appeared before a military court charged with "banditism, instigating the people of the Ottoman Empire to mutual hatred, pillage, rapine, devastation of the country and homicide in divers places."[19] He was sentenced to fifteen years of hard labor![20]

Weizmann was convinced that the mob was deliberately inflamed to jeopardize Zionist prospects at the San Remo Conference scheduled for a few weeks later. It was at San Remo that the Allied Powers met to discuss the fate of the territories previously under Turkish rule. There is also cause to suspect that members of the upper echelons of the military regime conspired with the rioters. For example, in Colonel Meinertzhagen's diary there is a damning account of the reported insidious behavior of Water-Taylors, a high-ranking British official. On April 26, 1920, Meinertzhagen wrote:

Water-Taylors saw Haj al Amin on the Wednesday before Easter and told him that he had a great opportunity at Easter to show the world that the Arabs of Palestine would not tolerate Jewish domination in Palestine; that Zionism was unpopular not only with the Palestine Administration but in Whitehall and if disturbances of sufficient violence occurred in Jerusalem at Easter, both General Bols and General Allenby would advocate the abandonment of the Jewish Home.... On the day of the rioting Waters-Taylor absented himself in Jericho for the day. Two days after the rioting he sent for the Mayor of Jerusalem—Moussa [sic] Kasim Pasha and said, "I gave you a fine opportunity; for five hours Jerusalem was without military protection: I had hoped that you would avail yourself of the opportunity but you have failed."[21]

Water-Taylors and his friends seem to have made a strategic error, for in the wake of the Jerusalem riots, a storm of indignation arose in Britain against the Palestinian authorities. By arresting and convicting Jabotinsky, the military had overreached themselves and tilted the balance toward their own demise. An embarrassed British government resolved to terminate military rule. They turned to Sir Herbert Samuel with an offer to appoint him as high commissioner of Palestine. After some soul searching, in which he reflected whether as a Jew with well-known Zionist sympathies he would be able to secure the cooperation of the Arab population, Samuel accepted.

THE ADVENT OF CIVIL ADMINISTRATION AND THE ORGANIZATION OF THE YISHUV

On July 1, 1920, a day after arriving in Palestine, Samuel assumed official duties and thereby inaugurated the country's civil administration.[22] All administrative and legislative powers were vested in him but to maintain a degree of local participation, Samuel formed an Advisory Council consisting of ten government officials, seven Arabs and three Jews.

Two of Samuel's top-ranking officials, were clearly pro-Zionist, that is, Colonel Wyndam Deedes and Norman Bentwich. But as if to prove to the Arabs that they could count on him as being an objective and fair-minded ruler, he also appointed Sir Ronald Storrs and Ernest Richmond. Storrs and Richmond were both uncompromisingly pro-Arab and regarded the Balfour Declaration as a political error of the first order of magnitude. Richmond, in particular, is on record as explicitly interpreting his role as one of thwarting the administration's official objectives.[23] The inclusion of Storrs and Richmond in Samuel's inner advisory circle, heartened other British civil servants in Palestine with similar views.

In attempting to be conciliatory toward the more extreme elements among the Arab nationalists, Samuel made a hasty and ill-considered decision, the effects of which resounded for years to come. In the spring of 1921 with the death of the old mufti of Jerusalem, Kamel Effendi al-Husseini, an election for the new mufti took place. Four candidates vied for the position. Of these, Haj Amin al Husseini, who had been implicated in the 1920 Jerusalem riots, secured the least number of votes. Since Haj Amin al Husseini's candidacy had been endorsed by many prominent individuals including the Greek Orthodox patriarch and the powerful Husseini clan, Samuel allowed himself to be persuaded that he ought to be the new mufti.

By convention, the government could only nominate a person from among the top three candidates. That being the case, the withdrawal of one of them was engineered, thus clearing the way for Samuel to elevate Haj Amin al Husseini. By such means, on May 8, 1921, Haj Amin al Husseini became the grand mufti of Jerusalem. (The appointment was never formally published and the term "grand" was never an official one.) Al Husseini, whose clerical accreditations in fact were minimal, was to prove himself to be an implacable enemy, not only of the Zionists but also of the British. His capacity to hold sway over the Arab community was enhanced in January 1922 when he was chosen (again by dubious means) to head the newly formed Supreme Muslim Council. The Council, which had a large, nonaudited, government-financed budget, had been entrusted with official control of all Muslim religious trusts and courts. By assuming its presidency, with permanent tenancy, al Husseini not only became the recognized head of the country's Muslim community, but also the most powerful political force in the Arab Palestinian movement.[24]

With regard to Jewish affairs, an eight-member Rabbinical Council, consisting equally of Sephardi and Ashkenazi rabbis, was officially sanctioned. From its ranks, two co–chief rabbis were selected, namely Yaakov Meier for the Sephardim and Avraham Yitzhak Kook for the Ashkenazim. The Rabbinical Council was granted exclusive jurisdiction over Jewish residents in all matters concerning marriage and divorce, alimony and confirmation of wills.[25]

In early 1920, a few months before Samuel's arrival, the Yishuv, with Government permission, constituted itself as an entity known as *Knesset Israel* (the Community of Jews). Until then, a Provisional Executive, formed in December 1917 at a meeting in Petah Tikva, had acted on the Yishuv's behalf. Members of Knesset Israel elected a parliamentary-type body called *Asefat Hanivharim* (Assembly of Delegates), which in turn selected the *Va'ad Leumi* (National Council). Within the Va'ad Leumi all political parties present in the Asefat Hanivharim were represented. In both bodies, members were elected on the basis of proportional representation. The Va'ad Leumi established a number of departments concerned with the Yishuv's health, education and local community services. Within education, there were initially two recognized autonomous streams, one catering to the general secular public and the other to religious adherents. In the mid-1920s, a third stream with emphasis on Labor Movement values, was also incorporated.

Given Samuel's background, it would have been natural to assume that he would actively promote Zionist objectives. Yet his government did not allocate

significant resources for such purposes. Instead of "facilitating" the establishment of a Jewish National Home, the Mandatory government (at least during
its first two decades) merely "allowed" it to incubate.[26] By contrast, the Arabs
whom Samuel regarded as being relatively disadvantaged, were singled out for
public assistance and patronage. As opposed to the Jewish community, their
health, education and general social welfare was in no small way government
funded.

At first, Samuel was able to govern the country with a reasonable degree of
cooperation from both Arabs and Jews. The April 1920 disturbances, which effectively brought him to power, appeared to be a thing of the past and everyone
seemed to go about their business in an orderly manner. However, behind the
scenes, Arab resentment of increasing Jewish immigration intensified.

THE 1921 RIOTS

Arab-Jewish violence recurred just over a year after the 1920 Jerusalem
pogrom. It originated on May 1, 1921, in Tel Aviv and, oddly enough, the seeming catalyst for the disturbances was an intra-Jewish brawl. Two Jewish May Day
processions collided with one another. One, organized by *Ahdut Ha'Avodah* (a
Zionist labor party) and legally sanctioned, clashed with a smaller unauthorized
procession of *Mopsim* (communists), who were bearing banners (in Yiddish) calling for a Soviet Palestine. The police interceded and drove the communists onto
sand dunes between Jaffa and Tel Aviv. Affronted by the Jewish activists' slogans
and by their very presence in Palestine, Arabs gathered to watch the encounter
between the police and the communists. Unable to join in the fray and to lash out
at the Jewish communists who were protected by a British police cordon, the
Arab mob, with assistance from Arab police, turned their attention to Jewish
shops and then to a migrant hostel where they killed fifteen young Jewish pioneers. Other Jews in the vicinity were similarly dealt with. By the end of the day,
27 Jews and 3 Arabs were dead and 104 Jews and 34 Arabs were injured.[27]

The *Haganah* (Jewish Defense Organization) in Tel Aviv appealed to the
thirty remaining soldiers of the Jewish Legion who were stationed at Sarafend,
an army base nearby, to come to their aid. They responded immediately, taking
absence without leave. Their Jewish commander, Colonel Margolin soon
rounded them up, sought and gained official permission for them to defend the
Yishuv and in the bargain secured eighteen old Turkish rifles for that purpose.
Seemingly, their intervention further inflamed Arab passions. Violence continued on May 2, claiming, among others, the lives of Haim Brenner (the eminent
writer) and five of his friends. The following day martial law was proclaimed
and both the Arab police and Jewish legionnaires were disarmed. By then the
death toll had risen to forty-three Jews and fourteen Arabs. Most of the Arabs
were killed by British troops.

On May 5, Petah Tikva was besieged by approximately 2,000 Arabs from thirty-two nearby villages.[28] They approached the settlement from two different directions, arriving with camels and wagons to gather anticipated spoils and with cans of gasoline to burn down the houses. The assailants, who were well armed and who were guided by Arabs who had worked in the settlement, mounted a frontal attack against the defendants who had taken up positions in newly dug trenches. For a short while, the settlers were able to ward them off, but being heavily outnumbered and outgunned, their situation soon became desperate. They were saved in the nick of time by the arrival of (British) Indian troops and then by the subsequent appearance of a British armored vehicle equipped with a mounted machine gun. The battle claimed the lives of four settlers and at least twenty-eight assailants.

An Arab mob then turned against Hadera. Despite an exchange of fire between them and the settlers, they managed to reach the perimeters of the settlement and laid waste to a few of its houses. As in the case of Petah Tikva, Hadera was relieved by British forces, two of whose planes bombed and strafed the attackers. Lastly, an attempt to overwhelm Rehovot was frustrated by resolute defenders firing from three separate fortified houses. By May 7, when the violence eventually subsided, the final death toll stood at forty-seven Jews and forty-eight Arabs.[29]

Samuel responded to the civil unrest with due diligence. Suspected rioters were detained and punitive fines were imposed on entire Arab villages believed to have been implicated. Nonetheless, not all violators were punished. Arab policemen who sided with the perpetrators were not disciplined, stolen Jewish property was not returned and the murderers of Brenner and his companions were never apprehended.[30]

To maintain an aura of impartiality in relation to both Arabs and Jews, Samuel felt the need to counter his stern handling of the rioters by introducing measures that would restore Arab confidence in him. For a short while, Jewish immigration was suspended and then on June 3, in a speech commemorating the king's birthday, Samuel provided an interpretation of the Balfour Declaration that downplayed its true meaning. He denied that it implied the formation of a Jewish National Home in Palestine, claiming that "the translation of the English words into Arabic does not convey their real sense."[31] He gave his audience the impression that, in essence, the Balfour Declaration favored the rights of some Jews to "come to Palestine in order to help by their resources and efforts to develop the country, to the advantage of all the inhabitants."[32] Samuel then affirmed that local conditions were not conducive to mass migration and that Jewish entry into the country in the future would be determined by the ability of the economy to absorb newcomers. The Jewish community was up in arms. Ben Zvi angrily resigned from the Palestine Advisory Council, while Berl Katznelson wrote that Samuel's speech heralded faintheartedness, a frightful surrender and fawning before hostile forces and rioters.[33]

Samuel believed that the Arab nationalists would be mollified by constitutional changes involving the transformation of the Advisory Council into an elected legislative body, in which they would constitute a majority. But since such a forum would have been precluded from enacting legislation contrary to the Mandate, the Arabs refused to cooperate. They conducted a successful boycott of an election that the British organized in 1922. Subsequently, no elected Palestinian assembly in which both Arabs and Jews participated, was ever convened. Instead, from December 1923, the country was administered by the high commissioner with the help of an Advisory Council composed entirely of British officials.[34] For the Jews, this was no ground for distress, since they feared that had an elected Legislative Assembly been established, not only would they have had minority representation (two out of twelve elected delegates) but in due course, the Assembly might have evolved into a nucleus for an independent Arab-dominated Palestine. Only out of a general sense of weakness and unwillingness to antagonize Samuel was Jewish cooperation forthcoming. It was to the Jews' good fortune that the Arabs did not appreciate the political benefits that potentially could have accrued to them had they gone along with Samuel's constitutional proposals.

THE 1922 CHURCHILL WHITE PAPER AND IMMIGRATION POLICY

With efforts to placate the Arabs by the introduction of an elected Legislative Council being stymied and in light of Samuel's revised migration policy, the British sought to redefine their objectives in Palestine. In 1922 Samuel was summoned to London, where, in cooperation with officers of the Colonial Office, he drafted a document that became known as the Churchill White Paper.

The Churchill White Paper detached Transjordan from the area of Zionist operation and determined that immigration was not to exceed the economic absorptive capacity of Palestine. The placement of Transjordan beyond the reach of potential Jewish settlements was justified as being in accordance with previous British commitments made to the Arabs by Henry McMahon. It had, in fact, already been decided on by Churchill in March 1921 at a conference of British officials held in Cairo. To some extent, events beyond British control forced Churchill's hand. In 1920, Faisal was unceremoniously deposed by the French in Syria. In response, his brother, Abdullah gathered a force of Bedouin and entered Transjordan as a prelude to a retributive encounter with Faisal's enemies. Realizing that the French would easily have routed Abdullah, Churchill devised a stratagem designed both to compensate the Sherifian family[35] and to ease British misgivings for not fulfilling previous pledges. Faisal was made king of Iraq (for which Britain had a Mandate) and Abdullah king of Transjordan.

In providing some consolation to the Zionists, the 1922 White Paper explicitly affirmed that the Balfour Declaration was not subject to change and that "the

Jewish people will be in Palestine as of right and not on sufferance."[36] Two categories of Jewish migrants were recognized. The first applied to "persons of independent means" who could prove that they had sufficient capital to sustain themselves in Palestine. This generally meant that they had to possess at least £1000. The other category related to unskilled workers who could only gain entry on the basis of the Labor Schedule. That schedule was periodically adjusted in accordance with the country's economic capacity to absorb labor. Once a figure was determined the government would issue a corresponding number of immigration certificates that were distributed by the Executive of the Zionist Organization and ultimately by the Jewish Agency (discussed further below).

Not until the late 1930s, did the immigration schedules meaningfully restrict Jewish entry. Occasional reductions in Jewish immigration were almost exclusively caused by a lack of willing entrants or a lack of the funds to finance them. For instance, in 1920, the inaugural year of Samuel's high commissionership, the Jewish migrant quota was set at 16,500, yet only 8,223 arrived, a fact that greatly embarrassed the Zionist Organization. A year earlier, Weizmann had confidently informed the Peace Conference that annual rates of Jewish immigration on the order of 70,000 to 80,000 could reasonably be expected.[37] But at no time during the 1920s were rates like these ever achieved. At the 1920 Zionist Conference in London, Weizmann, who appreciated that a large amount of money was needed to absorb migrants, proposed an annual budget of £2 million. More realistically, the American delegates made it clear that no more than £100,000 per year would be forthcoming. As Mossek observed, "This state of affairs more than anything else determined Zionist immigration policy for the coming decade."[38] In the absence of adequate financial resources, it was impossible to fund economic activities that would yield sufficient income to sustain masses of unskilled laborers. Even the small number who actually arrived presented the Zionists with intractable employment problems. The formation of agricultural settlements was held in check, not because of a shortage of disposable land but for want of sufficient startup and working capital. Within urban areas, industrial employment was severely limited by the nature of the country's inchoate manufacturing sector.

Despite all its shortcomings, the 1922 White Paper was endorsed by the Zionist Executive. The British made it clear that, had the Zionists not done so, they would not have submitted the Palestine Mandate for the approval of the League of Nations.

The Mandate, which came into force on September 25, 1923, was clearly based on the principles of the Balfour Declaration. In its preface it was stressed that the Mandate was issued in recognition of the historic connection between the Jewish people and the Land of Israel. Clause 2 read in part: "The Mandatory authority will be responsible for furthering the political, administrative and economic conditions which will facilitate the foundation of the Jewish National Home."

During the 1920s, the British more or less adhered to the essence of the Mandate. When Samuel retired in 1925, both Jews and Arabs conceded that he had been a good and honest administrator. He was succeeded by Field-Marshall Plumer, an army commander who, until the end of his term in 1928, administered Palestine impartially and efficiently. He, in turn, was followed by Sir John Chancellor, who took up his post just when the country's period of inner peace, which lasted from the end of 1921, abruptly ended. Chancellor lacked the stature and presence of his two predecessors and had the misfortune of assuming his position at a critical juncture.

THE THIRD ALIYAH (1919–1923)

In 1919 nearly 2,000 Jews arrived in Palestine and within the following four years the annual inflow exceeded 8,000. All told, during the Third Aliyah just over 35,000 Jews immigrated, raising the Jewish population in Palestine from a total of 56,000 in 1919 to 90,000 by the end of 1923.

In most, if not all of the migratory waves in Israel's short history, persecution was the main driving force. The Third Aliyah was no exception. Between 1915 and 1921, against the background of the First World War, the Russian Civil War and the general state of anarchy that existed at the time, "perhaps a quarter of a million Jews—men, women and children—were slain or allowed to starve to death," in the Ukraine and in White Russia.[39] The major instigators of that bloodbath were nationalist Ukrainian troops under Petlura (who killed more than 70,000 Jews), soldiers of Denikin's volunteer army (with approximately 50,000 murders to their credit),[40] miscellaneous Cossack regiments and ad hoc militia of both right- and left-wing varieties. In 1903, the Kishinev pogrom, involving a far smaller number of casualties, aroused a storm of international protest, but in the context of the carnage just witnessed during the First World War, the postwar pogroms excited little general interest.[41] Nevertheless, in one year alone, the number of Jews murdered exceeded the death toll of the Chmielnicki massacres that had occurred 270 years earlier and that figure prominently in Jewish martyrology.[42] The intensity and extent of the pogroms impressed upon Third Aliyah migrants the fact that the Jewish people would only be redeemed through Zionism and certainly not by means of universal social progress and enlightenment.

The Third Aliyah migrants hailed mainly from Russia, the Ukraine, Galicia, Poland and Lithuania. In addition, there were minor contingents from Austria, Germany, Czechoslovakia and the Balkans. Those from Russia and the Ukraine were swept up in the maelstrom of the Bolshevik revolution and the ensuing civil war. While the new Soviet regime did not immediately outlaw the Zionist Movement, it was obvious that its days were numbered. Jews who wished to leave for Palestine discovered that emigrating was both hazardous and, in most cases, forbidden. All the major thoroughfares were crowded with military traffic, and travel permits were required even for the simplest of journeys. Those approaching border areas were subject to keen scrutiny. In the chaos and state

of flux that prevailed, potential emigrants were suspiciously regarded as enemies fleeing from the clutches of whoever was in control of a particular area at
a given point of time.

The youth arriving in Palestine were enthusiastic idealists par excellence
who, in a very real sense, represented a continuation and reinforcement of Second Aliyah aspirations. Although the two migration streams shared common
goals, of which the need to create a strong Jewish working class with firm agricultural roots took pride of place, they nonetheless differed in certain ways. The
Third Aliyah migrants were very much children of both the First World War
and of postwar revolutionary movements. They believed they were witnessing
a new dawn for humankind as a whole, in which the national liberation of the
Jews would be included.

By contrast with Second Aliyah migrants, those of the Third Aliyah arrived
in Palestine within the framework of well-organized, tightly knit groups,
whose members were committed to the establishment of farming collectives.
The idea of engaging in the Conquest of Labor on an individual basis did not
appeal to them. Rather, they sought to found their own agricultural settlements
in which they would be self-employed. Most ventured to Palestine under the
auspices of a youth organization called *Hehalutz* (the Pioneer).

Hehalutz was an all-embracing movement that welcomed into its ranks
youth of various ideological persuasions, provided they aspired to become
farming pioneers in Palestine and subscribed to principles of equality, self-labor
and collective living. It sponsored a number of training farms within the diaspora and generally required of its members that, before migrating to Palestine,
they spend time on those farms, acclimating themselves to the rigors of manual work and learning the essence of agronomy.

On entering Palestine, the Third Aliyah migrants, like their Second Aliyah
predecessors, were faced with limited job prospects. The country's cities were by
no means thriving centers of manufacturing. Between 1920 and 1921, no more
than 4,750 Jews worked in "factories," which were mostly small workshops. In
two-thirds of them, no more than one worker was hired.[43] In the countryside,
the First Aliyah settlements (such as Petah Tikva, Rishon Letzion and so on)
maintained their traditional bias in favor of cheap Arab labor. In 1920, of the
4,000 workers that they employed, only about 200 were Jews.[44]

Fortunately for the Third Aliyah migrants, the Zionist Movement managed
to persuade the government to hire them on public works projects and, by the
end of 1920, approximately 2,000 Jewish workers were employed in road and
railway construction.[45]

THE ROAD AND RAILWAY BUILDERS

The new roads were mainly built in the Galilee. Notable among them were
those between Tiberius and Tzemach, Nazereth and Afula, and Haifa and

Pounding rocks for road construction (Central Zionist Archives).

Gedah. Two branch railway lines were also laid between Lydda and Sarafend and between Rosh Ha'Ayin and Petah Tikva. The first road construction work, which involved the Tiberius-Tzemach route, was contracted to an organization of Ahdut Ha'Avodah called *Merkaz Haklai* (Agricultural Center). In negotiating with the government, the Merkaz Haklai team soon realized that their knowledge of road-building methods was, to say the least, sparse.[46] They had no understanding of the technical terms and were unfamiliar with the nature of the various stones, gravel or other material required. Even so, they undertook full responsibility for the completion of all facets of the project. Before the work began, their supervisor signed up as an anonymous laborer on another road that was being laid by Arabs and Egyptians. There he noted and recorded the processes of road construction. A week later, he assumed the management of the Merkaz Haklai project. The operation was subdivided into various tasks, which were then subcontracted to groups of worker collectives.

On every road construction site, there were a number of worker encampments sporting white British army bell tents. At dawn, the workers, who would be roused from their sleep by the sound of a hammer clanging against a metal pole, would make their way to a square marquee that served as their dining room. There they would have a cup of tea or coffee with some bread and jam. Then, shouldering their various implements, they would head for their work sites. Those who toiled in the stone quarries were regarded as the true labor aristocrats. They were the strongest and bravest. They worked in pairs, with one holding an iron stake against a rock while the other slammed into it with a sledge hammer. When a hole of sufficient length was opened, it was filled with gunpowder and the wick placed in its center was lit with a lighted cigarette. Often half a dozen or so separate charges would be set simultaneously. The fragmented rocks would be carted away by wheelbarrows or even on corves. They were piled on a section of or next to the road in the making. Sitting astride each pile, young women would pound the rocks into small gravel stones, which would then be spread on the road to be compressed by a steamroller.

All the laborers were subject to the searing Palestinian heatwaves that inevitably occur each summer and that were exacerbated by the nature of the materials that they had to handle. In winter, the rain loosened their tent pegs, allowing strong gusts of wind to sweep away their canvas covers. The food provided was barely edible, but worst of all were the effects of widespread malaria and dysentery, which often incapacitated about a fifth of the work force. Some compensation was found in the feelings of solidarity that abounded and in communal singing and dancing; even so, being a road worker was no easy feat.

Of the various groupings that coalesced on the road works, two were particularly noteworthy, namely *Gedud Avodah* and *Hashomer Hatzair*.

GEDUD AVODAH (THE LABOR BATTALION)

Gedud Avodah was founded on August 25, 1920 along the banks of Lake Kinneret, at a meeting called to commemorate Trumpeldor's death at Tel Hai.[47] (Its full title was "Gedud Avodah in the name of Yosef Trumpeldor," or, in more precise English, "The Joseph Trumpeldor Labor Battalion.") The Gedud's founders belonged to Hehalutz. Prominent among them were workers from the Crimea who had previously established personal ties with Trumpeldor and who were among his most dedicated devotees. Three in particular were most noteworthy—Yehuda Almog, Mendel Elkind and Yitzhak Sadeh, who ultimately organized and headed the Palmach, a strike force in the Israeli War of Independence. The Gedud's initial membership totaled 40 but within a year it expanded to incorporate 560[48] and during the first six years of its existence, approximately 2,200 pioneers passed through its ranks.[49] While a constant membership turnover had a demoralizing effect, the core members were still able to sustain its pioneering ideals.

Most Gedud Avodah members were Third Aliyah migrants from Russia and until its adherents gradually mastered Hebrew, the Russian language resonated throughout its ranks. They were organized within a series of labor companies, each of which operated semi-autonomously and under its own democratic management. All companies were represented in a federal governing body and were subject to its overriding direction. The organization did not require uniformity of political views and was characterized by the philosophical heterogeneity of its membership. Within some companies, there was no dominant political orientation, but, in others, a common world view prevailed. All that was required of each recruit was a commitment to strive for a Jewish society based on productive labor free from exploitation.

The Gedud tried to uphold equality of earnings of all its members. Within each company, everyone was paid the same amount, in kind. Where some companies earned more than others, a transfer from better to worse off ones was to be effected. It was hoped that, in time, the entire Yishuv would, in effect, constitute one large Gedud Avodah collective.

The Gedud was very prevalent in the road and rail construction gangs mentioned above. It was also very active in urban development and played an important part in fostering Jewish building worker cooperatives. It was a disciplined organization that required of its members a willingness to serve where and in whatever capacity the national needs of the day dictated. Many individual companies operated in a variety of locations, dismantling their camps and re-establishing themselves further afield in response to the organization's central executive's decrees or to short-term contracts tended on their behalf by the *Histadrut* (Labor Federation).

As explained further below, the advent of the Fourth Aliyah (1924–1929) brought in a large wave of lower-middle-class migrants who wished to retain their previous diaspora lifestyles. Their impact on the social composition of the Yishuv, as well as the severe economic crisis in 1926–1927, forced the Gedud Avodah to consider whether it was still feasible to strive for a pan-national collective. After some bitter wrangling, the organization divided into two camps. One began to place more emphasis on traditional class conflict, as espoused by classical Marxists. The other adhered to the Gedud's original aims of building a Zionist socialist society in Palestine purely by means of constructive endeavors. The Marxist-leaning faction tended to make common cause with anti-Zionist communists. In 1926 about eighty of the left-wing faction, under Elkind's leadership, returned to Russia. There they hoped to establish a collective farm in what they thought was a true communist society. At first, they seemed to realize their objective. They formed a *Kolkhoz* (collective) in the Crimea, which they named *Via Nova* (New Way). However, the exclusive Jewish character of their settlement was short-lived. They were forced to incorporate neighboring anti-Semites, who ironically renamed the settlement the Brotherhood of Nations. During the Stalinist purges of the 1930s, Elkind and other leading figures were executed. Those who survived were eventually handed over by their "brotherly comrades" to the invading Germans. All, except one or two who managed to flee, were murdered.

The defection of Elkind and his followers effectively put an end to the Gedud Avodah. In 1929 the remnants were absorbed into Kibbutz Hameuhad and Ahdut Haavodah (discussed further below).

HASHOMER HATZAIR (THE YOUNG WATCHMAN)

From its earliest days in Lvov, Galicia, which date from 1913, Hashomer Hatzair began to take shape as an amalgam of a European Jewish youth movement called *Hashomer* (the Watchman) and an organization called *Tzierei Zion* (Young Zionists). Hashomer was very much influenced by Baden Powell's scouting ethos, with its emphasis on sport and physical fitness. It encouraged Jewish youth to "cultivate physical strength and to establish a rapport with the world of nature."[50] Tzierei Zion, by contrast, concentrated on the world of ideas, on Zionist theory and on the diffusion of Hebrew and Jewish history.

Hashomer Hatzair was also molded in the image of the German *Wandervogel* (wandering bird) Movement. From the Wandervogel it derived the notion that adolescents had their own unique set of qualities and that they needed to be autonomous and free of the corrupting effects of civilization. Like the Wandervogel, Hashomer Hatzair extolled simplicity in dress, modesty and clean living.

During the World War I years, Hashomer Hatzair's main founding fathers were, by force of circumstances, located in Vienna, where they came face-to-face with poverty in the midst of pockets of wealth. To them, the Jewish pillars of society were materialistic, degenerate and uncouth. They, in turn, mounted a spiritual revolt against the Jewish status quo. Dreaming of a renewed healthy existence in Palestine, where they hoped to become pioneers, they not only evolved an outlook embracing abstract political concepts but also one dealing with the sum total of humanity, including concern for the well-being of the individual. They intended to transform themselves into a new breed of Jewish farmers, who would not only cultivate their land with joyful enthusiasm but who would also mentally enrich themselves by delving into the best of the world's literature and philosophy. Their all-encompassing approach to human physical and cultural needs, was a decisive factor that created the movement's unique character. The movement captivated Jewish teenagers searching for a life with a new meaning and who eagerly adopted its cult of purity, beauty and youth.[51]

At first, Hashomer Hatzair was nonpolitical, totally unaffiliated with any other body and devoid of any internal ideological coherence. While groping for its own identity, the movement tended to stand aloof from other pioneering groups. A premium was placed on forming close-knit friendships within its own circles and its independence was closely guarded. On the road works, it formed its own body, which was named *Shomria*. Eventually, after the movement took root in Palestine, it did in fact become completely politicized. It constituted its own party, which stood on the extreme left of the Zionist political spectrum. At one time the party even adopted all the intellectual baggage of the Third International Communists, with the significant exception that it never deviated from its pioneering Zionist vision.

THE DEMISE OF THE ROAD CONSTRUCTION PROJECTS AND THE STATE OF THE ECONOMY UNTIL 1924

The public works programs did not last long, and by 1923 they were almost completely wound down, yielding employment for no more than 2 percent of the Jewish work force.[52] Labor encampments that once dotted the north Palestine landscape disappeared from sight. Instead, workers moved with their tents to urban areas, particularly to Haifa and Tel Aviv.

By inducing many Jaffa-based Jews to relocate in Tel Aviv, the 1921 riots stimulated a large demand for new houses. This, in turn, facilitated the entry of young Jewish laborers into the building industry, which until then had been a strictly Arab domain. Continuing the practices that they had adopted while on the roads, the new urban laborers adhered to worker collectives that provided their members with employment, income-sharing arrangements and mutual assistance. Each collective would contract for some specific building process. Since its members were not trained artisans, the collectives generally hired experienced builders, not infrequently Arabs, to guide and to teach them the tools of their trade.

The stability and inner harmony of the building communes were far less assured than those which were based on road making. On the road sites, the work was largely of an unskilled nature and the maintenance of income equality was moderately easy to sustain. By contrast, within the building sector, a large range of specific skills was required, involving trained carpenters, bricklayers, plumbers, roof tilers, masons, painters and so on. As individuals acquired a measure of expertise, often within the framework and support of their collective, they tended to abandon the group that had nurtured them. In the process, they struck out on their own, demanding a higher wage than that paid to unskilled workers.

In addition to the penetration of Jewish labor into housing construction and its allied industry, stone quarrying, inroads were also made in other areas. In Haifa, seventy-five Jews were taken on as port stevedores, while others secured jobs on the railways and within the post and telephone network services. The urban private sector also produced a measure of employment. In 1921 a brick factory named Silicat opened in Tel Aviv. A year later, a salt plant was established at Atlit and in Haifa a large flour mill and a soap factory (Shemen) was formed. Then in June 1923 Pinhas Rutenberg built the country's first electrical power station at Tel Aviv. (This was followed in 1925 by power stations erected in Haifa and Tiberius.) Also of note, in 1924, the construction of a cement plant (Nesher) began.

The Haifa flour mill was hard pressed to produce even a reasonable return. The importation of flour was duty free, whereas wheat imports were subject to very high tariffs. In other words, the mill experienced what economists term "negative effective protection." The government rejected arguments in favor of an industry protective tariff system on the grounds that it had to stand by consumers who needed access to goods at low prices.[53] Apart from the lack of import protection, industrialization of the Jewish economy was initially impeded by the limited internal market.

During the first quarter of 1923, general employment prospects reached a low ebb. Approximately 1,200 workers representing 12–13 percent of the labor force were unemployed. By the year's end, the number of unemployed rose to 2,300, a quarter of the organized Jewish work force. Some shared jobs, working two to three days per week. Many experienced outright hunger and feelings of depression, giving rise to increasing levels of emigration. In 1923, 3,500 left the country, followed by over 2,000 a year later.[54] The 1923 recession was partly induced by a lessening of private capital inflows and by the termination of the building boom once the upsurge in the demand for housing was fully met.[55] But the dominant influence was a severe contraction of the government's development expenditures, which fell from 588,000 Palestinian pounds in 1922 to 167,000 in 1923.[56] The government's development budgets were dependent on funds borrowed from London. In 1923, in the interests of fiscal expediency, the British treasury severely restricted such loans. Compounding the country's economic misfortunes, total Zionist outlays in Palestine contemporaneously declined by 28 percent.[57]

POLITICAL PARTIES AND THE LABOR FEDERATION (*HISTADRUT*)

Soon after the war, in February 1919, at a meeting in Petah Tikva, a new political party was founded under the stewardship of Berl Katznelson and David Ben Gurion, called *Ahdut Ha'Avodah* (the Unity of Labor). It sought to unify the disjointed labor groupings of the Second Aliyah, namely Poalei Zion, Hapoel Hatzair, the Organization of Farm Workers and the "nonparty" activists. However, Hapoel Hatzair declined to merge into it, as did a very small group of more radical Poalei Zion stalwarts, who formed their own tiny party, which became known as the Left Poalei Zion. Hapoel Hatzair's reluctance to link up with Ahdut Ha'Avodah emanated both from an anxiety not to forgo its separate identity and from serious reservations about the ideological orientation of the new party. A deciding factor was Ahdut Ha'Avodah's insistence that it maintain an affiliation with the Marxist-leaning World Poalei Zion Movement.

The upshot of it all was that the Yishuv was still endowed with essentially two competing parties, Ahdut Ha'Avodah and Hapoel Hatzair, except that the first had a much more solid following. Despite Hapoel Hatzair members' misgivings, there was not much to choose between their respective platforms. The leaders of Ahdut Ha'Avodah had, in point of fact, little inclination to be tarred with a socialist brush and rarely did they liken themselves to socialists, preferring instead to be considered as "Social Zionists."[58] Their desire to retain links with the Poalei Zion movement was based purely on power politics, for they hoped to mobilize that movement's support to gain a wider representation within the World Zionist Organization. Perhaps the only serious difference between the two parties was that Hapoel Hatzair's leaders were somewhat more moderate and less militant in their general bearing.

The two main parties were avid competitors. They both sought to cajole new Third Aliyah arrivals into their respective camps, meeting them at the country's ports of entry and offering them temporary accommodation and assistance in finding work. This led to a wasteful duplication of effort, with the establishment of rival trade unions and labor exchanges. In December 1919, noting that the party rivalry was sapping the meager resources of the budding Jewish labor movement, Joseph Trumpeldor publicly appealed to both parties to arrive at a modus vivendi that would facilitate joint cooperation. He envisioned the establishment of "a nonparty council that would create the common institutions of: (a) a labor bureau, (b) an information office, (c) a health fund, (d) immigrant hostels, (e) workers' kitchens, (f) evening classes and (g) a loan fund. The council would also assist in organizing nonparty–political professional associations. Apart from this, the council would be authorized to implement decisions based on the approval of all the various party delegates."[59]

Both Ahdut Ha'Avodah and Hapoel Hatzair indicated their willingness to work together on the basis of Trumpeldor's suggestions. In July 1920, they formed a commission to consider ways and means of forging a working-class alliance that would not impinge on each party's basic independence. The commission paved the way for a General Workers' Conference in December 1920, at which Ahdut Ha'Avodah had thirty-seven delegates, Hapoel Hatzair twenty-six, New Third Aliyah workers and Hashomer Hatzair sixteen and the Left Poalei Zion six. After a stormy debate, a new organization, known as the General Federation of Jewish Labor in Eretz Israel (*Histadrut*) was inaugurated. By means of a proportional voting system, its executive council reflected the relevant strength of its constituent bodies.

The Histadrut not only assumed standard trade union functions but took upon itself the responsibility for catering to the general needs of working people. It provided its members with universal health care, education, cultural facilities, low-priced consumer goods, a bank (Bank Hapoalim), job-placement advice, migration absorption facilities and in time, it also established numerous productive enterprises, many of which assumed commanding heights in the Palestine economy. A large proportion of building workers were employed through the medium of the Histadrut's Office of Public Works, which in 1924 was recast as a company named Solel Boneh. Solel Boneh rose to quite some prominence. For a time, it became the Histadrut's largest single concern and between 1924 and 1925, it provided jobs for over 2,000 members. In the cultural arena, in 1925 the Histadrut inaugurated a daily newspaper, *Davar*, edited by Berl Katznelson. This was followed a year later by the establishment of a workers' theater company *Ohel*.

The Histadrut was not comparable to the trade union federations that existed in Europe and North America. Above all, it regarded itself as an indispensable vehicle for realizing key Zionist objectives entailing the ingathering of the exiles and the creation of a democratic, worker-based Jewish state. Essentially, it was more like a state within a state, providing a comprehensive system of social welfare in the widest sense of the term. Therein lies the key to its success in attracting a large following. By the end of the 1920s, the Histadrut's general membership rose to more than 25,000, nearly a sixth of the entire Yishuv. Throughout almost all of its formative period, from 1921 to 1935, the Histadrut was led by Ben Gurion, who as its general secretary, steered the organization through stormy waters and ensured that it adhered to its basic charter.

Many observers believed that both in theory and in practice, a very strong egalitarian ethos pervaded the Histadrut. It was even suggested that as late as the 1940s, "A doorman at the Histadrut main building, father of seven children, was likely to get a higher salary than the chief executive of that body."[60] This assertion was based on what Histadrut executives would have been paid had their salaries been determined on the basis of official schedules, which made allowances for the number of an employee's dependents. In reality, income inequality prevailed even from as early as the 1920s, when Histadrut high fliers took home at least three times as much as low-ranking workers.[61] Most managers of Histadrut organizations enjoyed a comparatively high standard of living, even to the extent of engaging house maids.[62] In 1927, a report was submitted to the Histadrut's Central Committee detailing blatant instances of the misuse of Histadrut funds for personal gain. The report was never published and the leadership fended off criticisms on the basis that it was unfair to attack officials whose reputations for hard work and loyalty were beyond reproach.[63]

By the end of the 1920s, differences between the two workers' parties narrowed sufficiently for a merger to be considered a realistic proposition. After a series of protracted negotiations, the two parties united on the basis of full parity. Considering Ahdut Ha'Avodah's numerical superiority, this represented a rather generous concession on its part. On January 5, 1930, their unity heralded a new party named *Mapai*, a Hebrew acronym for the Workers' Party of the Land of Israel. Led by Ben Gurion, Mapai enjoyed many years of unrivaled political dominance.

Outside of the workers' political arena, there were, at least in the first half of the 1920s, no other organizations that could legitimately be described as political parties. Rather, there were a number of transitory alliances based less on ideological considerations and more on economic-professional or regional-local interests. The absence of any parliamentary body and of an independent Palestinian sovereignty, militated against general political party formations. In addition, since the merchant classes were not dependent on Zionist funds, they saw no need to form political organizations to lobby for allocations. The *Mizrahi* (religious) party had established itself in Palestine but in the 1920s, its sole concern was with the sponsoring of general religious observance and religious education. Even though it drew most of its support from members of the middle or lower-middle class, it did not, at that time, have any specific economic or political platform. Parallel to the Mizrahi party was Hapoel Hamizrahi, established in 1922. Hapoel Hamizrahi was, in effect, the labor movement of the religious bloc and cooperated with the Histadrut in a number of spheres. It strove to provide its adherents with working conditions that were compatible with their religious convictions.

In 1925, Jabotinsky founded the Zionist Revisionist movement (discussed at length in chapter 7) in Paris. As the Revisionists entrenched themselves in Palestine, partly through the auspices of Betar, its youth movement, the conflict between them and the labor movement became increasingly bitter and even violent. The first exchange of blows occurred in July 1929 at a meeting of the *Asefat Hanivharim* (the Yishuv's elected assembly) where Revisionist delegates assaulted labor members for supposedly impugning Jabotinsky's honor.[64] For his part, Jabotinsky likened Histadrut leaders to gypsy horse thieves, canaille, despicable riffraff who "pollute the air with the venom and cynicism of class hatred."[65]

Finally, on a different matter but one which ultimately played a critical role in the Yishuv's striving for political independence, the Jewish Agency was formed in 1929. It was established for the purpose of advising and cooperating with the Palestine administration in matters relating to the Jewish National Home and the Jewish population. Its main offices were located in Jerusalem, with a branch in London. Initially, half the members of the Jewish Agency were selected from the ranks of non-Zionists. The inclusion of non-Zionists was regarded as being of cardinal importance in ensuring the overall support of world Jewry. Most of the non-Zionist delegates appeared in their own personal capacity. As they retired, they were replaced by Zionists,[66] so that in time the Jewish Agency effectively became a full-fledged Zionist body.

FROM HASHOMER (THE WATCHMAN) TO HAGANAH (DEFENSE)

In June 1920, noting the lessons of the Jerusalem pogrom, which indicated that the military authorities could not be relied on to provide adequate security, Ahdut Ha'Avodah, assumed responsibility for the Yishuv's protection. All agreed that the Yishuv ought to demand that Jewish lives and property be officially safeguarded and that Jews be accepted into the ranks of all law enforcement agencies. But regardless of the government's response, Ahdut Ha'Avodah believed that it was incumbent on the Yishuv to ensure that it had a defense organization of its own, on which it could depend regardless of circumstances.

The party favored an arrangement that would ensure that defense matters were placed firmly under (Jewish) civilian control. Technical military leadership was allowed for, provided that, in the final analysis, high-ranking commanders were accountable to a democratically elected public institution. On the other hand, veteran Hashomer members would have liked defense matters to have been entrusted exclusively to them. They believed that, as an elitist band, Hashomer ought to have continued to operate as an autonomous group unbeholden to outsiders. Even though Hashomer unilaterally dissolved itself to pave the way for the creation of its successor organization, the Haganah, the issue tended to fester for years to come. Certain ex-Hashomer members formed a secret faction that operated both within and outside of the Haganah and only after the 1929 riots was the matter resolved.

At its 1920 founding convention, the Histadrut incorporated the Haganah as one of its subsidiary organizations. To manage the Haganah's affairs, which by force of circumstances had be conducted clandestinely, a five-man defense committee, consisting of Israel Shochet, Eliyahu Golomb, Yosef Baratz, Haim Sturman and Levi Eshkol, was appointed. They were soon joined by both Zvi Nadav and Yitzhak Sadeh.

Officially, the Haganah was a nonparty, all-embracing body, open to all who were committed to Jewish self-defense, but throughout the 1920s, it was effectively organized and led by Ahdut Ha'Avodah activists. Members of Hapoel Hatzair were at first mostly wary of anything that seemed to be tainted by militarism. Whereas for various other reasons, the nonlabor-affiliated Yishuv opposed the formation of an independent Jewish paramilitary force. Some, who simply placed their trust in the British Mandatory regime, argued that it would be spendthrift to invest scarce resources in an unnecessary organization. Between 1921 and 1929, Palestine was blessed with a period of tranquillity. In that light, many potential recruits thought that time spent undertaking military training exercises could be put to better use elsewhere. Farmers of the traditional First Aliyah villages believed that a (Jewish) national or countrywide defense association would be overtly provocative and would most likely incur the wrath of their Arab neighbors. They preferred to organize informal local defense units, hoping that by so doing, they would be officially licensed to maintain a reasonable quantity of weapons. At one point, it seemed that their hopes were being realized, for the government instituted a system of "sealed armories" that contained authorized rifles and pistols to be used in times of emergency. In addition, the nonlabor Yishuv in general were convinced that the Haganah, a Histadrut affiliate, would be beyond their control and that only those among the left wing of the political spectrum would hold commanding positions. For all these reasons, popular support for the Haganah was at first rather limited.

From the point of view of recruitment, the Haganah had at its disposal a reservoir of Third Aliyah migrants who had seen action of one kind or another during the First World War. Of those who came from Germany, Austria, Galicia and Hungary, there were a number who were battle-seasoned officers. Another potential source of manpower lay in the Jewish Legion, small remnants of which were encamped at Sarafend under Margolin until their demobilization in 1921.

In its early days, the Haganah was loosely organized. Its state of military preparedness was often dependent on the relative ability and strength of character of local commanders. Naturally, this varied from region to region. When it was first put to the test in the 1921 riots, it did not exactly pass with flying colors. As soon as the disturbances commenced and Jewish casualties began to mount in Jaffa, it was decided to open its Tel Aviv arms caches. Two boxes of hand grenades had been hidden in the ground adjacent to the home of a prominent Haganah official. But the wind had long since altered the contours of the sand dunes and it was found to be impossible to locate them. Their last hope lay in securing a quantity of revolvers that were supposedly encased in the cellar of a certain house. When it was discovered that the box in question was in fact empty, the two Haganah members sent to retrieve the weapons burst into tears. As Slutsky recounted, "Because of the negligence and complacency of those responsible for the city, Tel Aviv stood helpless before the Arab pogrom that raged in the heart of the New Yishuv."[67]

A few months thereafter, the Haganah had an opportunity to redeem itself. On November 2, 1921 (Balfour Day), a rampaging Arab mob, incited by rabble-rousing orators, headed from the Al Aqsa mosque toward the Jewish Quarter of the Old City of Jerusalem. Their path was blocked by ten members of the Haganah, who held the high ground of an alley through which the mob hoped to enter the Jewish area. At first, the crowd was undeterred by the sight of young Jews standing with revolvers in their hands. They too had weapons and, brandishing swords, daggers and revolvers, they followed their leader, Sheik Abu Said, who hugged the sides of the alley for cover. Just as they were within thirty paces of the defenders, they were confronted by the discharge of a couple of hand grenades and crude bombs, which set off a deafening explosion and a thick haze of smoke. With their leader having been killed and with others having been wounded, their enthusiasm for assaulting the Jewish Quarter instantly evaporated and they rapidly withdrew.

During the first few years of the Haganah's existence, the acquisition of weapons was regarded as a matter of urgency. For that purpose, Vienna was used as a base from which the organization could make contact with European arms suppliers. With the aid of modest sums of money donated by supporters in Poland, Romania, Germany, Belgium and Italy, a limited supply of revolvers and ammunition was procured. These in turn were brought into Palestine by certified migrants, whose luggage at that period of time was not scrutinized. Shipping weapons by such means entailed an unsatisfactory transmission rate. To expedite matters, pistols were hidden in the walls of refrigerators and in double-sided wooden crates. The latter ruse was far from foolproof. In December 1921, an Arab dock worker in Haifa accidentally dropped one of the crates which split open and poured out its contraband under the very eyes of the customs officials. Some 300 pistols and 17,000 bullets were seized. This was most embarrassing to the Zionist Organization, which was committed to the upholding of the law and the Haganah was prevailed upon to cease such activities. For a while it diverted its supplies via Beirut; thereafter, weapons were illicitly purchased from sources within Palestine. Among the consignments from Beirut were twenty-five machine guns, which were housed in cement mixers and road compressors. The weapons were stored in various secret makeshift armories but despite elementary precautions, many of them rusted and became inoperable.

The Haganah and the Israel Defense Force, which later emerged from it, both prided themselves on upholding the concept of "the purity of arms." By this was meant that their fighters were to observe the rules of warfare, which restricted military action exclusively to combatants. Whenever adhered to, such a principle tended, in part, to offset the brutalizing effects of generations of strife with the Palestinians and with the Arabs in general. However, actual practice did not always conform to theory and, from its very inception, incidents occurred that brought the name of the Haganah into disrepute. Recalling the 1921 riots, Golomb cited one such case where Haganah members, in a fit of rage over Arab atrocities, murdered a physically disabled Arab and his children in an orange grove.[68] A year later when an Arab youth was killed to avenge the death of a Jew, many within the Yishuv were appalled by such a senseless and immoral act of reprisal. (It is not clear whether or not the avenger was indeed a Haganah member.) Leading the protests was Ahad Ha'Am who wrote:

What are we and what is our future life in this country for which we make infinite sacrifices, without which the land would not be built? Is it just to add another small Levantine nation in a corner of the East that would compete with other Levantine states in terms of blood lust, revenge and rivalry, which has constituted the life's essence of such people? If this is the Messiah—may he not come![69]

To their credit, whenever such outrages occurred, the Haganah command usually stressed their unacceptability and the need to discipline offenders. That is not to say that individuals who either had Jewish blood on their hands or who were believed to be a serious threat to the Yishuv were not assassinated. In 1923, Tufik Bei, suspected of being responsible for the 1921 massacre of Jews in the Jaffa migrant hostel, was tracked down and shot by a member of the unofficial Hashomer faction.[70] Mainstream Haganah officials were even prepared to target Jews. One such person was Dr. Israel Jacob de Hahn, a Dutch Jew who, after migrating to Palestine in the early 1920s, came under the spell of the ex-

treme orthodox community in Jerusalem. Imbibing their anti-Zionism, he dedicated himself to the formation of a united front of the Old Yishuv with the
Palestinian Arab Executive Committee. The Central Office of the Haganah issued an order to assassinate him and on June 30, 1924, he was slain as he
emerged from the synagogue of Sha'arei Tzedek Hospital.[71] Three years later,
in an act reeking of terrorism, Arabs living near the Western Wall, who were
molesting Jews on their way to pray there, were "cautioned" by the placing of
a primitive mine in their street. The device was packed with explosives and
metal fragments but, fortunately, when it was detonated, no injuries were sustained.[72]

By and large, the Haganah was composed of dedicated idealists, decent men
and women who regarded military action as a necessary evil. They would have
preferred to live in peace with their Arab neighbors but ultimately they were
caught up in a cycle of violence that was perhaps an inevitable outcome of their
attempts to establish a Jewish National Home in a country already populated.

THE FORMATION OF NEW LAND SETTLEMENTS

By the end of 1918, when the British took possession of the whole of Pales-
tine, a sum total of fifty-one Jewish agricultural settlements were in existence.
Of these, thirty were moshavot (First Aliyah–style settlements like Rishon
Letzion, Petah Tikva, etc.), ten were kvutzot (collective farms such as Degania,
Kfar Giladi and Tel Hai), two were originally workers' auxiliary farms (Ein
Ganin and Nahalat Yehuda), eight were standard farms in the normal Western
sense and one, Mikvah Yisrael, was an agricultural school.[73]

In 1920, when the Palestine Zionist Office drafted its initial plans for the economic development of the Jewish sector, few resources were assigned for land
purchases. Of its total 1918–1921 budget of £983,000, only £123,000 were allocated to agriculture and land settlement.[74] The Zionists optimistically believed
that they would have free access to large stretches of publicly owned land—a
belief that was soon belied by the government making provisions for public
land transfers to Arabs but not to Jews. For the Zionists, that meant that every
dunam of land had to be bought in the open market.

At the first postwar World Zionist Conference held in 1920 in London, in
which the Jewish National Fund (JNF) was given prime responsibility for the
acquisition of land in Palestine on behalf of the Jewish people, an additional
fund, the *Keren Hayesod* (Foundation Fund) was founded. The Keren Hayesod,
which was charged with financing settlement projects, was expected to raise £25
million within a period of five years. This assumption proved to be entirely unrealistic and, in hindsight, it is easy to understand why. Potential donors were
more inclined to contribute toward the rehabilitation of pogrom victims in
Eastern Europe. The Russian Revolution quarantined some key wealthy supporters, not to mention the entire Russian Jewish population. Europe was un-

Breaking ground in the Jezreel Valley (Central Zionist Archives).

dergoing an economic crisis and, in America, the Zionist ideal did not yet galvanize the majority of the Jewish population. Even within the American Zionist Movement, opinions were sharply divided as to whether or not the main thrust of economic development in Palestine ought be borne by private capital. As it happened, between 1921 and 1923, the Keren Hayesod only secured just over £1 million, of which nearly £700,000 came from the United States.[75] Nonetheless, enough was accumulated, at least in the very early 1920s, to sponsor a modest amount of settlement activity.

In September 1920, the Land Registries were reopened and the Zionists lost little time in making what turned out to be the largest purchase of land during the entire Mandatory period. This involved the greater part of the Jezreel Valley in the Lower Galilee. The newly acquired land effectively consisted of two large blocs. One, the Mahalul bloc (straddling the Haifa-Nazareth Road), amounted to 18,600 dunams; the other, the Nuris bloc (between Givat Hamoreh and Gilboa), covered 29,400 dunams. They both were secured by Yehoshua Hankin, who devoted his life to the acquisition of Palestinian land on behalf of the Jewish people, and they provided the means for the establishment of a series of new settlements.

The land in question, which had been neglected over many generations, was for the most part barren. It was remote, strewn with rocks, covered with weeds and thistles and rife with snakes and scorpions. The lower parts (in the case of the Mahalul bloc, about a fifth of the total and almost all of the Nuris bloc) were swamp-infested. During the day, there were few, if any, trees to provide shade and at night, the sound of howling jackals and the constant expectation of attacks from roving Bedouin provided an uneasy rest to the pioneering settlers.

Draining the swamps was given top priority. The settlers stood waste deep in water, digging channels and then laying grids of clearance pipes. All around them swarmed mosquitos and in the initial year, practically no one escaped the scourge of malaria. Kadman Kufman recorded that from a high vantage point he would, from day to day, perceive how the area became increasingly dry as the swamps receded. Fields which were once waterlogged were transformed into a landscape of magnificent verdure.[76]

In terms of personal sacrifice, the cost of the land reclamation far exceeded the thousands of pounds invested by the Zionist Movement. Many were unable to survive a malarial attack, while those who did were chronically enervated. The two non-Jewish villages that were previously in the area, an Arab and a German one, were entirely eradicated on account of that dreadful disease.[77]

THE MOSHAV

Both shortly before and during the First World War, various Jewish farm workers began to take an interest in creating a new type of agricultural settlement that would bear many of the positive hallmarks of a cooperative venture without what they considered were some of the excesses of the fully collectivized kvutza. Under the influence of Eliezer Joffe, who had studied agronomy in the United States, they hoped to found a settlement (the moshav) which would have the following features: It would have a membership range of between 50 and 100 families, each of which would be allocated an equal-sized plot of land, which they would cultivate as they saw fit (except that outside labor, of any kind, was not to be employed). Ownership of the land would be permanently vested in the Jewish National Fund, which meant that it would not be subject to speculation or unauthorized private transfers. The settlement would provide communal education and health services as well as agricultural ones, such as marketing and input sourcing. Whereas a common levy would be exacted for the welfare services, for the economic ones, members would be charged a fee according to use. In addition, arrangements would be made to assist families in distress.

Quite a number of the leaders of the moshav movement had themselves at one time or other, lived in a kvutza. They granted the kvutza certain advantages in opening up new land areas and in absorbing unskilled workers, who acquired agricultural knowledge within a mutually supportive framework. However, they had grave doubts as to whether a kvutza could be anything more than a

Moshav Nahalal (Central Zionist Archives).

temporary arrangement. They perceived difficulties relating to the sustaining of personal initiative and, above all, they saw few solid prospects for maintaining a reasonable family life within the confines of a fully collectivized society. (At that stage, the kvutzot had not satisfactorily addressed the problems of child rearing and parenting.)

In 1919, members of Hapoel Hatzair, compiled a list of eligible moshav members and began negotiating with the Palestine Office of the Zionist Movement and the JNF for suitable land. Nearly three years were to pass before the first moshav, Nahalal, was established on September 11, 1921, in the Jezreel Valley on land that, as mentioned above, Hankin had negotiated.[78] All of its twenty original members were Second Aliyah workers belonging to Hapoel Hatzair, some of whom were even among Degania's founders. The settlement was planned on the basis of ultimately housing eighty families. It was built in the form of concentric circles in which the building structures were centrally located and each farmer's land radiated outwards.

A second moshav, named Kfar Yechezkel (composed of Ahdut Ha'Avodah members), made its appearance on December 18, 1921, in the Nuris bloc, near Ein Harod. From then onward, the moshav presented itself as an attractive alternative to the kibbutz, rivaling it for manpower and capital resources.

THE KIBBUTZ

Eleven days after Nahalal was put on the map (that is, on September 22, 1921), members of the Gedud Avodah, at Hankin's insistence, took possession of a stretch of land in the Nuris bloc, near a brook known in Hebrew as Ein Harod. They arrived as a comparatively large group of seventy-five workers and lost no time in pitching their tents, erecting a barbed-wire enclosure and digging defensive trenches. Gradually their numbers rose, as more workers joined them. Most were Third Aliyah pioneers. Under Shlomo Lavi's inspiration, the Gedud Avodah planned to create a very large collective farm to be subdivided into several spatially separate nodes, each concentrating on specific agricultural and even on nonagricultural undertakings. In keeping with that objective, an additional encampment was soon set up on a hillside roughly four kilometers from Ein Harod. It was named Tel Yosef (the Hill of Joseph) after Joseph Trumpeldor. The Gedud Avodah was hoping to be allotted the entire Nuris area, but other settlement groups were also given the green light to move in. Included among these was Bet Alfa, Hashomer Hatzair's first kibbutz.[79] The three above-mentioned settlements—Ein Harod, Tel Yosef and Bet Alfa—effectively constituted the country's first kibbutzim, as opposed to the early kvutzot, such as Degania. The difference between these two settlement forms lay in their size. The kvutza wished to limit its work force to no more than thirty to forty in order to ensure a high degree of personal intimacy among members, whereas the kibbutz was prepared to widen its intake to 100 and even more. It substituted the quest for intimacy with the quest for a greater diversity of economic options and as a byproduct, it offered a less restricted personal lifestyle. Of the other settlements that arose in 1922 in the Nuris bloc, namely Geva, Haftzi-Ba, Ginnegar and Yagur, all were of the kvutza variety.

The Gedud Avodah's farming strategy soon became contentious. A conflict arose over the issue of settlement autonomy. Lavi and his supporters argued that the investment funds that the Zionist Organization provided for the Gedud's agricultural ventures ought to go to them directly and not be deposited into the Gedud's general fund. Such a demand not only conflicted with the Gedud Avodah's tendency to be centrally regulated but it also was at odds with the organization's cardinal principle of ensuring an equality of resources and income to all its component bodies. However, Lavi and his followers maintained that if the settlements were underfinanced, they would eventually falter. In June 1923, after a bitter dispute in which the opposing sides failed to agree, the Gedud's settlement in the Nuris bloc bifurcated. Those abiding by the Gedud's official policy (numbering 225 workers) all moved to Tel Yosef, while the rebels (who had 110 members and who were almost all of the Second Aliyah) took exclusive possession of Ein Harod. They were soon joined by like-minded pioneers who had formed their own independent grouping, known as *Havurat Ha'Emek* (the Association of the Emek).

A youngster at Kibbutz Ein Harod, in the late 1920s (Central Zionist Archives).

By the end of the Third Aliyah in 1924, there were seventy-one Jewish agricultural settlements, of which twenty had been established since the war. Aside from those already mentioned, among the other key Third Aliyah settlements were Degania Bet and Kiryat Anavim. In total, they included some 650 working members. The contribution of Third Aliyah migrants was not confined to the new settlements. They also buttressed and sustained many collectives initiated by Second Aliyah Zionists. In so doing, they soon outnumbered the original Second Aliyah farmers and infused a renewed spirit of hope and idealism into potentially moribund communities.

KIBBUTZ FEDERATIONS

The kibbutzim and kvutzot came under attack by hostile elements in the Zionist Movement who looked on them as an extravagantly costly and needless socialist experiment. Typical of the disparaging remarks made about them was the comment of a Mizrahi leader, who, at a Zionist Congress held in 1925, referred to the kibbutz pioneers as "guest children," meaning that they were like orphans living on handouts. More threatening were the conclusions of a study commission sponsored by the Zionist Organization to investigate economic conditions within the Yishuv. It recommended that no more kibbutzim be established and that recently formed ones be converted into moshavim.[80]

Kibbutz critics did not appreciate that the settlements were underfunded, and, primarily for that reason, they experienced difficulties in achieving a basic measure of consolidation. Nor, given their inherent dislike of socialist projects, would they have cared to be reminded that the private First Aliyah moshavot were long-time recipients of Rothschild's benevolence. Kibbutz living standards remained at a very low level and many of them experienced a large membership turnover. It was hoped that a large kibbutz umbrella organization would best advance their cause by filling a need for the provision of mutual assistance and support to individual collective farm units. But differences in outlook and objectives precluded the formation of a single kibbutz federation and, instead, three separate bodies came into being.

In August 1927, the founding convention of *Hakibbutz Hameuhad* (United Kibbutz) took place. It was based on a merger of Ein Harod with Havurat Ha'Emek. Later, in December 1929, the Gedud Avodah kibbutzim of Tel Yosef, Kfar Giladi and Ramat Rahel also joined the association.

By 1927 five Hashomer Hatzair kibbutzim formed a countrywide association known as Kibbutz Artzi and in November 1928, the small kvutzot (such as Degania) joined forces to form a federation of their own called *Hever Hakvutzot* (Association of kvutzot).

Hakibbutz Hameuhad sponsored the formation of large, all-compassing kibbutzim based on agriculture, industry and even earnings from outside employment. Hever Hakvutzot favored small compact settlements with not more than a few dozen members, which would engage exclusively in agriculture. Kibbutz Artzi generally restricted its intake to members of the Hashomer Hatzair youth movement so that a "collective outlook" would prevail. Their optimal-sized kibbutz consisted of 100 to 150 members. Most of the founders of Kibbutz Hameuhad had originally belonged to Ahdut Ha'Avodah party, most of Hever Hakvutzut were members of the Hapoel Hatzair party, while Kibbutz Artzi was in the process of evolving its own distinctive political ideology.

THE FOURTH ALIYAH (1924–1929) AND MORE ON GENERAL ECONOMIC TRENDS

The Fourth Aliyah was characterized by a sudden upsurge, in 1924, of immigration from Poland. In that year, the Polish government, headed by Grabsky, introduced legislation that severely undermined Jewish economic activities. Normally, most Jews so affected would have chosen to go to America, but just as the Polish legislation came into force, the United States drastically restricted its total migrant intake. This was facilitated by the imposition of a system of quotas, determined on the basis of much earlier migratory flows from each overseas country.[81] Many Jews who would otherwise not have done so were then compelled to consider setting up home in Palestine. By 1925, for the first time in Zionist history, Jews arriving in Palestine exceeded by a wide margin those that entered the United States. The respective figures were 34,386 and 10,292.

Of the 62,133 Jews arriving in Palestine between 1924 and 1926, at least half originally came from Poland, 20 percent from the Soviet Union (that is, Jews of Russian origin then resident in Poland and elsewhere), 10 percent from Romania and Lithuania, with the remainder from a variety of other places including Yemen and Iraq.[82] Most were mature aged small traders who did not wish to forsake their previous callings. Their attitude evoked some resentment on the part of the Yishuv's labor establishment. Ben Gurion referred to them in rather harsh terms, suggesting that, unlike the young pioneers, "They came to Palestine to continue their Polish ghetto way of life. A way of life of middlemen, speculators, shopkeepers and money lenders."[83]

Although the Fourth Aliyah is correctly perceived as having a petit bourgeois coloration, there was indeed no letup in pioneer migrants. Their absolute numbers exceeded those of the Third Aliyah and, in that sense, there was some overlap between the Third and Fourth Aliyot (Hebrew plural for *Aliyah*). Had the Soviet Union not hermetically sealed its borders, the pioneers might well have constituted a majority of the Fourth Aliyah.

Since most Fourth Aliyah migrants were drawn to urban areas, the population of Tel Aviv rose from 16,000 in 1923 to 40,000 by 1926, transforming it from a small town into a vibrant city. Elsewhere, in Haifa and Jerusalem, new Jewish localities were established. All this brought about a sharp rise in the demand for new homes and buildings for commercial purposes. In the process, the previously flagging labor market was reinvigorated. The building industry alone employed 45 percent of the labor force directly. Indirectly, it provided an additional employment boost because of the demand it created for the provision of building inputs and for building workers' consumer requirements. As is typically the case with such sudden spurts in building activity, speculation was rampant. Beginning in May 1924, the price of land allotments in the center of Tel Aviv rose within a matter of months, from 30–40 to 150–175 Palestine pounds per dunam.[84]

The Fourth Aliyah augmented the supply of private capital, which financed the country's large trade deficits (the excess of imports over exports). This permitted consumption and investment spending to be far greater than what would normally be expected, given Palestine's then economic stage of development. Since the capital transfers were almost all unilateral ones, they neither burdened the country with a growing foreign debt nor with fixed interest payments.[85]

Tangible economic progress was achieved in the industrial and services sectors, aided, in part, by a gradual modification of the import tariff structure. The cement factory *Nesher* was established in 1925, as were a number of textile plants, printing plants and some enterprises based on leather. In Tel Aviv alone, workshops and factories expanded from a total of 61 in 1924 to 170 in 1926. During the same period, their combined staff roster rose from 837 to 1,780.[86]

However, most individual Fourth Aliyah "entrepreneurs" possessed rather limited means and the business ventures they generally entered into were very small-scale affairs. In Tel Aviv more than 100 new restaurants and lodging houses of various kinds opened, and the city was graced with a profusion of seltzer kiosks. The flimsy fiscal foundations of many of these businesses made them prime candidates for bankruptcy at the first sign of a general economic downturn.

A recession was certainly not slow in coming. It was already discernible at the close of 1925, and by 1926 it was well under way. Critical conditions in the Polish economy were mainly responsible for the adverse turn of events. The country was caught up in an inflationary spiral and new legislation was introduced that tightened foreign exchange controls. This led to a sharp drop in the number of people migrating to Palestine with even the most modest amount of capital, as well as a decrease in financial transfers from Poland. The rate of immigration dropped by half in 1926 and then in the following two years dropped to even lower levels, reaching, in 1928, the smallest intake throughout the entire Mandatory period.[87] (See Table 6.1.)

The combination of fewer migrants and a growing capital shortage spelled the end of the Tel Aviv building boom. Because the building industry played such a central role in the Tel Aviv economy, laid-off workers found it next to impossible to relocate elsewhere. Workers listed as unemployed rose from 1,000 in October 1925 to 8,440 in August 1927.[88] With one-third of wage earners being without a job, the unemployment rate was unbearably high, especially in Tel Aviv, where it was above the overall Jewish average. Solel Boneh's short life ended in bankruptcy (in June 1927)[89] as did Silicate, the brickmaking plant. With the general fall in buying power associated with the rising level of unemployment, many other firms also failed. A classical example of structural unemployment unfolded. The boom in economic activity that had previously taken place did not foster appropriate investments in long-term, income-generating enterprises. In 1925, for example, 64 percent of all investments went to the building industry.[90] As with the situation that existed in 1920, a disproportionate effort was directed toward satisfying immediate demands for accommodation. Once such needs were met, or once effective demand collapsed, there were precious few other avenues open to workers to produce goods for recurrent consumption. A healthy and sustainable economic environment had yet to materialize.

Faced with little prospect of attaining regular sources of income, people began to leave the country in droves. In 1927 Jewish emigration exceeded Jewish immigration and many wondered whether the Zionist enterprise was on the verge of disintegration. However, the Jeremiahs proved to be wrong. The economic crisis receded in 1928, with the number of unemployed falling in the third quarter of that year to 1,400. The following year immigration flows picked up from the 1927–1928 trough and once again exceeded emigration figures by a reasonable margin. Visible signs of an economic recovery were evi-

Table 6.1
Jewish Migration to and from Palestine

Year	Immigration	Emigration
1919	1,806	Not Known
1920	8,223	1,300
1921	8,294	1,200
1922	8,685	1,503
1923	8,175	3,500
1924	13,892	2,000
1925	34,386	2,151
1926	13,855	7,300
1927	3,034	5,000
1928	2,178	2,100
1929	5,249	1,764

Sources: Encyclopaedia Judaica (Jerusalem 1972); Gvati, *Hundred Years,* 1985, p. 78; Erez, *Third Aliyah,* 1964, pp. 44, 94; Giladi, *Jewish Palestine,* 1973, p. 38.

dent in the restoration of the 1929 real wage rate to precrisis levels and in an increase in private capital inflows.

In addition to the economic gains generally recorded in the urban sector, there was discernible progress in agriculture. But as with manufacturing, farming activities were not at first crowned with success. In the early twenties, the agricultural yields of the collective farms were rather low. The pioneers were largely novices, lacking the kind of knowledge and experience that traditional farmers generally inherited from a long line of previous generations. Realizing their limitations and applying their superior education, the Jewish farmers were not reluctant to accept expert advice. In this respect, they had access to at least twenty agronomists of the Zionist Organization.[91]

Innovations in farming practice were liberally adopted, with wheat yields rising to surpass those of the surrounding Arab farmers. In 1925, the latter averaged between 70 and 90 kilograms per dunam, while the Jewish collectives normally produced 100 to 130. In some settlements, like Ein Harod and Geva, wheat yields were normally no less than 140 to 150 kilograms per dunam, respectively.[92] Apart from advances in wheat, a number of new crops were introduced. These included table grapes, fruit trees, bananas (in Kinneret and Degania) and dates.

Improvements were not confined to field crops. Dairy-product yields, especially in milk, rose spectacularly, with the collectives becoming the regular source of supply to Jewish city dwellers. Distribution was managed by a new Histadrut body, formed in 1926 and named *Tnuva.* By maintaining its own series of dairies, Tnuva relieved the settlements of the expenses and bother involved in milk processing and ensured a uniformly high product quality, which reassured consumers. Furthermore, since Tnuva became the collectives' exclusive dairy marketing agency, it circumvented, from their point of view, the harmful effects of market competition.

Of all agricultural endeavors, the cultivation of citrus products seemed to be the most promising. The amount of land devoted to citrus farming rose from 30,000 dunams in 1924 to 56,000 in 1927, with the Jewish share increasing from 37 percent to 43 percent.[93] Exports, of which most went to Britain, rose from 1.5 million cases in 1923–1924 to 2.5 million in 1930–1931.[94] To some extent, Palestinian oranges, which were seedless and sweet, were able to compete with South American producers because of seasonal variations associated with the different hemispheres. The local industry attracted a number of Fourth Aliyah migrants who wished to engage in farming and who had the means to wait out the eleven-year gestation period needed for the young trees to become sufficiently prolific.

In general terms, the Fourth Aliyah was the first of the truly mass migratory waves into Palestine. Between 1924 and 1928, some 67,345 newcomers arrived, and by the end of the decade there were 157,000 Jews in the country, constituting 17.7 percent of the total population.[95] The Fourth Aliyah not only stimulated the Jewish economy but it also spurred the Yishuv's cultural and educational activities. In 1924, the Technion in Haifa began operating and a year later, in 1925, the Hebrew University in Jerusalem was officially opened. New theater companies came into being and books and daily newspapers began to appear in profusion.

THE 1929 RIOTS AND THEIR REPERCUSSIONS

As the decade of the 1920s drew to a close, Palestine experienced an outbreak of wanton violence of unprecedented levels of ferocity. Essentially, it was ignited by appeals to religious passions and by the spreading of false rumors that the Jews were about to usurp and destroy Muslim holy shrines.

The events that touched off the disturbances took place in Jerusalem. They originated in an Arab complaint (which was encouraged by the deputy governor of Jerusalem) that during the 1928 Jewish Day of Atonement, the Jews had breached the status quo. It seems that their transgression lay in their erecting a screen to separate men and women worshipers at the Western Wall. Acting on the Arabs' objections, the police removed the screen. The Jews were appalled. The Wall, the remaining vestige of their Second Temple, was their most venerated site. Unyieldingly, the Muslim authorities asserted that they were its rightful owners and that Jews were only permitted to approach it on sufferance.[96] Months later, as if to emphasize the extent of their powers, they provocatively began to build on and around the Wall. In early August 1929, a few hundred young Revisionist Zionists assembled at the Wall, raised the Zionist flag and sang *Hatikvah* (the Hope, the Zionist anthem). This was shortly followed by a counterdemonstration of 2,000 Arabs, who in the process, assaulted a Jewish beadle and burned Jewish prayer books. Two days later, a young Jew was stabbed when a football landed on an Arab's tomato patch. Ultimately, on August 23, widespread rioting broke out.

In the period of nearly a year between the initial partition incident and the commencement of rioting, the entire Arab community was subject to an endless stream of anti-Jewish calumny. All avenues were utilized, including the press, public meetings and, above all, religious pulpits. Not once did the local authorities intervene to curb the barrage of anti-Jewish incitement. When through the inspiration of the mufti, Arabs began to organize "religious" ceremonies adjacent to the Wall, which involved ululating, singing and dancing to the sound of drums and cymbals, the authorities turned a blind eye to so blatant a violation of the status quo. As the intercommunal tension mounted, the British set about removing the "sealed armories" from almost all the Jewish settlements, an act that was either one of extreme folly or, more likely, mischievously devised. The period in question was one of an interregnum between High Commissioner Plumer's departure and Chancellor's settling in. At the most critical juncture, when Sir John Chancellor was away on vacation, Palestine temporarily came under the control of Charles Luke, a thoroughgoing anti-Zionist, born of Hungarian Jews who had converted to Christianity. To anglicize his name, he changed it from Lukacs to Luke. On the eve of the riots, when the Jews were being stripped of their licensed weapons, they appealed to Luke to confiscate knives and clubs from Arabs who were swarming into Jerusalem in response to a call by the mufti to defend the Muslim holy places. Luke replied, "Such a step is likely to be fraught with danger, since it would inflame people carrying clubs who are without malicious intent."[97]

As the 1929 riots unfolded, it became evident that they were not spontaneous eruptions of Arabs venting their anger on Jews supposedly bent on desecrating Muslim shrines; rather, they were well planned and well coordinated. In the region of Jerusalem, numerous villages in their entirety, supported by Bedouin from the Judean Desert, converged on outlying Jewish settlements. They were fully armed and they attacked in neatly ordered formations, which unquestionably would have necessitated prior preparation.

The disturbances, which lasted for almost a week, wrought tremendous havoc. Ramat Rahel, an encampment on the outskirts of Jerusalem, went up in flames. Motza, in which horrendous acts of violence were perpetrated, was almost completely destroyed, as were the small settlements of Ein Zeitim, Hartuv, Kfar Uria, Be'er Tuvia and Hulda. In Tel Aviv and Jaffa, clashes were suppressed by the British police but in Haifa they assumed the character of an internecine civil war, with the Haganah giving as good as it got. The large prewar settlements, such as Rehovot and Petah Tikva, were bypassed, since they were known to be well protected. All in all, 133 Jews lost their lives and several hundred were injured.[98]

The overwhelming majority of Jewish victims were defenseless, anti-Zionist, religious Jews, who presented no threat whatsoever to Palestinian Arab national interests. Sixty-seven Jews of Hebron were murdered and in Safed forty-five—mostly women and elderly men—were killed or wounded. The mob in Hebron was particularly savage. Bearing knives, axes and swords, they swooped down on house after house, slaughtering and disfiguring cowering Jews regardless of age or sex. As bad as things were, they would have been even worse had it not been for the intervention of individual compassionate Arabs. Some in Hebron stood guard for six solid hours in front of Rabbi Slonin's home, in which sixty Jews congregated, until British police arrived. Elsewhere in Hebron, another Arab, with the help of his brother and son, gathered a number of Jews and hid them in his cellar.[99] Based on records lodged in the Zionist Archives, it would seem that at least two-thirds of Hebron's Jewish population were saved by righteous Arabs.[100] The provision of assistance by Arabs on behalf of their Jewish neighbors was not confined to Hebron. Similar acts of mercy were recorded throughout the country. The Haganah reciprocated and intervened to save Arab lives and property from Jews incensed by events in Hebron and Safed. In Jerusalem, it organized young runners to report on threats to Arabs in Jewish areas. Unfortunately, this did not prevent some Jews from killing innocent Arabs. To counter such senseless acts of retribution, the (Jewish) National Council issued a decree indicating that Jews taking the law into their own hands would be regarded as traitors.[101] In the bitterness that has ensued from generations of Jewish-Arab conflict, in which national stereotyping has become so ingrained, such acts of consideration have receded from most people's consciousness.

Two months after the riots, the British government sent the Shaw Commission to Palestine to inquire into their immediate causes and to make appropriate recommendations. Its findings were published in March 1930. Although the Shaw Commission acknowledged that responsibility for the disturbances could be fully attributed to the Arabs, it exceeded its brief by taking upon itself the presentation of the Arab anti-Zionist case. Essentially, it argued that Jewish immigration, which was of course a prime objective of the Palestine Mandate, was adversely affecting the Arab population. It was alleged that many Arabs had been evicted from their land as a result of the Zionist Movement's efforts to provide Jews with farm holdings. Considering that the area of arable land was rather limited, the Shaw Commission surmised that, as a result of a continuation of large-scale Jewish immigration, a large class of landless Arab peasants would arise. Such a conclusion was based on an assessment that, under prevailing farm practices, Palestine could not sustain a larger agricultural population. To allay what were considered legitimate Arab fears, the government was called on to issue a statement indicating just how Arab rights were to be assured.

A comprehensive and critical response to the Shaw Report was issued by the Jewish Agency and other Jewish bodies. The Va'ad Leumi described it as "one of the most unjust documents which our people have had to face in the course of

2,000 years of persecution. ... Every heinous Arab crime is presented in the Report as a mere error of judgment, whilst every Jewish merit is belittled into insignificance."[102] Weizmann and other Zionist leaders tried to intercede personally with the British authorities but the colonial secretary, Lord Passfield (Sydney Webb), turned a deaf ear. (Sykes describes him as "the most anti-Zionist Secretary of State with whom Zionists had to deal at any time.")[103] Lord Passfield's wife, Lady Passfield (Beatrice Webb), when conversing with Dr. Weizmann, echoed her husband's sentiments by declaring, "I can't understand why the Jews make such a fuss over a few dozen of their people killed in Palestine. As many are killed every week in London in traffic accidents and no one pays any attention."[104]

In order to temporize while finessing his own policy, Lord Passfield invited Sir John Hope Simpson to prepare a report on the Palestine economy. This was duly delivered in August 1930 and published on October 20 of the same year. The Simpson Report painted a bleakly unrealistic picture of the economic capacity of the country. It cast doubt on prospects for industrialization and incorrectly asserted that, at most, not more than 20,000 additional families could be settled on the land. Answering charges that Arab peasants were being impoverished as a result of Jewish land purchases, the Zionists asserted that although 93 percent of the land that they had acquired came from wealthy effendis, the tenant farmers were generously compensated. Arab farmers within the vicinity of Jewish settlements made tangible economic progress, either through emulating Jewish farming methods, selling some of their surplus vegetables to the Jews or by gaining employment in the large First Aliyah villages.

The Simpson Report was immediately overshadowed by the simultaneous release of the government's new Palestine policy, embodied in the Passfield White Paper. The Paper reflected the colonial secretary's deep-seated animus toward Zionism. It effectively annulled the Balfour Declaration by asserting that Britain's obligations to the Arabs were just as weighty as those of its obligations to the Jews. Accordingly, the special status of the Jewish Agency was abrogated. For the time being, the Jews were to rest content with land already in their possession. Migration was to be determined not simply on the basis of the absorptive capacity of the Palestine economy but also on the basis of the general state of Arab unemployment. Although not explicitly stated, it was abundantly clear that, as far as the British government was concerned, the building of the Jewish National Home had run its course and that its future, if any, depended on Arab approval.[105]

The Passfield White Paper met with stiff parliamentary censure, not only from Conservative and Liberal members outside the government but also from within the ruling Labor ranks. Bowing to strong political pressures, the Cabinet decided to back down. Instead of actually withdrawing the White Paper, it hit on the device of issuing another document providing an official interpretation of Lord Passfield's policy. This took the form of a letter from the Prime Minister, Ramsey MacDonald, to Dr. Weizmann, the contents of which were determined by a committee consisting of government and Jewish Agency officials. For all intents and purposes, Britain once again reaffirmed its commitment not only to the Jews already in Palestine but also to all those in the diaspora. In accordance with standard practice, ongoing Jewish immigration to Palestine was to be based only on Palestine's economic absorptive capacity and not on any political criteria.

Although an Arab political victory was narrowly averted and the Jewish migratory flow gained momentum throughout most of the 1930s, the fact that major British politicians were willing to pay heed to anti-Zionist views was not lost on the Palestinian Arabs. As shall be shown in the following chapter, when considerably more Arab pressure was eventually brought to bear, Britain finally acceded to their demands.

From the Zionist perspective, the 1929 riots produced a short-term sequel which brought a ray of hope and comfort to the movement. Diaspora Jewry, which in the main had not shown undue interest in the building of a National Home in Palestine, was deeply moved by the violent turn of events. Their hearts went out to the victims but what really brought about an unprecedented measure of empathy with the Yishuv were reports of the exemplary defense mounted by members of the Haganah. In Hulda, in particular, 35 defenders held out against close to 2,000 assailants, until they were relieved and evacuated by British police. Their resolve mirrored that of the Tel Hai defenders nine years earlier. As they would once again respond years later in the wake of the 1967 Six-Day War, world Jewry aided the Yishuv by raising more than £600,000 for an emergency fund that was used to finance the cost of restoring demolished and damaged settlements. Never before had so much money been collected within such a short period of time (a matter of a few months). Most settlements and homes, with those in Hebron being the main exception, were rebuilt and, as in the case of Ramat Rahel, were even fitted with imposing new buildings. Be'er Tuvia was completely overhauled. The older farmers who by then had lost the will to start life anew, left and were replaced by former members of the Gedud Avodah. The latter were provided with solid homes, inventory and working capital and by 1932, the settlement was re-established on a more sound footing. Even settlements that did not sustain any significant damage were upgraded. They received funding to build school facilities, modern dining rooms, children's living quarters and access roads. Most had telephone lines installed and those that were particularly vulnerable were equipped with sturdy fences. As Bein concluded, "Despite all the damage imposed on the settlements, in the final analysis, the riots inadvertently resulted in an outcome that was the opposite of what was intended."[106]

THE PALESTINIAN ARABS AND THE DYNAMICS OF ARAB NATIONALISM

In the 1920s nearly 90 percent of Palestinian Arabs were Sunni Muslims and most of the rest were Christians. The Druze, who originated from Shiite Muslims in the eleventh century and who numbered about 1 percent of the Arabs, formed an independent community.

Most Arabs were illiterate peasants who engaged in dry land farming. Their major winter crops were wheat and barley and in the summer, sorghum and sesame. Their general level of agricultural productivity was low, falling short of the average levels that prevailed in Syria and Egypt.

Two-thirds of the population dwelled in villages. Most of the land that they cultivated was designated in Ottoman times as Miri. The occupier of Miri land enjoyed a usufruct, which could be bequeathed, but in the absence of an heir or in the event of the land being neglected, it would revert to the state. Of more relevance, in the early 1920s, over half the villages adopted the practice of Musha, whereby all the land was treated as common property. Each fellah was allocated a patch for his own use but after a short interval, of no more than two years, it was reissued by the drawing of lots. This meant that no one had any incentive to invest in land improvements. Another complicating factor arose from land fragmentation. Many farmers had access to several small parcels of land, scattered around the neighborhood.

It is thought that about a third of the arable land belonged to effendis (large landowners) whose estates were hired out to tenant farmers, who in turn constituted close to a quarter of the farming population.[107] The tenants usually paid rent amounting to 30 percent of the value of their yields.

Most of the effendis lived in the cities. Some even had foreign domiciles. It was basically the effendis who assumed leadership of the Palestinian Arab Nationalist Movement. Two prominent families, the Husseinis and the Nashashibis, contested the movement's leadership. While the Husseinis were outspoken and uncompromising nationalists, the Nashashibis presented a more moderate facade and, on occasion, were prepared to cooperate with Jews, at least on certain parochial issues. This made the Jews think that they were more amenable to their point of view; in reality, however, they were no less nationalistic than their Husseini rivals. Being more militant, the Husseinis seized the political initiative and soon dominated the Palestinian National Movement. They certainly had a significant advantage in their kinsman, Haj Amin al Husseini, being both the mufti of Jerusalem and head of the Muslim Council. Haj Amin al Husseini lost no time in placing his relatives in key posts, which in turn helped to strengthen the Husseinis' grip on Arab affairs.

In December 1920, about forty effendis and various other educated Arabs assembled in Haifa in what was officially known as the Third Palestinian Congress. (The first two had been held in Damascus, when Faisal still reigned in Syria and when Palestine was regarded as an integral part of that country.) Among other things, they demanded a cessation of Jewish immigration, the establishment of a national government responsible to an assembly elected by Arab-speaking citizens present in Palestine before the First World War. All senior administrative posts were to be entrusted to Christians and Muslims only, "since Palestine was holy to Christians and Muslims," and, by implication, not to Jews.[108] The Congress appointed a standing committee, known as the Palestine Arab Executive, which was to be its permanent official representative body. It was headed by Musa Kazam Husseini, who had been mayor of Jerusalem during the 1920 riots, and consisted of seven Muslims and two Christians. In the following three years, congresses were held annually. In 1923, 115 delegates gathered in Jaffa where the term *Southern Syria*, which was taken to refer to Palestinian territory, was replaced by *Palestine*, indicating the emergence of a distinct local national consciousness. A separate Palestinian nationalism resulted from the collapse of pan-Arabism, which was to be incarnated in a large Sherifian empire. Such dreams were shattered by the ejection of Faisal from Syria and by the formation of local kingships in Iraq and Transjordan. Needless to say, the Zionist challenge played a crucial role in stimulating Palestinian nationalism.[109]

As far as the Palestinian Arabs were concerned, they were the exclusive owners of the country. They rejected the Zionist claim that the Jews had an historical connection to their land. Apart from hostility to Zionism on ideological grounds, many Arabs were disquieted by what they perceived as a strangeness in culture, customs and lifestyle exhibited by the young Jewish pioneers. In particular, the tendency of young Jewish women to dress in clothes that were regarded as being far too immodest and revealing affronted the moral sensibilities of most of the local inhabitants. In a seminal work on Palestinian nationalism, Porath concluded that "There is no doubt that for the Arab masses, lacking in education and political national consciousness, this variance, this strangeness and these apprehensions were a most important factor—perhaps the primary factor—in the growth of their hatred for Zionism."[110] Porath's views notwithstanding, even if the Jews had conformed to local customs, the fact that they strove for Jewish political dominance was sufficient to elicit a negative Arab reaction.

Between 1924 and 1928, with next to no achievements to its credit, the prestige of the Husseini-controlled Palestine Arab Executive reached a low ebb. The large Jewish migratory inflows of the Fourth Aliyah came about without any serious resistance on the part of the Arab leadership. The Palestine Arab Executive seemed to have lost its verve. Annual strikes on Balfour Declaration Day diminished and the financial resources of the Arab Executive began to be depleted. In turn, disillusioned Arabs turned to Nashashibi candidates during the 1925–1926 municipal elections and in 1927, the office of the Arab Executive closed.

With the Palestinian National Movement seemingly dormant and even beginning to show some signs of moderating its attitude toward the Zionists, the Husseinis, under the mufti of Jerusalem's leadership, decided to play the religious card, pure and simple: they inflamed latent anti-Jewish passions and thus prepared the groundwork for the outbreak of the 1929 riots.

Up until the 1929 riots, the country enjoyed a period of internal calm and peace in the wake of the 1921 disturbances. The absence of violence was due partly to the condign punishment that the government meted out to offending individuals and villages alike and to the fact that influential pro-Arab British politicians recommended a moderate course of action as the sure and only way to advance the Palestinian cause.[111] In addition, having been elevated in 1922 to the presidency of the Supreme Muslim Council, the mufti, Haj Amin al Husseini, bided his time by consolidating his position as the most pre-eminent Palestinian. To achieve that objective, he initially needed to court the good will of the government; therefore, for the time being, he moderated his stand on violent political action.[112] Not only did the mufti aspire to reach the pinnacle of Palestinian leadership, but he also skillfully presented himself to non-Palestinian Muslims from as far afield as India, as being their faith's defender of Jerusalem's holy places. He assumed the role of custodian of the two mosques on al-Haram al-Sharif (the Temple Mount) and coordinated an international fund for their renovations. By eventually suggesting that the Zionists were planning to replace the mosques with a restored temple, he placed himself at the head of a more virulent anti-Zionist movement.

BRIT SHALOM (COVENANT OF PEACE)

In 1925, a small group of Jewish intellectuals established an organization called *Brit Shalom* (Covenant of Peace). Under the inaugural chairmanship of Arthur Ruppin, and with other luminaries such as Dr. Judah Magnes and Professor Hugo Bergmann, Brit Shalom sought to cultivate Arab-Jewish good will. It hoped to allay Arab fears of being swamped by continued Jewish immigration by suggesting that Jewish aspirations to become a majority in Palestine need not necessarily be realized. As an alternative to the strivings of each national group for unencumbered Palestinian hegemony, Brit Shalom proposed a compromise. The two nations were to live amicably together in the framework of a binational state. Each would organize its affairs autonomously, sharing joint state sovereignty without regard to numerical considerations. It was hoped that, in the course of time, both peoples would uphold Palestinian citizenship, which would supplant their particular national loyalties.[113]

Although Brit Shalom's platform represented a magnanimous gesture on the part of a minute handful of Jews (it never exceeded more than a few dozen members), it never stood any chance of being taken seriously by either the Jewish or Arab masses. Zionism, which sought to extricate its followers from the hazards of the absence of Jewish sovereignty, was not expending prodigious efforts simply to attain some sort of autonomous entity that would depend on the willing cooperation of an Arab majority. Similarly, the Arabs saw no reason why they should forfeit what they regarded as their inalienable national rights to the whole of Palestine in order to accommodate the political demands of non-Arab migrants. This point was well appreciated by Arthur Ruppin, who in a letter dated May 30, 1928, wrote "There is no parallel in history to the aim of Zionism—to settle the Jews peaceably in a country which is already inhabited.

... So far, no nation has ever been willing to tolerate another nation settling beside it and claiming complete equality and national autonomy."[114] Not surprisingly, there was never even a hint of a parallel Brit Shalom–type movement within the Arab camp and by 1933, even Brit Shalom had ceased to exist.

BRIEF SUMMARY

Violent anti-Jewish rioting took place both in the beginning and at the end of the decade of the 1920s. In the interlude, Palestine was blessed with a period of tranquility, during which the Yishuv began to consolidate itself. The labor movement established the Histadrut, which in turn oversaw the development of the Haganah and a number of new collective farms, both of the kibbutz and moshav variety. Additional areas of land were acquired and settled, while in the urban sector, a growing Jewish presence in Tel Aviv and Haifa was clearly discernible. The overall Jewish population rose rapidly as a result of the Third and Fourth Aliyot (Aliyahs). During those two migratory waves, there was a flurry of activity, especially in the building industry, which rapidly declined when capital and/or migrant inflows suddenly abated. However, the Yishuv emerged enriched with an enhanced reserve of labor and new enterprises, which enabled it to absorb even larger numbers in the decade that followed. Progress in other spheres, such as the establishment of the Hebrew University in 1925, a school network, hospitals and clinics, as well as newspapers and political parties, not to mention the formation of the Jewish Agency, all fostered the feeling that the Yishuv was indeed a state in the making.

NOTES

1. In September 1921 the Commission's functions were assumed by a body called the Palestine Zionist Executive. Soon afterward, the Palestine Office of the Zionist Organization was incorporated into the Palestine Zionist Executive, which in turn became the exclusive representative in Palestine of the World Zionist Movement.

2. Faisal was the son of Hussein, then ruler of most of what is now Saudi Arabia.

3. Stein, *Balfour Declaration*, 1961, p. 638.

4. As reported by Weizmann, *Trial and Error*, 1949, p. 307.

5. As quoted by Stein, *Balfour Declaration*, 1961, pp. 641–42.

6. Laqueur, *History*, 1989, p. 237.

7. See Cohen, *Israel*, 1964, p. 149.

8. As quoted by Stein, *Trial and Error*, 1961, p. 646.

9. As quoted by Wasserstein, *British in Palestine*, 1978, p. 41.

10. Almost all the information in this segment is derived from Laskov, *Trumpeldor*, 1972. There are a number of alternative versions of the dynamics of the battle of Tel Hai. This is not surprising. As in all such skirmishes, each participant saw and recorded

things from his or her own perspective and subsequent writers adopted alternative accounts. Laskov's rendition may or may not be the most authentic but her biography of Trumpeldor is very well researched, authoritative and overshadows prior studies.

11. Quoted by Shapira, *Land and Power*, 1992, p. 99.

12. From Trumpeldor's diary, as published by Yaari, *Memoirs*, 1947, p. 1134.

13. Even-Shoshan, *History*, 1955, p. 340.

14. Laskov, *Trumpeldor*, 1972, p. 243.

15. Ibid., p. 247.

16. Ibid., p. 248.

17. Halpern, *Idea of a Jewish State*, 1961, p. 294.

18. Weizmann, *Trial and Error*, 1949, p. 319.

19. Patterson, *With the Judeans*, 1922, p. 271.

20. A few months later he was amnetised by Palestine's First High Commissioner, Herbert Samuel.

21. Meinertzhagen, *Middle East Diary*, 1959, p. 82. The authenticity of these statements has not been verified, but they are certainly consistent with the behavior of the British authorities.

22. By and large, the terms *Old* and *New Yishuv* will henceforth by replaced simply by the term *Yishuv*. This does not mean to imply that differences between the two communities no longer existed. Rather, in the early post–World War I period, the New Yishuv began to outnumber the Old one by a considerable margin and, within its orb, almost all the main subsequent historical events took place.

23. Kedourie, "Sir Herbert Samuel," 1969, p. 53.

24. Wasserstein, *British in Palestine*, 1978, p. 131.

25. Abramov, *Perpetual Dilemma*, 1976, pp. 95–96.

26. Esco Foundation for Palestine, *Palestine*, 1947, vol. 1, p. 256.

27. Wasserstein, *British in Palestine*, 1978, p. 101.

28. Esco Foundation for Palestine, *Palestine*, 1947, vol. 1, p. 270.

29. Wasserstein, *British in Palestine*, 1978, p. 102.

30. Shapira, *Land and Power*, 1992, p. 114.

31. As quoted by Sykes, 1965, p. 62.

32. Ibid.

33. Even-Shoshan, *History*, 1955, Book 2, p. 37.

34. Esco Foundation for Palestine, *Palestine*, 1947, vol. 1, p. 290.

35. That is, Faisal, his two brothers and his father.

36. As quoted by Weizmann, *Trial and Error*, 1949, p. 361.

37. Esco Foundation for Palestine, *Palestine*, 1947, vol. 1, p. 161.

38. Mossek, *Palestine Immigration Policy*, 1978, p. 9.

39. Sachar, *Course*, 1990, p. 566.

40. Gilbert, *Exile and Return*, 1978, p. 121 puts the figure at more than 60,000.

41. Laqueur, *History*, 1989, p. 441.

42. Gilbert, *Exile and Return*, 1978, p. 121.

43. Erez, *Third Aliyah*, 1964, pp. 22–23.

44. Ibid., p. 76.

45. Even-Shoshan, *History*, 1955, p. 387.
46. G. Harovi, "The Tiberius-Tzemach Road," in Erez, *Third Aliyah*, 1964, pp. 247–50.
47. Bein, *History*, 1970, p. 200.
48. Ibid.
49. Gvati, *Hundred Years*, 1985, p. 67.
50. Horowitz, *My Yesterday*, 1970, p. 30.
51. Ibid., p. 45.
52. Erez, *Third Aliyah*, 1964, p. 38.
53. Giladi, *Jewish Palestine*, 1973, p. 22.
54. Erez, *Third Aliyah*, 1964, p. 44.
55. Gross, "The 1923 Recession," 1979, p. 37.
56. Ibid., p. 38.
57. Ibid., p. 41.
58. Shapiro, *Formative Years*, 1976, p. 28.
59. Quoted by Laskov, *Trumpeldor*, 1972, p. 202.
60. Laqueur, *History*, 1989, p. 312.
61. Giladi, *Jewish Palestine*, 1973, p. 196.
62. Shapiro, *Formative Years*, 1976, p. 171.
63. Ibid., pp. 207–9.
64. Ibid., p. 371.
65. Ibid., p. 373.
66. After 1937, no non-Zionist was elected to the Jewish Agency.
67. Slutsky, *From Defence to Strife*, 1964, p. 96.
68. Ibid., p. 104.
69. As quoted by Slutsky, *From Defence to Strife*, 1964, p. 272.
70. Ibid., p. 227.
71. Ibid., p. 252.
72. Ibid., p. 253.
73. Gvati, *Hundred Years*, 1985, p. 62.
74. Bein, *History*, 1970, p. 151.
75. Erez, *Third Aliyah*, 1964, p. 21.
76. L. Kadman Kufman, "Settlement in the East Emek," in Erez, *Third Aliyah*, 1964, p. 481.
77. Even-Shoshan, *History*, 1955, Book 2, p. 69.
78. Gvati, *Hundred Years*, 1985, pp. 64 and 72.
79. The term *kibbutz*, as opposed to the term *kvutza*, was initially introduced by a member of Hashomer Hatzair shortly after encountering Baraslov Hassidim in Jerusalem. Although of a secular outlook, he was moved by the piety of the Hassidim and noted that they termed gatherings in memory of their founding rabbi a *kibbutz*. "Why not do likewise?" he asked. His suggestion was well received and their road construction collective was henceforth named "Kibbutz Hashomer Hatzair." Similarly, dozens of other collectives referred to themselves as kibbutzim. As it happens, the atheistic pioneers were generally moved by Hassidic melodies and were wont to incorporate

them in their rich song repertoire. See Y. Yaari, "The Road Full of Obstacles," in *Erez, Third Aliyah,* 1964, p. 890.

80. Giladi, *Jewish Palestine,* 1973, pp. 228–29.

81. Each country was allocated only 2 percent of the number of its citizens who had taken up U.S. residence in 1890.

82. Giladi, *Jewish Palestine,* 1973, p. 44.

83. Ben Gurion, *Israel,* 1971, p. 375.

84. Giladi, *Jewish Palestine,* 1973, p. 48.

85. Ibid., p. 13.

86. Bein, *History,* 1970, p. 264.

87. Giladi, *Jewish Palestine,* 1973, p. 39.

88. Bein, *History,* 1970, p. 266.

89. It did in fact continue to exist on paper only to rise like a phoenix in 1935.

90. Halevi, "Economic Development," 1979, p. 21.

91. Bein, *History,* 1970, p. 287.

92. Ibid., p. 288.

93. Giladi, *Jewish Palestine,* 1973, p. 77.

94. Gvati, *Hundred Years,* 1985, p. 79.

95. Giladi, *Jewish Palestine,* 1973, p. 36.

96. Laqueur, *History,* 1989, p. 255.

97. Slutsky, *From Defence to Strife,* 1964, p. 309.

98. Laqueur, *History,* 1989, p. 490.

99. Slutsky, *From Defence to Strife,* 1964, p. 323.

100. See article by Tom Segev, "The Year 1929 of Raymond Cafferata," in the *Haaretz* Weekly Supplement, June 11, 1999, p. 62.

101. Slutsky, *From Defence to Strife,* 1964, p. 349.

102. As quoted by Esco Foundation for Palestine, *Palestine,* 1947, vol. 2, p. 629.

103. Sykes, 1965, p. 121.

104. Weizmann, *Trial and Error,* 1949, p. 411.

105. Laqueur, *History,* 1989, p. 492.

106. Bein, *History,* 1970, p. 334.

107. Giladi, *Jewish Palestine,* 1973, p. 26.

108. Slutsky, *From Defence to Strife,* 1964, p. 61.

109. For example, see Gorny, *Zionism,* 1987, p. 84.

110. Porath, *Emergence,* 1974, p. 60.

111. Ibid., p. 134.

112. Ibid., p. 135.

113. Shapira, *Land and Power,* 1992, p. 167.

114. Ruppin, *Memoirs,* 1971, p. 237.

Chapter 7

Foreboding Times: Palestine in the 1930s

The decade of the 1930s represented a watershed for the Jews in Palestine. During that period, they secured a firm economic, social and defense footing but, as is outlined below, they also encountered tremendous political uncertainty. In fact, as the reader shall shortly discover, the early successes of the Yishuv were partly responsible for the deterioration of its relations, first with the Arabs and then with the British. This chapter commences with a description of the Yishuv's internal consolidation, which was, of course, mainly facilitated by the advent of the Fifth Aliyah.

THE FIFTH ALIYAH

The inflow of Jewish migration throughout the entire decade of the 1930s is known as the Fifth Aliyah. It constituted the largest migratory wave in the Yishuv's prestate history. Between 1930 and 1939, more than 270,000 Jews entered the country. By the end of 1939, the Jews in Palestine, who numbered 475,000, accounted for slightly more than 30 percent of the entire population. Their proportional share would have been even greater had it not been for the remarkable natural increase of the Palestinian Arabs, which was among the world's highest. As the Esco Foundation concluded, such a phenomenon could largely be attributed to "better conditions resulting from the development of the Jewish national home."[1] Malcolm MacDonald, the British colonial secretary in the late 1930s was even more emphatic. He declared that "If not a single Jew had come to Palestine after 1918, I believe the Arab population of Palestine today would still have been round the 600,000 figure, at which it had been stable under Turkish rule. It is because the Jews who have come to Palestine bring modern health services and other advantages that Arab men and women who would be dead are alive today, that Arab children who would never have drawn breath have been born and grow strong."[2]

The steadily worsening situation of the Jews, first in Poland and then in Germany and Austria, were the Fifth Aliyah's obvious causes. Given that the Jews of Eastern and Central Europe were in desperate straits and that the doors of alternative countries were being slammed in their faces, it is little wonder that so many streamed into Palestine.

As can be seen in Table 7.1, the peak inflows of Jewish immigration occurred from 1933 to 1936. Hitler had assumed high office, the Palestinian economy was booming and the administration was rather generous in determining acceptable migrant levels. Before then, the economy had been sluggish and the position of European Jews, though bad, was not seemingly catastrophic. In 1937 and thereafter, the migrant intake was significantly curtailed on account of changes in British policy.

Not only was the Yishuv enriched in manpower but the quality of its work force was significantly upgraded. As with the Fourth Aliyah, most migrants came from Poland, but in the wake of the 1933 Nazi accession to power, German Jews appeared both in increasing absolute and relative terms. While between 1920 and 1932, German Jews represented only 2.5 percent of all Jewish immigrants, between 1933 and 1938, their share rose to 27.7 percent.[3] Generally speaking, the German Jews tended to be members of the free professions, such as medicine, law, engineering and architecture. They also included many scientists and individuals who were au fait with commerce and industry and who had a flair for sound organization and order.

An important and innovative component of German Jewish immigration was the emergence of youth aliyah. This involved the organized dispatch to Palestine of youth between the ages of 15 and 17. In 1932 Racha Freier conceived the idea and, a year later, the Jewish Agency established a special Youth Aliyah Bureau headed by Henrietta Szold. As the scheme unfolded, youth were sent to Palestine in the framework of organized groups. Upon their arrival, the teenagers were billeted in either a kibbutz, a moshav, a training farm or a youth village. Over an initial two-year period, their days were more or less equally divided between agricultural work and formal study, including the learning of Hebrew. In February 1934, the first group was absorbed by Kibbutz Ein Harod and by the outbreak of the Second World War some 5,000 Jewish youth had settled in the country.

German Jews generally brought in more capital per person than other migrants. Until 1938, they were able to transmit funds to Palestine through an arrangement Chaim Arlossoroff and the Anglo Palestine Bank made with the Nazi regime. Prospective migrants deposited their capital into the bank's branch in Germany. On arrival in Palestine, they could claim a sum in local currency equivalent in value to their German account. The money originally lodged in Germany was utilized by the Anglo Palestine Bank to finance imports on either the migrants' behalf or on behalf of other Yishuv enterprises. Com-

Table 7.1
Jewish Immigration into Palestine in the 1930s

Year	Number of Immigrants
1930	4,944
1931	4,075
1932	9,553
1933	30,327
1934	42,359
1935	61,854
1936	29,727
1937	10,536
1938	12,868
1939	27,561

This table specifies only the numbers of authorized migrants. In addition, during the period in question, nearly 40,000 Jewish migrants entered the country illegally. In 1932, for instance, thousands of "tourists" arrived, ostensibly to view the Macabee Games, but most stayed on permanently. Also, between 1930 and 1939, only 6,517 Jews were recorded as having emigrated.

Sources: Even-Shoshan, *History,* 1955, Book 2, p. 264; Esco Foundation for Palestine, *Palestine,* 1947, vol. 2, p. 674.

pared with the period of 1921 to 1931, in which individual Jews introduced no more than 20 million Palestine pounds into the country, between 1932 and 1935, £30 million Palestine pounds were transferred. There was in fact a high correlation between capital inflows and immigration, with both peaking in 1935.[4]

The Fifth Aliyah made a big impact on Jewish urbanization, especially in Tel Aviv and Haifa. Between 1931 and 1935, Tel Aviv's population, which was virtually 100 percent Jewish, rose from 46,000 to 135,000. In Haifa during the same period, the number of Jews increased from 16,000 to 50,000. Within the urban areas, the manufacturing sector thrived and became more diversified. New industries included metals, chemicals, pharmaceuticals, textiles, clothing, machinery, electrical products, beer and fruit canning. Although the Jewish manufacturing sector blossomed, it did not become the Yishuv's economic frontrunner. That position was assumed by the tertiary sector, consisting of services (especially in passenger and freight transport), commerce and finance, which in 1935 collectively accounted for 71 percent of Jewish economic output. Within the realm of finance, dozens of new banks appeared, bringing the 1936 total to seventy-nine.[5] However, most were based on shaky foundations and by the end of the following year, only thirty-two had survived.

Elsewhere in the country, the economy's basic structure widened. Throughout the 1930s the generation of electrical power for industrial purposes rose seven-fold. In 1930, the Palestine Potash Company was founded. Operating at the Dead Sea, its potash output increased from 9,000 tons in 1932 to 63,500 tons in 1939.[6] That product, combined with bromine, which the company also produced, became significant export earners. In 1935, a new deepwater harbor was completed in Haifa and, within a couple of years, over three-quarters of the country's trade passed through its gates. In 1936, on account of Jewish Arab friction in Jaffa, a new port was opened in Tel Aviv, which handled some of the country's citrus exports. Finally, by 1937, the country had forged links with five international air transport carriers, which made use of its airports at Lydda, Haifa and Gaza.

In the first half of the 1930s, or, more precisely, between 1932 and 1935, the economy of the Yishuv flourished to such an extent that, despite the massive inflow of Jewish migrants, per capita incomes did not flag. Just when the rest of the world was experiencing the worst depression in modern history, the Palestine economy was assisted by a large infusion of capital, the 1931 devaluation of the Palestine pound, a fall in world commodity prices that lessened the country's import bill and a sharp rise in the demand for citrus fruit.[7]

In 1935 the economic tide in Palestine turned. Building activities virtually ground to a halt, there was a general reduction in the planting of citrus groves, which had previously buttressed exports, and a financial crisis that resulted from Italy's invasion of Ethiopia. General world prices began to rise, and countries such as France, Czechoslovakia, Italy and Syria depreciated their foreign currencies, which adversely affected Palestine's competitive standing. In 1936 matters worsened. The country was plagued by an Arab rebellion, accompanied by a general strike of six months' duration. Subsequent attempts to pacify the Arabs by drastically limiting Jewish immigration caused the economy to be in the doldrums for the remainder of the decade.

In contrast to economic activity in the Yishuv as a whole, the agricultural sector developed rapidly during the entire Fifth Aliyah period. At first, citrus farming recorded the most startling gains. The land area devoted to citrus orchards rose from 100,000 dunams in 1931 to 300,000 in 1935. Approximately half the orchards in question were in Jewish hands. Most of the output was sold abroad, with exports rising from 2.5 million crates in 1930–1931 to over 15 million in 1938–1939. By the latter period, citrus fruit constituted 75 percent of all Palestine exports.

The Palestine citrus industry was not without its problems. It had to compete in an international arena in which there was a marked tendency toward overproduction. With Palestine excluded from the Imperial Preference Scheme, its oranges were subject to higher import duties in Britain than those of the dominion countries. Considering that Britain was Palestine's main citrus buyer, this amounted to a significant export impediment.

The internal market for Jewish farm produce received a welcome boost, when, from 1936 onward, the Arabs withheld deliveries to Jewish clients. As an unintended consequence, the Jews made rapid strides in the supply of vegetables, poultry and milk products. For instance, while in 1935 only 2,000 dunams were allocated to vegetable growing, by 1937 the area was increased to 7,000 dunams.[8] Similarly, in 1931, Tnuvah, the Histadrut's agricultural marketing cooperative, sold on behalf of Jewish settlements 3 million liters of milk and 1.6 million eggs. In 1938, the figures had risen to 1.75 million in each case.[9] Discernible progress was also recorded in the realm of fishing. Trawlers were acquired for operation along the Mediterranean coast, and some settlements near Lake Kinneret and Lake Huleh also ventured into this sphere.

In general, farming in Palestine was encumbered with numerous difficulties. Lacking tariff protection, the country's agriculture was handicapped by competition from outsiders. It had great difficulty in meeting challenges from countries such as Switzerland that had natural comparative advantages in producing products like butter, or from other European sources where farmers enjoyed export subsidies. Alternatively, neighboring countries, such as Syria, were able to undersell Palestinian vegetable growers on account of their cheaper labor. Because of the low standard of living of Palestine's Arab population, internal outlets were rather limited. Even among the Jews, the consumption of certain essential food products, was small.[10] To improve farm productivity, expensive modern equipment was required. This, in turn, necessitated access to credit. Within the Jewish sector, most of the capital was derived from Zionist institutions, but in the mid-1930s, recourse to borrowed funds financed over 30 percent of capital outlays. As a consequence, the farmers bore a large debt servicing burden. Despite all these impediments, the Jewish agricultural sector performed well, with the overall number of its settlements increasing from 124 in 1931 to 252 in 1939.[11]

POLITICAL DEVELOPMENTS WITHIN THE ZIONIST MOVEMENT AND THE YISHUV

In April 1925, under Jabotinsky's leadership, the Revisionist Party was founded in Paris, where Jabotinsky then lived. It stood for the establishment of a Jewish state on both sides of the Jordan River, to be achieved by a sustained process of mass immigration funded by a national loan. One of the major bones of contention between the Revisionists and the Labor movement revolved around the use of force in attaining Zionist objectives. Almost every Yishuv Zionist adhered to the view that it was legitimate to use force to ensure the Yishuv's survival. However, the Revisionists parted company from others by giving absolute priority to establishing an officially sanctioned military body over general constructive endeavors. Jabotinsky held that the Arabs would never reconcile themselves to a growing Jewish presence in Palestine unless they were presented with an "iron wall" of Jewish resistance. This meant that it was imperative that the Jews possessed sufficient military means to dispel all Arab hopes and illusions that the Jews could be overpowered and that Zionism in Palestine could be eliminated.

The Revisionists insisted that the Zionists openly demand a sovereign Jewish state and not fudge their objectives by merely calling for a Jewish National Homeland. Since such a view was not shared by the World Zionist Movement, Jabotinsky decided that the Revisionists would have to act independently. In 1933 he withdrew the bulk of the Revisionists from the World Zionist Movement. (A small faction, known as the *Jewish State Party*, remained behind.) The timing of the Revisionist withdrawal was precipitated by a devastating electoral defeat in a poll choosing delegates for the 1933 Eighteenth Zionist Congress. Their share of the vote slumped from 25 percent for the previous Congress to 14 percent for the current one. Heralding a significant shift in the political composition of the World Zionist Movement, the Labor Zionists increased their representation from 29 percent to 44 percent. Two years later, the Revisionists established their own World Zionist Organization, which they named the New Zionist Organization.

Among the Revisionists in Palestine was a cabal of hotheads who referred to themselves as the *Biryonim*. They were led by Abba Achimeir, who justified political assassinations and who argued that all means were valid in achieving the Zionist end.[12] Other luminaries included Dr. Yeivan and the poet Uri Greenberg. In Achimeir's view, those concerned with ethical considerations "had no place in the new Hebrew Nation."(Such an opinion still resonates among many West Bank Jewish settlers, religious and secular alike.) The Biryonim were great admirers of fascism and a regular newspaper column by Achimeir was titled "From a Fascist's Notebook." Although they had few followers, they certainly achieved a certain notoriety for political hooliganism. Along with other Revisionists, they excoriated the Labor Movement, denouncing its leaders as "renegades" and "despicable lackeys of the British."[13] Much of their hostility was vented against Dr. Chaim Arlosoroff, a brilliant young Mapai intellectual who headed the political department of the Jewish Agency. Arlosoroff was certainly at odds with the Revisionists regarding the use of force as a means of attaining Zionist objectives. He categorically stated that the use of strongarm tactics never really yields long-term benefits and that "Since Jews and Arabs find themselves squeezed into one trajectory, a political process seeking some agreement is needed."[14] But it seems that Achimeir's main grudge against Arlosoroff was that, contrary to the Revisionists' campaign of imposing an embargo on German trade and not dealing with the Nazi regime, Arlosoroff was in the process of negotiating with them to transfer German Jewish capital to Palestine.

On June 16, 1933, while taking an evening stroll with his wife along Tel Aviv's foreshore, Chaim Arlosoroff was fatally shot. That very morning Achimeir's screed, *Hazit Ha'am* (the National Front), which often referred to Arlosoroff by the Hebrew pun, "Aral Zeh Rav," meaning "poison is abundant," carried a major article denouncing Arlosoroff as a traitor to the Jewish people. It suggested that Arlosoroff ingratiated himself with the Nazis simply to enrich himself and ended with the following statement: "The Jewish people have always known how to evaluate those who sell out their nation's honor and Torah. Also today, it will know how to respond to such an outrage, executed in the full light of day and in the eyes of the entire world."[15]

In the wake of the murder, Mrs. Arlosoroff reported to the police that one of the two assailants spoke Hebrew without an accent, using a Yiddish turn of phrase. Before shooting Arlosoroff, a flashlight was directed toward her husband's face and the movement of the flashlight enabled Mrs. Arlosoroff to discern the physiognomy of one of the men. On the basis of her description, which was widely publicized, two people independent of each other and of Mrs. Arlosoroff, advised the police that the description matched that of Avraham Stavsky, a rough-and-ready Revisionist newly arrived from Poland, who shared accommodations with Achimeir. Stavsky was identified by Mrs. Arlosoroff both visually and by his voice. He and two others, including Achimeir, were arraigned for murder. The other two were found not guilty, but Stavsky was sentenced to death. At his appeal trial, he was acquitted by the three presiding judges, who argued that although Mrs. Arlosoroff's evidence was compelling, they were obliged to find for the defendant on the grounds that Palestine law deemed that one witness alone was insufficient. Had the trial taken place in Britain, they added, they would have upheld Stavsky's conviction.

The trial split the Yishuv into two camps. The Labor Movement was convinced that the murderers were incited by a Revisionist hate campaign, while the Revisionists believed that they were the victims of a Labor blood libel. The Revisionists claimed that Arabs were behind it all, but the assassination did not bear the hallmarks of an Arab criminal attack. No one was robbed and Mrs. Arlosoroff was not harmed, and as the eminent historian Slutsky emphasized, Arab terrorism, as opposed to the European variety, was distinguished by not being directed against specific Jewish leaders. Rather, it sought to implant widespread fear within the Yishuv as a whole.[16] For years to come, the aftermath of the trial left a bitter taste in the Yishuv body politic. Many were of the view that the rift between the two camps could readily have degenerated into a Jewish civil war.

In 1934, the Revisionists established their own National Labor Federation, which lost little time in competing with and denigrating the Histadrut, which Jabotinsky called "a malignant tumor."[17] Their main concern with the Histadrut was that it did not confine itself exclusively to standard trade union affairs. Furthermore, the Revisionists preferred resolving all worker claims through compulsory arbitration, rather than resorting to strike action. With the support of some employers, they readily indulged in strikebreaking activities, which resulted in violent confrontations with workers legitimately pursuing industrial grievances. As it happened, the National Labor Federation did not flourish, and numerous individual Revisionists continued to stand by the Histadrut as a more reliable protector of worker rights and benefits. Within the general Palestinian Jewish political arena, the Revisionists became a formidable body, obtaining in 1931 23 percent of the vote for the *Va'ad Hanivharim* (the

Assembly of Delegates). Although in subsequent years the size of their following declined, they continued to be a force of some reckoning. Having been denied re-entry into Palestine in December 1929, their leader, Jabotinsky, had to
steer Palestinian Revisionist affairs from abroad.

It has often been said of the Revisionists that they were all bluff and blus-
ter and made little contribution to the practical building of the Yishuv. Amazingly, Jabotinsky and his supporters inadvertently endorsed such a viewpoint.
Jabotinsky railed against the colonizing process of the Labor Movement on the
specious grounds that once pioneers possessed homesteads and associated ac-
couterments, property of that nature would gradually become more precious to
them than the ultimate goal of conquering Palestine. As his biographer and
most loyal lieutenant attested, "The Revisionist party and its affiliates were the
only ones who (with a few minor exceptions) possessed no settlements, economic enterprises, or institutions of their own. *This enabled them to preserve
the integrity of their Zionist ideal.*"[18] Had the rest of the Yishuv thought likewise, it is highly unlikely that the state of Israel would ever have seen the light
of day.

Apart from Mapai, Hashomer Hatzair, Mizrachi and the Revisionists, there
was one other major party within the World Zionist Movement and within
Palestine: this was known as the General Zionists. They were, at first, simply
Zionists without any ideological agenda. In 1935 they split into two bodies,
known, respectively, as General Zionists A and General Zionists B. The A group,
led by Weizmann, cooperated with all sections of the Yishuv and was even associated with the Histadrut. The B General Zionists, by contrast, were very much
in favor of free enterprise and allied themselves with others of the right wing of
the political spectrum. In the course of time, the A group formed the Progressive
Party, while the B group simply became known as General Zionists. Many years
later, in 1961, the two parties merged to form the Liberal Party.

THE BEGINNING OF THE ARAB UPRISING

After the 1929 riots ended, sporadic attacks on Jews and their property continued uninterruptedly. Such incidents tended to be locally based and undertaken by individuals or small groups acting on their own volition. But in
October 1933, mass Arab violence made a fleeting reappearance, when a series
of riots flared up in Jaffa, Nablus, Haifa and Jerusalem. The disorders were
quickly suppressed, at a toll of twenty-six Arab lives and one British policeman.

Then on November 20, 1935, as a prelude to events that were soon to follow,
Sheik al-Din al-Kassem and his men were surrounded by British forces in their
retreat near Jenin. Refusing to surrender, the sheik and a few of his followers
were killed in the ensuing skirmish. This aroused a convulsive wave of anger
among thousands of Arabs, who regarded the sheik as a saintly man. At his funeral, Palestinian youth resolved to emulate his deeds. Ben Gurion shrewdly

observed that al-Kassem's last battle was tantamount to an Arab Tel Hai.[19] Al-Kassem was a Syrian dervish who migrated to Palestine, where he advocated a holy war against the Jews and the British. Operating in the Haifa area, al-Kassem led a small group that not only indiscriminately attacked Jews but also threatened Arabs selling land to them. Until his untimely death, he was a shadowy, marginal figure but, as so often happens, his heroic final stand transformed him into a potent symbol of Palestinian resistance. Al-Kassem and his men were revered as being the first within the Arab movement to fight until death for the sake of national and religious ideals.

A few months later, in April 1936, the country was plunged into widespread and prolonged violence. Many factors were responsible for the disturbances, but, unquestionably, the main underlying cause was the rapid rise, through immigration, of the Jewish population. By the mid-1930s, the Jews accounted for nearly a third of the country's total population. Extrapolating the then–extraordinarily rapid expansion of the Jewish presence in Palestine into the not-too-distant future, the Arabs concluded that they were on the verge of becoming a minority in their own homeland. From their perspective, they had to act decisively in order to halt and then reverse that trend. Their resolve to do so was strengthened by recent international events and by favorable developments in the Arab world. The cementing of the Berlin-Rome Axis and the Italian campaign in Ethiopia seemed to presage a weakening of Britain as a world power. Iraq had gained independence in 1931, while within Syria and Egypt, the Arab nationalist movement was on the rise. In Syria, following a brief strike, France acceded to Arab national demands and committed itself to Syrian independence. In Egypt, Britain concluded a treaty with the local regime, advancing its freedom of action. Quite naturally, Palestinian Arabs increasingly began to feel that the time was ripe for them too to press for national autonomy, if not outright independence. What especially affronted them was the fact that, unlike them, their neighboring kinsmen in Iraq, Syria and Transjordan were all provided with at least some trappings of self-government. Comparing themselves with the Transjordanians, who were generally less well equipped, from an educational or cultural standpoint, to assume control of their own destiny, the Palestinians felt particularly aggrieved. A few years previously, they had begun to revise their attitude toward the formation of a legislative assembly and petitioned the high commissioner, Sir Arthur Wauchope, to establish one. (Wauchope replaced Chancellor in November 1931.) Wauchope accepted the Arab overtures with enthusiasm, but pro-Zionist British members of Parliament scotched the idea. On April 8, 1936, in the face of formidable internal opposition, the government announced that it was no longer considering introducing new constitutional measures into Palestine. This led the Arabs to believe that the Zionists controlled the British government and they would have to pursue their demands by means of direct action.

The onset of mass disorder was neither preplanned nor centrally orchestrated. It simply arose from fortuitous incidents. The first occurred on April 15, when, on the Tulkarem-Nablus road, highway robbers waylaid a series of vehicles. On discovering that three of the accosted passengers were Jews, the bandits shot them, killing two of their victims. The following night, as an act of revenge, two Arabs sleeping in a hut near Petah Tikvah were murdered. Then, as one of the slain Jews was being buried in Tel Aviv, enraged mourners manhandled a number of Arabs. This led to the spread of rumors that Arabs were being slaughtered. As a result, on April 19, Arab mobs in Jaffa fatally vented their spleen on nine local Jews and injured fifty-seven others.[20]

On April 20, a general strike was called by an Arab national committee that assembled at Nablus. The strike was to continue until three basic demands were met; that is, until there was a complete halt to Jewish immigration, until land sales to Jews were prohibited and until an Arab-controlled government was installed. On April 25, to coordinate the strike action and other forms of Arab protest, a supreme Arab committee, which soon became known as the Arab Higher Committee, was established. It incorporated all Arab parties and groupings throughout the country. The mufti of Jerusalem, Haj Amin al-Husseini, was its president and effective leader. One of the Higher Committee's first deeds was the issuing of a proclamation, which read in part:

We call upon you, O Arab, to sacrifice yourself, to cease your work and commerce, to make do with merely a piece of bread ... in order to safeguard your homeland so that Arab Palestine will not be lost and that you will not be banished from it as a refugee in the midst of destruction and disgrace.[21]

At the beginning of May, the Arab Higher Committee decreed that all government taxes were to be withheld. Thereafter, there were a series of indiscriminate acts of destruction involving Jewish farms, houses, stores and other business enterprises. Crops and orchards were set ablaze and approximately 200,000 trees were uprooted.[22] Jews, British soldiers and police all came under fire.

The slaughter of Jews reached a peak in August, when thirty were killed. The victims were selected quite indiscriminately. Included among them was a father and his three children in Safed, two nurses working in a Jaffa hospital, and four laborers returning home from work. They were all struck with wanton ferocity by ignorant peasants beguiled into believing that the Jews had decapitated innocent Arabs and were planning to dispossess them all. Such canards were the daily staple that emanated from the pulpits of Palestinian mosques. Perversely, the murderers believed that they were acting in pre-emptive self-defense.

Also in August, Arab terrorists, operating from a "Muslim Sports Club" in Jaffa, began devising letter bombs that were sent to Jews living in Tel Aviv. This prompted an official warning not to open unsolicited mail. Up until the end of October, it was estimated that Arabs planted or hurled close to 1,400 explosive devices or primitive bombs.[23]

The Arab rebels were largely recruited from workers made unemployed by the general strike and from volunteers from neighboring countries, especially

Syria and Iraq. They formed a series of independent gangs, one of which was commanded by Fawzi al Kauwakji, a Syrian who had served as an officer in the Turkish army. Married to a German woman, al Kauwakji was a staunch Nazi admirer.[24] He assumed the role of generalissimo of all the rebel forces and, like his Syrian compatriot, al-Kassem, he set up his command headquarters in the Jenin area. From there he coordinated the rebellion. Its foot soldiers were organized according to their geographic origins. Locals were given leeway to plan actions from within their own regions, while at al Kauwakji's immediate disposal were three companies, made up of Iraqis, Syrians and Druze, respectively.

Apart from targeting Jews and their property, the Arab bands sabotaged public utilities, wrecking roads, railway and telegraph lines and damaging the oil pipeline running from Iraq to Haifa. They endeavored to paralyze the country's communication and transport facilities by firing on passing vehicles and trains. The railway system alone sustained close to 100 attacks.[25] This meant that, for the most part, setting out on an interurban excursion became a life-threatening exercise. As a precaution, Jews attached armored plating to their vehicles and traveled in convoys. At no time did they yield the roads to their Arab adversaries. To cripple the Yishuv's economy, a total ban was imposed on the sale or purchase of goods by Arabs to or from Jews. Arab laborers were ordered to sever their ties with all Jewish employers and the port of Jaffa was brought to a complete standstill. In Haifa, where there were a significant number of Jewish stevedores and of other Jews ready and willing to replace striking Arab workers, the port continued to function without interruption.

Despite all signs to the contrary, the uprising took the Yishuv by surprise. No specific preparations had been made for such a contingency. The Hebrew press criticized the Zionist leadership for their ostrich-like attitude. As one correspondent summarized the situation, "During good times, we are not interested in communicating with the Arabs and when times are bad, we declare that at such moments a dialogue is out of the question."[26] The rebellion certainly shook the Jews out of their complacency. Turning to his diary on April 27, 1936, Dr. Ruppin made the following prophetic entry: "It seems that we are destined to a state of perpetual strife with the Arabs and there is no escaping blood sacrifices. . . . In that light, I am of the opinion that the question of determining the causes of the current disturbances is of secondary significance. They would doubtlessly have erupted for one reason or another."[27]

Initially, the Haganah maintained a policy of self-restraint (havlaga). Refraining from undertaking organized acts of reprisal, the Jews stood aside while the British attempted to restore order. It seemed that there were two major reasons for acting in that way. First of all, the Jews wished to contain the violence and prevent it from becoming a general Arab-Jewish bloodbath. Second, they wanted the British to appreciate clearly that they were the victims and that the full strength of the official armed forces had to be brought down on Arab violators of the law. The policy of self-restraint was generally enforced, except for a brief lapse in August when, as already mentioned, an unusually large number of Jews were killed. Self-restraint certainly reaped handsome dividends. It won for the Jews British public support and, as a result, Britain took a number of measures to provide Jews with arms and with some weapons training.

In light of the arrival in September of 20,000 British troops sent to Palestine as reinforcements and the imposition of military law, the Arab Higher Committee decided to call off the strike. Seemingly, it did so in response to a joint request made by the Arab rulers of Iraq, Transjordan and Saudi Arabia. This, of course, was merely a face-saving device, since the strike failed to attain any of its objectives and was merely harming the interests of Arab traders and workers. The involvement of the neighboring Arabs, which presaged continued outside and unwarranted interference in Palestinian affairs, stemmed in part from some genuine concerns about events in Palestine. The Iraqis had an interest in guaranteeing the security of the oil pipeline from their country to Palestine and in a free flow of traded goods through Haifa port, while the emir of Transjordan had little to gain from widespread anarchy on his doorstep. As for the Saudis, they simply wished to ingratiate themselves with the British. In any event, the mufti, Haj Amin al-Husseini, had skillfully cultivated growing support for the Palestinian cause, not only on the part of fellow Arab states but also on the part of Muslims the world over. In 1931, he organized a World Islamic Congress in Jerusalem with delegates arriving from, among other places, Iraq, Transjordan, Egypt, Persia, India, the Far East and North Africa. To ensure that Jerusalem was ingrained on the Muslim mind as a central focus of attention, the mufti arranged for the internment of Muhammad Ali, the previous leader of the Indian Caliphate Committee, and of the late Hussein, king of the Hefaz, within the precincts of the *Haram al-Sharif* (the Jewish Temple Mount). The 1931 Congress sponsored the establishment of a Muslim university in Jerusalem but although this particular project was never realized, the Congress did at least elevate the importance of Jerusalem in Muslim eyes.

The general Arab strike ceased in October 1936, with Palestinians anticipating a diplomatic resolution of their grievances. Al Kauwakji and his men, who had been surrounded by British forces and who were on the verge of being annihilated, were given safe passage into Transjordan. As they left, posing as victors, no effort was made to disarm the rest of the general Arab population. Meanwhile, the members of the government-appointed Peel Commission left Britain for Palestine to investigate and report on the underlying causes of the civil unrest. At that point, some 80 Jews, 197 Arabs and 28 British personnel had been killed.

THE ARAB UPRISING RENEWED
WITH INCREASED VIGOR

The resumption of the Arab revolt may be dated from September 26, 1937, with the murder of Lewis Andrews, the district commissioner for Galilee, as he left a church service. Andrews, an Australian, was a warm supporter of Zionism. His assassination triggered a strong British military response. The Arab Higher Committee was disbanded and many of its members and key supporters, excluding the grand mufti who fled to Lebanon, were detained.

The renewal of the uprising was largely precipitated by the British government's decision in July 1937 to endorse the Peel Commission's recommendation that Palestine be partitioned. As the Palestinian Arabs perceived the situation, a section (albeit a small one) of their country was due to be wrenched from them, to be handed over to the Jews. They had suspended their insurrection in October 1936 to enable the Peel Commission to conduct its inquiry. Once it became clear that its findings did not favor their objectives, they felt that they had no recourse other than to resume belligerent activities.

Many Zionists chose to believe that the Arab revolt was either the fruit of a British imperialist divide-and-rule strategy or engineered by effendis in fear of social change.[28] The divide-and-rule hypothesis was not entirely without foundation. As a case in point, in January 1938 the Jewish Agency and Abdullah, the emir of Transjordan, concluded a deal providing for Jewish settlement on 17,500 acres of Transjordanian land. A thirty-three-year lease (renewable for two more similar periods) was agreed on. According to Abdullah, he was motivated by the wish to afford his country the opportunity of developing along the same prosperous lines as in Palestine.[29] As soon as the British received wind of the plans afoot, they immediately and successfully brought pressure to bear on both the Zionists and the emir to nullify the agreement.[30] The British were obviously not prepared to countenance an open rapprochement between the Zionists and Abdullah to which they were not an active party.

All that notwithstanding, the Arab Palestinian uprising was intrinsically a national one with broad popular support. Perceptive Zionists realized that, but most refrained from openly acknowledging it in order not to undermine their own national cause. Moshe Sharett was one of the few exceptions. He candidly wrote that were he an Arab, he "would rebel even more vigorously, bitterly, and desperately against the immigration that will one day turn Palestine and all its Arab residents over to Jewish rule."[31] Others dwelled on the criminal nature of the Arab activists. "As far as they were concerned," noted Teveth, the "disturbances" "were nothing more than dastardly acts of murder, robbery, looting, and destruction."[32] This does not mean to say that the revolt was, in reality, untainted by base and extraneous elements. Gilbert Mackereth, who was then the British consul in Damascus, observed that the Arab nationalists had hired known criminals in Syria who crossed the frontier to join bandit groups in Palestine. There they blew up passenger trains, menaced and murdered both soldiers and civilians alike and, at the point of a gun, indiscriminately robbed Arabs, Christians and Jews.[33] Moreover, the Husseinis took advantage of those turbulent times to settle old scores with their Nashashibi rivals, so that "about a quarter of the Arabs that lost their lives were murdered by their own people."[34]

Most of the standard rebel forces were recruited from the ranks of the peasantry. They had little military training and maintained imperfect intergroup coordination. Some participants rallied to the call to arms for specific localized actions only. The rest of the time, they attended to their farm work. Urban Arabs were expected to finance the uprising and arbitrary "taxes" were collectively imposed on them. In 1938, for instance, the Arabs of Jaffa were presented with an order to hand over 60,000 Palestinian pounds. On account of the commercial crisis that the rebellion engendered, the urban dwellers were hard pressed to meet such demands. The conservative rural insurgents also tried to impose strict Islamic norms on the entire Arab community. They singled out for censure and punishment imbibers of alcohol and prevailed on women to wear veils.

With the growing ascendancy of the Axis powers and the sellout in September 1938 by Britain and France of Czechoslovakia, the Arabs, inspired by the mufti, increasingly drew closer to Nazi Germany. Many were well disposed toward the Nazi anti-Semitic philosophy and in a number of Arab towns, swastikas and portraits of Hitler were openly displayed.[35] More significantly, the Nazis assisted in the revolt by means of donations of finance and technical support. Templar German settlers, who migrated to Palestine in the late nineteenth century, acted as a significant conduit for such Nazi penetration. For his part, the Italian dictator, Mussolini, declared himself the "defender of Islam." Axis subversion was not confined to Palestine. It also found fertile ground in Egypt, Iraq, Syria and other Arab countries.

The intensity of fighting in the second phase of the revolt was considerably higher than in the beginning. Armed bands were able to shelter among villages in the hilly regions of Palestine, especially in the vicinity of Nablus. They were well provisioned with the supply of weapons from neighboring Arab states and were emboldened to ambush isolated British troops. Specific British targets included military installations, police stations and, above all, the oil pipeline that ran from Iraq to Haifa. Terror attacks against Jews intensified. Roads and paths were mined and, on occasion, Jews were kidnapped for ransom.

By August 1938, the rebel offensive yielded startling gains. The Arab irregulars captured Hebron and Beersheba. They even occupied the Old City of Jerusalem, where they hoisted the Palestinian flag on a gate opposite government offices. The civil administration outside Jewish areas and most of the large towns, simply collapsed. In Nablus, Arab rebels brazenly strolled around fully armed without any let or hindrance.[36] All the railway stations between Jerusalem and Lod went up in flames, and trains between these two points stopped running. On October 2, hundreds of rebel forces penetrated into the Jewish quarters of Tiberias, where for a two-hour period they razed many buildings and killed nineteen Jews, eleven of whom were children.

Shortly thereafter, a turning point in the battle against the general Arab rebellion was reached. Strong British military reinforcements under the command of General Bernard Montgomery arrived and, by the end of October, the army in Palestine amounted to two divisions. British troops regained total control over all of Jerusalem and, resorting to stern and some might say, highly questionable methods,[37] they methodically routed the enemy in its hill and village strongholds. Most of the Arab guerrilla leaders fled, taking with them large sums of cash that they extorted from their kinsmen. Although the backbone of the rebellion was crushed, sporadic, small-scale acts of terror lingered on until the beginning of the Second World War.

The Arab uprising left the Jews with 545 fatalities and the Arabs with 2,176.[38] In addition to the Jewish losses of property mentioned above, approximately 200 Arab homes were detonated by the British and roughly £30,000 were extracted as fines from rebellious Arab villages.

THE REVOLT AND THE HAGANAH

Neither the Arab General Strike, the Arab Economic Boycott nor the Arab terror broke the morale of the Yishuv. On the contrary, it emerged with a greater military capability and confidence in its ability to fend for itself. Indeed, were it not for the Arab rebellion, which compelled the Yishuv to realign and reorganize its military resources, it is highly unlikely that the Jews would have prevailed in their War of Independence ten years later.

In 1936, inspired and guided by Yitzhak Sadeh, groups of field troops, known in Hebrew as *Plugot Sadeh,* or by its Hebrew acronym, *Fosh,* began to make sorties beyond the confines of Jewish agricultural settlements. Using the slogan, "going beyond the fence," these groups pounced on Arab guerrillas at their point of assembly and, taking them by surprise, routed them. Initially, Sadeh's men operated as mobile units within the Jerusalem area. It took a large measure of courage to undertake the first Fosh-type actions. At first, the settlers were rather reluctant to leave the relatively safe confines of their enclosed buildings to engage the enemy out in the open. They feared that should a section of their forces embark on a raiding mission, the remaining defenders would be placed in a more vulnerable position. Above all, they were infused with cautious hesitancy, exemplified by an old-timer who, in advising younger farmers that it was not worthwhile risking their lives to safeguard their crops, declared "One of your fingernails is more precious to me than all the vegetables outside."[39] However, under Yitzhak Sadeh's prodding and personal example, the settlers began to appreciate the value of moving from a passive to an active stance, especially once they perceived how their change of tactics successfully threw the Arabs off balance. In 1937, the Haganah formally decided to incorporate Sadeh's mobile patrols (Fosh) as an autonomous unit to function whenever and wherever the need arose. By March 1938, Fosh had more than 1,000 men attached to thirteen different sections.

Their mode of operation was vastly improved, thanks to the involvement of Orde Wingate, an unabashedly pro-Zionist British officer. Wingate, whose parents were devout Christians, had a profound knowledge of the Old Testament. He could readily recount ancient Israelite battles and felt destined to lead the Jews in their struggle to establish their homeland. Upon his arrival in Palestine in 1938, he immediately offered the Haganah his services. Considering that he was a military intelligence officer, his overtures were at first viewed with some suspicion, but his sincerity was soon appreciated and he began to be referred to with affection as "the *yadid*" (the friend). Operating from a base in Kibbutz Ein Harod and with the permission of Sir Archibald Wavell, the British force commander, Wingate took members of Fosh under his wing and organized Special Night Squads to defend the oil pipeline that ran from Iraq to Haifa and to ambush unsuspecting Arab guerrillas. He personally participated in most of his planned raids and on one occasion, when he was wounded, he resisted being hospitalized until his Jewish subordinates prevailed on Wingate's superiors to order him to do so. The success of the Special Night Squads had a tremendous effect on the military capability of the Yishuv. It fortified the confidence of the Haganah and encouraged its hierarchy to think confidently in terms of bold and imaginative forays. With such an approach becoming the hallmark of the future Israeli army, many contemporary Israelis gratefully refer to Wingate as being among their defense force's founders. Not only did he train and lead his men, but he subjected them to hours of lectures, imparting to them much of his own formal education in military theory and practice. His fellow British officers took a dim view of his activities, and, in 1939, on the eve of his enforced departure from Palestine, he addressed his Jewish trainees at Ein Harod in Hebrew promising that he would return. However, fate declared otherwise, for he died in 1944 in a plane crash in Burma.

Apart from the honing of new tactical strategies, which effectively transformed the Haganah from an organization concentrating on static guard duty to a mobile offensive fighting force, two other developments require mention. The first concerned the emergence of a special Mandatory auxiliary force, manned by Jewish volunteers. These combatants (known in Hebrew as *Notrim*), who were armed and trained by the British, were charged with defending Jewish positions. In practice, practically all the Notrim were Haganah members and by the spring of 1939, the combined Jewish auxiliary police forces numbered about 21,000 men.[40] For the Haganah, the organization of the Notrim was a godsend. It legally provided its members with lessons in the use of arms, and its various stations were used as fronts for its own activities. The second factor related to the substantial progress made during the late thirties regarding the establishment of a subterranean armaments industry. In disguised workshops scattered about the country, hand grenades, mines, mortars and explosive materials were manufactured. Although many of the production techniques were at first rather primitive, the Yishuv had taken a decisive step in guaranteeing some measure of self-sufficiency in weapons procurements.

THE REVOLT AND THE IRGUN

In 1931, a number of Haganah members resigned to establish an alternative body, which they initially called Haganah B and then *Irgun Zvai Leumi* (National Military Organization). The latter appellation is commonly referred to simply as the *Irgun* or by its Hebrew acronym, *Etzel*. Various shortcomings in the performance of the Haganah during the 1929 riots brought about an exodus from its ranks. Those leaving wished to form an organization based on stricter discipline and with all the trappings associated with military rankings. Within the Haganah, an air of informality prevailed and it was generally accepted that officers had to cultivate and retain the respect and loyalty of their subordinates by virtue of their own performance and example. Although Haganah B was not a Revisionist body and its commander, Tehomi, was not a party member, it was soon dominated by Revisionists. In April 1937, realizing the futility of the Yishuv sustaining two separate defense organizations, Tehomi and close to 1,500 like-minded comrades, returned to the Haganah fold.

Those remaining in Haganah B, now known as the Irgun, were all diehard Revisionists. Within its circles, opposition to the practice of *havlaga* (self-restraint) gained currency and before long the Irgun emulated the Arab terror campaign. The turning point appears to have been the hanging, by the British, of Shlomo Ben-Yosef, a young Revisionist, for a botched attempt at ambushing an Arab bus. The execution took place in June 1938. A month later, the Irgun detonated an explosive device in an Arab market, killing fifty people.[41] Similarly, a bomb was thrown at an Arab bus at Mahaneh Yehuda in Jerusalem, causing the death of five passengers. Such acts were unequivocally condemned by the Labor Movement not merely because they were immoral but also because they were self-defeating, since they drove moderate Arabs into the arms of the extremists.[42] Summarizing Labor's position, Ben Gurion maintained that random terror would faze neither the Arab military irregulars nor their leadership. "What would the mufti care," he asked, "if an Arab boy or a poor fellah was killed in Tel Aviv?"[43] More to the point, it seemed to Ben Gurion that those advocating pure terror were not concerned with organizing efficient and all-embracing self-defense forces, nor were they anticipating direct confrontations with large, armed Arab concentrations.

TOWER AND STOCKADE SETTLEMENTS

After the 1929 riots, the Jewish National Fund (JNF) acquired a fair amount of land in areas remote from other Jewish settlements. In the interest of preventing neighboring Arabs from encroaching on the unattended Jewish land and then claiming it as their own, the JNF hired groups of Jewish workers to ward off trespassers and to undertake a small measure of farming. But with the advent of the 1936–1939 Arab uprising, temporary bands of Jewish workers making desultory attempts to cultivate clusters of land surrounded by hostile forces were no longer tenable. An alternative arrangement was called for, which became even more imperative once the possibility of partitioning Palestine began to be canvassed. In light of such circumstances, the Jews had an urgent need to widen the area of their landholdings to strengthen their claims for a reasonable share of the country. Rising to the occasion, the JNF began amassing as much additional land as possible. It no longer regarded soil quality or price factors as being of paramount importance. Rather, strategic and political considerations determined its acquisition strategy. Accordingly, whenever available, land was snapped up alongside or near the country's borders and in areas where a Jewish presence was either nonexistent or very sparse.

As already intimated, with the pervasive anti-Jewish violence that prevailed during the Arab uprising, buying land was one thing; cultivating it was another. The solution the Zionists formulated entailed the almost instant transformation of prospective settlements in vulnerable regions into garrison-like complexes. In short order, a regular procedure was established. Prior to the settlers assuming occupation of the land assigned to them, intensive preparations were undertaken in a nearby kibbutz or moshav. At the staging base, sections of the future settlement's outer walls, the walls and roofs of its living quarters and of its watchtower were constructed from wooden material. Everything, including large amounts of gravel stone, was then loaded onto lorries and wagons. At dawn of the appointed day, or even hours beforehand, a convoy containing all the prefabricated material and accompanied by armed guards and numerous workers would set out for the new settlement site. On arrival, everyone, including nonsettlement volunteers, would frenetically undertake prearranged tasks. Top priority was given to the installation of the perimeter walls. These were made up of two panels spaced approximately 30 centimeters apart. Into the intervening cavity, gravel stones were compressed so that the structure was rendered bullet-proof. Along with the settlers' huts, a tall watchtower would be erected. It would be equipped with a powerful searchlight, activated by an electrical generator. By the day's end, everything would be in place, the outer wall, the living quarters, a dining room and the watchtower. Surrounding the settlement, there would also be a barbed wire fence. In most cases, the local Arabs would be taken unawares and before they could grasp what was occurring, a tower and stockade settlement would be firmly implanted within their midst. However, this was not always the case and not every new kibbutz or moshav arose without incident.

The establishment, in March 1938, of Hanita was rather eventful. Hanita was the first Jewish settlement to take root in the upper western Galilee, close to the Lebanese border. It was situated in a remote, mountainous region entirely populated by Arabs. On the day of its formation, a group of 91 pioneers, accompanied by 40 armed Jewish supernumerary police plus 400 volunteer helpers, gathered at its designated location. Despite such a strong contingent, armed encounters with local Arab irregulars occurred from the outset. During the construction of its basic superstructure and access road, 10 workers were killed.

Model of tower and stockade settlement (Central Zionist Archives).

Elsewhere and nearly four months later, a Polish contingent of the youth movement Gordonia (after A.D. Gordon) took possession of an elevation above Kibbutz Kiryat Anavim, near Jerusalem. In the process, five of its members fell and in their memory, the settlement was named *Ma'aleh Hahamisha* (the Elevation of the Five).

One tower and stockade settlement, *Tirat Zvi*,[44] was even attacked some eight months after it had been founded. The incident occurred in February 1938, when, under cover of darkness, Arabs penetrated its barbed wire fence. As they approached its inner defense positions, they were pelted with grenades, which caused them to panic and withdraw.

Throughout the tower and stockade period, that is from 1936 to 1939, fifty-six new settlements were formed, of which thirty-six were kibbutzim. During

May 1939 alone, with the release of the infamous White Paper announcing Britain's abnegation of the Balfour Declaration, twelve new settlements arose, seven on a single day. The majority were in areas in which there had been little or no previous Jewish presence. Jewish farmers secured toeholds in far-flung places such as Hanita in the north, Negba in the south and Ein Gev on the eastern banks of Lake Kinneret. In particular, the Emek Beth Sha'an (south of Lake Kinneret) and the Upper Galilee were transformed into additional regions of Jewish settlement.

ILLEGAL IMMIGRATION (ALIYAH BET)

From the commencement of the First Aliyah in 1882, many Jews migrated to Palestine illegally. This continued to be the case even under the British administration entrusted with the task of facilitating the establishment of a Jewish National Home. At no time during the Mandatory period were the gates of Palestine freely open to any Jew wishing to enter the country. Those without immigration certificates typically resorted to overstaying allotted tourist deadlines, arranging fictitious marriages with Palestinian citizens or, for the more daring, crossing the country's borders illicitly.

In 1934, the Hehalutz movement in Poland successfully hired a Greek ship, *Velos*, to transport 350 illegal pioneer migrants to Palestine. (Subsequently, all such ventures became known as Aliyah Bet, that is, "B" Immigration or *Hapala*, meaning "daring.") Since a second attempt undertaken a few months later ended in failure and considering the large sums of money involved and the political pressures not to antagonize the British, Hehalutz decided to suspend its maritime operations. Only at the end of 1937, when Britain began to curtail Jewish immigration quotas, did it resume such missions. To coordinate Aliyah Bet, a clandestine organization of that name, affiliated with the Histadrut, was formed. It was headed by Shaul Avigur of the Haganah and was staffed by members of Hehalutz and of the various kibbutz organizations, especially Kibbutz Meuhad.

The resumption of Aliyah Bet activities was marked by the landing of sixty-five pioneers in Palestine at the beginning of 1938. Gradually the sea passage of unauthorized migrants gathered momentum, reaching a peak in 1939, by which time eighteen vessels of various dimensions were utilized. Landings were undertaken under cover of darkness by resourceful volunteers who rapidly dispersed the incoming migrants among surrounding settlements. By such means, up until World War II, Aliyah Bet succeeded in bringing 6,000 Jews to Palestine.

The Histadrut was not the only player in stealthily shepherding Jews into Palestine. Between 1937 and September 1939, the Revisionists shipped some 6,000 immigrants, in fourteen voyages,[45] while private operators, working for profit, contributed another 9,000 to the illegal migrant tally.[46]

As for the British, they stepped up their coastal patrols, scanned the seas with spotter planes, sent spies to various ports of migrant embarkation, unremittingly pursued those who landed and treated migration transgressors far more harshly than common criminals. The severe and callous way in which detained illegal migrants were handled was exacerbated by the appointment, in March 1938, of Sir Harold MacMichael as Palestine's high commissioner. Unlike his predecessor, Wauchope, MacMichael was a narrow-minded, mean-spirited administrator, who lacked the slightest shred of sympathy for Zionism. He zealously deducted estimated numbers of illegal arrivals from the official Jewish immigrant quotas.

THE PEEL COMMISSION

On July 29, 1936, the British government responded to the initial Arab strike and disturbances by appointing Lord Peel as chairman of a Royal Commission to investigate their causes. In November 1936, the Commission arrived in Palestine to conduct its inquiry. It took evidence from a number of prominent Zionists, who tried to place Arab claims on Palestine into what they regarded as an appropriate perspective. The first to present the Zionist case was Weizmann, who pressed for continued Jewish immigration into Palestine. He drew the Commission's attention to the fact that in Eastern Europe and the Baltic countries, there are "six million Jews doomed to be pent up in places where they are not wanted, and for whom the world is divided into places where they cannot live, and places into which they cannot enter."[47] Later, when Jabotinsky appeared (in London), he emphasized that the Arabs already had several states that they either controlled or that they were about to control. That being the case, when their claim on Palestine "is confronted with our Jewish demand to be saved, it is like the claim of appetite versus the claim of starvation."[48]

At first the Arabs boycotted the Peel Commission's hearings, but they eventually condescended to articulate their views. When the mufti was asked whether Palestine could indeed assimilate and absorb the 400,000 Jews already in the country, he emphatically answered "no." Then, in reply to a follow-up question inquiring whether he would forcibly evict the Jews, he suggested that that was a matter to be determined in the future.[49]

The findings of the Peel Commission were made public on July 7, 1937. Among its main recommendations was a proposal to partition Palestine into a Jewish state and an Arab state, with a corridor, from Jaffa sweeping through Lod and Ramala and encircling Jerusalem and Bethlehem, remaining under British Mandatory control. The Jews were to be allotted most of the coastal plain from Ber Tuvia in the south and stretching northward to embrace almost all of the Galilee, except the region east of Lake Kinneret. Haifa, Acre, Safed and Tiberias were to remain "temporarily" under British control; Nazareth permanently. Jaffa was to be part of the Arab state, as was the rest of the country other than the area Britain wished to retain. (See map.) The Commission did not envision the establishment of a new Palestinian state. It thought in terms of expanding Transjordanian sovereignty into the areas allocated to the Arabs. (Not surprisingly, Emir Abdullah was widely known to favor partition.)

The proposal was rejected outright by the Palestinian Arabs. Apart from anything else, the powerful Husseini family had no intention of becoming subjects of Emir Abdullah, whom they detested. The Jews, as might be expected, indicated a willingness to consider the proposal but, to the dismay of the colonial secretary, this willingness did not arise spontaneously. The matter was heatedly debated at the Twentieth Zionist Congress held in Zurich in August 1937. At that gathering, Ussishkin, who was president of the Congress, forcefully argued the case for not accepting anything other than Palestine as a whole. In this respect, he was strongly supported by the religious Zionists, who asserted that the Jewish demand for all of Palestine was founded on a fundamental right (based on the Bible) and that "partition should never be accepted even in return for a peace settlement with the Arabs."[50] Other delegates feared that the proposal might result in the premature termination of the British Mandate before a separate Jewish state could be securely established, thus leaving the Jews high and dry. Marshaling all his powers of persuasion, Weizmann managed to obtain an outcome that gave him some scope for negotiating with the British. While the Congress resolved to reject the actual partition proposal outlined in the Peel Commission's Report, which merely indicated how partition could theoretically be implemented, it authorized the Zionist Executive to establish just what the British government was actually prepared to offer and then to refer the matter to a specially convened Congress for further discussion.

The thin sliver of land along the coastal plain, plus the Galilee, which the Peel Commission proposed for the Jews, was a far cry from what many of the draftsmen of the Balfour Declaration had in mind. Most thought in terms of a Jewish homeland on both sides of the Jordan River. What drove many Zionists to consider the Peel proposal was the desperate state of European Jewry and their movement's deteriorating political strength. Thrown such a small lifeline, they were not prepared to discard the opportunity of saving thousands of their brethren. Both Weizmann and Ben Gurion regarded the immediate founding of a Jewish state on such a paltry amount of land not as the end of the matter but as a basis for arriving at a more viable state in the future. Weizmann believed that even with the land area in question, such a state "would be able to absorb 100,000 immigrants a year, and sustain a Jewish population of 2.5–3 million."[51] In Ben Gurion's opinion, the proposed Jewish state "would constitute a decisive *stage* on the road to the achievement of Greater Zionism."[52] Elaborating on this, Ben Gurion described the partition scheme as providing a "decisive initial stage in our complete redemption and an unequaled lever for the gradual conquest of all of Palestine."[53] For their part, the Arabs, through the medium of their press, correctly sensed that the Zionists would not permanently rest content with a tiny state on a small portion of the disputed country.[54]

The Peel Commission's Partition Proposal

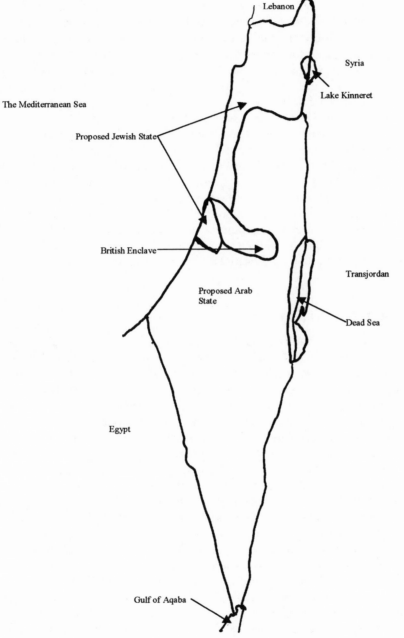

Even had both parties been amenable to the notion of partition, the scheme submitted by the Peel Commission would have provided for a very slender Jewish majority in the territory assigned to them. Realizing this, the colonial secretary, Ormsby Gore, suggested that Arabs in the future Jewish state be transferred to their own region. The acquiescence of the transferees was to be secured by financial inducements, but alternate means of persuasion were not ruled out. What Gore had in mind, was the post–World War I precedent of Greeks being transferred from the Turkish mainland. As Gore reasoned, the evacuees would "be going only a comparatively few miles away to a people with the same language, the same civilization, the same religion."[55]

Apart from its partition recommendations, the Peel Commission advocated severe restrictions on Jewish land purchases and on Jewish immigration. It was suggested that only 12,000 Jews per year be allowed entry into Palestine. Such measures were to be applied either as a stopgap measure until the precise terms of partition were determined or, in the event of the general notion of partition being discarded, they were to be enforced in order to assuage the Arabs. Previous British pledges that only the country's economic absorptive capacity would govern annual immigration rates were to be annulled. Instead, it was proposed that political and psychological factors be taken into account.

THE BRITISH BETRAYAL

Because the Arabs had rejected the Peel Commission's partition plans, they had effectively become inoperable. In any case, the British themselves were losing interest in the matter. The Colonial Office, which was at first genuinely supportive of partition, was soon discouraged by criticism of the scheme aired in Parliament and elsewhere. It met with sustained opposition from the Foreign Office, which believed that partition could in practice only be attained by force and, had the British persevered, they would have incurred the enmity of the entire Arab world. There certainly could be no mistaking Arab opinion. At a pan-Arab conference held in Syria in September 1937, attended by over 400 delegates from Palestine and all existing Arab states (save Yemen) it was declared that "Palestine was an integral part of the *Arabian* homeland and no part of this territory would be alienated with Arab consent."[56] Then, adopting a comminatory tone, the conference declared that unless the government in London saw the error of its ways, the Arabs would side with other European powers who were aligning themselves against Britain.

By December 1937, after months of equivocation, the British government decided to set up yet another Commission, this one to be headed by Sir Charles Woodhead. Supposedly, the Commission was to confine its deliberations to examining alternative partition arrangements, but the government also let it be known that if no politically feasible partition plan were conceivable, the Commission ought to be up front in such matters. In practice, the government had already decided to withdraw its earlier support for partition and was counting on the Woodhead Commission, whose four members were chosen accordingly, to provide it with a pretext to announce its change of heart.[57]

In November 1938, the Woodhead Commission's report was released. It was distinguished by its ambiguity and the lack of consensus among its members. The only major point of common agreement was the belief that the Peel Commission had been unduly generous in its land allocations for the proposed Jewish state. The commissioners had two alternative partition suggestions in mind, each of which would have left the Jews with considerably attenuated land areas than had originally been envisioned. All this proved to be academic when, a few weeks later, the British government officially washed its hands of the whole affair. Instead, it called for a conference to be held in London, to which representatives from the Jewish Agency, Palestinian Arabs and also notables from neighboring Arab states would be invited. (The latter included delegates from Egypt, Saudi Arabia, Iraq, Yemen and Transjordan.) By incorporating non-Palestinian Arabs, Britain formally widened the internal Jewish–Arab Palestinian conflict into one in which the Arab world as a whole seemingly had a legitimate interest. Ever since then, the Yishuv and the future Jewish state have had to contend with outside Arab intervention, even in areas that patently have had no bearing on Palestinian Arab welfare. More ominously, Britain let it be known that, in the absence of an agreement, it would impose its own solution.

The gathering, which went by the name of the London Round Table Conference, opened on February 7, 1939. The Arabs refused to be seated in the same room as the Jews and, in accordance with their wishes, arrangements were made for them to enter St. James' Palace, where the conference was held, through a separate entrance. The British met exclusively with either the Arab or the Jewish delegations on alternative days. Throughout the entire proceedings, the Arabs clearly wanted to be seen as negotiating only with the British. Under such circumstances, a joint Arab-Jewish understanding was obviously unattainable. As the conference proceeded, it became clear that the British had already decided to adjust their policies in accordance with the essence of the Arab demands. At the same time, they indulged in duplicity, praising the Jewish delegation for its moderation while dropping hints about their frustration with the Arabs. When they would meet with the Arabs, they would offer sympathetic understanding of their standpoint, embellished with unsavory comments about the Jews. (Unbeknownst to the British, the Jews had access to the original shorthand transcripts of the Arab sessions.)[58]

On March 15, the conference ended in a British proposal that allowed for an independent Palestinian state after a transition period of about ten years. The Jews were to be provided with some form of constitutional guarantee as a protected minority whose numbers were not to exceed a third of the total population. Both Jews and Arabs rejected the proposal—the Jews because it denied them their promised national homeland and the Arabs because they were neither prepared to wait another ten years nor were they prepared to countenance even a token amount of additional Jewish immigration. Finally, on May 17, two months after Hitler invaded Czechoslovakia, the notorious White Paper, which revoked the Balfour Declaration and which denied the Jews all hope of becoming a sovereign nation, was published. In essence, it once again declared Britain's intention to cede independence to Palestine within ten years. Jewish immigration was to be limited to 75,000 over the following five years; thereafter, Jewish immigration was to occur only with Arab consent. Jewish settlement was to be prohibited in certain parts of Palestine and strictly limited elsewhere. In short, the Zionist enterprise was to be terminated. All this, asserted Ben Gurion, was "the greatest betrayal perpetrated by the government of a civilized people."[59]

The Yishuv protested against the White Paper by means of mass street demonstrations in Tel Aviv and Jerusalem. Within the Haganah, a unit known as Special Actions was commissioned to sabotage British installations, especially motorized craft that were utilized to intercept oncoming vessels bearing illegal migrants. In general, there was widespread agreement that the Yishuv had to mobilize all its military capabilities to counter by force any attempt to make Palestine an independent Arab state.

For its part, with a Second World War looming, Britain felt the need to secure the friendship of the Arabs, or, if that was not feasible, at least to placate them. Crucial interests, including the Suez Canal, air links with India and Iraqi oil supplies were at stake. Potential Arab hostility seemed to pose a far greater strategic threat than did Jewish anger and, in any case, the Jews were hardly likely to side with the Germans.

Reflecting on the White Paper, Weizmann recalled that immediately after Hitler occupied Prague, Chamberlain rhetorically asked why Britain should have risked war for the sake of "a far away country of which we know very little and whose language we don't understand." If, as Weizmann mused that "was the way the Czechs were spoken of, what could we Jews expect from a government of that kind."[60]

By 1939, the British government and the rest of the civilized world were given clear notice of the fate that Hitler had in store for the Jews. On January 30, 1939, in a speech before the Reichstag, Hitler declared:

If the international Jewish financiers in and outside Europe should succeed in plunging the nations once more into a world war, then the result will not be the bolshevization of the earth, and thus the victory of Jewry, but the annihilation of the Jewish race in Europe![61]

There was no reason whatsoever to doubt Hitler's intentions. As it happened, in September 1942, almost eight months after the Nazis formally decided to embark on the "final solution" of the Jewish people at the Wannsee (Berlin) Conference, Hitler, appearing at the Berlin Sports Palace, gleefully announced:

In my Reichstag speech of September 1, 1939, I have spoken of two things: first, that now that the war has been forced upon us, no array of weapons and no passage of time will bring us defeat, and second that if Jewry should plot another world war in order to exterminate the Aryan peoples of Europe, it would not be the Aryan peoples which would be exterminated, but Jewry.... At one time the Jews of Germany laughed about my prophecies. I do not know whether they are still laughing or whether they have already lost all desire to laugh. But right now I can only repeat: they will stop laughing everywhere, and I shall be right also in that prophecy.[62]

Throughout the 1930s, a constant flow of information, in large part through official diplomatic channels, was reaching Britain and other countries, detailing the widespread atrocities being committed against innocent German Jews. In 1933 in a dispatch to the *New York Times*, Birchall reported that "Aryanism is now the keystone of Nazi policy. ... Its corollary is persecution even to extermination—the word is the Nazis' own—of the non-Aryans, if that can be established without too much world disturbance."[63] As 1933 drew to a close, Lord Marley, deputy speaker of the House of Lords, estimated that in Germany, 2,000 people had already been assassinated.[64] In 1936, in Nuremberg, Julius Streicher addressed a closed meeting of anti-Semitic journalists from Europe and the United States. Some of his listeners conveyed his text to outsiders and it was published, among other papers, in the *New York Times*. Not mincing his words, Streicher stated that, ultimately, extermination was the only real solution to the Jewish problem.[65] Even a year before Hitler's 1939 infamous Reichstag speech, *Das Schwarze Korps*, the organ of the Gestapo, in a front-page article, predicted "the definite end of Jewry in Germany and its complete extermination."[66]

By as early as April 1933, Jews were totally excluded from all posts in the German civil service. They were no longer permitted to practice law and their rights to work as doctors or dentists were severely constrained. Shortly thereafter, Jews were barred from journalism and from the performing and creative arts. As the months rolled by, Jews were excluded from agriculture, industry and commerce. The events of the *Kristallnacht*, which occurred on November 9, 1938, in which many Jews were murdered, more than 20,000 incarcerated and 195 synagogues destroyed, were well documented and were never even challenged by the Nazis. To add insult to injury, the Jews were collectively fined a billion marks for "their hostile attitude to the German people and its state."

Assuming that one could not have anticipated the actual fate that ultimately befell them, there was no room for any doubt whatsoever that, at the very best, the Jews of Germany were being consigned to a living hell. By the close of the 1930s, apart from anything else, they were forbidden to enter parks, museums and concert halls. Within some cities, their telephones were disconnected and their radios impounded. In Munich, Leipzig and Nuremberg, they were not allowed to buy food. Sir George Ogilvie-Forbes of the British embassy in Berlin informed the British foreign secretary that the German Jews were faced with misery and, being deprived of sufficient resources, "Their end will be starvation."[67] When in March 1939, the Germans occupied Czechoslovakia, non-German Jews (in addition to those in Austria) likewise found a noose tightening around their necks.

Turning a blind eye to the fate of European Jewry and having opted for a policy of Arab appeasement, the British assiduously tried to ensure that not one more Jew than the White Paper prescribed would enter Palestine. With utter ruthlessness, they tracked and impounded incoming vessels bearing unauthorized migrants and peremptorily sent them packing with little, if any, consideration for their welfare and safety. When Palestinian Jews cited the circumstances in which Jews in Greater Germany and other European countries were placed as a justification for facilitating their entry into Palestine, the Colonial Office responded egregiously. It proclaimed that the Jews, "like so many other lawbreakers, are thinking only of themselves, and fail to realise that what they are doing is fundamentally anti-social—as anti-social as the German persecution of which they complain."[68]

As the war clouds darkened, the British persisted in hounding Jews who had made desperate attempts to seek the safety of Palestine's shores. On August 4, 1939, as a means of punishing the Zionists for persisting in lending a hand to their persecuted kinsmen, the colonial secretary, Malcolm MacDonald, authorized the suspension of legal Jewish immigration into Palestine for a six-month period starting in October 1939. Just over a month later, after Hitler invaded Poland and Britain declared war on Germany, Dr. Weizmann pleaded with MacDonald to allow 20,000 Polish Jewish children to enter Palestine. The appeal was submitted in terms of the White Paper's provision for a special quota for 25,000 refugee migrants. MacDonald turned down the request on the spurious grounds that the special quota allowed for persecuted Jews from all countries and not just Poland and that, in any case, distress in Poland was being borne equally by Christians and Jews alike.[69] With a stroke of his pen, MacDonald inadvertently let 20,000 Jewish children, who might otherwise not have done so, face the prospect of the Holocaust. It was not that MacDonald was inherently an unkind and uncaring person. Rather, he, like so many other British politicians, was simply enmeshed in the politics of expediency.

Nor were the British alone in being basically unresponsive and insensitive to the plight of European Jewry. Most other nations were prepared to admit only token numbers. For example, in 1935, merely 6,252 Jews immigrated to the United States, 3,159 to Argentina, 1,758 to Brazil, 1,078 to South Africa and only 624 to Canada.[70] Acting on President Roosevelt's initiative, in July 1938, delegates of thirty-two countries participated in a conference in Evian to coordinate their efforts on behalf of German Jewish refugees. At Britain's insistence, Palestine, as a potential haven for Jews, was deliberately not taken into account. Except for the Dominican Republic, all the spokesmen generally indicated that their countries could not accept more than a small handful of Jews. Some, such as the Australian representative, openly declared that they had no intention of importing a racial problem.

In May 1939, 930 German Jewish refugees set sail for Cuba in a luxury liner, the *St. Louis*. They all held official Cuban landing certificates and 734 of them possessed U.S. immigration quota numbers that would have allowed them to enter America three months to three years after disembarking in Cuba. On arrival at Havana, almost all the passengers were denied entry on the grounds that their landing papers had subsequently been rescinded. After unsuccessfully negotiating with the authorities in Havana, the ship's captain turned toward Miami in the hope that the U.S. government would relent and take in the Jewish immigrants ahead of their scheduled time. Instead, Washington issued strict instructions to prevent any of the passengers from setting foot in the United States. Having no other recourse, the *St. Louis* returned to Europe, where, except for 287 Jews who were given asylum in England, the rest were left to the mercy of the Nazis. According to Bishop James Cannon Jr. of Richmond, Virginia, the failure to rescue the *St. Louis* passengers "was one of the most disgraceful things that has happened in American history."[71] The episode of the *St. Louis*, and other similar occurrences, starkly highlighted the perils of Jewish statelessness.

NOTES

1. Esco, *Palestine*, 1947, vol. 2, p. 666.
2. As quoted by Koestler, *Promise and Fulfillment*, 1983, p. 31.
3. Bein, *History*, 1970, p. 343. Migrants were classified on the basis of their citizenship. Many Jews living in Germany had Polish citizenship and, accordingly, were counted as Polish migrants. This implies that more Jews arrived from Germany than the figures indicate.
4. Even-Shoshan, *History*, 1955, Book 3, p. 308.
5. Halevi, "Economic Development," 1979, p. 38.
6. Esco, *Palestine*, 1947, vol. 2, p. 695.
7. Horowitz and Hinden, "Economic Survey," 1938, pp. 10–12.
8. Halevi, "Economic Development," 1979, p. 41.
9. Esco, *Palestine*, 1947, vol. 2, p. 686.
10. Horowitz, *Development*, 1948, p. 55.
11. Ibid., p. 686.
12. See, for instance, Shapira, *Land and Power*, 1992, p. 194.
13. Laqueur, *History*, 1989, p. 319. Their hate-ridden rhetoric was replicated by their political offspring, who, in the early 1990s, demonized Itzhak Rabin shortly before his assassination.
14. As quoted by Cohen, *Israel*, 1964, p. 228.
15. As quoted by Teveth, *Murder*, 1982, p. 42.
16. Slutsky, *From Defence to Strife*, 1964, p. 449.
17. Schechtman, *Fighter and Prophet*, 1961, p. 240.
18. Ibid., p. 232. Italics added.
19. Teveth, *Ben-Gurion*, 1987, p. 512.
20. Dothan, *Struggle*, 1981, p. 106.
21. As quoted by Dothan, *Struggle*, 1981, p. 106.

22. Sykes, *Crossroads*, 1967, p. 191.

23. Slutsky, *From Defence to Strife*, 1964, p. 652.

24. Bauer, "The Arab Revolt," 1966, part 1, p. 56.

25. Slutsky, *From Defence to Strife*, 1964, p. 646.

26. Cohen, *Israel*, 1964, p. 244.

27. As quoted by Dothan, *Struggle*, 1981, p. 114.

28. See, for example, Laqueur, *History*, 1989, pp. 263–64.

29. Esco, *Palestine*, 1947, vol. 2, p. 767.

30. Ibid., p. 767.

31. As quoted by Teveth, *Ben-Gurion*, 1987, p. 544.

32. Ibid., p. 544.

33. As expressed in a letter dated November 15, 1937, cited by Gilbert, *Exile and Return*, 1978, p. 187.

34. Sykes, *Crossroads*, 1967, p. 191.

35. Shapira, *Land and Power*, 1992, p. 231.

36. Porath, *Palestinian Arab National Movement*, 1977, p. 238.

37. These included the use of torture, arbitrary executions in the field and the imposition of collective punishment. For example, see Segev, *One Palestine*, 2000, pp. 420–26.

38. Cohen, *Israel*, 1964, pp. 203–4.

39. Slutsky, *From Defence to Strife*, 1964, p. 690.

40. Bauer, "The Arab Revolt," 1966, part 2, p. 26.

41. Slutsky, *From Defence to Strife*, 1964, p. 812.

42. Bauer, "The Arab Revolt," 1966, part 2, p. 26.

43. As quoted by Even-Shoshan, *History*, 1955, Book 3, p. 111.

44. Kiryat Zvi was founded by Hapoel Hamizrahi, a religious party.

45. Near, *Kibbutz Movement*, 1992, vol. 1, p. 333.

46. Ibid., p. 334.

47. As quoted by Sykes, *Crossroads*, 1967, p. 169.

48. As quoted by Laqueur, *History*, 1989, p. 370.

49. Esco, *Palestine*, 1947, vol. 2, p. 816.

50. Gorny, *Zionism*, 1987, p. 274.

51. Weizmann, *Trial and Error*, 1949, p. 475.

52. As quoted by Even-Shoshan, *History*, 1955, Book 3, p. 70. Italics added.

53. As quoted by Teveth, *Ben-Gurion*, 1987, p. 613.

54. Dothan, *Struggle*, 1981, p. 146.

55. As quoted by Gilbert, *Exile and Return*, 1978, p. 185.

56. From a resolution of the conference, as reported by Sykes, *Crossroads*, 1967, p. 188. Italics added.

57. Kleiman, *Divide or Rule*, 1983, p. 107.

58. Horowitz, *My Yesterday*, 1970, p. 235.

59. As quoted by Laqueur, *History*, 1989, p. 528.

60. Weizmann, *Trial and Error*, 1949, p. 501.

61. As quoted by Gilbert, *Exile and Return*, 1978, p. 220.

62. As quoted by Morse, *While Six Million Died*, 1983, p. 17.

63. Ibid., p. 156.
64. Ibid., p. 160.
65. Ibid., p. 194.
66. Ibid., p. 239.
67. Ibid., p. 224.
68. As quoted by Gilbert, *Exile and Return,* 1978, pp. 238–39.
69. Ibid., p. 244.
70. Laqueur, *History,* 1989, p. 507.
71. Morse, 1985, p. 280.

Chapter 8

World War II Years

The commencement of the Second World War on September 3, 1939, augured ill for the Yishuv. Germany had seized large stretches of Poland and, in so doing, ensnared a substantially increased number of Jews. Although the Mediterranean was considered safely navigable in the war's early days, the British obdurately denied all but a minuscule number of refugees sanctuary in Palestine. Even the paltry quota determined in the 1939 White Paper was not realized in the specified time. Over the period 1940–1945, merely 53,000 were admitted.[1] In retrospect, considering the fate that ultimately awaited European Jewry, the process of deliberately barring their entry into their officially designated homeland amounted to indirect Holocaust complicity.

Notwithstanding the imposition of stringent immigration controls, many desperate Jews headed for Palestine. At the beginning of September 1939, the ship *Tiger Hill*, bearing Jewish refugees, was fired on by the British Coast Guard, causing the death of three passengers. All the others were turned away. Over a year later, in November 1940, 1,770 Jews arriving at Haifa on the *Pacific* and on the *Milos* were forcibly transferred to the *Patria* for deportation to the Indian Ocean island of Mauritius. On November 25, the *Patria* exploded in Haifa harbor, leading to the loss of life of more than 200 people. This disaster was an unintended byproduct of an act of sabotage undertaken by the Haganah. A time bomb was smuggled on board and placed along the lower inner sidewall of the ship. The charge had been set simply to disable the *Patria* but no allowance had been made for its decrepit and rusty state. When the bomb was detonated, it blew a three-by-two-meter hole in the outer plating and water rushed in so swiftly that the boat sank within fifteen minutes.[2] Due to a strong public backlash in both Britain and the United States, MacMichael, the high commissioner, who had planned to evict the stricken survivors at the next available opportunity, reluctantly allowed them to stay. No such compassion was shown to the 1,645 refugees who appeared, at about the same time, on the *Atlantic*. At first, all the *Atlantic* passengers were interned at a camp at Atlit. Then suddenly, one daybreak, the camp was surrounded by a large detachment of troops. As soon as the detainees realized what awaited them, they resisted fiercely but to no avail. Many were beaten unconscious and were carried out on stretchers. Others, including the elderly, women and children, all of whom were naked and barefoot, were roughly handled by a select group of army thugs and, as a result, were bleeding profusely.[3] The distraught Jews were bundled onto waiting army lorries and then onto two ships that sailed for Mauritius.[4] On the island, men and women were separated into two camps and only after two years, were the womenfolk allowed brief visits to their husbands, fathers and sons.

By far the worst incident related to the *Struma*, which was over 100 years old and originally served as a cattle boat plying the waters of the Danube. In December 1941, it left the Romanian port of Constanza with 769 Jews on board, 669 more than its normal complement. It was certainly ill-equipped to carry such a large number of people, for it contained only one toilet, no washing facilities and had grossly inadequate sleeping quarters. Passengers wishing to breathe fresh air had to wait their turn to stand on the packed upper deck. Worst of all, no provision was made for life preservers or for any other means of rescue.[5] By mid-December, the *Struma* had reached Istanbul, where it was held up for repairs. It had a leaking hull and defective engines. Since the passengers lacked appropriate documentation, the British indicated that none of them would be permitted to enter Palestine. The Turks, for their part, similarly held them at bay. For weeks on end, the Zionists conducted frantic negotiations to persuade MacMichael to relent. They begged him to permit the passengers to land in Haifa, either under the various immigration categories or as war refugees. MacMichael was informed that the U.S. (Jewish) Joint Distribution Committee stood ready to finance the absorption of all concerned. At the eleventh hour, the high commissioner condescended to make an exception for the children but by then the Turks had ordered the ship back to the Black Sea. On February 24, 1942, only four or five miles from the entrance to the Bosporus, the *Struma*, which either hit a mine or was attacked by a torpedo, blew up and sank. All but one of the passengers perished.

Later, Moshe Shertok in a letter to the British colonial secretary of state, summarized the events of the *Struma* as follows:

A group of Jews manages to escape from death and torture at the hands of their Nazi oppressors.... All the resources of the democratic world which is fighting Nazi oppression, including the Mandatory Government of Palestine, fail to provide them a haven of refuge; all avenues of rescue being closed to them, they are forcibly sent back into the inferno from which they have fled: in the end ... fate administers them the coup de grâce and they all drown.... *Jews cannot possibly conceive that anything of that sort could have happened if those fugitives had belonged to a nation which has a government—be it even one in exile—to stand up for them.*[6]

One ray of light in the general immigration saga stemmed from the rescue of the "Teheran children." Seven hundred young Jewish boys and girls who had fled from German-occupied Poland to the Soviet Union were transferred to Teheran, where they were housed in a transfer camp. Many had personally witnessed the murder of their parents. The Yishuv assumed responsibility for them and managed to secure permission for their entry into Palestine. In February 1943, after a six-month journey that entailed traveling overland to India, sailing to Egypt and then proceeding by train to Palestine, they arrived, almost all in need of either medical or psychological treatment.

On February 28, 1940, as if to compound the limitations imposed on the Yishuv's ability to sustain a reasonable population increase, the British government arbitrarily restricted Jewish access to land. Only in one tiny area amounting to 5 percent of Palestine, were the Jews entitled to unencumbered land acquisitions. Given that they already owned half the land area in question, not more than 2.5 percent of the country was theoretically within their future grasp. But since virtually all of the remaining holdings were occupied and cultivated by Arabs, the Esco Foundation concluded that "the opportunity to buy land in the so-called free zone approached the vanishing point."[7] In March, thousands gathered in the streets of Tel Aviv and other cities to protest against such a blatantly inequitable policy. They encountered a violent police reaction in which 2 people were killed and 400 injured.

In keeping with their new anti-Zionist stance, the British began to suppress the Haganah. Toward the end of September 1939, forty-three of its members (including Moshe Dayan) were arrested while walking in the countryside for illegally bearing arms. One was sentenced to life imprisonment (for pointing his rifle at members of the arresting party), while the others were imprisoned for ten years. Thereafter, arms searches were conducted in various settlements and the Yishuv was ordered to surrender its entire arsenal, which, of course, it refused.

More drastic measures were about to be applied, but abrupt changes in the course of the war necessitated their temporary suspension. With Italy entering the fray as Germany's ally in June 1940 and, when, in early 1942, Rommel's forces were in the ascendancy in North Africa, military cooperation with the Yishuv momentarily served Britain's interest. A tolerant disposition was shown to the Haganah, both to free British soldiers stationed in Palestine for service elsewhere and to increase the reservoir of anti-Axis fighting forces that remained in the country. Virtually all jailed Haganah members were released.

By 1943, after the German Afrika Corps was overwhelmed, the harassment of the Haganah resumed. Those possessing unauthorized arms were severely dealt with. For example, on October 7, 1943, a military court consigned a Jew to seven years' imprisonment for possessing one bullet more than his official allocation. That only Jews were harshly punished is indicated by the light treatment meted out to an Arab tried exactly four days later. Found with an unlicensed rifle, rounds of ammunition and a bayonet, he was deprived of liberty for only six weeks.[8]

Jewish settlements suspected of housing arms were thoroughly combed. On November 16, 1943, British forces accompanied by Polish military police entered Ramat Hakovesh, on the pretext of looking for deserters from the Polish army. The settlement, which was located in a remote part of the country and which was exposed to potential Arab attacks, was certain to contain a number of weapons for its legitimate defense. In this particular raid, 800 troops with fixed bayonets, backed up by forty military vehicles, surrounded the settlement, which housed only 140 members. When the Poles discovered that the male settlers, including those dragged from their sickbeds, were corralled in the heat of the day into a barbed-wire enclosure, pending the ransacking of the collective, they withdrew in disgust. The settlers were viciously beaten with clubs and rifle butts. Fourteen were hospitalized and one, whose skull was fractured, subsequently died. When the British finally took leave of the area, it appeared as if it had been hit by a whirlwind.[9] After the Ramat Hakovesh incident, punitive anti-Haganah activities eased somewhat, but they continued nevertheless.

THE YISHUV AND THE WAR

The moment Britain declared war on Germany, roughly a quarter of the Yishuv indicated their availability for immediate military service. Far from welcoming them with open arms, the British begrudgingly accepted Jewish volunteers at a rate commensurate with that of Arab enlistments. Since relatively few Arabs stepped forward, the formation of Palestinian units, which were incorporated into the East Kent Regiment or "Buffs," advanced at a slow pace. Only in May 1941, when German forces were poised to sweep across the Suez Canal and into Palestine, did the Army High Command abandon the principle of Arab-Jewish parity to establish within the "Buffs," battalions of Palestinian Jews.

Jewish volunteers primarily served as trench diggers, drivers, stevedores, mechanics, quartermasters, map drafters, camouflage constructors, technicians and radio operators. Some obtained partial entry into the Navy, artillery units and the R.A.F. in which twenty were trained as pilots. Of these, three would ultimately, at one time or another, head the future Israeli Air Force. In general, they were very much involved in frontline activities in France, Greece, Crete and North Africa and, following the German invasion of Greece and Crete, some 1,200 Palestinian Jews fell into captivity.

In September 1940, the reality of the war was brought home to the Yishuv by an Italian Air Force bombardment of Tel Aviv, which took the lives of more than 100 people.[10] Two years later, with the likelihood of Palestine falling to Rommel's Afrika Corps, the Yishuv faced the grim prospect of sharing the fate of Polish Jewry. The impending German invasion created quite a stir, especially when it was ascertained that, should Alexandria be lost, the British would not defend Palestine. Some members of the Jewish Agency counseled surrender, believing that their lives might be spared. But others talked in terms of fighting to the end and planned for a final stand in the Mount Carmel region, where the entire Yishuv was to be relocated. Fortunately, toward the end of 1942, in the wake of Rommel's defeat at the battle of El-Alamein, the direct threat to the Yishuv receded.

Finally, after years of delay, the British, in September 1944, acceded to a Zionist request for the formation of a Jewish Brigade. When the idea was first mooted in the early stages of the war, calls were made for either a Jewish army or a Jewish division. Churchill warmly supported the proposal, as did his colonial secretary, Lord Lloyd, who on October 17, 1940 wrote to Weizmann informing him that the scheme met with the government's approval.[11] By the end of December, a commanding officer had been appointed and preparations were being made regarding the unit's formation, its flag, its insignia and so on. The untimely death of Lord Lloyd on February 8, 1941 and his replacement by the anti-Zionist Lord Moyne, put a long-lasting hold on the plan. Under Moyne's guidance, all the arguments of British officials and officers in the Middle East who opposed a distinctly Jewish force were submitted to the cabinet. As a result, the scheme was first "postponed" and then officially canceled, ostensibly due to a lack of equipment and shipping. The ultimate establishment of a Jewish Brigade reflected years of persistent lobbying, both by the Zionists and by a group of sympathetic non-Jewish politicians.

Brigadier Ernest Frank Benjamin was appointed as the Jewish Brigade's senior officer and approval was given for its flag to be that of the Zionist Movement; that is, one centered by a blue Star of David, flanked by two blue horizontal bands against a white background. Soldiers wore a blue-and-white shoulder flash bearing a gold Star of David. The three Jewish battalions of the Palestine "Buffs" Regiment constituted its major source of manpower.

In February 1945, the Brigade, which consisted of some 6,500 soldiers, assumed active duty in Italy within the framework of the British Eighth Army under the command of General Mark Clark. Contrary to the hopes of the Zionist leadership, the tardy formation of the Brigade prevented it from playing a meaningful role in the defeat of the Nazis. However, at the close of the war, it served as a beacon of light to many Holocaust survivors, directing them to ports of embarkation for their illegal sea crossings to Palestine. From the point of view of the Yishuv's defensive potential, members of the Brigade were able to acquire training in the use of heavy weapons and artillery and gleaned valuable combat experience. Above all, they were exposed to organizational issues involving the coordination of large concentrations of troops and logistics. Such know-how, which was indispensable for the running of a modern army, was not at the time available to the Haganah.

In reviewing the Yishuv's contribution to the war effort, one cannot but make special mention of a group of thirty-two Jewish paratroopers recruited by the British. In 1943 and in the first half of 1944 they were air-dropped into the enemy-held countries of Romania, Hungary, Slovakia, Yugoslavia, Italy and Bul-

The Jewish Brigade at morning prayer (Central Zionist Archives).

garia. On behalf of British intelligence, they willingly assumed the hazardous task of making contact with local partisan groups and securing vital military information, which was to be relayed by portable radio transmitters. More to the point, they also regarded themselves as Zionist emissaries, with a duty to locate the remnants of European Jewry. It was hoped that their appearance out of the blue, so to speak, would breathe new life into dejected survivors and fortify them in their resolve to reach Palestine. Of the thirty-two, twelve were captured and seven, including two women, Hana Senesh and Haviva Reik, were executed.[12] Although the paratroopers did not make any significant impact in the countries in which they landed, they exemplified an outstanding spirit of willing self-sacrifice, for they all appreciated the high risk of death that their mission entailed. They served as a moving source of inspiration for Jewish youth in Palestine, who a few years later were called on to fight for Israel's newfound existence.

By the war's end, the number of Palestinian Jews who had enlisted in the British armed forces as a whole, exceeded 26,000.[13] Of these, approximately 280 were killed in action or died in captivity.[14]

THE PALMAH

On May 15, 1941, the Haganah, under Yitzhak Sadeh's initiative, inaugurated the first of a series of groups, known by the Hebrew acronym *Palmah*, from *Plugot Mahatz* (shock companies). As soon as Sadeh began recruiting and training the inaugural contingent, the British called on his men to assist them in their June invasion of Syria and Lebanon. Thirty-three members of the Palmah, plus a non-Palmah member from Kibbutz Dan, linked up with two Australian brigades. Dividing into two squads, one led by Yigal Allon and the other by Moshe Dayan, they were required to guide forward units of the British army, cut telephone lines and secure strategic bridges. The weapons issued to them by the British were so decrepit that they returned them and utilized their own. In the Palmah's baptism of fire, Moshe Dayan's party overran a key police station manned by Vichy troops. During the encounter, an Australian soldier was killed and three Palmahniks (Palmah members) were wounded, including Moshe Dayan, who lost an eye.

By November, four Palmah companies had been formed, comprising 460 members, most of whom had served in the late 1930s, either with Orde Wingate or Yitzhak Sadeh. Training was undertaken over weekends and, except for a small cadre of officers, its fighters continued with their normal civilian activities. The Palmah was hard-pressed for funds and equipment, general morale was low and its future was very much up in the air. What saved the day was the closing in of Rommel's forces in North Africa in early 1942 and the additional possibility that the Germans might enter the Middle East from the north. These factors induced the British to approach the Haganah with a request for special volunteers to undertake sabotage and scouting operations behind enemy lines. Members of the Palmah were duly put forward and in return they received tuition from British officers at Kibbutz Mishmar Ha-Emek. Recalling that critical period, Yigal Allon noted that "the necessity to prepare for a campaign against a modern military machine such as the German one gave the Palmah commanders an opportunity to think, to plan and to train their men along the most modern lines."[15]

Nonetheless, the Palmah continued to experience budgetary problems, which made it all but impossible to maintain itself, as it would have liked to have done, as a permanent fully mobilized force. A solution was presented by Tabenkin and adopted in August 1942. It entailed the attachment of Palmah units to various kibbutzim, mostly to kibbutzim belonging to the Kibbutz Meuhad Federation. Within each kibbutz, members of the Palmah would work 14.5 days a month and would devote another 8.5 days to full-time military activities.

Such an arrangement influenced the basic character both of the Palmah and of its members. For in keeping with the kibbutz's egalitarian ethos, all its soldiers were subject to exactly the same living conditions, regardless of rank. They shared a common mess and, although their superior officers had the last word, they freely participated in their units' general decision-making process. Following a series of backbreaking hikes, where orientation skills were honed, as well as numerous evenings huddled around campfires, where privates and officers sat, shoulder to shoulder, listening to lectures, singing songs, telling tall stories, brewing coffee and eating roasted potatoes, a unique camaraderie emerged. By their distinctive experience, mode of dress and use of their own special slang, laced with Arabic expressions, members of the Palmah recognized each other as brothers and sisters (women were fully incorporated as active combatants).[16]

As the war progressed, the Palmah was faced with a new challenge. Noting that Jewish youth were volunteering by the thousands for service in the British army, many wished to do likewise. In their judgment, not only would they have become full-time soldiers in the true sense of the term, but they would have been able to make a more direct contribution to the defense of Palestine and to the general Allied war effort. A not insignificant number of Palmahniks broke ranks to join the British army and it took a tremendous amount of persuasion to convince the rest not to do the same. The crucial necessity of the Yishuv maintaining a kernel of a standing army of its own was emphasized.

Those remaining loyal to the Palmah had to contend with numerous irritants. Since they did not wear army uniforms, not only were they denied all the benefits associated with military service, such as discounts at coffee shops and cinemas, but the general public, unaware of their situation, perceived them as draft dodgers, and, on occasion, even assaulted them.[17]

THE ARABS AND THE ALLIES

Within Palestine, the Arab revolt had died down entirely, probably as a result of previous defeats and of the massive British military presence in the country. Jewish migration was effectively staunched and the White Paper held out to the Arabs prospects of an independent Palestinian state. As a beneficial byproduct of all this, from late 1939 until late 1947, Arab-Jewish strife was quiescent and the Yishuv once again enjoyed the internal calm that it experienced throughout most of the 1920s.

The Arabs were, to say the least, tentative British allies. They either tended to withhold their support until it was evident that the democracies would triumph, or they prematurely threw in their lot with the Axis powers, when the latter momentarily gained the upper hand.

Even though the British-Egyptian Treaty stipulated that Egypt was to come to Britain's aid in time of war, Egypt simply declared itself a non-combatant ally. The country was infested with Axis spies and supporters (including King Farouk)[18] and only by active intervention did Britain prevent the establishment of a pro-Axis cabinet.

In Iraq, the British army had to unseat Rashid Ali al Gailani, who, in 1941, intended to place the Mosul oil fields at Hitler's disposal. His efforts to do so were assisted by the Germans who provided a number of fighter planes.[19] Rashid's actions have variously been described by British sources as amounting to a "revolt," as if it were some aberration that needed to be set right. In truth, Rashid, whose rise to power was confirmed on April 10 by the Iraqi parliament, was effectively Iraq's leader, and his hostile activities amounted to nothing less than an Iraqi declaration of war against Britain. Rashid received strong backing from Haj Amin al Husseini, who falsely charged that Churchill had stated that "the world would not know peace as long as the Koran prevailed."[20]

Once Iraq was subdued, the British and Free French invaded Vichy Syria, where Axis activists had run riot. Even though the invaders, who were assisted by a small contingent of the Yishuv, declared that they intended to grant Syria independence, very few of the country's inhabitants rallied to their side. It would seem that their pro-Nazi sentiments smothered their own sense of national pride.[21]

As for the Palestinian Arabs, their leader, Haj Amin al Husseini, briefly assisted Rashid Ali al Gailani, then fled to Europe via Iran to further the Axis cause. He met with both Hitler and Mussolini, endorsed the Nazis' final solution for the Jews, organized Arab and Muslim volunteers to fight alongside the Germans and broadcast Nazi propaganda to the Middle East and North Africa. In a draft declaration, which he prepared for German adoption, he wrote that the Arabs in both Palestine and other countries should be accorded the right to handle the Jewish problem "by the same method that the question is now being settled in the Axis countries."[22] After the war, he escaped from French arrest to find asylum in Egypt. His popularity among the Palestinians never waned and, to his death, he was revered by them. Of no mean significance, noted Wistrich, "Palestinians and other Arabs have rarely if ever criticized the mufti's complicity in the Holocaust."[23]

Only after Rommel's defeat at El-Alamein did Iraq, in January 1943, declare war on Germany. Then, in February 1945, as the war was drawing to a close, Syria, Lebanon, Egypt and Saudi Arabia belatedly followed suit. By so doing, all of the above-mentioned Arab states became eligible for UN membership.[24] Later, in what can only be described as a travesty of natural justice, these lackluster Arab "allies" participated in a crucial UN General Assembly that determined the fate of the Yishuv.

In September 1944, with British prompting and under the leadership of Nahas Pasha of Egypt and Nuri Said of Syria, heads of Arab states gathered in Alexandria to discuss the possibility of establishing an Arab League. The following March, having reached general agreement, a League Convention was signed in Cairo by Egypt, Syria, Lebanon, Iraq, Transjordan and Saudi Arabia. Yemen joined two months later, and a special representative status was granted to the Arabs of Palestine. The latter decision reflected the League's determination to make Palestine its major source of concern.[25]

A REDEFINING OF OFFICIAL ZIONIST OBJECTIVES

The Zionists as a whole strove toward the formation of an independent Jewish state in Palestine. But to avoid adding unnecessary fuel to the movement's conflict, first with the Turks and then with the Arabs, official Zionist objectives, as opposed to those of the dissident Revisionists, were muted. Ever since the movement's inception, Zionist spokesmen consistently indicated that their final aims were merely the establishment of a Jewish National Home within Palestine, to be realized in the nebulous future.

However, with the entry of the United States into the Second World War in December 1941, a change in Zionist strategy was deemed desirable. As America was shouldering a large share of the burden of defeating the Axis powers, it was obviously destined to become a key player in postwar reconstruction talks. Given that Britain still adhered to its White Paper policy and that postwar Europe was expected to contain millions of displaced Jews (the extent of the ongoing Holocaust was then not fully appreciated), Katznelson, Weizmann and Ben Gurion all agreed that the Zionists ought to be more forthcoming in stating their final objectives. They sensed that only a very narrow postwar window of opportunity would be available to the Jews, and if they did not act decisively, they would miss that opportunity, perhaps for generations to come. Ben Gurion had in mind, the drafting of a bold and incisive program calling for a Zionist solution of the Jewish question. Taking into account the Arabs' inclination to side with the Nazis and of the growing world sympathy with the lot of the Jews, it seemed fitting for the Zionists to state their case unequivocally.

This they first did at an all-American Zionist Conference (which also included some participants from Canada, South America and Palestine), held in May 1942 at the Biltmore Hotel in New York. The conference urged "that the gates of Palestine be opened; that the Jewish Agency be vested with control of immigration into Palestine and with the necessary authority for upbuilding [sic] the country; including the development of its unoccupied and uncultivated lands; and that Palestine be established as a Jewish Commonwealth integrated into the structure of the new democratic world."[26] Later, in November 1942, the Biltmore Program was approved and adopted at a meeting in Palestine of the Zionist Organization's Executive Committee. Twenty-one members voted in favor and four, representing Hashomer Hatzair and Left Poalei Zion, opposed it on the grounds that they preferred the formation of a binational state in Palestine. Three members of Mapai's B Faction, composed of members of the Kibbutz Meuhad Federation, who would have liked to have voted against the motion, abstained.[27] They believed that it was still premature to issue sweeping demands, which in the circumstances of the time would have prompted an Arab backlash. That in turn would have encouraged the British to formulate a solution that would not be to the Yishuv's liking. In early 1944, the B Faction seceded to form its own party, called Ahdut Ha'Avodah (the same name as the party that fused with Poalei Hatzair in 1930 to form Mapai).

Binational-state advocates, who emanated from two like-minded associations, *Ihud* (Unity) and the League for Arab-Jewish Rapprochement, effectively did not radically differ from mainstream Zionists as far as their long-term goals were concerned. Hashomer Hatzair in 1942, for example, had actually advocated a postwar arrangement for Palestine whereby the Jewish Agency would have the right to determine Jewish immigration and to promote the development of the country, including the right of settling all state domains and waste lands.[28] However, they opposed calls for the immediate foundation of a Jewish state in Palestine because the Arabs would not countenance such a proposition. While sharing standard Zionist demands for unlimited Jewish immigration, they assumed that if the modalities of a binational state could be agreed on, in which neither nation would have absolute power over the other (through a system of guaranteed parity in one of the legislative bodies), the Arabs would no longer have feared for their future and the Yishuv would have been able to develop to its heart's content.

The Arabs, of course, were not naive. What the Jewish promoters of a binational state were effectively proposing was that the Arabs cede half the seats in a national assembly to the Jews, constituting 30 percent of the population, in return for a Jewish commitment not to dominate the entire country in the future.[29] Had the Arabs complied with the binationalists, unfettered Jewish immigration would have soon converted them into a minority. Their supposed equal control over the affairs of state would then have depended on the willingness of the new Jewish majority to abide by earlier agreements. Were the Jews to adhere to such an arrangement, they would have set a historic precedent. To their credit, the binational proponents were in fact genuinely seeking an honorable outcome. However, that would have necessitated the prevalence of people of extraordinary good will in both Arab and Jewish societies.

THE JEWISH TERROR CAMPAIGN

At the onset of the war, the *Irgun Zvai Leumi* or, more commonly, the *Irgun* (see previous chapter), agreed to suspend all anti-British actions to cooperate in the fight against the Axis powers. In May 1941, the Irgun's leader, David Raziel, accepted a request by British Intelligence to enter Iraq with three of his comrades to assess the possibility of blowing up vital fuel tanks and to engage in activity against the mufti. Shortly after their arrival there, Raziel was killed in an aerial bombardment. The loss to the Irgun was incalculable, for Raziel was its sole outstanding commander at that time. Only in January 1944, with Menachem Begin taking over its reins of control, was the Irgun once again led by a forceful and respected leader.

Not everyone in the Irgun was willing to collaborate with the British. In September 1940, a group directed by Avraham Stern that perceived Britain and not Germany as the Yishuv's main enemy, seceded to form an alternative militia. Regarding themselves as embodying the Irgun's original spirit, they referred to their organization, which never numbered more than a few hundred, as being the Irgun in Israel. Shortly thereafter, they renamed it the Israel Freedom Fighters, or more simply by its Hebrew acronym, *Lehi*.[30] In January 1941, Lehi sent an emissary to Beirut to negotiate with Nazi diplomats to propose the establishment of a totalitarian Jewish state linked by treaty to the German Reich. Lehi leaders had such an abiding hatred of the "British imperialists" that they totally misjudged the nature of the Nazi regime. They assumed that its anti-Semitism was secondary to its military strategy and that if an alliance with Jews would further Nazi global ambitions, it would readily enter into one.[31] Why Lehi contemplated that the Germans would prefer the Jews over a very much larger Arab multitude, more than willing to share their racial prejudices, remains a complete enigma. What is clear is that the Nazis were not the slight-est bit interested. Eventually, with an infusion of a new breed of members, Lehi began to associate itself with the Soviet Union and to view its organization as a revolutionary socialist one dedicated to the liberation of the entire Middle East.

Until 1942, Lehi was more of a hindrance to the Yishuv than to the Manda-tory government, in that it robbed Jewish banks and in the process killed or in-jured innocent bystanders.[32] Not surprisingly, it was widely regarded both by the public at large and by the police, as a group of gangsters or as the "Stern Gang." In February 1942, Avraham Stern met his death during a police raid and for almost all of the following two years, Lehi was in disarray until it regrouped under David Friedman-Yellin's leadership.

Against the background of continued police and military attempts to disarm the Yishuv and of the regime's inexorable adherence to the White Paper, even after the slaughter of European Jewry had become clearly evident, the Irgun and Lehi jointly launched a military campaign against the British. A deciding factor as far as the Irgun was concerned was the rejection of a proposal it had submitted at the end of 1942, which would have involved the parachuting into Europe of 300 Palestinian Jews behind enemy lines. The Irgun had hoped that its fighters would, in the name of the Jewish people, wreck havoc and revenge on the Germans and, with the British refusal to consider it, the Irgun concluded that the unilateral ceasefire that it had thus far been upholding had become pointless.

The opening of the new terrorist campaign occurred on the night of Febru-ary 12, 1944, when in both Jerusalem and Tel Aviv, offices of the Department of Migration were damaged by incendiary bombs. For the most part, the Irgun di-rected its activities toward the destruction of government buildings, whereas Lehi operated as a full-fledged terrorist outfit. Five days later, two British police officers were killed in a gunfight. On March 23, explosive devices, causing four fatalities, were detonated at police headquarters in Jerusalem, Haifa and Jaffa. Other acts of violence followed, but two sponsored by Lehi went well beyond the pale. The first, which occurred on August 8, involved an unsuccessful at-tempt on the life of MacMichael, the high commissioner. The second incident involved the actual assassination of Lord Moyne, who was then the British minister of state in Cairo. On November 6, Lord Moyne was struck down in Cairo by two Lehi gunmen, who were subsequently sentenced to death.

Of all the terrorist acts, the murder of Moyne was the most damaging to the Zionist cause. In reviewing Moyne's murder before the House of Commons,

Churchill declared: "This shameful crime has shocked the world and has affected none more strongly than those like myself who, in the past, have been consistent friends of the Jews and constant architects of their future. If our dreams for Zionism are to end in the smoke of an assassin's pistol and the labors for its future produce a new set of gangsters worthy of Nazi Germany, many like myself will have to reconsider the position we have maintained so consistently and so long in the past."[33]

Within the Yishuv, revulsion against the Moyne assassination was widely shared and reflected in condemnatory statements by leading secular and religious leaders. Weizmann went as far as to assert that it shocked him even more than the loss of his son, Michael, who had died in action while serving in the Royal Air Force.[34] With the willingness of the Jewish Agency to cooperate with the authorities, plus of course strong measures taken by the government itself, all Jewish terrorist activity was, for the time being, suspended. (Even before Moyne's death, the British had adopted severe countermeasures, the most draconian being the expulsion, on October 20, 1941, of 251 Jewish detainees to a prison camp in Eritrea.)[35]

In what became known as the *saison* (French for "season," or hunting season), members of the Irgun were ruthlessly hounded by the Zionist establishment. Ironically, Lehi, whose members gunned down Lord Moyne, were not targeted. Lehi escaped attention on the basis of a promise to lay low. Since Lehi was always only a peripheral body with a very limited following, cynics might well argue that the Mapai-led Yishuv, seized on a golden opportunity to deal a crushing blow to its main rival. Certainly, Ben Gurion pulled no punches. On November 20, 1944, in addressing an annual Histadrut Conference, he demanded that the dissidents (a euphemism for the Irgun and Lehi) and their active supporters be dismissed from all workplaces, that the public deny them shelter and that the Yishuv collaborate with the British in helping to stamp them out.[36] Responding to Ben Gurion's call, special units of the Haganah kidnapped Irgun members and supplied the British with the names, aliases and addresses of many others.[37]

Such actions were in fact primarily designed to further the Yishuv's intrinsic interests. A year earlier, the British Cabinet had appointed Herbert Morrison to head a secret ministerial committee to review the Palestine problem. It came down in favor of partitioning the country into two states. This information was imparted to the Jewish Agency, which in turn rejected the concept since it did not accord with the Biltmore Program of Jewish sovereignty over the entire country. However, it was hoped that an even better proposal would eventually arise.[38] Begin, who was taken into the Jewish Agency's confidence, was asked to suspend Irgun activities in order to smooth the way for a negotiated settlement. Since Begin refused point blank, it was felt that this left the Yishuv with no alternative other than to attempt to quash the Irgun. Anxious to prevent a Jewish civil war, Begin issued strict instructions to all Irgun members not to retaliate.

The *saison*, which effectively involved the persecution of brothers in arms for Jewish statehood, left an enduring bitter aftertaste in the Yishuv. The Morrison plan notwithstanding, the British Cabinet never actually abandoned its anti-Zionist policies, nor did it desist from hounding the Haganah. That being the case, the *saison*, which ended in March 1945, turned out to be a pointless gesture to what had become an implacable and uncompromising opponent of Jewish national aspirations.

ECONOMIC DEVELOPMENTS

The outbreak of the Second World War ushered in a brief period of severe economic dislocation. With ships being commandeered for the transportation of essential supplies, international trade was very much curtailed. The situation worsened when on June 10, 1940, Italy entered the war as Germany's ally. The Mediterranean was closed to most commercial traffic and the rate of unemployment in the Yishuv rose to alarming levels. By August 1940, it reached a record 27,000.[39] For the most part, the immediate cause was a precipitous decline in citrus exports and the building industry's newfound inability to access key materials. Imports in general became difficult to come by and the few supplies that were on hand were rationed under the watchful eye of a newly formed War Supply Council. To make matters worse, a crisis of confidence in the financial sector arose. As panic-stricken depositors rushed to withdraw their bank savings, the amount of money in circulation declined. A reduction in the availability of credit added a further downward pressure on the building industry.

The depressed state of affairs was not longlasting. Instead, the country experienced the most vigorous bout of economic growth that it had yet achieved. Over the entire war period, the average annual growth rate was 10.1 percent, exceeding, by a narrow margin, the growth rate of the booming American war economy.[40] Britain's main regional economic agency, the Middle East Supply Center, established in 1941 in Cairo, looked to the Yishuv as a source of supply for many of its military needs. It ensured, inasmuch as was humanly possible, that the Yishuv's industrial complex was provided with necessary raw materials.

Large troop concentrations in Palestine necessitated the rapid construction of additional camps, airfields, army hospitals, fortifications and roads, much of which was undertaken by the Histadrut's Solel Boneh.[41] Not only did Solel Boneh operate within Palestine, but it also fulfilled British Army building assignments in various other parts of the Middle East. In the process, the building industry was reinvigorated.

The seemingly insatiable military requirements (for infrastructure, equipment and the personal consumption of troops stationed in Palestine) caused aggregate demand to soar, and by 1943, only 3,500 were registered as unemployed. As most of the residual unemployed were not actually employable, a serious labor shortage emerged, exacerbated by the virtual cessation of immigration, and by the 26,000 Jews who had joined the British armed forces.

To ensure sufficient availability of food, the agricultural sector expanded rapidly. Grain acreage was substantially widened, as was the amount of land devoted to growing vegetables. Between 1939 and 1945, annual milk output rose from 35 million liters to 69 million and eggs from 59 million to 90 million.[42] Progress in the agricultural sector also received a strong boost from the development of a local food-canning and jam-making industry. For the most part, supply increases occurred in the Jewish settlements, whose numbers expanded and which relied upon a more extensive use of irrigation. Throughout the entire war, forty-five new Jewish settlements (of which most were kibbutzim) were created and between the war's end and the formation of the State of Israel in May 1948, another fifty were added. By then, more than 300 Jewish settlements were in place.

Of all economic sectors, industry benefited the most. With foreign sources of supply essentially being inaccessible, the Yishuv had to step into the breach by producing otherwise unobtainable products locally. It was as if the country's industrial sector had suddenly been protected by across-the-board import restrictions. A host of new industries and plants appeared, which included industrial machinery, automobile parts, textiles, agricultural equipment, medical and electrical instruments, chemical and pharmaceutical products, shipbuilding, a diamond polishing industry and an oil refinery at Haifa. In many individual industries, progress was phenomenal. For example, although diamond polishing in Palestine commenced only in 1941 (on the initiative of refugees from Belgium and Poland), it soon became a world contender, since it was entirely export oriented. In addition, it relied exclusively on locally made machinery. By 1942, the shipbuilding industry had launched twenty 100-ton concrete fishing trawlers powered by locally made diesel engines. In the country's budding iron and steel industry, a new foundry near Haifa began to produce steel comparable in quality to that made in Sweden.[43] The array of new products that the Yishuv suddenly began supplying was truly impressive. Included were items such as antitank mines, fuel containers, electrical batteries, coils of wire, water flasks, fire extinguishers, cranes, automobile parts, hydraulic tools, signaling lights, razors, tents, camouflage nets, life preservers, galvanized rubber, optic instruments, dry ice, acetone and modern state-of-the-art medical and pharmaceutical products.[44] As a result of all these developments, by 1943 the number of Jews employed in manufacturing had doubled, reaching a total of 61,000.

The remarkable growth and development of the Yishuv's economy, combined with the valuable military experience that many Palestinian Jews acquired during the war, placed the Zionists in a strong position in the immediate postwar period. They could enter the final stage of the struggle for a Jewish state with a measure of enhanced self-confidence and with some solid grounds for success.

NOTES

1. Gvati, *Hundred Years,* 1985, p. 104.

2. Slutsky, *From Defence to Strife,* 1964, p. 154.

3. Ibid., p. 157.

4. Esco Foundation, *Palestine,* 1947, vol. 2, p. 945.

5. A report by Shertok cited by Trevor, *Under the White Paper,* 1980, p. 26.

6. As quoted by Trevor, *Under the White Paper,* 1980, p. 32. Italics added.

7. Esco Foundation, *Palestine,* 1947, vol. 2, p. 934.

8. Ibid., p. 1037.

9. Ibid., p. 1038, and Slutsky, *From Defence to Strife,* 1964, p. 184.

10. Segev, *One Palestine,* 2000, p. 449.

11. Bauer, *From Diplomacy to Resistance,* 1973, p. 89.

12. There was one other woman parachutist, Sara Braverman, who managed to survive.

13. Slutsky, *From Defence to Strife,* 1964, p. 699.

14. Ibid., p. 700.

15. Allon, *Making of Israel's Army,* 1970, p. 16.

16. By 1944, there were approximately 300 women in the Palmah. See Bauer, *From Diplomacy to Resistance,* 1973, p. 343.

17. Slutsky, *From Defence to Strife,* 1964, p. 400.

18. Sachar, *History,* 1981, p. 228.

19. Esco Foundation, *Palestine,* 1947, vol. 2, p. 979.

20. Dothan, *Struggle,* 1981, p. 205.

21. Esco Foundation, *Palestine,* 1947, vol. 2, p. 51.

22. As quoted by Hurewitz, *Struggle,* 1950, p. 155.

23. Wistrich, *Antisemitism,* 1992, p. 246.

24. To qualify for inclusion in the UN, potential states had to have declared war against the Axis powers before March 1945.

25. Bauer, *From Diplomacy to Resistance,* 1973, p. 255.

26. As reported in Teveth, *Ben-Gurion,* 1987, p. 817.

27. Hurewitz, *Struggle,* 1950, p. 159.

28. Esco Foundation, *Palestine,* 1947, vol. 2, p. 1102.

29. Dothan, *Struggle,* 1981, p. 192.

30. The Hebrew title was *Lohamei Herut Yisrael.*

31. Shavit, *Jabotinsky,* 1988, p. 232.

32. Laqueur, *History,* 1989, p. 377.

33. As quoted in Esco Foundation, *Palestine,* 1947, vol. 2, pp. 1047–48.

34. Slutsky, *From Defence to Strife,* 1964, p. 515.

35. Ibid., p. 530.

36. Bar-Zohar, *Ben Gurion,* 1968, p. 76.

37. Bauer, *From Diplomacy to Resistance,* 1973, p. 331.

38. Slutsky, *From Defence to Strife,* 1964, p. 195.

39. Halevi, 1976, p. 46. Laqueur, *History*, 1989, p. 543, points to government statistics suggesting that 50,000 Jews were unemployed, but Halevi, an eminent Israeli economics professor, is more likely to be relied on.

40. Gross and Metzer, "Palestine," 1993, p. 63.

41. Although Solel Boneh had become bankrupt in the 1920s, it was subsequently rejuvenated.

42. Gvati, *Hundred Years*, 1985, p. 104.

43. Esco Foundation, *Palestine*, 1947, vol. 2, pp. 1054–55.

44. Slutsky, *From Defence to Strife*, 1964, pp. 206–9.

Chapter 9

The Postwar Struggle for Independence

When the British Labor Party gained power in July 1945, the Zionists were ecstatic, for its platform included an unequivocal commitment to their cause. The British Labor Party, in a conference held in December 1944, adopted a position that even the most pro-state of mainstream Zionists hesitated to take. Not only did it favor handing over Palestine in its entirety to the Jews, but it even suggested that "the Arabs be encouraged to move out as the Jews move in."[1] In astonishment, Weizmann noted that he and his colleagues "had never contemplated the removal of the Arabs."[2] Furthermore, recognizing the smallness of Palestine, which was "less than the size of Wales," the resolution in question concluded by suggesting that Britain "should re-examine also the possibility of extending the present Palestinian boundaries."[3] The following year, Dr. Hugh Dalton, addressing a Labor Party conference held a few weeks before the Labor ministers took office, explained that "it is morally wrong and politically indefensible to impose obstacles to the entry into Palestine now of any Jews who desire to go there." He added that Britain, in conjunction with the United States and the Soviet Union, should jointly support a policy "which will give us a happy, free and prosperous Jewish state in Palestine."[4]

However, in next to no time, the Labor government completely and utterly repudiated its party promises and slavishly kowtowed to the Arabs. Its newly adopted pro-Arab orientation was motivated by perceptions of self-interest. The Foreign Office, which had grave misgivings regarding communist intentions, was troubled about the possibility of the Soviets penetrating into Africa by way of the Middle East. Also, in accordance with an earlier agreement with Egypt, whose implementation was postponed because of the war, Britain had to withdraw all its forces stationed in Egypt to the canal zone. This enhanced the attractiveness of Palestine as an alternative base. On assuming office and in attempting to re-evaluate its Middle East policy, the Labor government sought advice from the Foreign Office, the War Office, the Palestine government, the Colonial Office, the Middle East Office in Cairo and from other Middle East centers. According to Kimche, they "all sang the same refrain: The Arabs in the Middle East were the key to the maintenance of Britain's position there; dire perils would follow if their good will was lost by accepting the Zionist outlook."[5] Some put their case even more churlishly. For example, Lawrence Grafftey-Smith, the British representative in Jidda (Saudi Arabia), suggested that Britain's enemies were seeking to promote immigration into Palestine of Jews who were none other than an "irritant of non-assimilable elements of Eastern European outlook and dubious ideology."[6]

That British security concerns did not materialize, is indicative of Palestine policy having been driven by functionaries who not only misread the international situation but who were also motivated by a deep antipathy to Zionism. At any rate, for a party supposedly committed to social justice and decency, Labor's abject obeisance to a clutch of reactionary and obscurantist Middle Eastern tyrants, almost all of whom were dubious allies in the fight against Germany, was to say the least, most unseemly.

Despite the Holocaust and the presence in Europe of thousands of physically and psychologically traumatized Jewish survivors, the Labor government resolved to adhere rigidly to the essence of the White Paper. To rub salt into the victims' wounds, the foreign minister, Ernest Bevin, had the effrontery to complain that the Jews "want to get too much at the head of the queue."[7] Bevin turned a blind eye to the unique and tragic circumstances in which the Jews were placed, preferring instead to regard them as "presenting a problem similar to that of the bombed-out cities of London or Coventry."[8] For all he cared, they could rebuild their lives in the charnels of Europe. Weizmann, who was particularly incensed by Bevin's heartless insensitivity, retorted that "No Jews should be forced to return to countries where they saw their wives mutilated and burned, their sons and daughters buried alive, their parents turned into white ash."[9]

At the war's immediate end, there were some 50,000 Jews in Germany and Austria. Their numbers were rapidly enhanced by the arrival of thousands of others who kept fleeing westward from Poland and from other areas under Soviet control. Many headed for U.S. displaced persons camps after having returned to their original homes to find that they were the sole survivors in their families and that their former communities had been completely eradicated. Their trek westward was facilitated by Zionist officials, sent mainly from the Yishuv. A vast network of guides and transborder smugglers directed them to transit camps and then to staging posts for illicit journeys to Palestine. This entire migratory process, which was both spontaneous and organized, was called *Bricha* (Flight). In Poland and other Eastern European countries, local inhabitants very much resented the return of Jewish survivors. Apart from their ongoing anti-Semitic prejudices, those who had gladly taken over abandoned Jewish property were either loathe to hand it back or to compensate the original owners. On July 3, 1946, in Kielce (Poland), they vented their feelings in a violent pogrom, which took the lives of forty-two Jews. This massacre, committed just a year after the Nazis were defeated, provided the Bricha with added momentum. It convinced Jewish survivors that Palestine and Palestine alone had to be their final destination. Between 1944 and 1948, some 250,000 Jews fled from Eastern Europe to Germany, Austria and Italy.[10]

In August 1945, with it becoming apparent that the gates of Palestine were not to be freely open to the Jews, *Hapala* (illegal migration to Palestine) was renewed with increased vigor by the Aliyah Bet organization (see chapter 7). The Aliyah Bet project involved an inordinate amount of finance and effort.[11] Since Aliyah Bet journeys usually resulted in the confiscation of boats, it was next to impossible to hire them. Therefore in most cases, Aliyah Bet had to acquire its own vessels. In the early postwar years, newly constructed ships were totally beyond its reach, so its fleet consisted entirely of old craft, some of which were of doubtful seaworthiness. They were gathered from numerous European sources as well as from the United States. Before undertaking their hazardous voyages, they were fitted out (in as much secrecy as possible) to accommodate the illegal migrants. Special bunks were constructed in their holds, furnished with straw-filled mattresses. An adequate supply of food and water was brought on board and carefully stored and when all was ready, the passengers, who were assembled in neighboring transfer camps, were allocated their specific sleeping quarters. In many instances, large numbers were involved, sometimes in excess of a thousand, and the passengers were grouped in distinct parties, led by a supervisor, who coordinated with other supervisors and an organizing committee. A doctor or two was usually included and special attention was given to ensure that inasfar as circumstances permitted, a reasonable measure of cleanliness and hygiene was maintained. Crowding was so intense that, even though special ventilators were installed, the air below deck was extremely stale. For most of the journey, out of fear of being spotted by British surveillance planes, the passengers had to remain under wraps. Haganah members were always on hand to attend to both internal and external security matters and by means of competent radio officers, contact was secured with Aliyah Bet stations in both Europe and Palestine. Most seamen were gentiles but there were some Jews both from the Palmah's sea division and from America who had served in the U.S. Navy.

If a ship succeeded in running the British Navy's gauntlet, Aliyah Bet would mobilize Haganah resources to meet it, offload its human cargo and place the migrants within neighboring settlements. The feat of receiving and caring for the newcomers was an operation in its own right, which required a coordinated effort to secure the roads, to watch out for the British Army and to have all the requisite means of land transport in place. In the more likely case of a ship being interdicted, passengers were advised to withstand efforts to detain them. However, they were no match for the British, who were equipped with tear gas and powerful water cannons and who indiscriminately truncheoned them.

The largest contingent of Aliyah Bet was borne by two American ships, the *Pan York* and the *Pan Crescent*, which were respectively renamed the *Gathering of Exiles* and *Independence*. Between the two of them, 15,240 potential migrants sailed from Romania. The journey, which began on December 22, 1947, represented the culmination of intricate organizational planning, which involved the funneling of thousands of passengers by rail and road transport to the port of embarkation. By agreement with the British, the two ships surrendered peacefully and allowed themselves to be escorted to Cyprus, where they appreciably added to the number of exiles under British custody.

Between May 1945 and the establishment of Israel, some 70,000 Jews sailed illegally in some sixty-five worn out, overcrowded vessels to Palestine.[12] Most were intercepted, even before reaching the country's shores and were detained in Atlit and then, from August 1946, in Cyprus. Although Aliyah Bet did not appreciably increase the Yishuv's population,[13] the constant drama played out at sea under international media scrutiny greatly enhanced world sympathy for the Zionist cause.

When in October 1945, Britain officially announced that only 1,500 Jews per month would be permitted to immigrate to Palestine, the Haganah cooperated with the Irgun and Lehi to create a unified national resistance movement. Rejecting Bevin's restrictive migration policy, Ben Gurion announced that, even at the cost of life, the Yishuv would not concede "the freedom of Jewish immigration, the right to build our desolate homeland, and the political independence of our people in its own land."[14] This was followed shortly by an operation to free illegal immigrant detainees as well as by widespread sabotage of the railway network. As might have been expected, the British responded with a series of punitive reprisals. In November, they swooped down on settlements in the Sharon coastal plain in search of illegal migrants. Hundreds of unarmed Jews in the surrounding area rushed to the scene to offer passive resistance and, in the process, British troops opened fire on them, killing eight and wounding twenty. Then in December, fifty-five Irgun and Lehi detainees were deported to a prison camp in East Africa, where the following February, Sudanese sentries shot two of them dead and injured eleven. Such unprovoked and indiscriminate slaughter evoked a growing desire within the Yishuv for even firmer anti-British initiatives. These were not slow in coming. In April, Lehi took the lives of seven British soldiers at an army camp near the Yarkon River. Thereafter, violent clashes between British forces on the one hand and Lehi and the Irgun on the other, occurred on a regular and ongoing basis. On some occasions, after encountering fatal losses in the wake of a Lehi or Irgun sortie, enraged British troops would take the law into their own hands by indiscriminately shooting or assaulting passing Jews.

Contempt for Jews was widely prevalent among both British troops and police, and in the postwar period, instances of Jews meeting their deaths at the hands of some brutal British official occurred with frightening frequency. With notorious Black and Tan veterans in leading positions and with former members of Mosley's fascist Blackshirts spread throughout its ranks, the Palestine Police was described by Arthur Koestler as "one of the most disreputable organizations in the British Commonwealth."[15] Often the anti-Semitism articulated by the police was no different from that of the Nazis. As a case in point, on September 21, 1945, the *Palestine Post* reported an incident of a Christian, by the name of George Elia, warding off a police dog that jumped on him while he innocently strolled in a Jerusalem street. As he was doing so, a British constable in uniform, mistaking him for a Jew asked "Who gave you permission to speak to another dog?" Then, silencing Elia by shouting "Shut up you dirty bloody Jew," the constable took him into custody where he was beaten unconscious.[16]

In August 1945, U.S. President Harry S. Truman approached Prime Minister Clement Attlee with a suggestion that 100,000 Jewish Holocaust survivors be granted immediate admittance to Palestine. Truman's overture emanated from a study by Earl Harrison, who was instructed to examine the plight of the wartorn Jewish refugees. Harrison discovered that the refugees were living in the same general conditions that prevailed under the Nazis, except that the Americans were not exterminating them.[17] Moved by Harrison's findings, Truman anticipated a positive British response. Not wishing to appear entirely uncooperative, Britain expressed some willingness to permit the entry of Jewish refugees into Palestine, provided that the United States lent armed support to subdue expected Arab resistance. As Britain was well aware, on account of strong Congressional opposition to the postwar stationing of U.S. troops abroad, Truman was unable to meet such a stipulation.[18]

On November 13, 1945, following Truman's refusal to let the UK off the hook, the Labor government agreed to the formation of an Anglo-American Inquiry Committee to study the question of the Jews in Europe, the possibility of their immigration to Palestine and to examine and make recommendations regarding Palestine's political future.[19] Consisting of six members from each country, the Committee commenced its proceedings on January 4, 1946.

Bevin, who had already decided that Palestine ought to have become a United Nations trustee state, as a prelude to its attaining full independence "as a Palestinian, not a Jewish state,"[20] was not at first enthusiastic about sponsoring the Anglo-American inquiry. But once it was determined that it was to be officially advised by Harold Beeley of the British Foreign Office and Evan Wilson of the U.S. State Department, both of whom were renowned for their staunch anti-Zionism,[21] he felt very much more reassured. With revised expectations that the Committee would produce a report in consonance with his own views, he volunteered that if the Committee were to reach a finding unanimously, he would willingly endorse its recommendations.

On April 20, 1946, after a comprehensive inquiry, the Anglo-American Committee delivered its verdict. It proposed that 100,000 displaced Jewish refugees be admitted into Palestine forthwith and that thereafter the Mandatory government should "facilitate Jewish immigration under suitable conditions." It also called for the rescinding of the 1940 land transfer regulations on the grounds that they flagrantly violated the basic principle of nondiscrimination. However, the Committee refrained from calling for the formation of a Jewish state. Rather, it suggested that a future independent Palestine preserve the interests of both Arabs and Jews and that British rule continue, pending the formulation of a UN trusteeship agreement.

On May 1, far from abiding by the unanimous recommendations of the Anglo-American Committee as Bevin had promised, Prime Minister Attlee announced that Britain would only consider implementing them after the Yishuv had completely emasculated itself by surrendering all its weapons. In addition, American military and financial assistance was requested since, according to Bevin, the absorption of the displaced Jews in Palestine was liable to cost the British taxpayers £200 million. As it happened, such a claim was blatantly untrue, for all expenses relating to the transport and settlement of Jewish migrants were exclusively borne by the Zionists.[22]

To make sure that it was fully understood that Britain would certainly not admit 100,000 displaced Jews into Palestine, Bevin went on to assert that a migration of that size would necessitate the deployment of another British division, *which he had no intention of authorizing*.[23] Since such an armed force would have been required to counter the Arabs only, one might well wonder why the complete surrender of Haganah arms was raised as a precondition for Britain's acceptance of the Anglo-American Committee's proposals. Bevin was certainly aware of the fact that General Darcy had testified to the Anglo-American Committee that he could implement a pro-Jewish policy without too much difficulty. If, on the other hand, a pro-Arab orientation were called for, Darcy maintained that at least three military divisions would have been required.[24]

Meanwhile, the national resistance movement intensified its activities. On February 2, 1946, the Irgun and Lehi audaciously raided Palestinian airfields, destroying twelve military airplanes valued at 750,000 Palestinian pounds.[25] Such deeds seriously undermined the oft-repeated assertion that Palestine presented itself as a tranquil and secure location for British bases. Then, on June 16, 1946, the Palmah set out to disable eleven bridges linking Palestine with its neighbors. The following morning, in a well-coordinated mission in which fourteen Palmahniks fell, ten of the bridges were either totally demolished or severely damaged. The next day, forty-five members of Lehi penetrated the Haifa railway workshops, where they wrecked locomotives and valuable machinery. Within the compound, two of the attackers were killed in encounters with sentries and nine more were mowed down by machine gun fire while trying to escape. All but six of the survivors were captured.[26] In the immediate aftermath, British soldiers fired on a group of unarmed Jews. They continued to shoot at them even after they had raised their hands. Two were killed on the spot and one died later as a result of his wounds.[27]

Having decided to repress the Yishuv, Britain swiftly applied draconian countermeasures, which culminated on June 29 (Black Saturday) with the arrest of the entire Zionist Executive currently in Palestine as well as nearly 3,000 others. The Jewish Agency offices were sealed and extensive searches were undertaken in the Yishuv's settlements and in other public institutions. Thirty settlements were ransacked in the quest for arms caches. Only in Kibbutz Yagur was one uncovered. In almost all the settlements in question, property was either looted or needlessly damaged.

Throughout Black Saturday, some troops were particularly abusive. Three kibbutz members were killed and many others were grievously injured. Rabbi Yehuda Fishman, the acting head of the Jewish Agency, who was among those detained, requested permission to walk to a police station on account of it being contrary to Jewish law to drive on the Sabbath. Instead, he was struck and forced into a car. As one lout of a soldier exclaimed, "I walloped him."[28]

Being unable to elicit Jewish quislings who would do its bidding and not wishing to jeopardize U.S.-UK relations by crushing the Yishuv with unbridled savagery, Britain gradually relented. Most of the detainees were freed within a couple of months and the rest by the following November. The full release of all the Zionists was secured by a Jewish Agency assurance, given in October, that the Haganah would refrain from further anti-British military activities.

On July 22, a wing of the King David Hotel was blown up by the Irgun. Six stories, which housed, among other things, the General Military Headquarters, collapsed under the force of the explosion. The hotel, as aptly described by Menachem Begin, had been "developed into a veritable fortress," closely guarded and protected.[29] Disguised as Arab delivery men, Irgun operatives placed milk cans, packed with a compound of 350 kilograms of TNT and gelignite, in a basement underneath the area to be demolished. Telephone warnings indicating that the hotel was about to be destroyed, were dispatched to the hotel, the *Palestine Post* and the French Consulate-General situated in the hotel's immediate vicinity. They were not heeded; consequently, there were unintended casualties amounting to ninety-one deaths and forty-five injuries. British, Jews and Arabs alike were among the victims. Although the bombing originally had prior Haganah approval,[30] the large death toll effectively resulted in the Haganah suspending combined operations with the Irgun and Lehi.

Seeking to track down members of the Irgun, some 20,000 troops converged on Tel Aviv where a twenty-four-hour curfew was enforced for a four-day period. Curfew violators were threatened with being shot on sight.[31] The soldiers conducted systematic house-to-house searches, but there was little to see for their efforts. The Yishuv took all this in stride, but what really rankled was a nonfraternization order issued by Lieutenant-General Sir Evelyn Barker, the British commander in Palestine. Barker viewed all Jews in Palestine as Irgun accomplices. In prohibiting social contact of any kind between British troops and Jews, he went on to express his desire to punish "the Jews in a way the race dislikes as much as any, by striking at their pockets and showing our contempt for them."[32]

Within Palestine, both the Irgun and Lehi stepped up their anti-British attacks. Having failed to stifle terrorist activities by the conventional use of emergency powers, the military authorities decided to employ additional means of deterrence. One of these included the administration of corporal punishment. The Irgun announced that the Yishuv would not tolerate such a barbaric infringement on human rights and dignity, and that should the army lay its hands on any Jew, it would respond appropriately. In simple terms, its message, "If you whip us, we will whip you," was inscribed on a multitude of street posters. On December 29, 1946, ignoring the Irgun's warnings, Benjamin Kimchin, a Jewish lad of seventeen, was given eighteen lashes in a Jerusalem jail. The Irgun promptly seized a British army major and three NCOs and paid them in kind. Thereafter, the British no longer inflicted corporal punishment on captive insurgents.

Ben Gurion, who was abroad at the time of Black Saturday, naturally evaded arrest. On August 1, he summoned the remnant of the Zionist Executive to Paris for a meeting. It was decided to modify the clear and uncompromising stand of the Biltmore Program by proposing a viable Jewish state, not in the whole of Palestine but in an adequate area of the country.[33] When the Biltmore Program was formulated in May 1942, the Zionists were still hoping that, in the aftermath of the war, millions of European Jews would survive and would eagerly migrate to Palestine. Now that only a small contingent was left, dreams of the Jews rapidly becoming a majority within Palestine as a whole, evaporated. Reviewing the situation more realistically, it was thought that perhaps the central hilly regions, which were thickly populated by Arabs, ought to be conceded, with the Jews assuming control of the remainder of the country.[34] Nahum Goldmann was authorized to approach the American administration to notify them of the Zionists' change of position, which, as it happened, was also partly motivated by a desire to appear more reasonable to the U.S. administration.[35] A few weeks later this resulted in a public statement by President Truman, in which he not only reiterated his call for Britain to allow 100,000 displaced Jews to migrate to Palestine but he also endorsed the Zionist Executive's new policy.

During the same period, Herbert Morrison, a British minister, explained to the House of Commons that an agreement had been reached, based on a report of a joint UK-U.S. committee of experts.[36] These experts were supposed to find common ground for implementing the Anglo-American Committee's proposals, but British civil servants subverted the proceedings to further the Labor government's own narrow objectives. The Committee's recommendations, which became known as the Morrison-Grady plan, provided for a federal Palestine state, headed by a high commissioner with authority to determine immigration. Within the federation, allowance was made for a Jewish and an Arab sector, plus two other regions (one of which included Jerusalem) that would have remained strictly within the British domain. The Jewish-designated area was the smallest ever proposed, but it would initially have been entitled to absorb 100,000 migrants. Thereafter, migratory inflows were to have been set according to the sector's economic circumstances.

Considering, among other things, that the Morrison-Grady plan explicitly excluded the entire Negev from Jewish control, the Zionists decided to expand their foothold there to strengthen their claims to that part of the country. Already, three Jewish observation points, established in 1942, were in place as well as two kibbutzim, Yad Mordechai and Nizanim. On October 6, 1946, after some careful planning, eleven new settlements were simultaneously erected. They were widely dispersed and, with only thirty settlers at each location, they were exposed to considerable security risks. A water pipeline began to be laid in January 1947, which was completed shortly before Israel became independent in May 1948. Within the period of 1946–1947, a total of eighteen new settlements were founded in the Negev.[37] Throughout Palestine as a whole, twenty-six new Jewish settlements arose in 1946, followed by fifteen a year later.[38] The unstinting efforts of the Negev settlers were reflected in a dramatic transformation of the land they cultivated. By 1947, their ability to make the desert bloom greatly impressed a UN investigative commission and was instrumental in ensuring that the Negev was included within the bounds of a future Jewish state. As Jorge Garcia-Granados, a member of the UN commission, put it, "When we visited the Negev, we realized how much the Jews could do with that wasteland, how eager they were to develop it, and how little the Arabs could do, or wished to do, with it."[39]

Neither the Jews nor the Arabs found any merit in the Morrison-Grady proposals; neither did President Truman, who on August 12 formally informed Prime Minister Attlee that they were unacceptable. This did not deter Bevin from presenting them at a British-orchestrated Palestine conference that met in London between September 10 and October 2, 1946 and then from January 17 to February 12, 1947. This conference was boycotted by the Jewish Agency but some of its members were available in London and their views were informally sought. Official Zionist opinion began to harden. In December 1946, gathering for the first time since the war, the Twenty-second Zionist Congress formally confirmed its adherence to the full Biltmore Program and declared that only through the formation of a Jewish state would the Mandate realize its original goals and be able to be terminated.

With an agreement between Arabs and Jews proving to be elusive, and with the United States adamant that it would not back the British position, Bevin, on February 18, 1947, announced that his government would refer the entire Palestine issue to the United Nations.

One can only surmise what drove Britain to appear to wash its hands of Palestine, after it had doggedly clung to the notion that it had to maintain a foothold there for strategic and geopolitical reasons. For one thing, the terrorist campaign had taken its toll. In the period from May 1945 to the end of the Mandate in May 1948, 338 British citizens met a violent death at the hands of the Irgun and Lehi.[40] As a result, the British press and various politicians, Churchill among them, began to clamor for "bringing the boys home." One hundred thousand British soldiers were stationed in Palestine, making the armed forces there four times as large as they had been at the height of the Arab revolt in the late 1930s. This cost Britain dearly. Between the time the Labor Party took office until the Mandate ended, it has been estimated that the budgetary expenses, associated with British rule in Palestine exceeded $220 million (US). It was not simply the maintenance of regular troops that ate into the budget, but the weighty burdens borne by combating illegal immigration. These entailed constant warship and aircraft patrols off the Palestine coast, the transporting of more than 50,000 intercepted migrants to Cyprus and the outlays associated with detaining them there. Such activities drained the treasury of £30 million a year, which was a colossal sum in those days, especially when Britain's financial reserves had to be propped up by the Americans. Within Britain itself, the economy was in a deep crisis. Coal supplies fell far below current needs, stocks of wheat dwindled, potatoes disappeared from the shops, factories closed for want of fuel and unemployment was on the increase. By the beginning of February, electricity cuts were imposed on the whole of southern England.[41] In short, Britain's presence in the Palestine quagmire was beginning to be less and less cost effective.

Yet Bevin remained reluctant to relinquish the country. In requesting UN involvement, he assumed that superpower rivalry would prevent the emergence of a consensus. With no alternative solution forthcoming, he expected the United States to be more accommodating to Britain's point of view and the Arabs and Jews less obstructionist. That would then have paved the way for him to implement a plan of his own choosing. On May 29, Bevin told the Labor Party annual conference that he would not be bound by any UN decision unless it were unanimous, and that it was a sure thing that such a proviso would never be fulfilled.[42]

Even were the UN to reach a general agreement, Bevin hedged his bets. At a press conference on April 4, the British UN delegation stated that it was not giving the world body carte blanche vis-à-vis Palestine. Rather, as Arthur Creech-Jones, the colonial secretary, maintained, it was merely seeking advice "as to how the Mandate can be administered."[43]

Accepting Britain's formal request, a special session of the UN General Assembly was convened between April 28 and May 15, 1947, at Flushing Meadow, near Lake Success in New York City. Sir Alexander Cadogan, Britain's UN envoy, requested that the session be devoted exclusively to the selection of a United Nations Special Committee on Palestine (UNSCOP) and to determine its charter. Instead of simply being restricted to reviewing alternative regimes suitable for introduction into Palestine, as Britain would have preferred, UNSCOP was commissioned to examine the "problem of Palestine and all questions and matters associated with it," including the problem of displaced European Jews. The Committee was not expected to confine its investigations to Palestine but "to every place deemed to be necessary."[44] Finally, the composition of UNSCOP was to consist of eleven members drawn from Australia,

Canada, Czechoslovakia, Guatemala, India, Iran (Persia), the Netherlands, Peru, Sweden, Uruguay, and Yugoslavia plus a nonvoting delegate representing the UN.

During the special session, delegates of the Jewish Agency and the Palestinian Arab Higher Committee were allowed to address the UN's political committee. Arab spokesmen lost little time in showing their true colors. Amil Gouri of the Arab Higher Committee, in defending the Palestinians' supreme leader, the Nazi collaborator and mufti, Haj Amin al Husseini, mistakenly thought that a dose of religious anti-Semitism would go down well. He complained that the mufti "was attacked by a representative of the very nation that crucified the Christian Messiah."[45] For good measure, Amil Gouri emphasized that the Arabs would "refuse to consider *any* solution which even implies the loss of their sovereignty over *any part* of their country."[46] He was followed by a member of the Syrian legation who explained that, under an Arab Palestinian regime, the Jews would all be expelled to their countries of origin. Such remarks planted seeds in many UN members' minds that the Jews could not be entrusted to Arab lordship and that awarding them a state of their own made both political and ethical sense. A day before the special session closed, this tendency was strongly, if not surprisingly, reinforced by Andrei Gromyko, the Soviet Union's UN diplomat. Deviating from the Soviet Union's traditional anti-Zionist position, Gromyko declared that "the aspirations of a significant sector of the Jewish people in the world are linked with Palestine and its future. The UN's investigative committee cannot ignore the aspirations of the Jews for their own state." What is more, he asserted that if a binational state were not a realistic proposition, "It would be necessary to consider a solution involving partitioning Palestine into two independent states."[47]

With prospects of the formation of a Jewish state seeming to be increasingly feasible, the Executive of the Jewish Agency wished to ensure that the Yishuv presented a united front before the UNSCOP team. In pressing their case for all of Palestine to be transformed into a Jewish state, they also wished to let it be known that if worse came to worst, they were prepared to accept some compromise formula that at least awarded them initial sovereignty in a reasonable part of the country. To minimize the submission of conflicting entreaties from within the Yishuv, the cooperation of the non-Zionist devout Agudat Israel association was sought. For its part, Agudat Israel wanted to be assured that in a future Jewish state, matters of personal status would be regulated according to religious practices, the Sabbath would be upheld, state institutions would ensure that all food supplied was strictly kosher and that the Agudat Israel would have autonomous control over its own educational bodies. The Executive of the Jewish Agency agreed to Agudat Israel's requests and, as a result, Rabbi Levin of Agudat Israel firmly advocated the case for Jewish statehood.[48]

While the UNSCOP delegation was collecting evidence in Palestine, three members of the Irgun—Avshalom Aviv, Meir Nakar and Yaacov Weiss—were sentenced to death. They had been involved in blasting open the walls of the Acre prison, where, on April 16, four of their comrades—Dov Gruner, Dov

Rosenbaum, Mordechai Alkoshi and Eliezer Kashani—were hanged. UNSCOP requested clemency to avert "possible unfavorable repercussions," but the British were in no mood for compromises and executed the three on July 23. They each walked to the gallows with their heads held high singing "Hatik-vah." Twice before, the Irgun was able to secure the suspension of death sentences by holding British soldiers as hostages and by threatening to execute them, should their comrades not be granted leniency. On this occasion, the government paid no heed to similar warnings. On July 24, in revenge for what was regarded as the murdering of prisoners of war, the Irgun hanged two British sergeants. While one of the bodies was being taken down, it fell onto and detonated a mine. (It was hoped that a third British soldier would be killed to level the score.)[49] The incident was widely viewed with abhorrence and stimulated anti-Semitic acts of arson and vandalism in Britain. Within Palestine, some British police and troops ran amok. Six Jews were randomly shot to death and at least twenty-four others were wounded.[50]

One other dramatic event unfolded while UNSCOP was in Palestine. In July 1947, a Chesapeake Bay ferryboat originally named *President Garfield* when it was built in 1918, and then renamed *Exodus* in 1947, left Port de Bouc, near Marseilles, for Palestine, with 4,500 Jewish Holocaust survivors on board. It was soon traced and escorted across the Mediterranean by the British Navy. About twelve miles off the coast of Palestine—that is, while still in international waters—it was surrounded by five destroyers and a cruiser. The *Exodus* was peppered with gunfire and then two destroyers approached it and rammed it from opposite sides, smashing into its upper deck onto which a group of sailors sprang. Some of them made for the pilot house where they clubbed the ship's captain to death. Two other Jews, including a fifteen-year-old boy, were also killed. Many more were wounded. The continued ramming of the *Exodus* threatened to sink it. This had the desired effect of bringing about its surrender. In Haifa, the British transferred the refugees onto three other vessels which made for Port de Bouc. In France, the passengers refused to disembark and the French were not prepared to compel them to do so. The ship was then ordered to proceed to Hamburg and in early September, a week before the UN began to consider UNSCOP's report, the refugees were dragged, kicking and screaming, into a detention camp in the heartland of Germany. All this made a deep impression on the UNSCOP visitors and was partly instrumental in convincing most members of the need to allow Jews into Palestine. The incident also generated a wave of anti-British sentiment in the United States and France. For some mysterious reason, the British invited scores of journalists to witness the forceful disembarkation of Jews onto their arch tormentors' soil. Almost all the reporters were sickened by the spectacle, with some Americans shouting "Stop it, stop it." The British officer in charge cautioned them that if they did not cease to voice their anger, their professional licenses would be revoked.[51]

Also not without repercussions were a series of demonstrations, organized in the same period by the Palestinian Arabs. These were held in Haifa, Jaffa and

The *Exodus* and some of its passengers at Haifa (Central Zionist Archives).

Jerusalem, and in one of them, a message was relayed from the mufti informing his supporters that the "Zionists must not have an *inch* of this country. It is your duty to gain back every *inch* of your land."[52] Such an unyielding approach, just when the Yishuv had indicated that it would be amenable to a partition compromise, encouraged the majority of UNSCOP to think along similar lines.

By August 31, 1947, UNSCOP issued both a minority and a majority report. The minority report (supported by India, Iran and Yugoslavia) proposed that, after a three-year period during which the country would be placed under UN supervision, Palestine ought to become an independent federal state. Jews and Arabs alike would have certain national rights but the federal authority would, among other things, control immigration, defense and foreign affairs. The Arab sector would encompass most of the territory, including Jerusalem and the Negev, and the lower legislative body would be elected on the basis of proportional representation. As a corollary of all this, the Jewish National Home would be stillborn. However, the majority (that is Canada, Czechoslovakia, Guatemala, the Netherlands, Peru, Sweden and Uruguay)[53] found in favor of partitioning Palestine into two independent states—one Jewish, the other Arab—with close economic ties between them (see map). Jerusalem was to be placed under an international trusteeship and the two new independent states were to see the light of day by September 1949.

As already mentioned, the Palestinian Arabs were categorically against any form of partition, or any other arrangement that would have meant sharing the

The UN Partition Scheme

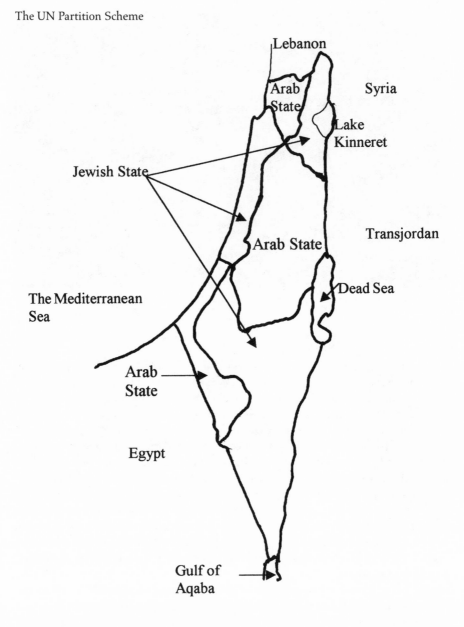

country with the Jews. Outnumbering the Jews by a ratio of two to one and counting on neighboring Arab states for direct military intervention, they believed that they had more than sufficient means to prevail by force. The Zionists, by contrast, went along with the majority report, even though it excluded large parts of the Galilee and Jerusalem and its environs, all of which contained

Jewish suburbs or settlements. Other serious shortcomings of the partition proposal, from the Jewish point of view, involved prospective borders that were extremely difficult to defend, the linkage of the Jewish state in a Palestine economic union and the sharing of a common currency, which would have restricted the state's economic freedom of action. On the other hand, the land designated to the Zionists, which included the Negev, was far more extensive than what Britain had offered in 1937 when it first toyed with the concept of partition. It also had the advantage that the Jews would have immediately formed a majority, albeit a very slender one, within the precincts of their proposed state.[54] The Zionist acceptance of the majority report was decided on September 2 by the Movement's executive committee, which met in Zurich. It was not endorsed unanimously but certainly by a very wide margin of fifty-one in favor to sixteen against. The naysayers consisted of Hashomer Hatzair, which still held out for a binational state, Ahdut Ha'Avodah and the Revisionists, who had returned to the mainstream Zionist fold in 1946. The latter two organizations remained committed to a Jewish state in all of Palestine. (In January 1948, Hashomer Hatzair and Ahdut Ha'Avodah merged to form a party called *Mapam* [United Workers' Party], which fully supported the establishment of a Jewish state in Palestine despite its members' earlier reservations regarding partition.)

On September 16, 1946, UNSCOP's findings were tabled at a session of the UN General Assembly. An ad hoc committee consisting of delegates from all UN members was appointed to examine UNSCOP's submission and to formulate its own recommendations for a plenary session of the General Assembly.

Although the Zionists were prepared to accept UNSCOP's majority report, it was by no means clear that the UN General Assembly would. Apart from outspoken opposition by the Arabs, most Asian countries and Britain, the stand that the United States might take seemed uncertain. The U.S. State Department and the military establishment were not in favor of an independent Jewish state. They believed that American support of the Zionist position would threaten U.S. access to Middle East oil and that alienated Arabs would throw in their lot with the Soviet Union. Truman himself was buffeted between the conflicting views of his State Department and a strident Zionist lobby. On October 9, after some hesitation, he ultimately declared in favor of partition.

A short while before the UN General Assembly vote for the partition of Palestine was due, the Zionists learned that the U.S. delegation, in its desire to sweeten the pill for the Arabs, was bent on removing the southern part of the Negev from the area to be allotted to the Jews. Desperate to forestall such a move, Weizmann went to America to persuade President Truman to abide by the essence of UNSCOP's original proposal.[55] After patiently hearing out Weizmann, Truman reassured him that the Jews would not be deprived of the section of the Negev providing access to the Gulf of Aqaba.

On November 25, the Ad Hoc Committee endorsed the partition proposal, with some minor modifications (such as the removal of Beersheba from the fu-

ture Jewish state), by a vote of twenty-five to thirteen with seventeen abstentions. Although it represented a sweeping victory for the Zionists, it fell short
of the two-thirds majority required for subsequent ratification by the General
Assembly to which the Ad Hoc Committee reported. Some member states had
not determined their final position and this provided the Zionists and their allies with a short interval in which to lobby energetically. Similarly, the Arabs
and their supporters also made good use of the time available. They were anticipating widespread Latin American backing on account of the Vatican's misgivings about Zionism. To add to the general uncertainty, the United States,
although committed to partition, was loath to act as the Zionists' advocate.
Only in the final days, in response to a directive by Truman, did the U.S. UN
delegates solicit votes. This was done in a rather perfunctory manner and without any heavy-handed methods.[56] Undersecretary of State Robert Lovett wrote
that Truman had issued strict instructions to the U.S. UN delegation not "to use
threats or improper pressure of any kind on other delegations to vote for the
majority report favoring partition."[57] In some countries a decision was very
much in the balance. France, which was concerned about possible negative re-
verberations in its North African Muslim colonies, was not inclined to favor
partition. Indeed, members of the Jewish Agency learned that the French foreign office had prepared a telegram that was to be wired to its UN delegation on
the voting day formally instructing it to abstain.[58] To counter that, Leon Blum,
a former French prime minister, pleaded the Zionist case with his president. In
Belgium, powerful Catholic interests seemed to presage lack of support,
whereas Ethiopia, which felt some sympathy for the Jews but which was subject to strong Arab pressure, was in a genuine quandary. A day before the final
vote was taken, the president of the General Assembly, Oswaldo Aranha, concluded that there was insufficient endorsement for partition.[59] Certainly, the
matter was not cut and dried. The Arabs had left no stone unturned and, considering their wartime associations with the Axis powers, they brazenly resorted to the libelous charge that Zionism was a form of Nazism, a charge that
has periodically been raised ever since. Referring to the Iraqi and Syrian UN
delegates who articulated such a calumny, Weizmann questioned their qualifications to pass judgment on Zionism, though he did "not dispute the right of
those two gentlemen to speak with intimacy on the nature of Nazism."[60]

When the UN General Assembly finally met on November 29, 1947, partition was approved by a vote of thirty-three to thirteen with ten abstentions,
which ensured the necessary two-thirds majority.[61] At the eleventh hour,
France and Belgium provided their assent and intensive last-minute Zionist efforts to win over the Philippines, Liberia and Haiti, which had not previously
favored partition, paid off. The Ethiopian delegate, who expressed solidarity
with both the Arabs and Jews, abstained.

The horrors of the Holocaust played little, if any, part in the voting behavior
of member states. Russia endorsed partition as a means of evicting Britain from
Palestine. South American countries did not subscribe to the view that they had

a moral obligation to support the Zionists because of Jewish suffering. Nor did Britain and France. Even within the United States, where internal Jewish pressures were most strongly felt, opponents of partition from the State Department, the military establishment and oil companies represented a potent threat to Zionist interests. In fact, as already mentioned, the Holocaust, by reducing European Jewry to a small fraction of its former size, cut the ground under the Zionists' feet in relation to their earlier claims that they needed Palestine in its entirety as a homeland for millions of persecuted Jews. What did seem to sway both the majority of UNSCOP and the UN General Assembly was the vibrant democratic and progressive society that the Yishuv had created and the patent injustice of consigning Jews to a minority status within an inevitably reactionary and repressive Palestinian unitary state.[62]

When word of how the vote went reached Palestine, the Yishuv erupted into a joyous celebration, with Jews dancing and singing in the streets. Unlike most of the revelers, Ben Gurion was not inclined to indulge in excessive gaiety. Later he recorded, "It never occurred to me that simply on account of a decision to form a state, that the state would arise. I realized that before that, we would have to endure severe trials, such as we had never experienced in the past."[63] Be that as it may, the UN decision had extremely important ramifications. It made it next to impossible for Britain to renege on a commitment, which it had subsequently given, to terminate the Mandate and withdraw from Palestine. It aroused world Jewry to rally to the aid of the Yishuv in terms of generous financial assistance and internally it encouraged people to heed the general dictates of its national councils, which were perceived as their government in the making. Of no small importance, it facilitated the eventual state's recognition in the international arena, which ultimately helped to ease some of Israel's pressing trade and supply problems.[64]

As Ben Gurion feared, the day following the fateful UN decision, some of the grim realities of life in Palestine once more came to light. Under the guiding hand of the Arab Higher Committee, the Arabs declared a three-day protest strike, which rapidly degenerated into rioting; by the end of the first day, seven Jews had been killed.

The civil unrest in Palestine marked the beginning of a long chain of Arab-Jewish internecine strife, which continued unabated during the rest of the Mandate. Local Arab protagonists were reinforced by the arrival of outside volunteers. At the beginning of 1948, four separate Arab forces were stationed in the country. In the north, under the Syrian officer Fawzi al Kauwakji, and consisting mainly of non-Palestinians, the Arab Liberation Army encamped. (Earlier, in July 1947, Kauwakji defined the coming battle between Jews and Arabs as a total one, with only one possible outcome: "the extermination of all Jews, whether they be in Palestine or in the rest of Arab countries.")[65] John Glubb (a British officer who became known as Glubb Pasha) commanded the Transjordan Arab Legion, which held ground in the Hebron and Ramalla region. The mufti's cousin, Abdul-el Kader Husseini, and his comrade, Hassan Salame, di-

Crowd in Tel Aviv celebrating the UN partition resolution (Central Zionist Archives).

rected local militia in the Jerusalem and Ramla-Jaffa sector, respectively. In the Negev, there was a band of volunteers from the Egyptian Moslem Brotherhood. Fortunately for the Jews, these forces were fragmented by keen rivalry and thinly disguised mutual enmity, which meant that their efforts were rarely co-ordinated. However, their presence in Palestine emboldened local Arabs to attack Jewish positions and to lay siege to Jerusalem.

For the most part, the center of gravity of the conflict revolved around the access roads to Jewish settlements and to Jerusalem. Jewish transport convoys were heavily attacked and only with extreme difficulty and loss of life did desperately needed supplies reach their destinations. The perils that Jewish drivers encountered were needlessly exacerbated by the authorities constantly impounding their weapons. Even when licensed guards were permitted to accompany a vehicle, the guards were required to ride alongside it, in an open jeep![66]

By the beginning of 1948 the Haganah consisted of the Palmah, which maintained a permanently mobilized force of about 2,000 fighters, a small number of specially trained "field soldiers" available for service on call but who otherwise continued with their normal civilian life and the Hebrew Settlement Police, which included 1,658 men officially licensed to bear arms.[67] On account of both severe budgetary constraints and serious shortfalls in weapons (until late April, the Jews had only one rifle for every two of its soldiers),[68] the Yishuv initially was able to mobilize no more than 30 percent of those who responded to the

Haganah's recruitment drive.[69] However, by February, the pace of mobilization began to gather momentum. Lacking coercive governmental powers, the Yishuv was unable to impose a compulsory draft. Nonetheless, potential shirkers were subject to strong moral suasion, which involved publishing their names in the newspapers and obtaining their dismissal from employment. The Haganah's ranks were also augmented by the timely arrival from Western countries of volunteer Jewish ex-servicemen and by a Jewish Agency decision, taken in March 1948, to transfer new migrants of military age directly to Haganah camps.

Having been outmaneuvered in the UN General Assembly and having determined to vacate Palestine, the British authorities virtually abdicated their responsibility to maintain law and order there. Many police and army units aided and abetted Arab insurgents. To its utmost discredit, Britain refrained from ejecting sections of the Arab Legion, which had taken up positions in the western part of Palestine. On April 16, 1948, in response to international concern, Sir Alexander Cadogon informed the UN Security Council that the Arab Legion would be withdrawn before the Mandate officially terminated. A similar pledge was given by Bevin in the House of Commons on April 28, but when British forces finally withdrew, the Arab Legion was well entrenched around Jericho and Hebron, with small bridgeheads in Beersheba, Lod and the hills between Nablus and Jerusalem. David Kimche noted that that was "probably the first—and, we may hope, the last—time in the history of the British Empire that a foreign army with hostile intentions was allowed to camp and organize itself undisturbed on territory for which Britain was responsible."[70]

Nor were the British prepared to facilitate the entry of a UN Operations Committee, which was to prepare the groundwork for the formation of both the Jewish and Arab states. Among its various duties, it was to supervise the formation of suitable militias, so that, upon the Mandate's termination, appropriate law-enforcement agents would be in place. On January 31, in total disregard of the letter and spirit of UN resolutions, Sir Alexander Cadogon announced that Britain would only deal with the committee two weeks before its final evacuation and, even then, permission for the constitution of the militias would be withheld while the Mandate was still in force. As for Jewish immigration, Britain intended to apply existing restrictions until the very end.

The Arabs had no difficulty in securing arms. Britain readily furnished the Arab Legion with all its military requirements and willingly sold heavy artillery and armor, including Sherman tanks, to both Iraq and Egypt.[71] By contrast, the Yishuv was hard-pressed to obtain even the most basic weapons. Shortly after the UN partition resolution, the United States imposed an embargo on armament sales to the Middle East and, as the Yishuv scrambled to find alternative sources of supply, the British shamelessly censured the Czech government for its willingness to help the Zionists. While the British were not for want of resources to deprive the Yishuv of its defensive needs that were arriving by sea, they seemed to lack the manpower to intercept the transfer of weapons to Arabs across Palestine's land borders. On February 1, 1948, a unit from Syria consisting of 700 Arab fighters, traveling in twenty Syrian-licensed trucks and bearing rifles and mortars, *openly* crossed into Palestine. As Jon and David Kimche observed, "No one objected. No one interfered."[72] Two weeks later, these very forces unsuccessfully attacked the Jewish settlement of Tirat Zvi.

Outlying settlements that were directly assailed by Arab forces generally succeeded in holding them at bay. The four settlements of the Etzion Bloc (*Gush Etzion*)—Kfar Etzion (founded in 1943, near a settlement that was abandoned in the 1929 riots), Masuot, Ein Tzurim and Revadim, all of which were located south of Jerusalem—constituted an exception. At first, on January 15, 1948, with help from a small Palmah detachment, they were able to repel an attack on Kfar Etzion. The Arabs, led by Abdul el-Kader el Husseini, actually managed to breach the settlement's outer defenses but were routed by a counterattack in which 120 of their men fell. The next day, the Haganah in Jerusalem sent off thirty-five reinforcements. As they were winding their way through wadis, a shepherd boy alerted the Arabs to their presence and, confronted by superior force, all were annihilated. This incident sent a shock wave through the Yishuv, temporarily undermining its self-confidence.[73]

Eventually, on May 12, the Etzion Bloc was stormed by the British-drilled troops of the Arab Legion, with the additional support of thousands of armed local Arabs. After a raging battle and the near depletion of the defenders' ammunition, the attackers, who were in possession of armored vehicles and heavy guns, burst into Kfar Etzion. In their wake were hordes of Arab villagers who massacred 127 settlers (including twenty-one women). Only four Jews were spared.[74] On May 14, the very day when the State of Israel was declared, the remaining three settlements succumbed. Their surviving 320 members, including eighty-five women were taken as war prisoners.[75]

In the first quarter of 1948, as Palestine became increasingly embroiled in bloody turmoil, U.S. support for partition began to waiver. The moment the Zionists sensed that the administration was preparing to backtrack, they clamored for an audience with the president. However, having been affronted by the brazen and abrasive behavior of some of their spokesmen, Truman refused to meet with any of them. In desperation, they summoned Eddie Jacobson to intercede on their behalf. Jacobson, who had previously been Truman's business partner in a haberdashery store, remained one of his closest personal associates. On March 13, in his encounter with his old pal, Jacobson found Truman to be uncharacteristically embittered, complaining of how mean and disrespectful some of the pillars of the Jewish community were toward him. Noting a small statue of Andrew Jackson in Truman's office, Jacobson remarked that he appreciated how much Truman admired Jackson and then went on to state that he too had a hero, that is Weizmann, the "greatest Jew who ever lived." Calling up all the debts of an old friendship, Jacobson admonished Truman for refusing to see Weizmann, saying, "It does not sound like you, Harry because I thought that you could take this stuff they have been handing out to you."[76] Truman, looking away, pondered for a while. He then suddenly spun around in his swivel chair and blurted out, "You win, you baldheaded son of a bitch. I will see him." Twenty-five minutes were allocated to the meeting with Weizmann, which took place on March 18, 1948. As the discussion proceeded Truman mellowed considerably and extended the time for an additional twenty-five minutes. Warming to Weizmann, whom he greatly respected, he gave him full assurances of his support and of his willingness to recognize a Jewish state should one be declared but requested that the conversation and its details be kept strictly confidential.

The very next day, on March 19, 1948, Senator Warren Austin informed the UN Security Council that a peaceful resolution of the conflict was seemingly not feasible and therefore the Operations Committee should discontinue its efforts to implement the November General Assembly Palestine Resolution. Truman, who had not previously vetted Austin's text, was highly embarrassed. Above all, he feared that Weizmann would regard him as a liar. Nonetheless, at that point, he did not intervene.

There were at least two factors behind the efforts undertaken by the U.S. State Department to place the UN November partition resolution on hold. The first relates to a renewed effort on the part of both the oil lobby and State Department officials to oppose U.S. backing for the formation of a Jewish state on the basis of perceived threats to America's commercial and strategic interests. In the second instance, on account of the unfolding events in Palestine, there were reasonable grounds for assuming that the Jews were about to be completely routed and possibly wiped out. It was believed that such a disaster could be averted by freezing the partition process. In that way, it was assumed, the Arabs would no longer feel the need to resort to arms.

It is by no means difficult to envision why in March 1948, outside observers in the United States and elsewhere judged the Jewish strategic position to be grim. Up to then, the Yishuv, which had been losing a large number of people per month,[77] had done little more than parry Arab attacks on its settlements and population centers. (Ben Gurion estimated that in the period between the UN partition decision on November 29, 1947 and the proclamation of the Jewish state on May 14, 1948, over 900 Jews were killed.)[78] On March 11, an Arab parked a van loaded with explosives in front of the Jewish Agency's headquarters in Jerusalem. Moments later, a violent blast not only shattered the building but also the confidence of the Yishuv that its key institutions were relatively secure. On March 26, a Jewish convoy returning from the Etzion Bloc was ambushed. Many were killed and those who survived did so as a result of the British coming to their rescue. (The price that the British exacted was the confiscation of the Jews' weapons and the transfer of the same to the Arabs.)[79] Three days later, another Jewish convoy traveling in the western Galilee was surrounded by Arab bands and, in the ensuing battle, forty Jews met their death. Then on March 30, on the winding ascent to Jerusalem, below the steep, wooded slopes of Bab-el Wad, the largest Jewish convoy ever mounted came under the withering fire of Abdul el-Kader el Husseini's forces. Dozens of vehicles were destroyed, Jewish casualties were considerable and access to Jerusalem was cut off. As Colonel Lund, a Norwegian member of the UN mission in Palestine saw things, the situation of the Yishuv was "worse than that of Norway in 1940."[80]

On account of the Soviet Union's opposition, the Security Council did not comply with Austin's suggestion, but it agreed to convene a special session of the General Assembly to reconsider the Palestine issue. Austin then articulated the U.S. State Department's alternative proposal, which entailed a UN trustee-ship covering all of Palestine and administered by a governor. Not only would such a move have represented an unwarranted disregard of what should have been taken as a binding UN resolution, but the plan with which Austin toyed was far less generous to the Jews than what even the British had previously suggested. It made no allowance for regularizing Jewish immigration, it did not include internal Jewish and Arab autonomous zones and it did not specify a time limit for the trusteeship's duration. Austin's proposal formed the basis of discussion in a specially convened General Assembly session, which met on April 16. Although the Assembly generally took a dim view of the U.S. trustee-ship scheme, it appointed a subcommittee to discuss a provisional international regime for Palestine.

During the month of April, while the UN was preoccupied with reappraising its position on Palestine, the tide in that country's "civil war" began to turn in favor of the Jews. As already mentioned, up to then the Haganah had refrained from attacking Arab targets. One consideration related to fears of provoking re-taliation on the part of the British, fears with which the Arabs seldom had to contend. There were certainly no lack of grounds for believing the British to be willing and able to hinder the Yishuv's fighting capacity. For example, during the opening weeks of hostilities in Jerusalem, a British patrol detained four members of the Haganah, disarmed them and then dropped them off in an Arab-controlled zone in the Old City, where they were instantly killed.[81] The Haganah was compelled to continue running as an underground organization, while the Arabs *openly* went about assembling fighting units across Palestine as a whole. But as the British presence in Palestine lessened, consequent on a steady evacuation, the likelihood of Britain foiling Jewish initiatives waned. Second, to refute allegations that the proposed Jewish state would be indefensi-ble, it was decided that no Jewish settlement or suburb would be yielded. This meant that the limited number of armed fighters at the Yishuv's disposal had to be spread thinly, precluding the Jews from amassing concentrated formations necessary to launch effective assaults. Only once the general mobilization of the Yishuv was put into high gear, the new recruits provided with basic train-ing and some additional armaments procured could the Haganah begin con-templating a series of new offensives.

On March 31, in a meeting with the Haganah's high command, Ben Gurion, who in December 1946 was charged with overall responsibility for the Yishuv's defense, called for a sharp military thrust to open the road to Jerusalem. Had the besieged city not been able to receive fresh stocks of fuel and food, its inhabitants would have been hard-pressed to sustain themselves. Supplies of water stored in renovated reservoirs were doled out daily on the basis of ten liters per person.[82] Likewise, bread was rationed. Neither meat, fish nor fruit was available and only a limited amount of milk and eggs were on hand for children and the sick. Responding to Ben Gurion's call, Yigal Yadin, the chief of staff, proposed that 500 men be made available but, to everyone's amazement, Ben Gurion insisted on no less than 1,500, the largest deployment of force that the Haganah had yet assembled. To meet the quota, units were drawn from numerous other fronts. That very night, the first consignment of arms from Czechoslovakia arrived in a Skymaster plane that had evaded British surveillance to land at a secret destination. It carried 200 rifles, 40 machine guns and thousands of bullets. All of these were expeditiously unloaded and forwarded to the assembled assault troops, who on the following morning, April 1, launched Operation Nachshon. After ten days of grueling combat, in which the Haganah's fortunes fluctuated considerably, the Yishuv's efforts were crowned with success. Free entry into Jerusalem was secured and three large convoys, one of which consisted of more than 250 vehicles, ferried needed food and ammunition to the city. However, by the end of April, the Arabs had regained some of the steep promontories overlooking the road arterial into Jerusalem and the city was once again fully encircled.

On the night of April 4, while almost all of the Haganah's reserves were tied up in Operation Nachshon, the Liberation Army's commander Fawzi el-Kauwakji gathered a force numbering a thousand men and attacked Kibbutz Mishmar Ha'Emek, which initially only mustered close to 170 defenders. The settlement, which lay alongside the main road to Haifa, guarded the approach to the Jezreel Valley. Bombarding the settlement with 75mm guns, Kauwakji, who took the defenders by surprise, failed to press his advantage. A twenty-four-hour truce, arranged by a British officer, enabled the kibbutz to summon reinforcements from neighboring settlements and to evacuate its women and children. Thereafter, intensive fighting ensued. The Jews, who had suffered heavy casualties and who were running out of ammunition, found that on April 9 they were saved by a sudden withdrawal by Kauwakji and his forces. Not realizing that he was on the verge of a victory, Kauwakji paused to gather a fresh influx of fighters. When on April 14, he resumed his advance, the Jews, who were very much better prepared, ambushed him. As a result, Kauwakji's troops flinched and retreated.

The Haganah's victory at Mishmar Ha'Emek proved to be a turning point in the general conflict, for the Jews went on to secure Tiberias, Haifa, Safed and Jaffa. On April 18, they gained control over Tiberias in the wake of a short battle that culminated in all of its Arab residents abandoning the city. Then on the morning of April 22, after some closely fought skirmishes and after having been deserted by their commander, Amin Izzedin, the Arabs of Haifa surrendered. Next Safed passed into Jewish hands on May 10, as did Jaffa on May 13. The battle for Safed was bitterly contested and was made problematic for the Haganah by a prior transfer from the British to the Arabs of a well-protected and strategically placed police station. All these victories enabled the Yishuv to consolidate its hold over the territory that the UN allocated to it. In addition, the Haganah swept into the northwest sector of the country to incorporate Acre, the township of Nahariya and its neighboring Jewish settlements.

As the Jewish offensive progressed, an outrage occurred at Deir Yassin, an Arab village located just west of Jerusalem near the road to Tel Aviv. Deir Yassin had recently undertaken neither to permit the entry of foreign Arabs nor to engage in hostile acts against the Yishuv. On April 9, in the belief that Iraqi irregulars had infiltrated Deir Yassin, against the wishes of its inhabitants, a combined group of Irgun and Lehi members assailed it. After a prolonged exchange of fire, the attackers prevailed. When the fighting died down, it was discovered that most of Deir Yassin's fatalities were the elderly, women and children.[83] The attackers claimed that the casualties resulted from the need to dynamite fortified houses or lob hand grenades through doorways and windows. However, there is strong evidence that most of the victims were shot.[84] A year after the event, David Friedman-Yellin, Lehi's commander-in-chief, stated that although he did not believe the slaughter to be premeditated, he understood that those involved acted to avenge their own dead and wounded.[85] According to this way of reasoning, if one enters into a battle and sustains casualties, one is entitled to take it out on enemy civilians. The exact number of Arab deaths has never been determined. For many years, it was believed that the tally amounted to 254, a figure proudly issued by an Irgun spokesman shortly after the battle. Recent research points to a smaller number, between 120 and 150.[86]

Glorying in their exploits, the Irgun and Lehi humiliated some of the survivors by publicly displaying them in a "victory parade" in West Jerusalem. Moreover, the village was thoroughly pillaged. The attackers removed everything of value, including livestock, gold, jewelry and clothes. To the disgust of Hadasah Avigdor, an Irgun member, some of her female comrades had draped themselves in looted traditional Palestinian embroidered dresses. When she established that the garments had been taken from Deir Yassin, she recalled, "I was stricken with loathing, shame, anger and anguish."[87]

The overwhelming majority of the Yishuv reacted to the carnage with shock and dismay. Ben Gurion expressed his sense of remorse to King Abdullah, while Jerusalem's chief rabbi officially excommunicated all the perpetrators.

The battle of Deir Yassin put the fear of God into the general Arab populace, inducing many of them to flee. Even so, the exodus of Arab refugees did not originate from the events at Deir Yassin. Three months earlier, the high commissioner reported that a considerable number of middle-class and well-heeled Arabs were leaving the country on account of the general unrest and prevailing lack of security.[88] However, the atrocities committed at Deir Yassin turned a large stream of refugees into a veritable flood.[89] The Arab exodus certainly benefited the Jews by relieving them of a large number of hostile elements and enabling them to constitute a clear majority in the areas under their control. While in many instances Arabs were deliberately edged out, it was not the Yishuv's intention to rid itself of all Arab inhabitants. At a meeting in Haifa between Jews and local Arab dignitaries, held immediately after the battle for the city, the Arabs were promised full and equal residency rights. On receiving the Jewish offer, the Arabs requested a brief adjournment to contact the Arab states for advice. Hours later they announced to everyone's disbelief, including that of Major-General Stockwell, a high-ranking British officer who acted as an observer, that rather than live under Jewish control, they would leave for Lebanon. In conclusion, they stated, "we do not recognize you and we shall return when you are no longer here." Stockwell, who was utterly astounded, asked them whether they had taken leave of their senses.[90] In vain, the Jewish mayor, Shabetai Levy, implored them to reconsider their decision, but it seems that they acted under instructions received from the Arab Higher Command. Only 5,000–6,000, out of Haifa's original Arab population of 65,000 remained.

The Arabs lost little time in exacting vengeance for Deir Yassin. On April 11, a medical convoy, en route to the Hadassah Hospital on Mount Scopus in Jerusalem, was ambushed. The Haganah in Jerusalem was so hard-pressed for manpower that it could not spare anyone to rush to the convoy's defense. For countless hours, the cornered Jews fought back desperately. Pleas for assistance conveyed to British forces stationed roughly 200 meters away were met with deaf ears and in the end, seventy-nine doctors, nurses and students perished. (Among the fatalities was the fiancé of Ben Gurion's youngest daughter.)[91]

On the civilian front, steps were taken in anticipation of Jewish independence. In early April, the Yishuv established a provisional government or National Administration (*Minhelet Ha'am*), headed by Ben Gurion, and a Provisional Parliament or National Council (*Moetzet Ha'am*). The first body had a membership of thirteen and the latter thirty-seven.[92] Allowance was made for Arab members who were prepared to come to terms with a Jewish state, but no Arab organization or party requested representation.

The new Jewish administration began to act as an autonomous government in areas under Jewish control. Among other things, it issued its own postage stamps, raised tax revenue and made allowances for an emergency supply of food and fuel. It also reactivated electricity and water supplies cut off by the British. The Yishuv's ability to present itself as a nascent state is reflected in the fact that, over the previous two decades, it had developed a wide-ranging series of social institutions as well as commercial, agricultural and industrial enterprises. It provided its own defense, education and welfare services and its vibrant economy was largely independent of the Arab sectors of the country.

Faced with the near certainty of a conflict with the future Jewish state's neighbors, the Zionists made some effort to avoid or reduce it. On November 17, 1947, that is, twelve days before the UN Palestine partition resolution, Golda Meir, representing the Jewish Agency, secretly met with King Abdullah of Transjordan at a location on the Jordan River. Abdullah, a long-term foe of the mufti, proposed a course of action whereby he would seize and annex the territory to be allotted to the Palestinians, with the understanding that, thereafter, he would come to peaceful terms with the Jewish state. (In actual fact, Abdullah wanted to occupy certain strategic parts of Palestine, such as Haifa and the Negev, which were meant to be part of Israel.)[93] For her part, Meir indicated that the Jews would formally remain neutral with regard to Abdullah's dealings with the Palestinians, but would accept the outcome that Abdullah claimed he was pursuing.[94] But as Arab-Jewish conflict within Palestine intensified, irrepressible pressures bore down on the surrounding Arab heads of state to intervene militarily. With the gathering of war clouds, Golda Meir (accompanied by Ezra Danin) paid one more visit to Abdullah. On May 11, 1948, disguised as an Arab woman, she slipped into Amman, where Abdullah received her at his chauffeur's home. He explained that the changed situation had made it impossible for him not to engage in battle against the future Jewish state and that the best he could hold out for the Jews was the provision of some regional autonomy in a united Palestine under his kingship.

As the end of the Mandate drew near, U.S. officials cautioned the Yishuv against declaring a Jewish state. Not being sanguine about its chances of survival, George Marshall, the secretary of state, informed Shertok (who acted as the Zionists' foreign representative) that if the tide turned adversely, the Jews could expect no assistance from the United States.[95] On the eve of Shertok's departure from the United States to Palestine, where a decision on a declaration was pending, Weizmann, bearing Truman's previous secret commitment in mind and never for once losing faith in his word, strongly urged Shertok to stress to Ben Gurion and others that the time had come to cast their die.

The National Administration, meeting on May 12, discussed Golda Meir's latest mission to Abdullah along with Shertok's account of George Marshall's admonition. Yigal Yadin of the Haganah general staff had judged the probability of the Yishuv warding off a combination of hostile Arab states at being no more than 50 percent. This was much more optimistic than the assessment of the Egyptian prime minister, who, relying on British experts, expected the Yishuv to be defeated within two weeks.[96] For his part, Ben Gurion, two days earlier, had publicly proclaimed that though the Yishuv's general strength was not up to par, its fighting reserves were inadequately prepared and only a small minority had been given sufficient training, with the entire Yishuv mobilized and with the timely arrival of even a small consignment of military supplies from abroad, there was no need to despair.[97] Under Ben Gurion's leadership, a decision to declare the state, without specifying its boundaries, was carried by a vote of six against four. At that time, the population of the Yishuv was estimated to be around 650,000.

Two days later, at 4 P.M. on May 14 at the Tel Aviv Art Museum, independence was officially declared. The Mandate had yet to expire at midnight and the reason why the declaration was not issued the day after is that the next day

Ben Gurion reading Israel's Declaration of Independence (Central Zionist Archives).

was a Saturday and that Jewish law forbade the signing of documents on the Sabbath. In any event, the high commissioner had already boarded the ship that was to convey him to the UK.

The ceremony itself was a very modest and short one, as would be befitting a community literally hours away from a full-scale war. It formally commenced with Ben Gurion striking a table with a wooden gavel and calling on all those in attendance to rise to sing "Hatikvah." Then when everyone resumed their seats, Ben Gurion, standing in front of a large portrait of Theodor Herzl, read out the proclamation of independence.

Among other things the declaration stated that:

The State of Israel will be open to Jewish immigration and to the gathering of the exiles. It will foster the development of the country for the benefit of all its residents; it will be based on principles of freedom, justice and peace, according to visions of the prophets of Israel; it will maintain absolute equality of social and political rights for all its citizens, without any distinction with regard to religion, race and sex; it will guarantee freedom of religion, conscience, language, education and culture; it will preserve the holy sites of all religions and will be faithful to the principles of the United Nations Charter.

The declaration also included a special appeal to the Arabs living within the State of Israel to share in the building of the new nation on "the basis of full and equal citizenship and on the basis of appropriate representations in all its institutions, whether they be temporary or permanent ones."

After Ben Gurion read the declaration, the entire assembly spontaneously leapt to their feet to acclaim it. Rabbi Fishman pronounced the traditional benediction thanking God for "giving us life, preserving us and bringing us to this point of time" and, to rapturous applause, the abrogation of the White Paper and all legislation associated with it was announced. Ben Gurion signed the declaration, as did all present members of the National Council. The proceedings then ended with Ben Gurion simply stating that, "the State of Israel has arisen, this concludes the session."

As the gathering began to disperse, strains of Hatikvah could be heard from the Palestine Philharmonic Orchestra (now the Israeli Philharmonic Orchestra), which, due to a lack of space in the ceremonial chamber, was assembled on the floor above. That afternoon, the anthem's final verse: "we have not lost our hope, the hope of two thousand years, to be a free nation in our homeland, the land of Zion and Jerusalem," was particularly moving, for, at that very moment, the hope was finally realized.

Hours later, unbeknownst to Austin and his staff at the UN who were still engaged in a UN discussion on Palestine, the United States, at Truman's insistence, recognized the new State of Israel de facto, with the Soviet Union recognizing it de juro three days later. This gracious act on Truman's part fortified the resolve of the Yishuv when, on the following day, it faced the invading armies of Egypt, Syria, Lebanon, Iraq and Transjordan. The Arabs' war objectives were chillingly enunciated by the Arab League's Secretary-General Abdul Rahman Azzam Pasha, who at a Cairo press conference on May 15, stated, "This will be a war of extermination and a momentous massacre that will be spoken of like the Mongolian massacres and the Crusades."[98] Israel did not succumb, and while it went on to gather millions of Jewish exiles and burgeon into a modern industrial welfare state, it has yet to enjoy the benefits of a peaceful existence that so many other countries take for granted.

NOTES

1. Weizmann, *Trial and Error*, 1949, p. 535.

2. Ibid.

3. As quoted by Sykes, *Crossroads*, 1967, p. 273.

4. As quoted by Crossman, *Palestine Mission*, 1947, p. 63.

5. Kimche, *Seven Fallen Pillars*, 1950, pp. 141–42.

6. As quoted by Kochavi, "The Struggle," 1998, p. 146.

7. Sykes, *Crossroads*, 1967, p. 289.

8. Ibid.

9. As quoted by Hurewitz, *Struggle*, 1950, p. 238.

10. Bauer, *Flight and Rescue*, 1970, p. vii.

11. See, for instance, Slutsky, *From Defence to Strife*, 1964, pp. 1107–11.

12. Slutsky, *History of the Haganah*, 1972, p. 1114.

13. Segev, 1991, p. 132. Some illegal migrants were eventually allowed to stay in Palestine, but their numbers were deducted from official migrant quotas.

14. As reported in Shapira, 1982, pp. 292–93.

15. Koestler, *Promise and Fulfillment*, 1983, p. 15.

16. Trevor, *Under the White Paper*, 1980, p. 133.

17. Segev, 1991, p. 116.

18. Hurewitz, *Struggle*, 1950, p. 230.

19. Snetsinger, *Truman*, 1974, p. 22.

20. As reported in Esco Foundation, *Palestine*, 1947, vol. 2, p. 1193.

21. Dothan, *Struggle*, 1981, p. 309.

22. Koestler, *Promise and Fulfillment*, 1983, p. 116.

23. Pollack, *Rise of the State of Israel*, 1955, p. 44.

24. Slutsky, *History of the Haganah*, 1972, p. 819.

25. Ibid., p. 871.

26. Ibid., p. 887.

27. Ibid.

28. Trevor, *Under the White Paper*, 1980, p. 218.

29. Begin, *Revolt*, 1979, p. 212.

30. Nearer to the time, the Haganah requested a postponement, but since the reasons for such a request were not given, the Irgun, which was fully poised for the mission, decided to proceed regardless.

31. Begin, 1977, p. 237.

32. Hurewitz, *Struggle*, 1950, p. 256.

33. Laqueur, *History*, 1989, p. 573.

34. Dothan, *Struggle*, 1981, p. 332.

35. Ibid., p. 334.

36. Pollack, *Rise of the State of Israel*, 1955, p. 44.

37. Near, *Kibbutz Movement*, 1997, p. 102.

38. Gvati, *Hundred Years*, 1985, p. 109.

39. As quoted by Near, *Kibbutz Movement*, 1997, p. 105.

40. Silver, *Begin*, 1984, p. 84.

41. Kimche and Kimche, *Both Sides*, 1960, p. 21.

42. Ibid., p. 30.

43. Halpern, *Idea of a Jewish State*, 1961, p. 361.

44. Pollack, *Rise of the State of Israel*, 1955, p. 71.

45. Ibid., p. 67.

46. As quoted by Sykes, *Crossroads*, 1967, p. 330. Italics added.

47. As quoted by Pollack, *Rise of the State of Israel*, 1955, p. 69.

48. See Abramov, *Perpetual Dilemma*, 1976, p. 127. There seems to be some disagreement on this matter. Pollack (*Rise of the State of Israel*, 1995, p. 88) had claimed that no agreement was reached and that Agudat Israel pleaded only for the elimination of Jewish immigration restrictions. Considering that Rabbi Levin represented Agudat Israel in Israel's provisional government, it would seem that Abramov's version has more credence, especially since, in practice, all of Agudat Israel's demands were subsequently met.

49. Silver, *Begin*, 1984, p. 79.

50. Slutsky, *History of the Haganah*, 1972, p. 929.

51. Ibid., p. 1163.

52. As quoted by Hurewitz, *Struggle*, 1950, p. 294. Italics added.

53. The Australian member did not sign either report.

54. In terms of the final UN plan, the proposed Jewish state would contain 515,000 Jews and 350,000 Arabs. See Pollack, *Rise of the State of Israel*, 1955, p. 113.

55. Although no longer president of the Zionist Organization, Weizmann remained its pre-eminent spokesperson.

56. Snetsinger, *Truman*, 1974, pp. 68 and 70.

57. As quoted by Benson, *Harry S. Truman*, 1997, p. 106.

58. Slutsky, *History of the Haganah*, 1972, p. 992.

59. Snetsinger, *Truman*, 1974, p. 71.

60. As quoted by Hurewitz, *Struggle*, 1950, p. 308.

61. Those states voting in favor of the resolution were: Australia, Belgium, Belorussia, Bolivia, Brazil, Canada, Costa Rica, Czechoslovakia, Denmark, Dominican Republic, Ecuador, France, Guatemala, Haiti, Holland, Iceland, Liberia, Luxembourg, New Zealand, Nicaragua, Norway, Panama, Paraguay, Peru, Philippines, Poland, South Africa, Sweden, Ukraine, Uruguay, United States, USSR and Venezuela, Those voting against were Afghanistan, Cuba, Egypt, Greece, India, Iran, Iraq, Lebanon, Pakistan, Saudi Arabia, Syria, Turkey and Yemen. Ten countries abstained. They were Argentina, Britain, Chile, China, Colombia, Ethiopia, Honduras, Mexico, Salvador and Yugoslavia. (The negative vote of Cuba, plus the presence of six Latin American countries among the abstainers, supports the view that they were not subject to arm twisting by the United States and that the Arabs were partly correct in assuming that many of them would not rally to the Zionists' cause.)

62. Dothan, *Struggle*, 1981, pp. 370–71.

63. As quoted by Pollack, *Rise of the State of Israel*, 1955, p. 111.

64. Pollack, *Rise of the State of Israel*, 1955, pp. 111–12.

65. As quoted by Slutsky, *History of the Haganah*, 1972, p. 1202.

66. Kimche and Kimche, *Both Sides*, 1960, p. 210.

67. Pollack, *Rise of the State of Israel*, 1955, p. 29.

68. Ibid., p. 134.

69. Ibid., p. 141.

70. Kimche, *Seven Fallen Pillars*, 1950, p. 202.

71. Ibid., p. 198.

72. Kimche and Kimche, *Both Sides*, 1960, pp. 85–86.

73. After Israel arose, a kibbutz called *Netiv Halamed He* (the Path of the Thirty-five) was established in their memory.

74. Slutsky, *History of the Haganah*, 1972, p. 1439.

75. Gvati, *Hundred Years*, 1985, p. 118.

76. As quoted by Snetsinger, *Truman*, 1974, p. 77.

77. Kimche, *Seven Fallen Pillars*, 1950, p. 208.

78. Ben Gurion, *Restored State*, 1969, p. 77.

79. Bar-Zohar, *Ben Gurion*, 1968, p. 103.

80. As quoted by Bar-Zohar, *Ben Gurion*, 1968, p. 104.

81. Kimche and Kimche, *Both Sides*, 1960, p. 78.

82. This water ration had to suffice for drinking, personal washing, laundering, cooking, cleaning of utensils and flushing toilets.

83. Ibid., p. 273.

84. Ibid., p. 270, refers to an eyewitness account of Dr. Engel who stated that in the years he served as a medic in the First World War, "I never saw such a gruesome sight."

85. Slutsky, *History of the Haganah*, 1972, p. 1548, where Friedman-Yellin is quoted verbatim.

86. Milstein, *War of Independence*, 1989, vol. 4, p. 274, and Silver, *Begin*, 1984, p. 95.

87. As quoted by Milstein, *War of Independence*, 1989, vol. 4, p. 266.

88. Sykes, *Crossroads*, 1967, p. 363.

89. The Arab refugee issue is to be treated in greater length in the author's subsequent book dealing with Israel since independence.

90. Kimche and Kimche, *Both Sides*, 1960, p. 122.

91. Bar-Zohar, *Ben Gurion*, 1968, p. 108.

92. The political lineup of the National Administration, chaired by Ben Gurion, consisted of four members from Mapai, two from the General Zionists, Mapam two, Mizrahi one, Hapoel Hamizrachi one, Agudat Israel one, Aliyah Hadasha one, and Sephardim one.

93. Kimche and Kimche, *Both Sides*, 1960, p. 48.

94. Shlaim, *Iron Wall*, 2000, p. 32.

95. Benson, *Harry S. Truman*, 1997, p. 133.

96. Kimche, *Seven Fallen Pillars*, 1950, p. 199.

97. Pollack, *Rise of the State of Israel*, 1955, p. 190.

98. Sykes, *Crossroads*, 1967, p. 364.

Glossary

Agudat Israel: An association of non-Zionist orthodox Jews.

Ahdut Ha'Avodah: "United Labor," a socialist party.

Aliyah: Literally "ascent"; in practice, it relates to immigration to Palestine.

Aliyah Bet: An organization sponsoring illegal migration to Palestine.

Aliyot: Plural of Aliyah.

Alliance Israelite Universelle: An organization founded in Paris in 1860 to further Jewish civil and religious rights and to promote Jewish vocational training.

Ashkenazi: A Jew who hailed from Central or Eastern Europe and who spoke Yiddish.

Ashkenazim: Plural of Ashkenazi.

Betar: Youth movement of the Revisionists.

Bilu: A Zionist youth organization of the First Aliyah fostering migration to Palestine.

Biluim: Members of Bilu.

Communa: A collective.

Dunam: A quarter of an acre.

Eretz Israel: The Land of Israel.

Feuilleton: Section of newspaper devoted to literature and criticism.

Gedud Avodah: A Jewish labor battalion in Palestine in the 1920s.

Haapalah: The process of migrating illegally to Palestine in the 1930s and 1940s.

Haganah: Successor defense organization to Hashomer.

Haham Bashi: Chief Sephardi rabbi in Ottoman Palestine.

Hanukkah: Jewish Festival of Lights commemorating the victory of the Hasmoneans.

Hapoel Hamizrachi: Religious Zionist Workers' Party.

Hapoel Hatzair: "The Young Worker," a Second Aliyah labor party.

Hashomer: "The Watchman," a Second Aliyah Jewish defense organization.

Hashomer Hatzair: "The Young Watchman," a Zionist socialist youth movement.

Haskallah: "Enlightenment," the term used for spreading modern European culture among the Jews.

Hasmonean: Priestly family that in 166 B.C.E. (Before the Common Era) directed a popular revolt in Palestine against the Syrian king Antiochos Epiphanes.

Hassid: Singular of Hassidim.

Hassidim: Members of a Jewish religious movement founded in the early eighteenth century.

Hatikvah: "The Hope," the Zionist anthem.

Havlagah: Self-restraint.

Heder: Primary Jewish religious school.

Hehalutz: An umbrella Zionist youth pioneering organization.

Hever Hakvutzot: A federation of kvutzot.

Hora: A circular dance originating in the Balkans.

Hovevei Zion: Lovers of Zion.

Irgun: "National Military Organization," a Jewish militia.

Judea: Name given by the Romans to their vassal kingdom in Palestine.

Keren Yayesod: Fund for the promotion of the Yishuv's development.

Khan: An oriental inn with a large inner court that accommodated camel caravans.

Kibbutz: A large collective farm.

Kibbutz Artzi: The kibbutz federation of Hashomer Hatzair.

Kibbutz Ha-Meuhad: A kibbutz federation favoring large settlements.

Kibbutzim: Plural of kibbutz.

Kvutza: A small collective farm.

Kvutzot: Plural of kvutza.

Lehi: The "Freedom Fighters of Israel," a Jewish militia.

Mapai: "The Israel Workers Party," formed by the merger of Ahdut Ha'Avodah and Hapoel Hatzair.

Mitnagdim: Theological opponents of the Hassidim.

Mizrahi: Religious Zionist Party.

Moshav: A cooperative farming settlement with private ownership of land-holdings.

Moshava: A large First Aliyah settlement.

Moshavim: Plural of Moshav.

Moshavot: Plural of Moshava.

Palmah: A special fighting force of the Haganah.

Palmahnik: A member of the Palmah.

Peabody: After George Peabody, an American philanthropist.

Poalei Zion: "Workers of Zion," a Second Aliyah labor party.

Sephardi: Singular of Sephardim.

Sephardim: Jews who lived in the Middle East, North Africa and others, such as those from Turkey, who originated from the Spanish Jewish community.

Shekel: A Jewish coin current in the time of the Hasmoneans.

Shofar: Ram's horn blown at the Jewish New Year and on the Day of Atonement as well as on other special occasions.

Shtetl: Eastern European town or village where Jews predominated or that had a large, close-knit Jewish minority.

Talmud: Compilation of Jewish law and rabbinical commentaries.

Torah: The Five Books of Moses. (The term also refers to the totality of Jewish Law embodied in both the Books of Moses and the Talmud.)

Yeshiva: A rabbinical seminary.

Yeshivot: Plural of yeshiva.

Yiddish: German-based language with a mixture of Hebrew and other words spoken by Ashkenazi Jews.

Yishuv: Jewish population in Palestine.

Bibliography

WORKS IN ENGLISH

Abramov, S.Z. *Perpetual Dilemma: Jewish Religion in the Jewish State*. Cranbury, NJ: Associated University Presses, 1976.

Ahad Ha'am. *Selected Essays*. Philadelphia: Jewish Publication Society of America, 1912.

Allon, Y. *The Making of Israel's Army*. London: Valentine Mitchell, 1970.

Antonius, G. *The Arab Awakening*. Beirut: Librairie du Liban, 1969.

Avineri, S. *The Making of Modern Zionism: The Intellectual Origins of the Jewish State*. New York: Basic Books, 1981.

Avneri, A. *The Claim of Dispossession: Jewish Land-Settlements and the Arabs 1878–1948*. New Brunswick, NJ: Transaction Books, 1984.

Bar-Zohar, M. *Ben Gurion: The Armed Prophet*. Englewood Cliffs, NJ: Prentice Hall, 1968.

Batal, J. "Truman Chapters on the Middle East," *Middle East Forum* (December 1965).

Bauer, Y. "The Arab Revolt of 1936." *New Outlook* (July–August 1966; Part One) and (September 1966; Part Two).

———. *Flight and Rescue: Brichah*. New York: Random House, 1970.

———. *From Diplomacy to Resistance*. New York: Atheneum, 1973.

Begin, M. *The Revolt*. London: W.H. Allen, 1979.

Bein, A. *Theodore Herzl*. Philadelphia: Jewish Publication Society of America, 1940.

Beit-Hallami, B. *Original Sins: Reflections on the History of Israel and Zionism*. New York: Olive Branch Press, 1993.

Ben Gurion, D. *Israel: A Personal History*. New York: Funk and Wagnalls, 1971.

Ben-Zvi, I. *The Hebrew Battalions: Letters*. Jerusalem: Yad Itzhak Ben-Zvi, 1969.

Benson, M.T. *Harry S. Truman and the Founding of Israel*. Westport, CT: Praeger, 1997.

Brenner, Y.S. "The 'Stern Gang' 1940–48." *Middle Eastern Studies* (October 1965).

Burns, M. *Dreyfus: A Family Affair 1789–1945*. London: Chatto and Windus, 1993.

Collins, L., and Lapiere, D. *O Jerusalem*. London: Pam Books, 1973.

Crossman, R. *Palestine Mission*. London: Hamilton, 1947.

Cunningham, A. "Palestine: The Last Days of the Mandate." *International Affairs*, Vol. 24 (1948).

Davitt, M. *Within the Pale.* New York: Arno Press, 1975.

De Haas, J. *Theodor Herzl.* Chicago: The Leonard Company, 1927.

Dubnow, S. *History of the Jews in Russia*, vol. 1–3. Philadelphia: Jewish Publication Society, 1918.

Eban, A. "Tragedy and Triumph." In Weisgal and Carmichael, *Chaim Weizmann*, 1962.

———. *An Autobiography.* London: Weidenfeld and Nicolson, 1977.

Ebner, M. "Memories of the First Zionist Congress." *Zion* (August 1951).

Elon, A. *The Israelis: Founders and Sons.* London: Weidenfeld and Nicolson, 1971.

———. *Herzl.* New York: Holt, Rinehart and Winston, 1975.

Engle, A. *The Nili Spies.* London: Hogarth Press, 1959.

Esco Foundation for Palestine. *Palestine: A Study of Jewish, Arab and British Policies.* Vols. 1 and 2. New Haven: Yale University Press, 1947.

Frankel, J. *Prophecy and Politics: Socialism, Nationalism and the Russian Jew, 1862–1917.* New York: Cambridge University Press, 1981.

Friedman, I. "The System of Capitulations and Its Effects on the Turco-Jewish Relations in Palestine, 1856–1897." In Kushner, *Palestine*, 1986.

Gerber, H. "A New Look at the Tanzimat: The Case of the Province of Jerusalem." In Kushner, *Palestine*, 1986.

Ghory, E. "An Arab View of the Situation in Palestine." *International Affairs* (September 1936).

Gilbar, G.D. "The Growing Economic Involvement of Palestine with the West, 1865–1914." In Kushner, *Palestine*, 1986.

Gilbert, M. *Exile and Return: The Struggle for a Jewish Homeland.* New York: Lippincott, 1978.

———. *Jerusalem: Rebirth of a City.* London: Chatto and Windus, 1985.

———. *The Holocaust.* London: Fontana, 1986.

———. *Israel: A History.* London: Doubleday, 1998.

Gillon, D.Z. "The Antecedents of the Balfour Declaration." *Middle Eastern Studies* (May 1969).

Gorny, Y. "Zionist Socialism and the Arab Question, 1918–1930." *Middle Eastern Studies* (January 1972).

———. *Zionism and the Arabs: 1882–1948.* Oxford: Oxford University Press, 1987.

Gross, N. "The 1923 Recession and Public Sector Finance in Palestine." Maurice Falk Institute for Economic Research in Israel, Discussion Paper no. 794, Jerusalem (October, 1979).

———. "A Note on the Periorization of the Yishuv's History During the Mandatory Period." Maurice Falk Institute for Economic Research in Israel, Discussion Paper no. 801, Jerusalem (January 1980).

Gross, N., and Metzer, J. "Palestine in World War Two: Some Economic Aspects." Maurice Falk Institute for Economic Research in Israel, Research Paper no. 207, Jerusalem (1993).

Gvati, H. *A Hundred Years of Settlement.* Jerusalem: Keter, 1985.

Halevi, N., Gross, N., Kleiman, E. and Sarnat, M. *Banker to an Emerging Nation.* Jerusalem: Shikmona, 1977.

Halpern, B. *The Idea of the Jewish State.* Cambridge: Harvard University Press, 1961.

Halpern, B., and Reinharz, J. *Zionism and the Creation of a New Society*. New York: Oxford University Press, 1998.

Hertzberg, A. *The Zionist Idea*. Westport, CT: Greenwood Press, 1970.

Herzl, T. *Complete Diaries*. Vols. 1–5. New York: Herzl Press and Thomas Yoseloff, 1960.

———. *Old New Land (Altneuland)*. New York: Markus Weiner and Herzl Press, 1987.

———. *The Jewish State*. New York: Dover, 1988.

Hess, M. *Rome and Jerusalem*. New York: Bloch Publishing Company, 1918.

Heymann, M. "Max Nordau at the Early Zionist Congresses, 1897–1905." *Journal of Israeli History*, vol. 16, no. 3 (1995).

Horowitz, D. "Aspects of Economic Policy in Palestine." Economic Research Institute, Jewish Agency, Jerusalem, 1936.

Horowitz, D. *State in the Making*. New York: Knopf, 1953.

Horowitz, D., and Hinden, R. "Economic Survey of Palestine." Economic Research Institute, Jewish Agency, Tel Aviv, 1938.

Hurewitz, J.C. *The Struggle for Palestine*. New York: Norton, 1950.

Jabotinsky, V. *The Story of the Jewish Legion*. New York: Ackerman, 1945.

Kark, R. "The Contribution of the Ottoman Regime to the Development of Jerusalem and Jaffa, 1840–1917." In Kushner, *Palestine*, 1986.

Katz, S. *Days of Fire*. London: W.H. Allen, 1968.

———. *Battleground: Fact and Fantasy in Palestine*. New York: Bantam, 1973.

———. *Lone Wolf: A Biography of Vladimir (Ze'ev) Jabotinsky*. Vol. 1. New York: Barricade Books, 1996.

Kedourie, E. *England and the Middle East: The Destruction of the Ottoman Empire 1914–1921*. London: Bowes and Bowes, 1956.

———. "Sir Herbert Samuel and the Government of Palestine." *Middle Eastern Studies* (January 1969).

Kimche, J. *Seven Fallen Pillars*. London: Secker and Warburg, 1950.

———. "Bridge to Statehood." In Weisgal and Carmichael, *Chaim Weizmann*, 1962.

Kimche, J., and Kimche, D. *The Secret Roads*. London: Secker and Warburg, 1954.

———. *Both Sides of the Hill: Britain and the Palestine War*. London: Secker and Warburg, 1960.

Kochavi, A.J. "The Struggle Against Jewish Immigration to Palestine." *Middle Easten Studies* (July 1998).

Koestler, A. *Promise and Fulfillment: Palestine 1917–1949*. London: Macmillan, 1983.

Kurland, S. *Biluim: Pioneers of Zionist Colonization*. New York: Scopus, 1943.

Kushner, D. *Palestine in the Late Ottoman Period*. Jerusalem: Yad Itzhak Ben-Zvi, 1986.

Laqueur, W. *The Israel-Arab Reader*. Middlesex: Penguin Books, 1970.

———. *A History of Zionism*. New York: Schocken Books, 1989.

Leonard, L. "The United Nations and Palestine." *International Conciliation*, no. 454 (October 1949).

Lindeman, A.S. *The Jew Accused*. Cambridge: Cambridge University Press, 1991.

Lipovetzky, P. *Joseph Trumpeldor: His Life and Works*. Jerusalem: World Zionist Organization, 1953.

Lipsky, L. "A Portrait in Action." In Weisgal and Carmichael, *Chaim Weizmann*, 1962.

Lowe, H. *The Tsars and the Jew*. Basel: Harwood Press, 1978.

Mandel, N.J. "Ottoman Practice as Regards Jewish Settlement in Palestine: 1881–1908." *Middle Eastern Studies*, vol. 11, no. 1 (1975).

————. *The Arabs and Zionism before World War One.* Berkeley: University of California Press, 1976.

Margalit, E. "Social and Intellectual Origins of the Hashomer Hatzair Youth Movement, 1913–20." *Journal of Contemporary History* (April 1969).

Mattab, P. "The Mufti of Jerusalem and the Politics of Palestine." *Middle East Journal* (Spring 1988).

Meinertzhagen, R. *Middle East Diary, 1917–1956.* London: The Cressett Press, 1959.

Morse, A.D. *While Six Million Died.* New York: Overlook Press, 1983.

Mossek, M. *Palestine Immigration Policy under Sir Herbert Samuel.* London: Frank Cass, 1978.

Naiditch, I. *Edmond de Rothschild.* Washington, DC: Zionist Organization of America, 1945.

Near, H. *The Kibbutz Movement: A History, Volume One Origins and Growth, 1909–1939.* Oxford: Oxford University Press, 1992.

————. *The Kibbutz Movement: A History.* Vol. 2. London: Mitchell and Co., 1997.

Nedava, J. "The Tragedy of the House of Herzl." *Zionist Quarterly* (Spring 1952).

O'Brien, C.C. *The Siege: The Saga of Israel and Zionism.* New York: Simon & Schuster, 1986.

Patterson, J.H. *With the Zionists in Gallipoli.* London: Hutchinson and Co., 1916.

————. *With the Judeans in the Palestine Campaign.* London: Hutchinson and Co. 1922.

Pawel, E. *The Labyrinth of Exile: A Life of Theodor Herzl.* New York: Farrar, Straus and Giroux, 1989.

Perlmutter, A. "Dov Ber-Borochov: A Marxist Zionist Ideologist." *Middle Eastern Studies* (January 1969).

Peters, J. *From Time Immemorial.* New York: Harper & Row, 1984.

Pinsker, L. *Auto-emancipation.* London: Federation of Zionist Youth, 1936.

Porath, Y. *The Emergence of the Palestinian-Arab National Movement, 1918–1929.* London: Frank Cass, 1974.

————. *The Palestinian Arab National Movement: From Riots to Rebellion, 1929–1939.* London: Frank Cass, 1977.

Preuss, W. *The Labour Movement in Israel: Past and Present.* Jerusalem: Rubin Mass, 1965.

Reinharz, J. "The Balfour Declaration and Its Maker: A Reassessment." *Journal of Modern History* (September 1992).

————. *Chaim Weizmann: The Making of a Statesman.* New York: Oxford University Press, 1993.

Rinnot, M. "Capitulations: The Case of the German-Jewish Hilfsverein Schools in Palestine, 1901–1914." In Kushner, *Palestine,* 1986.

Roi, Y. "The Zionist Attitude to the Arabs, 1908–1914." *Middle Eastern Studies* (April 1968).

Rubinstein, A.Z. *The Arab-Israeli Conflict.* New York: Praeger, 1984.

Ruppin, A. *The Agricultural Colonisation of the Zionist Organization in Palestine.* London: Martin Hopkinson, 1926.

————. *Three Decades of Palestine.* Jerusalem: Schocken, 1936.

————. *Memoirs, Diaries, Letters.* London: Weidenfeld and Nicolson, 1971.

Sachar, H.M. *A History of Israel.* New York: Alfred Knopf, 1981.

————. *The Course of Modern Jewish History.* New York: Vintage, 1990.

Schechtman, J.B. *Rebel and Statesman: The Vladimir Jabotinsky Story, The Early Years.* New York: Thomas Yoseloff, 1956.

———. *Fighter and Prophet: The Vladimir Jabotinsky Story, The Last Years.* New York: Thomas Yoseloff, 1961.

Segev, T. *The Seventh Million: The Israelis and the Holocaust.* New York: Hill and Wang, 1993.

———. *One Palestine Complete.* New York: Metropolitan Books, 2000.

Shafir, G. *Land, Labor and the Origins of the Israeli-Palestinian Conflict, 1882–1914.* Cambridge: Cambridge University Press, 1989.

Shapira, A. *Land and Power: The Zionist Resort to Force.* New York: Oxford University Press, 1992.

Shapiro, Y. *The Formative Years of the Israeli Labour Party: The Organization of Power, 1919–1930.* London and Beverly Hills: Sage, 1976.

Shavit, Y. *Jabotinsky and the Revisionist Movement 1925–1948.* London: Frank Cass, 1988.

Shilo, M. "The Immigration Policy of the Zionist Institutions 1882–1914." *Middle Eastern Studies,* vol. 30, no. 3 (July 1994).

Shlaim, A. *The Iron Wall.* New York: Norton, 2000.

Silver, E. *Begin: A Biography.* London: Weidenfeld and Nicolson, 1984.

Snetsinger, J. *Truman, the Jewish Vote and the Creation of Israel.* Stanford: Hoover Institution Press, 1974.

Speigel, S. *Hebrew Reborn.* Cleveland: Meridian Books, 1962.

Stein, L. *The Balfour Declaration.* London: Valentine-Mitchell, 1961.

Sternhell, Z. *The Founding Myths of Israel.* Princeton: Princeton University Press, 1998.

Sykes, C. *Crossroads to Israel.* London: The New English Library, 1967.

Szereszewski, R. "Essays on the Structure of the Jewish Economy in Palestine and Israel." Maurice Falk Institute for Economic Research in Israel, Jerusalem (June 1968).

Tasse, R.L. "Great Britain and Palestine Towards the United Nations." *Middle Eastern Studies* (July 1994).

Tessler, M. *A History of the Israeli-Palestinian Conflict.* Bloomington: Indiana University Press, 1994.

Teveth, S. *Ben-Gurion: The Burning Ground 1886–1948.* Boston: Houghton Mifflin, 1987.

Trevor, D. *Under the White Paper.* Munich: Kraus, 1980.

UK Government. "Report of the Commission on the Palestine Disturbances of August 1929" (Shaw Report), HMSO, CMD 3530, London, March 1930.

———. (A). "Palestine: Report on Immigration, Land Settlement and Development" (Hope Simpson Report), HMSO, CMD 3686, London, October 1930.

———. (B). "Palestine: Statement of Policy by His Majesty's Government in the United Kingdom" (Passfield White Paper), HMSO, London, October 1930.

———. "Palestine: Statement of Policy," HMSO, CMD 6019, London, May 1939.

Vital, D. *The Origins of Zionism.* London: Oxford University Press, 1975.

———. *Zionism: The Formative Years.* London: Oxford University Press, 1982.

Viteles, H. *A History of the Co-Operative Movement in Israel, Book Two; The Evolution of the Kibbutz Movement.* London: Valentine Mitchell, 1967.

Wasserstein, B. *The British in Palestine: The Mandatory Government and the Arab Jewish Conflict 1917–1929.* London: Royal Historical Society, 1978.

Weintraub, D., Lissak, M., and Azmon, Y. *Moshava, Kibbutz and Moshav.* Ithaca, NY: Cornell University Press, 1969.

Weisgal, M.W., and Carmichael, J. *Chaim Weizmann.* London: Weidenfeld and Nicolson, 1962.

Weizmann, C. *Trial and Error.* London: Hamish Hamilton, 1949.

Weltsch, R. "The Fabian Decade." In Weisgal and Carmichael, *Chaim Weizmann,* 1962.

Wheatcroft, G. *The Controversy of Zion: How Zionism Tried to Resolve the Jewish Question.* London: Sinclair-Stevenson, 1996.

Wigoder, G. *The New Standard Jewish Encyclopedia.* Jerusalem: Massada Press, 1977.

Wistrich, R.S. *Antisemitism: The Longest Hatred.* London: Mandarin, 1992.

Zborowski, M., and Herzog, E. *Life Is with People: The Little Town of Eastern Europe.* New York: International Universities Press, 1952.

WORKS IN HEBREW

Almog, S. *Zionism and History.* Jerusalem: Mangus Publishers, The Hebrew University, 1982.

Arenson, R. "Stages in the Establishment of First Aliyah Settlements and Their Development." In Eliav, *The First Aliyah,* vol. 1, 1981.

Avinom, R. *Twenty Years of Revival and Independence.* Jerusalem: Defence Office, 1968.

Avistur, S. "Agriculture, Craft and Industry." In Eliav, *The First Aliyah,* vol. 1, 1981.

Be'eri, E. *The Beginning of the Israeli-Arab Conflict.* Tel Aviv: Sifriat Poalim, 1985.

Bein, A. *A History of Zionist Settlement: From the Time of Herzl to the Present Age.* Ramat Gan: Masada, 1970.

Belkind, I. "In the Path of the Biluim: Memories of Israel Belkind." Jerusalem: Ministry of Defence, 1983.

Ben Arye, Yeshua. "Geographic Aspects during the Beginning of the Development of Hebrew Settlements in the Land of Israel." In Eliav, *The First Aliyah,* vol. 1, 1981.

Ben Gurion, D. *The Restored State of Israel.* Tel Aviv: Am Oved, 1969.

———. *Memoirs.* Tel Aviv: Am Oved, 1971.

Berlovitz, Y. "Literature of the First Aliyah." In Eliav, *The First Aliyah,* vol. 1, 1981.

Carmel, A. "The Jewish Settlement, the Ottoman Rule and the Foreign Consulates." In Eliav, *The First Aliyah,* vol. 1, 1981.

Cohen, A. *Israel and the Arab World.* Tel Aviv: Sifriat Hapoalim, 1964.

Dinor, B. *Book of the History of the Haganah.* Jerusalem: Hasifriya Hatzionit, 1964.

Dothan, S. *The Struggle for Eretz-Israel.* Tel Aviv: Ministry of Defence Publishing House, 1981.

Druyen, N. "The Immigration and Striking of Roots of Yemenite Jews during the First Aliyah." In Eliav, *The First Aliyah,* vol. 1, 1981.

———. *Without a Magic Carpet: Yemenite Immigrants in Eretz Israel 1881–1914.* Jerusalem: Ben-Zvi Institute for the Study of Jewish Communities in the East, 1981.

Eliav, M. "Early Tribulations of Petach Tikva." *Cathedra,* no. 9 (1978).

———. *The First Aliyah.* Vols. 1 and 2. Jerusalem: Yad Izhak Ben Zvi, 1981.

Ellsberg, P. "The Arab Question in the Policies of the Zionist Executive Before World War One." In Diner, B., and Heilpren, Y., *Shivat Tzion.* Vol 4. Jerusalem: Tsifria Hastsionit, 1965.

Erez, Y., *Book of the Third Aliyah*. Tel Aviv: Am Oved, 1964.

Ettinger, S., and Bartel, I. "Roots of the New Settlement in the Land of Israel." In Eliav, *The First Aliyah*, vol. 1, 1981.

Even-Shoshan (Rozenstein), Z. *The History of the Labour Movement in Eretz Yisrael.* Vols. 1, 2 & 3. Tel Aviv: Am Oved, 1955.

Gal, A. "Brandeis' Views on the Upbuilding of Palestine." *Ha-Tziyonut*, no. 6 (1981).

Gershuni, Z. *Memoirs.* Jaffa: Eitan and Shoshani, 1919.

Gidon, S. *Pathways of the Kvutzah and the Kibbutz.* Vol. 1. Tel Aviv: Am Oved, 1955.

Gidon, S. "The Aspiration for a Collective Life and Its Realization in the Second Aliyah." *Cathedra* (July 1980).

Giladi, D. *Jewish Palestine during the Fourth Aliyah Period, 1924–1929.* Tel Aviv: Am Oved, 1973.

Gross, N. "The Economy of Eretz Israel at the End of the 19th Century and Beginning of the 20th Century." In Halevi et al., *Banker to an Emerging Nation*, 1977. (Hebrew text)

Habbas, B. *Book of the Second Aliyah.* Tel Aviv: Am Oved, 1947.

Halevi, N. "The Economic Development of the Jewish Community in Palestine 1917–1947." Maurice Falk Institute for Economic Research in Israel, Paper No. 7914, Jerusalem (November 1979).

Harel, C. "The Zionist Movement and the Yishuv in Eretz Israel Towards the End of the First Aliyah." In Eliav, *The First Aliyah*, vol. 1, 1981.

Harmeti, S. "The Revival of Spoken Hebrew in the Settlements." In Eliav, *The First Aliyah*, vol. 1, 1981.

Horowitz, D. *The Development of the Palestine Economy.* Tel Aviv: The Bialik Institute, 1948.

———. *My Yesterday.* Jerusalem: Schocken, 1970.

Kellner, Y. "The First Aliyot—Myth and Realities: Two Examples." *Kivunim* (November 1978).

———. "The Firstcomers in Their Own Eyes." In Eliav, *The First Aliyah*, vol. 1, 1981.

Kleiman, A. *Divide or Rule.* Jerusalem: Yad Yitzak Ben Zvi, 1983.

Kniel, Y. (A). "The Old Yishuv and the New Colonization." In Eliav, *The First Aliyah*, vol. 1, 1981.

———. (B). "The Early Formation of the New Yishuv in Jerusalem." In Eliav, *The First Aliyah*, vol. 1, 1981.

Kollet, Y. "Workers of the First Aliyah." In Eliav, *The First Aliyah*, vol. 1, 1981.

Krack, R. "The Rise of Jaffe as the Centre of the New Yishuv—Social and Cultural Aspects." In Eliav, *The First Aliyah*, vol. 1, 1981.

Laskov, S. *Trumpeldor: A Biography.* Haifa: Shikmona, 1972.

———. "Chovevei Zion in Russia on Behalf of Settlement in Eretz Yisrael." In Eliav, *The First Aliyah*, vol. 1, 1981.

Levontin, Z.D. *To the Land of Our Fathers.* Tel Aviv: Eitan and Shushani, vol. 1, 1924; vol. 2, 1925; and vol. 3, 1928.

Meir, Y. *The Zionist Movement and the Jews of Yemen.* Tel Aviv: Sifriat Afikim, 1983.

Meirowitz, M. *In the Days of the Bilu.* Jerusalem: Rubin Mass, 1942.

Metzer, J., and Kaplan, O. "The Jewish and Arab Economies in Mandatory Palestine: Product, Employment and Growth." Maurice Falk Institute for Economic Research in Israel, Jerusalem (1990).

Milstein, U. *The War of Independence.* Tel Aviv: Zmora Bitan. Vols. 1–2, 1989; Vols. 3–4,
     1991.
Pollack, A.N. *The Rise of the State of Israel.* Tel Aviv: Sefarim, 1955.
Roi, Y. "Jewish Arab Relations in the First Aliya Settlements." In Eliav, *The First Aliyah,*
     vol. 1, 1981.
Salmon, Y. *Religion and Zionism: First Encounters.* Jerusalem: Hassifria Haziyonit,
     1990.
Shalmon, J. "The Bilu Movement." In Eliav, *The First Aliyah,* vol. 1, 1981.
Shapira, A. *Berl Katznelson.* Tel Aviv: Am Oved, 1981.
Sharret, M. *In the Forum of Nations.* Tel Aviv: Am Oved, 1958.
Shidorsky, D. "Public Libraries During the First Aliyah." In Eliav, *The First Aliyah,* vol.
     1, 1981.
Slutsky, Y. *From Defence to Strife.* In B. Dinor, *History of the Haganah,* vol. 2, 1964.
Slutsky, Y. "The Role of Ideology in the Formation of the Kvutza in Eretz Israel."
     Baderech (April, 1968).
————. In B. Dinor, *History of the Haganah,* vol. 3. Tel Aviv: Am Oved, 1972.
Stein-Ashkenazi, E. "The Beginnings of Rechovot 1890–1900." *Cathedra,* no. 17 (1980).
Teveth, S. *The Murder of Arlosoroff.* Tel Aviv: Schocken, 1982.
Tzemach, S. *First Year.* Tel Aviv: Am Oved, 1965.
Vitkin, J. "Proclamation to Youth of Israel Whose Hearts Are With Their People and
     Zion." In Eliav, *The First Aliyah,* vol. 2, 1981.
Vlack, Z. "The Development of National Education in the Settlements." In Eliav, *The
     First Aliyah,* vol. 1, 1981.
Yaari, A. *Memoirs of Eretz Israel.* Vols. 1 & 2. Jerusalem: Department of Youth Affairs
     of the Zionist Organization, 1947.
Yavnieli, S. *The Era of Hibat-Zion.* Vols. 1 & 2. Jerusalem: Bialik Institute, 1961.

Index

About the Author

LESLIE STEIN is a Senior Research Fellow at Macquarie University in Sydney, Australia.